New Directions in Psycholegal Research

New Directions in Psycholegal Research

Edited by

Paul D. Lipsitt

Laboratory of Community Psychiatry
Harvard Medical School
Boston, Massachusetts

Bruce Dennis Sales

Department of Psychology and
College of Law
University of Nebraska, Lincoln

Sponsored by the American Psychology-Law Society

 VAN NOSTRAND REINHOLD COMPANY
NEW YORK   CINCINNATI   ATLANTA   DALLAS   SAN FRANCISCO
LONDON   TORONTO   MELBOURNE

Van Nostrand Reinhold Company Regional Offices:
New York   Cincinnati   Atlanta   Dallas   San Francisco

Van Nostrand Reinhold Company International Offices:
London   Toronto   Melbourne

Library of Congress Catalog Card Number: 79-18106
ISBN: 0-442-26267-1

Manufactured in the United States of America

Published by Van Nostrand Reinhold Company
135 West 50th Street, New York, N.Y. 10020

Published simultaneously in Canada by Van Nostrand Reinhold Ltd.

15   14   13   12   11   10   9   8   7   6   5   4   3   2   1

Library of Congress Cataloging in Publication Data

Main entry under title:

New directions in psycholegal research.

"Developed out of the Third National Conference
of the American Psychology-Law Society which was
held in Snowmass, Colorado in June 1977."
   Includes index.
   1. Psychology, Forensic—Congresses.   2. Insanity
—Jurisprudence—Congresses.   3. Law—Psychology—
Congresses.   4. Criminal psychology—Congresses.
I.   Lipsitt, Paul D.   II.   Sales, Bruce Dennis.
III.   American Psychology-Law Society. [DNLM:
1. Forensic psychiatry—Congresses.   W740 N532]
K487.P75N48   347.06′6   79-18106
ISBN 0-442-26267-1

Contributors

Eugene Borgida, Department of Psychology, University of Minnesota.

John S. Carroll, Department of Psychology, Loyola University, Chicago.

Ebbe B. Ebbesen, Department of Psychology, University of California, San Diego.

David P. Farrington, Institute of Criminology, University of Cambridge, England.

Paul P. Freddolino, School of Social Work, Michigan State University.

Thomas Grisso, Department of Psychology, St. Louis University.

Lynn R. Kahle, Survey Research Center, Institute for Social Research, University of Michigan.

Martin F. Kaplan, Department of Psychology, Northern Illinois University.

Barry J. Knight, Institute of Criminology, University of Cambridge, England.

Vladimir J. Konečni, Department of Psychology, University of California, San Diego.

Paul D. Lipsitt, Laboratory of Community Psychiatry, Harvard Medical School.

Sam Manoogian, Department of Neurology, Bowman Gray School of Medicine, Wake Forest University.

Daniel McGillis, Center for Criminal Justice, Harvard Law School.

Robert G. Meyer, Department of Psychology, University of Louisville.

John Monahan, Program in Social Ecology, University of California, Irvine.

Erin Maria Mulcahy, Department of Psychology, University of California, San Diego.

Raymond W. Novaco, Program in Social Ecology, University of California, Irvine.

Daniel Perlman, Department of Psychology, University of Manitoba, Canada.

Bruce Dennis Sales, Department of Psychology and College of Law, University of Nebraska, Lincoln.

Cynthia Schersching, Department of Psychology, Northern Illinois University.

Debora E. Willage, Department of Psychology, University of Louisville.

Preface

This book developed out of the Third National Conference of the American Psychology–Law Society which was held in Snowmass, Colorado in June, 1977. The majority of the chapters represent an expansion and development of a select portion of the papers originally presented at that time. Five of the chapters, while not presented at the conference, were specifically requested because of their appropriateness to the central theme of the volume.

As the title to the book indicates, we were interested in putting together a collection of writings that represented new directions in psycholegal research. The chapters of Section I of the volume present both theoretical and empirical approaches to studying the decision making of participants within the legal process and system. Chapter 1 by Monahan and Novaco presents a theoretical and conceptual rationale for studying the decisions of corporate executives which result in violence to the public. Farrington and Knight, in Chapter 2, test the value of the subjectively expected utility model for explaining a person's decision to steal. Perlman, in Chapter 3, then argues for the theoretical and heuristic value of using attribution theory to study the decision making of various participants within the criminal justice process and system. In the next chapter, Carroll examines some psychological principles used by parole boards in predicting the recidivism of offenders. He points out that the boards can use both clinical information concerning the specifics of a particular case, as well as statistical prediction aids. His chapter particularly focuses on the use of this latter body of information. Finally, in Chapter 5, Konečni, Mulcahy and Ebbesen take a radically different approach to analyzing legal decision making. By ignoring traditional social psychological theories and, instead, by statistically analyzing the covariation between the information available to the participants in the legal decision and the actual decisions that they reach, they argue that this approach will yield an empirically derived theory that can be used to predict legal decision making.

The second section to the book focuses on another major development within psycholegal research—namely, research used to identify critical problems within the legal process and system and approaches for ameliorating those deficiencies. Grisso and Manoogian investigate juveniles' comprehension of Miranda warnings and demonstrate that the assumption that they provide an important right to juveniles is not warranted in many cases, since the juveniles do not understand the intended warnings. They go on to point out how this research can be potentially valuable to the courts and policy makers in determining the capacity of particular juveniles to both understand the warnings and waive their rights. In Chapter 7, Kaplan and Schersching illustrate the utility of information integration theory for potentially minimizing the effects of bias on judge and juror judgments. Borgida, in Chapter 8, then examines the impact of the common law rules of evidence in rape cases versus two types of revised evidentiary rules on the decisions of simulated juries. As the first of a series of studies in this area, this programmatic effort should be valuable to legislators who are concerned with making laws more just for both rape victims and their alleged assailants. The section ends with a chapter by McGillis who provides a comprehensive review and discussion of the alternatives to the traditional processing of disputes through the courts. There can be no question that the excessive delays that often typify the processing of both civil and criminal cases make this an important area for further research that should ultimately improve our justice system.

The last section sharply diverges from the previous two. In this section we wanted to focus on one substantive topic in depth, rather than broadly covering the use of major conceptual approaches of psychology in the study of the law. Because of psychology's long standing interest and involvement with mental health, we chose to investigate some psycholegal issues in the care and treatment of the clients of mental health services. Each chapter in this section uses different research methodologies to focus on how the law can intimately affect both the therapist's behavior and the potential patient recovery. Meyer and Willage present two studies that probe whether therapists understand the relevant concepts of privileged communication and confidentiality and whether differing conditions of confidentiality would affect the type of information a patient would disclose during therapy. The remaining three chapters explore the impact of recent modifications in involuntary civil commitment law upon the processing of subjects of such commitment and patients within mental hospitals. In Chapter 11, Lipsitt focuses on whether recent statutory modification of the civil commitment law affects the kinds of information that mental health professionals will present to substantiate the use of involuntary emergency hospitalization. Kahle and Sales then present the results of a national survey that assesses the attitudes of psychiatrists, clinical psychologists and lawyers toward the various approaches that past and current involuntary civil commitment statutes dictate in this area. Finally, in the last chapter, Freddolino assesses the attitudes of mental health professionals and other workers in a state mental health hospital towards patients' rights.

Paul D. Lipsitt
Bruce Dennis Sales

Contents

New Directions in Psycholegal Research

I
DECISION MAKING OF PARTICIPANTS WITHIN THE LEGAL PROCESS AND SYSTEM

1

Corporate Violence: A Psychological Analysis

John Monahan
Raymond W. Novaco

A group of stockholders recently filed suit against 17 executives of the McDonnell Douglas Corporation. The suit alleges that the executives had prior knowledge of a defect that was responsible for the 1974 crash in Paris of a DC-10 in which 346 persons were minced into 18,000 pieces after the plane's rear cargo door had blown out (Associated Press, March 5, 1977). Two years before the crash, officials at McDonnell Douglas are claimed to have had incontrovertible evidence that the door had failed factory testing and had in fact blown out on a flight over Canada. The officials were quoted at the time as conceding that "We have an interesting legal and moral problem," but decided to take no corrective action (Johnson, 1976; Eddy, Potter, and Page, 1976).

Kriesberg (1976), in a recent Note in the *Yale Law Journal*, documents the fact that legislative and judicial policies for responding to such alleged corporate malfeasance are in a period of transformation. He argues that "effective legal policy concerning corporate crime must be founded on an understanding of the decision-making process underlying corporate action" (p.1092).

Despite the web of penal statutes surrounding corporate entities and employees, the capacity of the criminal law to control corporate crime has been widely discounted. The basic problem is that the law is not founded on an understanding of the decision-making process that the law must shape in order to deter

We would like to thank Thomas Lalley, Scott Armstrong, Robert Meier, Vladimir Konečni, Bruce Sales, and Paul Lipsitt for their helpful comments on a previous draft of this chapter.

3

corporate lawbreaking . . . [L]egal policy has not been based on a systematic analysis of corporate decision-making that sets out the factual patterns and deterrence strategies implied by the various assumptions. As a result, the assumptions of legal policymakers are usually unarticulated and untested, and the actions based on those assumptions are often misguided (p. 1099).

Monahan, Novaco, and Geis (1979) have attempted to expand the empirical study of corporate decision-making to include the most extreme forms of corporate crime described by Kriesberg (1976). They defined corporate violence as "behavior producing an unreasonable risk of physical harm to consumers, employees, or other persons as a result of deliberate decision-making by corporate executives or culpable negligence on their part." [1] They suggested that the lack of behavioral science research on the topic was the result of individualistic and political biases on the part of researchers and a relative lack of access to data bases and funding sources. Finally, they proposed a three-pronged research strategy of intensive case studies, quasi-experimental analyses of existing naturalistic data, and laboratory simulations to bring this neglected form of violent behavior under empirical scrutiny.

This chapter will extend the analyses of Monahan, Novaco, and Geis (1979) by presenting a series of reasoned hypotheses regarding the aspects of corporate decision-making which relate to the occurrence of violent behavior. We believe that it will be profitable to approach the subject of corporate violence as Goldstein, Heller, and Sechrest (1966) approached research in psychotherapy, i.e., to examine research in related areas and attempt to deduce empirically testable hypotheses concerning the phenomenon of interest. In the case of corporate violence, three bodies of literature appear to be most directly and face-validly relevant. It may be argued that corporate decision-making which results in harm is a form of violence, and hence the existing research on *individual violence and aggression* may provide a source of hypotheses that can be applied to the corporate arena. Corporate violence, by definition, is also a form of corporate decision-making. Studies of corporate behavior in the literature on *organizational and management theory* may thus provide leads for research directions. Finally, corporate violence in many ways constitutes a moral problem for the decision-makers, and the developing research area of *moral reasoning* may provide insights into its nature.

We will consider each of the above research areas, focusing upon major findings, and attempt to derive testable hypotheses concerning corporate violence. Anecdotal evidence to support the hypotheses will also be presented wherever possible. We see this analysis as a logical prerequisite to the development of a body of empirical research on corporate forms of violent behavior.

I. INDIVIDUAL AGGRESSION AND VIOLENCE

A. Reinforcement Control

Individual aggression and street and family violence have been among the most studied topics in the history of the social sciences. One of the most frequently verified and straightforward hypotheses in the literature is that aggressive or violent behavior can be shaped and maintained by reward and punishment contingencies. The conditions of reinforcement may be either direct (Geen and Pigg, 1970; Geen and Stonner, 1971) or vicarious (Bandura, 1965). The instrumentality of aggressive behavior, i.e., its function in obtaining a desired outcome, is a powerful determinant of aggression and its intensity (Buss, 1963; 1966). By systematically rewarding compliance and punishing noncompliance, aggressive behavior can be brought under instructional control (Bandura, 1973). The obedient aggression demonstrated in Milgram's (1963) research followed from the subject's displacement of social values in response to the requests of a perceived, legitimate authority. When the demands of the instructing authority are more immediate and salient than the demands of the victim, there is a greater probability of an obedient response (Milgram, 1965).

Economic contingencies bearing on decisions within corporations appear to define the situation as one that is especially conducive to the instructional control of behavior (Armstrong, in press). Baumhart (1961) found that the behavior of a person's superiors in the company was ranked as the primary determinant of unethical decision-making by executives. As one of his respondents put it, "The constant, everyday pressure from top management to obtain profitable business, unwritten, but well understood, is the phrase 'at any cost.' To do this requires every conceivable dirty trick" (p. 132).

Brenner and Molander (1977), in their 15 year follow-up of Baumhart's (1961) survey, found that superiors were still ranked as the primary influence on unethical decision-making. "Respondents frequently complained of superiors' pressure to support incorrect viewpoints, sign false documents, overlook superiors' wrongdoing, and do business with superiors' friends" (p. 60). Fully half of the executives surveyed in the 1977 study believed that superiors often do not want to know how results are obtained, as long as the desired outcome is achieved.

In addition to heightening the salience of superiors' instructions, the economic contingencies bearing on corporate decisions appear to constrict the consideration of non-economic factors in the decision-making process. Brenner and Molander (1977) reported that "only" 28 percent of the executives surveyed agreed with the position of economist Milton Freedman (1962), who has stated that "few trends could so thoroughly undermine the very foundation of our free society as the acceptance by corporate officials of a social responsibility other than to make as much money for their stockholders as possible" (p. 132). Many other executives undoubtedly resonate to the sentiments of management theorist Peter Drucker (1974) who states that managers must negotiate "trade-offs" between product safety and corporate profit.

It is interesting to note how these "trade-offs" are resolved in practice; Linowes (1972), for example, suggests that corporations should produce an annual "Socio-Economic Operating Statement." In his proposed scheme, under the category of "Relations with People," one would take the costs of *Improvements,* such as "training program for handicapped workers" and "extra turnover costs because of minority hiring," and subtract from it the dollar value of such *Detriments* as "postponed installing of new safety device on cutting machines" to arrive at a figure for the *Net Improvements in People Actions for the Year.* Even Estes' (1976) sympathetic review notes the "ambiguities" involved in setting dollar equivalents to physical injuries. How many handicapped workers need to be trained to make acceptable the "trade-off" that other workers are losing their limbs on unprotected cutting machines?

Typical of this state of affairs is the conclusion of the Center for Auto Safety (1972) that the Volkswagen corporation's "definition of a safety defect is very narrow, admitting only those deficiencies which are so severe that the company's legal liability would outweigh the cost of the recall campaign" (p. 84) and therefore would result in a net reduction in corporate profit if the defect were not corrected. The numerous case studies cited elsewhere (Monahan, Novaco, and Geis, 1979; Geis and Monahan, 1976) illustrate that safety decisions are balanced against the financial costs of implementing them.

B. Ethical Standards

Net reinforcement value, or absolute cost-benefit considerations, alone do not fully describe the contingency matrix confronting the potential aggressor. An additional consideration is whether the aggressive act violates the ethical criteria that an individual has set for his or her own behavior. Decision-making "hinges on self-evaluations and self-administered outcomes contingent upon one's achieving or violating one's own standards'' (Mischel and Mischel, 1976, p. 98). The relevance of self-imposed standards to the performance of both aggressive (Bandura and Walters, 1963; Bandura, 1973) and moral behavior (Aronfreed, 1968; 1976) has been amply demonstrated. With respect to corporate decision-making, there would appear to be several factors influencing the development of standards regarding the degree of harm to be tolerated without self-condemnation: the harm tolerated by the corporation in the past, the harm tolerated by other corporations in the same industry, and the individual decision-maker's own ''moral code.'' Put another way, the decision-maker may compare the amount of harm generated by a given decision with his or her company's *historical* standards, with the *comparative* standards of the industry, and with *absolute* standards as judged by the decision-maker's personal, moral goals. Anecdotal evidence exists to support all three sources of performance standards.

Stone (1975) cites worker safety records in coal mines operated by the traditional coal mining companies and those from mines more recently purchased and operated by steel companies. He found twice as many deaths and over five times as many injuries in the mines operated by the coal companies as in the mines operated by the steel companies; the reason appears to lie in historically based performance standards adopted in the two industries.

> Traditionally, the steel company's top corporate executives, being used to a relatively good safety record in their steel mills, have never been willing to tolerate poor safety performance in their mines. 'There's a paternalistic attitude (in the steel companies) that you don't find prevalent in (coal),' admits the head of one large commercial coal operation (cited in Stone, 1975; p. 138).

The steel companies never adopted the ''coal mining mentality'' of accepting high death and injury rates among their employees.

Social comparison processes (Festinger, 1954) have also been found to influence the setting of ethical performance standards. Baumhart (1961) reported that corporate executives rated ''industry climate'' as one of the primary factors giving rise to unethical decision-making. The same survey found that ''personal codes'' of morality were seen as the chief influence when ethical decisions were made.

C. Diffusion of Responsibility

The probability of individual aggression increases as aggressors can exempt themselves from self-devaluation and liability of punishment by diffusing responsibility to others for harm-doing behavior (Bandura,

Underwood and Fromson, 1975; Diener, 1976; Diener, Endreson, Beaman, and Fraser, 1975). Analogously, diffusion of responsibility relieves individuals of a felt need to engage in prosocial behavior, such as aiding a person in distress (Darley and Latane, 1968). Corporate organizations appear designed to distribute responsibility in as many directions as possible (Sutherland, 1949). "The buck," as Mintz and Cohen (1971; p. 295) have stated, "seems to stop nowhere." As Bandura (1973) has put it:

> [One] bureaucratic practice for relieving self-condemnation for aggression is to rely on group decision-making, so that no single individual feels responsible for what is eventually done. Indeed, social organizations go to great lengths to devise sophisticated mechanisms for obscuring responsibility for decisions that affect others adversely . . . Through division of labor, division of decision-making, and collective action, people can be contributors to cruel practices and bloodshed without feeling personally responsible or self-contemptuous for their part in it (p. 213).

What Hannah Arendt (1965) referred to as "rule by nobody" is likely to play a significant role in corporate decision-making which results in harm (Nader, 1972; Geis and Monahan, 1976). In discussing corporate decisions in the automobile industry, McCarthy (1972) has observed:

> It is unlikely that G[eneral] M[otors] chairman James Roche ever sends out memos to his staff saying things like 'Make the exhaust systems out of cheaper metal this year,' or 'Order a lower-grade iron for the wheel disks on those three-quarter-ton trucks.' Yet in many such cases he might as well . . . [D]own the line of corporate responsibility someone had those thoughts about cheapening the exhausts and disks, someone else seconded those thoughts, and someone else carried them out. Death and injury resulted and surely GM regrets it. Yet many millions in that $22 billion profit [from 1947 to 1969] resulted also, and it is not likely that GM has regrets about that (p. 34).

D. Sex Differences

A fourth variable that has received a great deal of attention in the aggression literature is that of sex differences. According to Maccoby and Jacklin's (1974) definitive review of sex-linked behavior, the fact that males are more aggressive than females is one of only four sex differences that have been "fairly well established" by empirical research. They found that:

> The sex difference in aggressison has been observed in all cultures in which the relevant behavior has been observed. Boys are more aggressive both physically and verbally. They show the attenuated forms of aggression (mock-fighting,

aggressive fantasies), as well as the direct forms more frequently than girls. The sex differences are found as early as social play beings—at age two or two and a half. Although the aggressiveness of both sexes declines with age, boys and men remain more aggressive through the college years. Little information is available for older adults (p. 352).

Among persons over eighteen, however, males are still arrested for violent crimes nine times more frequently than females (Kelly, 1977), despite the fact that female violence has increased substantially in recent years. A recent review of laboratory research on aggression by Frodi, Macaulay, and Thorne (1977) has argued that sex differences in aggression are not as prevalent as commonly believed and that women may be as aggressive as men under certain conditions, such as when the aggressive act is perceived as justified. However, in their review of studies concerning aggression in *non-angered* subjects (which is most pertinent here), the authors found many studies showing clear-cut sex differences.

Objection might be taken to generalizing this sex difference in individual aggression to the corporate sphere. It has been alleged that female executives, in order to succeed in the male-dominated corporate hierarchy, are forced to suppress the more stereotypically "feminine" aspects of their personality (e.g., compassion). Hennig (1976), in the most comprehensive study to date on female corporate executives (Presidents and Corporate Vice-Presidents of major corporations), found that her subjects did indeed report that at the outset of their careers they were "determined to act as much as possible like the men around them" (vii–14). At approximately age 25, "all of the subjects took their femininity and 'stored it away for future consideration' " (vii–2). At 35–40, however, after achieving success in their business careers, these executives were able to reincorporate previously suppressed aspects of their personality, such as a desire for close, noncompetitive, personal relationships.

Given the changes that have occurred in American society in regard to women's rights since 1950—when Hennig's subjects were beginning their business careers—the initial "masculine" period for the prospective woman executive may be less mandated by current business climate.

II. ORGANIZATIONAL AND MANAGEMENT THEORY

An enormous literature exists in what might be loosely termed "organizational psychology" or "the sociology of organizations." It spans the continuum from the sweeping theories of Parsons (1960) and Merton (1957) on the nature of organizations and bureaucracies and their place in society, through the more limited and empirical approaches of Katz and Kahn

(1966), March and Simon (1958), and Argyris (1964), to the pragmatic prescriptions for effective management of Drucker (1974) and Townsend (1970).

A. Organizational Roles

While the literature on organizations and bureaucracies is difficult to summarize, there are several concepts that appear to recur in various theories and across levels of analysis. One such concept is that of "role" in an organization (e.g., Biddle and Thomas, 1966; Sarbin & Allen, 1968; Cyert and MacCrimmon, 1968). A role, according to Haas and Drabek (1973), is "a cluster of norms that applies to any single unit of social interaction" (p. 111). The norms defining a role in an organization need not be handed down from the leader of the organization; they may be supplied by one's organizational peers. Roles provide a set of *expectations* which "may include preferences with respect to specific acts and personal characteristics or styles; they may deal with what the person should do, what kind of person he should be, what he should think, or believe, and how he should relate to others" (Katz and Kahn, 1966; p. 175).

The effect that an organizational role may have on its occupants is demonstrated most vividly in a study by Lieberman (1956) of the attitudes of manufacturing employees. A group of persons went from the role of "worker" to the role of "foreman." Over a three year period, some of these persons remained foremen, and some were demoted back to the worker role, due to economic cutbacks. Lieberman assessed the subjects' attitudes toward a number of company issues at three points in time: when all were still workers; after all were promoted to foremen; and later when some remained foremen and some were returned to the worker role. The percentage of employees who believed that "management officers really care about the workers" was initially low in both groups (0–8 percent); it jumped to 25–33 percent for both groups one year after entry into the foreman role. Two years later, 67 percent of those who remained in the foreman role believed that management cared about workers, but the attitudes of those returned to the worker role reverted to their previous level of no one believing in management's concern.

Organizational role has also been held to have a major effect on corporate decision-making (Armstrong, in press). The most frequently suggested procedure to increase corporate accountability with regard to consumer issues (including product safety) has been the inclusion on the Board of Directors of major corporations of one or more persons with the role of a "Public Director" (e.g., Nader, 1971; Townsend, 1973; Stone,

1975). The proposal was first made by former Supreme Court Justice William O. Douglas in the 1930s when he was the chairman of the Securities and Exchange Commission. Douglas spoke of the need for "a public director, representing not only the present but the potential stockholder and representing the public as well" (quoted in Chamberlain, 1973; p. 195). The proposal has yet to be acted upon, despite intensive lobbying during Nader's "Campaign GM" (Nader, 1975). As might be expected, the notion of a public director has been vigorously resisted by corporate executives. The result of such a proposal, it has been held, is that "important corporate policy debates will be carried into the streets, just as has occurred, with much the same backing [i.e., by social "radicals"], in American universities" (Manne, 1975; p. 103; see also Roche, 1975).

The rationale in the demand for a public director is based on the belief that if a person specifically was given the role of considering the interests of the potential victims of hazardous products (or the victims of price gauging), he or she would bring such issues to the fore in board meetings and would engage in "whistle-blowing" publicity if those concerns were ignored. Whether this would actually occur, or whether the public director would gradually adopt the values of the other board members and disregard his or her role prescriptions, is not known.

B. Organizational Levels

In addition to the influence of organizational roles upon the attitudes and behavior of the individuals occupying them, the variable of organizational *level* has received scholarly attention (Indik, 1968; Porter, Lawler, and Hackman, 1976). Level here refers to the location in the corporate hierarchy at which a given decision is made. Stone (1975) has recently written that "one of the most effective ways to make a corporation more responsible (in the sense of being more deliberative and reflective) is to take decisions of large social concern out of the hands of lower-level functionaries and insist that they be put into the hands of others higher in the organization" (p. 217). There are several potential reasons to support such a position. Decision-makers at lower levels in the corporate hierarchy may be reluctant to be the bearers of bad tidings to their superiors concerning safety defects and therefore attempt to minimize or cover-up the potential harm where possible. They may have the expectation (indeed, they may be *given* the expectation) that part of their job is to "protect" their superiors from inconvenient information, so that the superiors can later claim ignorance (and innocence) if such information comes to light. It is interesting to note in this regard that the percentage of executives who reported that honesty in providing information to top management was a major source of ethical conflict has almost doubled in the past fifteen years (Baumhart, 1961; Brenner and Molander, 1977). It is now ranked as the primary source of conflict between company interests and personal ethics (Brenner and Molander, 1977). Finally, those at the top of the corporate hierarchy, having "made it" in the business world, may feel more of a *noblesse oblige* responsibility for the social consequences of their actions or at least a heightened sensitivity to public criticisms of their performance.

Support for the notion that the level at which decisions are made can influence safety-related decisions comes from a preliminary study by the National Institute for Occupational Safety and Health comparing companies high and low in employee accident rates (Cohen, Smith, and Cohen, 1975). After comparing the two groups on a large number of variables, the authors concluded that one of the sole factors distinguishing them was that "more of the low accident companies had their highest safety officials at top management levels of their firms" (p. 63). These top management officials were more aggressive than their lower-level counterparts in investigating minor work injuries, rather than waiting for a serious mishap to be brought to their attention.

Monahan, Novaco, and Geis (1979) also provide tentative support for the relevance of organizational levels to organizational decision-making. Investigating the recall procedure of the automobile industry regarding defective vehicles, they found that two of the "Big Four" Detroit automobile manufacturers make recall decisions at the middle-management level and two at the level of top-management (vice-presidents and members of the board). The most recent annual data from the National Highway Traffic Safety Administration reveals that the two companies whose recall decisions were made at the middle-management level were audited by the government for product safety violations a total of ten times, while the two companies where decisions were made at top management levels were audited only once. While many factors (e.g., differences in sales volume) confound a straightforward interpretation of this finding in terms of level of decision-making, it does suggest the possible operation of such an effect.

C. Organizational Security

A third and related area which has received some attention in the literature on organizational psychology and sociology is that of the status or security of the organization (Merton, 1957; Drucker, 1974). While the previous factor we discussed related to the level of the individual decision-makers within the hierarchy of the organization, security relates to the level of the organization on the hierarchy of its own need-fulfillment, usually expressed in financial terms. According to Stone (1975):

> [W]hile the corporation is *potentially* immune from a single-minded profit orientation, in any particular company that potentiality is able to become reality only after some satisfactory level of profits has been achieved. A corporation that is operating "on the margin" is going to cut as many corners as it can get away with on worker safety, product quality, and everything else (p. 234).

Such an inference might also be drawn from the psychological literature relating goal frustration to the willingness to engage in aggression and relating goal attainment to the performance of socially responsible behavior (Berkowitz, 1962; Berkowitz and Connor, 1966; Rosenhan, Moore, and Underwood, 1976).

Just as individuals low in the corporate hierarchy may perceive themselves as having more to lose by giving attention to "unprofitable" issues such as safety, so too organizations which have not achieved the level of success to which they aspire may lack concern for that which does not advance their fiscal status. It would not be difficult to interpret Drucker's (1974) popular management text in such a light; Drucker holds that the principal "limitation" on an executive's social responsibility is his "higher responsibility" to make a profit for the organization (p. 344).

Indeed, Lane (1953), in one of the earliest empirical studies of business ethics, concluded that "while it is generally (but not universally) true that economic gain is necessary for violation of the law to take place, marginal and declining firms are more likely to violate the law than prosperous firms" (p. 164).

III. MORAL REASONING

The study of moral reasoning, moral development, and moral behavior has attracted the attention of a growing number of psychologists (Lickona, 1976). The cognitive-developmental theory of Lawrence Kohlberg (e.g., 1958; 1976; in press) has been the principal approach to the processes by which people distinguish what is "right" from what is "wrong." In Kohlberg's view, moral reasoning must be understood in the broader context of cognitive development (Piaget, 1967). He holds that an invariant sequence of three levels of moral reasoning exists: The first is a *preconventional level,* where rules and social expectations are seen as something external to the self; the second is the *conventional level,* where the self identifies with or internalizes the rules of others, especially of persons viewed as "authorities"; the third is the *postconventional level,* where persons differentiate themselves from the rules and expectations of others and define values in terms of self-chosen principles (Kohlberg, 1976; p. 33). Each of these three levels of moral reasoning is subdivided into two separate stages, resulting in a six-stage sequence of moral development. Kohlberg has developed elaborate interview methods for assessing his stages of moral reasoning (Kohlberg, Colby, Speicher-Dubin, and Lieberman, 1975) and claims 90 percent interrater reliability. A paper and pencil instrument to assess moral reasoning has recently been developed by Rest (1976).

Several studies have reported associations between stage of moral reasoning and performance of moral behavior. Kohlberg (1970) found that 75 percent of Stage 6 "principled" subjects disobeyed orders to continue shocking a "victim" in a Milgram (1965)-type laboratory experiment on obedience to authority, while only 13 percent of lower-stage subjects disobeyed. Kohlberg (1970) also found less cheating by higher-stage subjects than by lower-stage subjects in a replication of the Hartshorne and May (1928) cheating studies. Haan, Smith and Block (1968) reported substantial relationships between moral stage and participation in sit-ins during the Berkeley free speech movement, with 80 percent of the Stage 6 subjects sitting-in and only 50 percent of the Stage 5 subjects. Leming (1974) found analogous results in a study of sit-ins by high school students opposing the Cambodian invasion. Finally, McNamee (in preparation) related differences in moral reasoning, as assessed by Kohlberg's scale, to the degree of help offered in a "Good Samaritan" bystander study. "Results showed that the frequency of giving help increased with each higher level of moral development: Persons at Stage 2 helped 11 percent of the time; those at Stage 3, 27 percent of the time; those at Stage 4, 38 percent; Stage 5, 68 percent; and Stage 6, 100 percent" (Huston and Korte, 1976; p. 277). Finally, Tapp and Kohlberg (1971) found that orientation to general issues of law and justice closely paralleled the Kohlbergian stages of moral development (see also Tapp, 1976).

Despite its confirmation in studies such as these, Kohlberg's theory has been vigorously criticized: Simpson (1974, 1976) finds it "a case study of scientific cultural bias;" Kurtines and Greif (1974) argue that both the reliability of the stage scoring and the construct validity of the six-stage model are seriously inadequate (see Kohlberg's reply, 1975); Mischel and Mischel (1976), reflecting a persistent criticism of Kohlberg, state that "sophisticated social science versions of stratification systems which categorize people in terms of their overall level of morality, unless carefully moderated, can lead to an elitism that is empirically unjustified as well as socially hazardous" (p. 107).

Lickona (1976b), in an excellent critique of Mischel and Mischel (1976) position, states that such claims have:

. . . much appeal both to ethical tolerance and to the strain of intellectual relativism that runs strong in American social science. But what logical problems are masked by that appeal? At the same time that Mischel and Mischel's essay rejects 'moral stratification systems,' it deplores the fact that people tend to be facile at using 'a wide variety of self-deceptive mechanisms . . . to facilitate and excuse the most horrendous acts . . . and extraordinarily cruel aggressions.' By what criteria are acts to be judged horrendous or cruel? If one does attempt to construct moral criteria that would identify horrendous acts as well as good ones, can 'stratifications' or levels of morality be avoided?

Of particular relevance to the topic of corporate violence, Lickona (1976b), in a critique of an early effort by Geis and Monahan (1976) to equate corporate decision making resulting in violence (such as in the manufacturing of defective aircraft) with street violence, argues that any form of social-moral advocacy presupposes an implicit commitment to a moral hierarchy. "One cannot demand equal treatment of those who kill by manufacturing dangerous aircraft and those who murder in the street and say that all value systems are relative or arbitrary" (p. 7). While the present authors have not come to a final resolution of the exceedingly complex theoretical and methodological issues raised by Kohlberg's theory of moral reasoning, the theory does appear to have sufficient heuristic value to justify its application to the study of corporate violence.

In the only study to date applying moral development theory to corporate executives, Erdynast (1974) states:

Popular opinion regarding moral reasoning of executives is clear and simple: there is none. The common view is that executives are by and large immoral and that there are no ethics in business. Executives are viewed as people who act only with their own materialistic self-interest or with the materialistic self-interest of their companies in mind. Even when executives are not caricatured as completely immoral persons, they are viewed as at least having two distinct sets of moral values, one for their private lives and a second set which governs their behavior at work (p. 43).

In contrast to this view, Erdynast found that a sample of 20 executives taking a course at Harvard Business School were scored at between Stage 4 and Stage 5 on Kohlberg's six-stage scale (comparing favorably with the general population) and that there were no differences between their reasoning on Kohlberg's "standard" moral dilemmas (presumably reflecting their "private life" standards) and on dilemmas specifically relevant to business practices. None of these dilemmas, however, related directly to decision-making which could result in injury to either consumers or employees.

A. Empathy and Dehumanization

Throughout the moral development literature, the claim is made that the ability to take the role of another (role reversibility or reciprocity) is a prerequisite in the development of moral reasoning (Simpson, 1976; Hoffman, 1976). In one study by Selman (1976), "each role-taking stage was found to be a necessary, but not sufficient, condition for the corresponding moral stage" (p. 308). The "emotional side" of role-taking ability is empathy or sympathy for others (Kohlberg, 1976). Studies by Liebhart (1972) and Schwartz and Clausen (1970) found that the degree to which subjects sympathize with the plight of victims correlated with their willingness to offer help to others in a "Good Samaritan" task.

Applied to the topic of corporate violence, these results suggest that the degree to which the corporate decision-makers can empathize with, or take the role of, the potential victims of their actions would relate to the amount of violence they would be willing to sanction. This hypothesis from moral development theory dovetails nicely with implications which could be drawn from the social learning theory of individual aggression. A number of studies find that when a victim is dehumanized (Bernard, Ottenberg, and Redl, 1971) (sometimes called "deindividuated" (Zimbardo, 1969)), aggression will increase (Bandura, 1973; Bandura, Underwood, and Fromson, 1975). However, Diener and his colleagues (Diener, 1976; Diener et al 1975) have found a general lack of correlation between measures of deindividuation and aggressive behavior.

Relevant to the dehumanization hypothesis, inhibitions to aggress or to make harm-doing decisions may be reduced by physical distance from the victim. Milgram (1965) found that obedient aggression varied with the sheer physical remoteness of the victim to the subject: Following the victim's protest, 66 percent of the subjects obeyed instructions to shock the victim when the victim was in another room; 40 percent obeyed when they were in the same room with the victim; and only 30 percent obeyed when they were in close proximity to the victim. Turner, Layton, and Simons (1975) also found that victim visibility inhibited aggression in a naturalistic setting.

The most dramatic examples of victim dehumanization leading to increased violence are found in war and in civil unrest (Bandura, 1973): Opton (1971) quotes one American soldier in Vietnam as saying of his colleagues, "A lot of these people wouldn't think of killing a man . . . I mean, a white man—a human, so to speak" (p. 66). Janis (1971) notes that meetings among top policy-makers in the Johnson Administration to plan the course of the Vietnam war "were characterized by a games theory detachment." The decision-makers "were able to avoid in their discussions with each other all direct references to human suffering and thus to form an attitude of detachment similar to surgeons" (p. 73).

While moral development theory emphasizes "role-taking" and "empathy" and social learning theory employs terms such as "depersonalization" and "dehumanization," the two approaches appear to be addressing essentially the same phenomenon, albeit in somewhat different languages. If one views the victims of violent acts as less than persons and less than human, one precludes reversing roles with them and decreases the possibility of empathy for them.

To the extent that the consumers (victims) of hazardous products or the employees of an hazardous industry are removed in space, time, and social class from corporate decision-makers, there exist conditions conducive to the development of depersonalization and lack of empathy. Speculation on why the Dow Chemical Company has maintained a relatively good record in avoiding occupational health hazards is relevant in this regard. "Part of the answer may be that Dow began as a family firm in Midland [Michigan] so that top executives had a strong sense of personal identification with Dow's activities and were not isolated from lower-level subordinates or production workers" (Cooper and Steiger, 1976b, p. 27). Furthermore, when the victims are perceived to have voluntarily chosen a hazardous work environment, such as a coal mine, or a hazardous product, such as a Corvair, they can be seen by decision-makers as having invited their own misfortune (Lowrance, 1976; Bennigson and Bennigson, 1974).

B. Personality Factors

Moral reasoning stages may be distinguished from what are generally referred to as "personality variables" or "traits" (Kohlberg, 1976). Whereas moral reasoning refers to the cognitive process by which an individual assesses the moral value of given behavioral options, personality traits are held to be propensities or predispositions to behave in certain ways (e.g., aggressively, honestly) across various situations. While personality traits and moral reasoning levels clearly share some properties (e.g., both are attributes of individual persons rather than of organizations), they are sufficiently dissimilar to warrant separate investigation of the role of personality factors in corporate violence.

A great deal of effort has been expended, to no avail, to locate the source of moral or prosocial behavior in the personality of the individual (Mischel, 1968). Elms and Milgram (1965), for example, found personality variables, as expressed in psychological test scores, to be wholly unrelated to the tendency to obey an instruction to shock a victim. Gergen, Gergen, and Meter (1972) concluded that "the search for general [personality] correlates of prosocial behavior is . . . shortsighted" (see also Mischel and Mischel, 1976; Rosenhan, Moore, and Underwood, 1976). This finding would compliment the conclusion of Megargee's (1970) extensive review of the psychological test correlates of violent or antisocial behavior. No test has been found "which will adequately *post*dict, let alone *pre*dict, violent behavior" (p. 145). In regard to corporate crime, Lane (1953) notes that in corporations which violated the law, "there was great consistency of behavior toward specific laws over long periods of time when the managing personnel changed several times over. It seemed to be the position of the firm, rather than any emotional qualities of its management which led it to violate" (p. 163).

The literature would appear to support Opton (1971) when he states that we must "pay attention to the factors that lead ordinary men to do extraordinary things. The American tradition is to locate the source of evil deeds in evil men. We have yet to learn that the greatest evils occur when social systems give average men the task of routinizing evil" (p. 51).

CONCLUSIONS

We have argued that corporate decisions which involve harmful consequences should be subject to the same empirical scrutiny as the decisions of individuals in society. As a first step in the development of a body of knowledge on corporate violence, we have reviewed the literature in the fields of individual violence and aggression, organizational and management theory, and moral reasoning to locate findings of possible relevance to the occurrence of harmful consequences in the corporate decision-making process.

The literature on individual aggression and violence suggests a number of factors that might facilitate or inhibit corporate decision-making that results in an unreasonable risk of harm. Reinforcement theory, as well as basic economics, would lead one to predict that harmful decisions are more likely to be made when the expected value of financial benefits exceeds the expected value of financial costs. However, from our psychological standpoint, it would be fruitful to investigate conditions related to these decision problems, such as compliance with the demands of superiors who perceive the financial cost/benefit ratio to favor harmful decisions. Diffusion of responsibility for organizational decisions and their consequences may foster decisions that result in harm. In addition, the origins and determinants of industry standards regarding "acceptable" levels of risk are intriguing areas for investigation.

Conditions of distance in space, time, and social class between the decision-makers and the potential victims may be conducive to a lack of empathy for the victims of harmful organizational decisions. While moral development theory suggests that the level of moral reasoning will determine the nature of executive decisions regarding threats to physical safety, there is reason to believe, on the other hand, that personality traits will not distinguish the decision-maker who perpetrates corporate violence from the one who does not.

The literature on organization and management theory also has heuristic value for the generation of research hypotheses. One's organizational level and role may have a powerful effect on the probability of decisions that we have termed corporate violence: persons at low levels in the organizational hierarchy may be most susceptible to overlooking the harmful consequences of company actions, and the presence of someone with the role of advocate for the potential victims may inhibit group decisions that result in harmful outcomes. The organizational literature also suggests that organizations that are fiscally marginal may be most tolerant of injurious effects due to their decisions.

We await the results of our own and others' research to verify, disconfirm, or refine these and other hypotheses suggested by our review, so that we might move closer to Kriesberg's (1976) goal of having social policies "founded on an understanding of the decision-making process that the law must shape in order to deter corporate law breaking."

REFERENCES

Arendt, H. *Eichmann in Jerusalem*. New York: Viking, 1965.

Argyris, C. *Integrating the Individual and the Organization*. New York: Wiley, 1964.

Armstrong, S. Social irresponsibility in management. *Journal of Business Research*, in press.

Aronfreed, J. *Conduct and Conscience*. New York: Academic Press, 1968.

Aronfreed, J. Moral development from the standpoint of a general psychological theory. In T. Lickona (Ed.) *Moral Development and Behavior*, pp. 54–69. New York: Holt, Rinehart & Winston, 1976.

Associated Press. Douglas executives blamed for crash. *Daily Pilot*, May 5, 1977.

Bandura, A. *Aggression: A Social Learning Analysis*. Englewood Cliffs, N.J.: Prentice-Hall, 1973.

Bandura, A. Influence of models' reinforcement contingencies on the acquisition of imitative responses. *Journal of Personality and Social Psychology* **1**:589–595 (1965).

Bandura, A., Underwood, B., and Fromson, M. E. Disinhibition of aggression through diffusion of responsibility and dehumanization of victims. *Journal of Research in Personality* **9**:253–269 (1975).

Bandura, A., and Walters, R. *Social Learning and Personality Development*. New York: Holt, Rinehart & Winston, 1963.

Baumhart, R. How ethical are businessmen? *Harvard Business Review*, July, 1961.

Baumhart, R. C. How ethical are businessmen? In G. Geis (Ed.) *White-Collar Criminal*. New York: Atherton, 1968.

Bennigson, L., and Bennigson, A. Product liability: Manufacturers beware. *Harvard Business Review* **52**:122–132 (1974).

Berkowitz, L. *Aggression: A Social Psychological Analysis*. New York: McGraw-Hill, 1962.

Berkowitz, L., and Connor, W. Success, failure, and social responsibility. *Journal of Personality and Social Psychology* **4**:664–669 (1966).

Bernard, V., Ottenberg, P., and Redl, F. *Dehumanization*. In N. Sanford and C. Comstock (Eds.) *Sanctions for Evil*, pp. 102–124. San Francisco: Jossey-Bass, 1971.

Biddle, B., and Thomas, E. (Eds.) *Role Theory: Concepts and Research*. New York: Wiley, 1966.

Brenner, S., and Molander, E. Is the ethics of business changing? *Harvard Business Review* **55**(1):57–71 (1977).

Buss, A. Physical aggression in relation to different frustrations. *Journal of Abnormal and Social Psychology* **67**:1–7 (1963).

Buss, A. Instrumentality of aggression, feedback, and frustration as determinants of physical aggression. *Journal of Personality and Social Psychology* **3**:153–162 (1966).

Center for Auto Safety. *Small-on Safety: The Designed-in Dangers of the Volkswagen*. New York: Grossman, 1972.

Chamberlain, N. *The Limits of Corporate Responsibility*. New York: Boise Books, 1973.

Cohen, A., Smith, M., and Cohen, H. Safety program practices in high versus low accident rate companies—An interim report to the National Institute for Occupational Health and Safety. Washington, D.C.: Government Printing Office, 1975.

Cooper, R., and Steiger, P. How one big firm fought health perils. *Los Angeles Times*, **1**:26–27 (b), June 27, 1976.

Cyert, R., and MacCrimmon, K. Organizations. In G. Lindzey and E. Aronson (Eds.) *The Handbook of Social Psychology*, pp. 568–611. Reading, Mass.: Addison-Wesley, 2nd Ed., Vol. 1, 1968.

Darley, J., and Latane, B. Bystander intervention in emergencies: Diffusion of responsibility. *Journal of Personality and Social Psychology* **8**:377–383 (1968).

Diener, E. Effects of prior destructive behavior, anonymity, and group presence on deindividuation and aggression. *Journal of Personality and Social Psychology* **33**:497–507 (1976).

Diener, E., Dineen, J., Endresen, K., Beaman, A., and Fraser, S. Effects of altered responsibility, cognitive set, and modeling on physical aggression and deindividuation. *Journal of Personality and Social Psychology* **31**:328–337 (1975).

Drucker, P. *Management: Tasks, Responsibilities, Practices.* New York: Harper & Row, 1974.

Eddy, P., Potter, E., and Page, B. *Destination Disaster—from the Tri-motor to the DC-10: The Risks of Flying.* New York: Quadrangle, 1976.

Elms, A., and Milgram, S. Personality characteristics associated with obedience and defiance toward authoritative command. *Journal of Experimental Research and Personality* **1**:282–289 (1966).

Erdynast, A. Improving the adequacy of moral reasoning: An exploratory study with executives and philosophy students. Unpublished dissertation, Graduate School of Business Administration, Harvard University, 1974.

Estes, R. *Corporate Social Accounting.* New York: Wiley, 1976.

Festinger, L. A theory of social comparison processes. *Human Relations* **7**:117–140 (1954).

Friedman, M. *Capitalism and Freedom.* Chicago: University of Chicago Press, 1962.

Frodi, A., Macaulay, J., and Thome, P. R. Are women always less aggressive than men? A review of the experimental literature. *Psychological Bulletin* **84**:634–660 (1977).

Geen, R. G., and Pigg, R. Acquisition of an aggressive response and its generalization to verbal behavior. *Journal of Personality and Social Psychology* **15**:165–170 (1970).

Geen, R. G., and Stonner, D. Effects of aggressive habit strength on behavior in the presence of aggression-related stimuli. *Journal of Personality and Social Psychology* **11**:149–153 (1971).

Geis, G., and Monahan, J. The social ecology of violence. In T. Lickona (Ed.) *Morality: Theory, Research, and Social Issues,* pp. 342–356. New York: Holt, Rinehart & Winston, 1976.

Gergen, K., Gergen, M., and Meter, K. Individual orientations to prosocial behavior. *Journal of Social Issues* **28**:105–130 (1972).

Goldstein, A., Heller, K., and Sechrest, L. *Psychotherapy and the psychology of behavior change.* New York: Wiley, 1966.

Haan, N., Smith, B., and Block, J. Moral reasoning of young adults. *Journal of Personality and Social Psychology* **10**:183–201 (1968).

Haas, J., and Drabek, T. *Complex organizations: A sociological perspective.* New York: Macmillan, 1973.

Hartshorne, H., and May, M. *Studies in the nature of character.* New York: Macmillan, 1928.

Hennig, M. Career development for women executives. Unpublished dissertation, Harvard Business School, 1976.

Hoffman, M. Empathy, role taking, guilt, and development of altruistic motives. In T. Lickona (Ed.) *Moral Development and Behavior*, pp. 124–143. New York: Holt, Rinehart & Winston, 1976.

Huston, T., and Korte, C. The responsive bystander: Why he helps. In T. Lickona (Ed.) *Moral Development and Behavior*, pp. 269–283. New York: Holt, Rinehart & Winston, 1976.

Janis, J. Groupthink among policy makers. In N. Sanford and C. Comstock (Eds.) *Sanctions for Evil*, pp. 71–89. San Francisco: Jossey-Bass, 1971.

Johnson, M. *The Last Nine Minutes: The Story of Flight 981*. New York: Morrow, 1976.

Katz, D., and Kahn, R. *The Social Psychology of Organizations*. New York: Wiley, 1966.

Kelley, C. *Uniform Crime Reports*. Washington, D.C.: U.S. Government Printing Office, 1976.

Kohlberg, L. The development of modes of moral thinking and choice in the years ten to sixteen. Unpublished doctoral dissertation, University of Chicago, 1958.

Kohlberg, L. Education for justice: A modern statement of the Platonic view. In N. F. Sizer and T. R. Sizer (Eds.) *Moral Education*, pp. 57–83. Cambridge, Mass.: Harvard University Press, 1970.

Kohlberg, L. The cognitive-developmental approach: New developments and a response to criticisms. Presented to the Annual Convention of the Society for Research in Child Development, Denver, 1975.

Kohlberg, L., Colby, A., Speicher-Dubin, B., and Lieberman, M. *Standard Form Scoring Manual*. Cambridge, Mass.: Moral Education Research Foundation, 1975.

Kohlberg, L. Moral stages and moralization: The cognitive-developmental approach. In T. Lickona (Ed.) *Moral Development and Behavior*, pp. 31–53. New York: Holt, Rinehart & Winston, 1976.

Kohlberg, L. (Ed.) *Recent Research in Moral Development*. New York: Holt, Rinehart & Winston, in press.

Kriesberg, S. Decisionmaking models and the control of corporate crime. *Yale Law Journal* **85**:1091–1129 (1976).

Kurtines, W., and Greif, E. The development of moral thought: Review and evaluation of Kohlberg's approach. *Psychological Bulletin* **81**:453–470 (1979).

Lane, R. Why businessmen violate the law. *Journal of Criminal Law, Criminology, and Police Science* **44**:151–165 (1953).

Leming, J. Moral reasoning, sense of control and social-political activism among adolescents. *Adolescence* **9**:507–528 (1974).

Lickona, T. Critical issues in the study of moral development and behavior. In T. Lickona (Ed.) *Moral Development and Behavior*, pp. 3–27. New York: Holt, Rinehart & Winston, 1976.

Lickona, T. (Ed.) *Moral development and behavior*. New York: Holt, Rinehart & Winston, 1976.

Lieberman, S. Effects of changes in roles on the attitudes of role occupants. *Human Relations* **9**:385–402 (1956).

Liebhart, E. Empathy and emergency helping: The effects of personality, self-concern, and acquaintance. *Journal of Experimental Social Psychology* **8**:404–411 (1972).

Linowes, D. An approach to socio-economic accounting. *Conference Board Record*, pp. 58–61, November 1972.

Lowrance, W. *Of Acceptable Risk: Science and the Determination of Public Safety*. Los Altos, Ca.: William Kaufman, 1976.

Maccoby, E., and Jacklyn, C. *The Psychology of Sex Differences*. Stanford: Stanford University Press, 1974.

Manne, H. Good for General Motors? In E. Bander (Ed.) *The Corporation in a Democratic Society*, pp. 100–108. New York: H. W. Wilson, 1975.

March, J., and Simon, H. *Organizations*. New York: Wiley, 1959.

McCarthy, C. Deciding to cheapen the product. In R. Heilbroner et al. *In the Name of Profit*, pp. 32–59. New York: Doubleday, 1972.

McNamee, S. Relation of moral reasoning to experimental helping behavior. In L. Kohlberg (Ed.) *Recent Research in Moral Development*. New York: Holt, Rinehart & Winston, in press.

Megargee, E. The prediction of violence with psychological tests. In C. Spielberger (Ed.) *Current Topics in Clinical and Community Psychology*. New York: Academic Press, 1970.

Merton, R. K. *Social Theory and Social Structure*. New York: Free Press, 1957.

Milgram, S. Behavioral study of obedience. *Journal of Abnormal and Social Psychology* **67**:371–378 (1963).

Milgram, S. Some conditions of obedience and disobedience to authority. *Human Relations* **18**:57–76 (1965).

Mintz, M., and Cohen, J. S. *America, Inc.* New York: Dial Press, 1971.

Mischel, W. *Personality and Assessment*. New York: Wiley, 1968.

Mischel, W., and Mischel, H. A cognitive social-learning approach to morality and self regulation. In T. Lickona (Ed.) *Moral Development and Behavior*, pp. 84–107. New York: Holt, Rinehart & Winston, 1976.

Monahan, J., Novaco, R., and Geis, G. Corporate violence: Research strategies for community psychology. In T. Sarbin (Ed.) *Community Psychology and Criminal Justice*. New York: Human Sciences Press, 1979, pp. 117–141.

Nader, R. Campaign GM. In E. Bander (Ed.) *The Corporation in a Democratic Society*, pp. 97–99. New York: H. W. Wilson, 1975.

Nader, R. Forward. In J. Esposito, *Vanishing air*. New York: Grossman, 1971.

Nader, R. *Unsafe at Any Speed*. New York: Grossman Publishers, 1975.

Opton, N. It never happened and besides they deserved it. In N. Sanford and C. Comstock (Eds.) *Sanctions for Evil*, pp. 49–70. San Francisco: Jossey-Bass, 1971.

Parsons, T. *Structure and Process in Modern Societies*. Glencoe, Ill.: Free Press, 1960.

Piaget, J. *Six Psychological Studies*. New York: Random House, 1967.

Porter, L., Lawler, E., and Hackman, J. *Behavior in Organizations*. New York: McGraw-Hill, 1976.

Rest, J. New approaches in the assessment of moral judgment. In T. Lickona (Ed.) *Moral Development and Behavior,* pp. 198–218. New York: Holt, Rinehart & Winston, 1976.

Roche, J. The threat to American business. In E. Bander (Ed.) *The Corporation in a Democratic Society,* pp. 89–93. New York: H. W. Wilson, 1975.

Rosenham, D., Moore, B., and Underwood, B. The social psychology of moral behavior. In T. Lickona (Ed.) *Moral Development and Behavior,* pp. 241–252. New York: Holt, Rinehart & Winston, 1976.

Sarbin, T., and Allen, V. Role theory. In G. Lindzey and E. Aronson (Eds.) *The Handbook of Social Psychology,* pp. 488–567. Reading, Mass.: Addison-Wesley, 2nd Ed., Vol. 1 (1964).

Schwartz, S., and Clausen, G. Responsibility norms and helping in an emergency. *Journal of Personality and Social Psychology* **16:**299–310 (1970).

Selman, R. Social cognitive understanding: A guide to educational and clinical practice. In T. Lickona (Ed.) *Moral Development and Behavior.* New York: Holt, Rinehart & Winston, 1976.

Simpson, E. A holistic approach to moral development and behavior. In T. Lickona (Ed.) *Moral Development and Behavior,* pp. 159–170. New York: Holt, Rinehart & Winston, 1976.

Simpson, E. Moral development research: A case of scientific cultural bias. *Human Development* **17:**81–106 (1974).

Stone, C. *Where the law ends: The social control of corporate behavior.* New York: Harper & Row, 1975.

Townsend, R. A modest proposal: The public director. In R. Nader and M. Green (Eds.) *Corporate Power in America,* pp. 257–259. New York: Grossman, 1973.

Tapp, J. Psychology and the law: An overture. *Annual Review of Psychology* **27:**253–404 (1976).

Tapp, J., and Kohlberg, L. Developing senses of law and legal justice. *Journal of Social Issues* **27:**65–91 (1971).

Turner, C. W., Layton, J. F., and Simons, L. S. Naturalistic studies of aggressive behavior: Aggressive stimuli, victim visibility, and horn honking. *Journal of Personality and Social Psychology* **31:**1098–1107 (1975).

Zimbardo, P. G. The human choice: Individuation, reason, and order versus deindividuation, impulse, and chaos. *Nebraska Symposium on Motivation,* 1969. Lincoln, Nebraska: 237–309, 1969.

FOOTNOTE TO CHAPTER 1

[1]We have adopted an "unreasonable risk" standard for designating a given decision as a case of corporate violence. Thus, we explicitly acknowledge the role of social judgments in determining culpability for harm-doing. Our point of departure is that corporate decisions that increase the risk of physical harm to people are socially undesirable. However, if one took *any* increase in the risk of physical harm as the standard, one would be faced with the dilemma that it is almost always possible to conceive of less harmful alternatives, but there comes a point at which such alternatives cease to be pragmatically feasible. For example, while one could always make safer automobiles out of thicker metal, failure to produce tank-like cars should not be considered "corporate violence."

The "unreasonable risk" standard derives from traditional criteria for negligence in tort law. People are liable if they do not behave as would "a reasonable man of ordinary prudence" (Vaughn v. Menlove, 1738, 132 Eng. Rep. 490). This person is "a personification of a community ideal of reasonable behavior determined by the jury's social judgment" (Prosser, 1971; p. 151). As described in the Second Restatement of Torts, "One who sells any product in a defective condition unreasonably dangerous to the user or consumer or to his property is subject to liability for physical harm thereby caused . . ." (Section 402A). According to Prosser, "the prevailing interpretation of 'defect' [in the above section] is that the product does not meet the reasonable expectation of the ordinary consumer as to its safety" (Prosser, 1971; p. 659).

Many factors must be taken into account in the determination of "unreasonableness" in the law, including the normative standards of the industry. Yet, as Judge Learned Hand noted in 1932, "In most cases, reasonable prudence is in fact common prudence; but strictly speaking, it is never its measure; a whole calling may have unduly lagged in the adoption of new and available devices . . . There are precautions so imperative that even their universal disregard will not excuse their omission" (Eastern Transp. Co. v. Northern Barge Corp., 60 F2d 470).

2

Four Studies of Stealing as a Risky Decision

David P. Farrington
Barry J. Knight

The decision to steal is a risky decision, since there is a certain probability that it will be followed by unpleasant consequences, such as apprehension by the police and legal penalties. The most influential theory of (single stage) risky decision making is the subjectively expected utility model (e.g. Becker and McClintock, 1967; Edwards, 1961; Rapoport and Wallsten, 1972; Slovic, Fischhoff and Lichtenstein, 1977) which has been derived and tested in gambling experiments. The subjectively expected utility (SEU) of an event or outcome is the product of the subjective probability of its occurrence and its utility, or subjective value or attractiveness. In a risky decision, each alternative choice has a total SEU, which is the sum of the SEUs associated with each possible outcome of the choice. The SEU theory suggests that a person chooses the course of action with the greatest SEU. It is inspired by the fact that, in gambling, a person can maximize his winnings by choosing the bet with the greatest expected value (the product of objective probability and objective value). Because of the maximization involved, it can be argued that the SEU theory prescribes the 'rational' course of action. It is not suggested that subjective probabilities and utilities are calculated and combined at the conscious level, but only that people behave as if they were maximizing SEU.

The four studies described in this chapter were designed to investigate whether the SEU theory can be used to explain the decision to steal. In the most direct application of the theory, it can be suggested that, given an opportunity to steal, a person will do so if and only if the SEU of stealing exceeds the SEU of every alternative course of action. This theory seems too simple, partly because it is deterministic, partly because it neglects individual or trans-situational factors, and partly because it assumes that every factor influences stealing only insofar as it has an SEU. However, it is worthwhile to begin with a comparatively simple theory and to see how far it can explain the observed findings and in what ways it might need extension and modification. A simple theory which explains a large number of findings may be more useful than a complex theory which can explain everything but predict nothing.

For a complete test of the theory, it would be necessary to measure the SEU of stealing and of each alternative course of action, to compare the SEUs to predict whether or not stealing would occur, and then to ascertain whether or not stealing did occur. For practical reasons, the studies described here concentrate on the SEU of stealing, and the prediction tested here is that the probability of stealing increases as the SEU of stealing increases. In turn, this means that the probability of stealing should increase with the subjective probability and positive utility of pleasant outcomes of theft and should decrease with the probability and negative utility of unpleasant outcomes of theft.

No other researcher has investigated the adequacy of the SEU theory in explaining stealing or any other kind of dishonesty or delinquency. Similar ideas can be found in a theoretical analysis by Short and Strodtbeck (1965), who argued essentially that the decision of a boy to take part in a gang fight depended on the subjectively expected utilities of the different outcomes. They suggested that there might be a rational balancing of the near certainty of immediate loss of status in the group against the remote possibility of punishment by the larger society. Cohen (1972) also emphasized the role of subjective probabilities and utilities in crime decision making but did not work within the framework of the SEU theory. He argued essentially that the offender staked the SEU of freedom against the quantity SEU (loot)/SEU (punishment). Piliavin, Vadum, and Hardyck (1969) and Phillips and Votey (1972) have also suggested that the commission of delinquent acts depends on the relative sizes of their rewards and costs, but they did not consider the role of subjective probabilities.

The assumption that crime is rational and that it varies with the severity and certainty of legal punishments is central to the concept of deterrence, but it is difficult to use the results of deterrence research to test the SEU theory. For example, some researchers (e.g. Chiricos and Waldo, 1970; Logan, 1972; Tittle, 1969) have carried out 'ecological' surveys in which crime rates in different states of the U.S.A. have been correlated with indices of the severity and certainty of legal punishments in these states. However, in addition to the problems arising from the biases in and noncomparability of official statistics (e.g. Hood and Sparks, 1970), ecological correlations cannot be used to draw conclusions about individuals (Robinson, 1950).

Surveys based on individuals are more relevant, and Willcock (1974) in England and Waldo and Chiricos (1972) in the U.S.A. found that youths who admitted to large numbers of delinquent acts gave low estimates of the probability of being caught by the police. Self-report measures of delinquency seem to be valid (e.g. Farrington, 1973), but it is difficult to establish causal order in these correlational studies. The SEU theory would suggest that a low probability of detection results in a high probability of delinquency, but the correlations are equally compatible with the hypothesis that those who commit large numbers of delinquent acts give low estimates of the likelihood of being caught, as a result of their experiences.

In testing any theory, it is desirable to carry out research with high internal and external validity (Campbell and Stanley, 1966). In testing the SEU theory, experiments with stealing as a dependent variable are likely to have the highest internal validity; field experiments with behavioral measures of stealing are likely to have higher external validity in relation to real life stealing than experiments in the laboratory or using verbal measures. Few experiments have ever been carried out with a behavioral measure of stealing or dishonesty as a dependent variable, but three of the four studies described here are of this kind.

Behavioral experiments in the related area of cheating have been carried out for many years, following the pioneering research of Hartshorne and May (1928). Some of the results obtained in these experiments are relevant to the SEU theory. For example, the likelihood of cheating increases with the rewards which are dependent upon it. Mills (1958) found increased cheating with a more valuable prize at stake; Dmitruk (1971) found more cheating with more attractive incentives; and Vitro and Schoer (1972) found more cheating in a test when the results of the test were made more important to the subject. The probability of cheating also varies with the likelihood and severity of negative consequences. Heisler (1974) varied the severity of the penalty for cheating by students by negatively sanctioning a confederate in front of them and found that cheating decreased as the consequences became more severe. Mills (1958) found that cheating decreased when he increased the likelihood of detection by suggesting to children that their scores would be checked, and similar results were obtained by Burton, Allinsmith, and Maccoby (1966), Hill and Kochendorfer (1969), Vitro and Schoer (1972), and Tittle and Rowe (1973). These results are in agreement with the SEU theory, suggesting that it may be useful in explaining other kinds of dishonesty.

Most theories of crime and delinquency have been historical theories in which present behavior is explained by reference to a sequence of past events. This is equally true of psychological approaches, such as social learning theory (e.g. Trasler, 1973) and sociological perspectives, such as labelling theory (e.g. Lemert, 1972). These theories emphasize individual consistency over situations and tend to neglect the immediate, situational determinants of crime. It is difficult to devise an adequate methodology to test historical theories. The typical method of comparing a group of convicted delinquents with an unconvicted group encounters many problems, both in the definition of the groups (e.g. the biases in official statistics) and in the measurement of historical factors (e.g. retrospective biases and faulty memory). Longitudinal surveys (e.g. West and Farrington, 1977) are more adequate, but they still encounter problems in drawing causal inferences. The SEU theory is a theory about the immediate factors influencing behavior, and as such it is much more susceptible to testing by the experimental method.

STUDY 1

This study was carried out by David P. Farrington, William S. Knapp, and Bonnie E. Erickson. Its aim was to investigate whether the probability of stealing increased as the SEU of stealing increased. In measuring the SEU of stealing, the number of possible outcomes was reduced to two, getting away with the theft and being caught by the police. The subjective probability and utility of each of these outcomes was measured, and the derived SEU was then compared with the estimated probability of stealing. The adequacy of the SEU theory in explaining stealing was also compared with its adequacy in explaining another kind of risky behavior.

The major focus of interest in the present research is on statements about likely behavior in hypothetical stealing and risk-taking situations, but these have been compared with statements about past stealing and risk-taking and also with actual stealing and risk-taking behavior. These comparisons are necessary, because statements about likely behavior in hypothetical situations may not always correspond with actual behavior in actual situations (e.g. Deutscher, 1973; Nisbett and Wilson, 1977). As an example of this occurring with stealing, Shaffer, Rogel, and Hendrick (1975) staged a theft in a university library to investigate bystander intervention and also described the theft to some students as a hypothetical situation. Many more students said that they would intervene to prevent the theft than actually did so (85 per cent as opposed to 40 per cent).

METHOD

Twenty-five Cambridge youths aged 16–18 were interviewed in a van parked in the street. They were recuited either at or near addresses where young adult delinquents were known to live. These addresses were obtained from reports of court cases in a local newspaper. Each youth was asked if he would like to take part in an anonymous survey about gambling and risk-taking and was told that he would have the opportunity to win some money by gambling. The interview was in four parts.

1. Actual Risk-Taking Behavior

The first part was designed to be a test of actual risk-taking behavior in gambling for money. Each youth was asked to choose which of two bets he would like to play, based on throws of a dice. One of the bets always involved a smaller chance of winning and a larger amount to be won, and this was operationally defined as the more risky bet. The expected value, or average amount which was likely to be won, was always the same for each of the bets in a pair. The youth was asked to choose between ten pairs of bets altogether, and the main measure of risky behavior was the number of risky bets chosen. After he had made all ten choices, he was given 50p and allowed to play all ten bets by throwing a dice, winning or losing money according to the fall of the dice. During this gambling task, the interviewer told the youth that the money was provided by a rich man who had won a lot of money from gambling and who was writing a book about gambling.

2. Actual Stealing Behavior

The second part of the interview was supposedly a coin-sorting test to see how fast the youth could think when he was handling money, but its real purpose was to provide an opportunity for the youth to steal. The youth was given a bag containing 2p, 5p, 10p and 50p coins and was told to sort these coins into the four compartments of a sorting box as fast as he could, not stopping if he made any mistakes. The interviewer explained that he was supposed to get out of the van while the sorting was in progress, so that he did not distract the youth. The youth had to time himself during the sorting by starting and stopping a stopwatch. After he had finished sorting, the youth was supposed to check through the piles of coins to take out any that had been sorted wrongly and then to call back the interviewer to the van. The interviewer told the youth in passing that he did not make up the bag and that he just collected the bag and gave it back, implying that he did not know very much about its contents. In fact, the interviewer knew exactly how many coins there should be in the bag and carefully checked through the coins after the interview to see if any had been stolen.

This method of measuring stealing was inspired by the research of Brock and Del Giudice (1963) in which children arrived one by one to find a female researcher in a state of apparent confusion with the contents of her purse scattered over the floor. She told each child that she had to go to a remote room; that she did not have time to collect everything together; and that she had no idea how much was in her purse, although she knew it was 'only pennies'. She asked the child to collect the things together and to put everything back in her purse while she was away. The researcher did in fact know how much money was scattered around, and, under these conditions, about 40 per cent of the children stole some.

3. Past Stealing and Risk-Taking

In the third part of the interview, the youth was asked a series of questions about past risky and delinquent activities. He was asked about the most he had ever lost in a week from gambling; whether he thought he took more or less risks in life than the average person; whether he had ever taken dares; whether he had risked getting involved in a fight; whether he had risked getting a girl pregnant; and whether he had climbed up the outsides of any buildings. He was also asked about being caught by the police; whether he had smoked pot or taken any other drugs; and whether he had stolen things from school or work or from a shop.

4. Hypothetical Stealing and Risk-Taking

In the final part of the interview, the youth was asked to estimate his likely behavior in two situations, one involving physical risk-taking and one involving stealing. In the stealing situation, he was asked to imagine that he was in a big store and that he did not possess a radio but would like to have one. It was pointed out to him that if he stole a radio from a store, he might get away with it and have something he wanted, or he might be caught by a shop assistant and reported to the police. He was asked to indicate, by placing a cross at some point on each of four lines, the likelihood that he would be caught by the police; how nice it would be if he successfully stole the radio; how nice it would be if he were reported to the police; and how likely he would be to steal the radio. The first and fourth of these lines were marked 'Definitely would not . . . . Definitely would' at the ends and were intended to measure subjective probabilities.

The position of the cross was converted into a probability by measuring its distance from the ends, set at .00 and 1.00, respectively. The second and third lines were marked 'The worst thing that could happen . . . . The best thing that could happen' at the ends and were intended to measure utilities. The position of the cross was converted into a utility by measuring its distance from the ends, set at −1.00 and +1.00, respectively. In the risk-taking situation, the youth was asked to place marks on the same four lines to indicate his subjective probabilities and utilities in connection with a physical risk, namely walking along a high wall in response to a challenge from his friends.

RESULTS

1. The Incidence of Stealing

The 25 youths could be divided into eight who could not possibly have known anything in advance about the interview and 17 who knew varying amounts about it, because they had been recommended by someone else who had already been interviewed and had told them something about it. Not one of the eight truly naive subjects stole anything during the coin-sorting test, but seven of the 17 who were more or less forewarned stole amounts ranging from one to seven 50p pieces. It seemed, therefore, that this stealing was, to some extent, premeditated, since it only occurred when a youth knew what was involved in the interview in advance. An attempt was therefore made to re-interview the eight naive subjects, on the pretext that the interviewer had lost their interview schedules. Five were re-interviewed, and three stole on the second occasion. For these subjects, all analyses are based on the second interview. In all then, ten of the 25 subjects stole during the coin-sorting test.

2. Past Stealing and Risk-Taking

On the basis of their own admissions, the 25 youths were a fairly delinquent group. Only seven of them denied ever having been caught by the police for committing an offence, while four had been to a penal institution. The main distinction used here is between the 11 who admitted being found guilty in court or cautioned for a standard list offence, such as burglary or theft (the 'delinquents') and the 14 who did not admit this. Nearly all the youths admitted stealing from school or work (21) or from a shop (22).

Again, nearly all the youths admitted past risky behavior, such as riding a bicycle with no hands (25); taking risks when crossing the road (23);

risking getting involved in a fight (22); risking getting a girl pregnant (19); and playing chicken on railway lines (17). Two distinctions are used here: firstly, between 12 youths who said that they had lost £3 or more in a week from gambling (the 'past risky gamblers') and the remaining 13; and secondly, between 14 who said that they took more risks than average (the 'risky youths') and the remaining 11.

3. Testing the SEU Theory in Hypothetical Situations

In the hypothetical stealing and risk-taking situations, the SEU of the act was correlated with the estimated probability of committing it. Taking a stealing example, subject 12 estimated his probability of being caught by the police as .45, which meant that his subjective probability of not being caught was .55. His utility of stealing successfully was $+0.2$ and of being caught by the police was 1.0; therefore, his SEU of stealing was ($+0.2$ × .55 1.0 × .45) or $-.34$. His estimated probability of stealing was .05. Over all 25 youths, the mean probability of being caught by the police was .48; the mean probability of stealing was .37; the mean utility of stealing successfully was $+.35$; and the mean utility of being caught by the police was $-.72$.

In agreement with the SEU theory, the SEU of stealing was significantly correlated with the subjective probability of stealing (Spearman $r = .36$, $p = .037$), and the SEU of risk-taking was significantly correlated with the subjective probability of risk-taking ($r_s = .50$, $p = .006$). In the risk-taking situation, 15 youths had an SEU of .00 or higher, and 14 of them had a probability of risk-taking of .80 or higher. Of the remaining ten youths, seven had a probability lower than .80. On the basis of the SEU of risk-taking, then, it was possible to divide the youths into two groups which overlapped very little in their probabilities of risk-taking. Much the same was true of stealing: fifteen youths had an SEU of stealing of $-.25$ or higher, and 12 of them had a probability of stealing of .20 or higher; only three of the remaining ten youths had such a high probability.

Of the individual probabilities and utilities, the probability of stealing was most closely correlated with the probability of being caught by the police ($r_s = -.38$, $p = .031$). It was less closely correlated with the utility of stealing and was unrelated to the utility of being caught by the police. It seems that the possible consequences of theft were much less important than the likelihood of being caught. A similar pattern of correlations was found with risk-taking. The probability of taking the risk and walking along the wall was especially related to the perceived probability of failing and falling off ($r_s = -.57$, $p = .002$); these results indicate that there are similarities between stealing and risk-taking.

4. Verbal and Behavioral Measures

The two verbal measures of stealing were significantly related, since the 11 delinquents gave a significantly higher mean subjective probability of stealing than the 14 nondelinquents (56.4 as opposed to 22.1: Mann-Whitney U = 41, p < .05). However, the behavioral measure of stealing was not significantly related to the subjective probability of stealing (mean 45.5 for ten thieves and 31.7 for 15 nonthieves: Mann-Whitney U = 55.5, N.S.). Furthermore, the delinquents were hardly more likely to steal than the nondelinquents (five out of 11 delinquents stole, as opposed to five out of 14 nondelinquents).

The measures of risk-taking were not significantly inter-related. The 13 youths who chose three or more risky bets actually gave a slightly lower mean probability of risk-taking than the remainder (70.0 as opposed to 86.7). The past risky gamblers also did not give a significantly higher mean probability (85.4 as opposed to 71.2). It could be argued that gambling and physical risk-taking are two different kinds of behavior; however, the past risky gamblers were no more likely to make risky betting choices than the remainder (six out of 12 as opposed to seven out of 13). The only relationship which approached statistical significance was the tendency of the past risky gamblers to see themselves as more risky than average (nine out of 12 past risky gamblers did so, in comparison with five of the remaining 13: Fisher exact p = .07).

5. Risk-Taking and Stealing

The probability of stealing was nearly significantly related to the probability of risk-taking (r_s = .32, p = .06). The utility of stealing was significantly related to the utility of taking the risk successfully (r_s = .43, p = .015). Other verbal measures of stealing were also significantly related to verbal measures of risk-taking; however, the behavioral measures of stealing and risk-taking were not significantly related. In fact, the thieves were, if anything, less likely to be risky gamblers than the remainder (four of the ten thieves chose three or more risky bets, in comparison with nine of the 15 nonthieves).

6. Comments by the Youths

The comments made by youths were sometimes illuminating; for example, one youth who was an exception in that he had a high SEU of stealing but a low subjective probability of stealing said, "If I really wanted a radio, I'd get somebody else to nick it." Another youth, who gave successful stealing a high negative utility, said that one radio wasn't anything much but that he might have stolen ten radios. The spontaneous comments of one or two youths indicated that their probability of stealing would depend on whether they were alone or with their friends.

DISCUSSION

On the basis of statements about likely behavior in hypothetical situations, this research shows that the SEU theory can be used to explain stealing and risk-taking. The subjective probability of stealing increased significantly with the SEU of stealing, and the subjective probability of risk-taking increased significantly with the SEU of risk-taking. Furthermore, verbal measures of stealing were related to verbal measures of risk-taking; however, the behavioral measures of stealing and risk-taking were not significantly related to the verbal measures. One possible reason for this is that the behavioral measures, which were taken first, biased the verbal measures in some way; for example, perhaps youths who had stolen in the coin-sorting test were reluctant to give high probabilities of stealing in case the interviewer should suspect that they had stolen.

The remaining three studies described in this chapter use behavioral measures of stealing or financial dishonesty and have experimental rather than correlational designs. As mentioned earlier, very few experiments have been carried out with stealing or financial dishonesty as a dependent variable: Feldman (1968) gave people an opportunity to dishonestly claim money which was said to have been dropped on the street; Feldman (1968) and Korte and Kerr (1975) gave cashiers and store clerks too much money when buying items, thereby giving them an opportunity to dishonestly keep the money; Bickman (1971) gave people an opportunity to dishonestly keep money left in telephone booths; White (1972), in an experiment intended to investigate the donating of gift certificates exchangeable at a local store, also observed children stealing these certificates, using a one-way mirror in a mobile laboratory; Diener, Fraser, Beaman, and Kelem (1976), after telling children that they could take one candy from a dish in a house, observed the stealing of extra candies or of money from an adjacent dish, using a peep-hole in curtains. In a campus-bound experiment, Penner, Summers, Brookmire, and Dertke (1976) left unobtrusively coded dollar bills in various locations where students would find them and recorded whether the dollars were returned, ignored or dishonestly taken. As an example of the problems likely to arise in campus-bound research, Coe, Kobayashi, and Howard (1972), in an experiment on the influence of hypnosis on stealing, asked a randomly chosen control group of unhypnotised subjects (students) to steal an examination paper on campus; none of them agreed, but the reaction of more than a quarter of them was to ask if it were a psychological experiment!

STUDY 2

This was a field experiment on financial dishonesty carried out by David P. Farrington and Robert F. Kidd (Farrington and Kidd, 1977). The measure of financial dishonesty was similar to that used by Feldman (1968). People in the central shopping streets of Cambridge, England, were given the opportunity of dishonestly accepting a coin which an experimenter offered them. For ease of exposition, the negative utility of an event or outcome, or its unpleasantness or unattractiveness, will be referred to as its 'cost' from now on; 'utility' will refer to positive utility.

METHOD

The experiment employed a 2×2 between-subjects factorial design, with two levels of utility (low or high) and two levels of cost (low or high). An attempt was made to vary the utility of dishonesty by offering either a 10p (low utility) or 50p (high utility) coin. An attempt was made to vary the cost of dishonesty by changing the experimenter's statement. In the low cost condition, the experimenter said 'Excuse me, I think you dropped this', while in the high cost condition he said 'Excuse me, did you drop this?' It can be argued that the cost of dishonesty was greater in the second condition, because it was more difficult and more unpleasant for the subject to have to tell a lie in order to claim the coin. In the first condition, it was easier for the subject to accept the coin passively. In the interests of simplicity, the design was intended to investigate the immediate cost of only one outcome, dishonestly claiming the coin. No attempt was made to make the subject aware of possible future outcomes or to vary their subjective probabilities. The SEU theory would predict more dishonesty in the high utility condition and in the low cost condition. One male and one female student, both neatly dressed and aged 20, served as experimenters.

The procedure was as follows: at the beginning of each trial, the experimenter consulted a stack of index cards to determine the experimental condition to which the next subject would belong. Each card contained the name of one of the four conditions, and the cards were arranged in a random order. Once the experimenter had determined the experimental condition, the next person (other than a child) who was alone and had at least one arm free was designated as the subject. The experimenter then positioned himself so that he and the subject would walk past each other.

When he was about 10 feet past the subject, the experimenter bent down as if picking something off the ground. He then turned and ran after the subject, calling "Excuse me," and, when he was parallel to the subject, he offered one of the two coins and made one of the two statements. The experimenter then waited for the subject's reply in silence. If the subject refused the coin, the experimenter prompted him once by saying "Are you sure?" and then turned and walked away. After the completion of each trial, the experimenter recorded the condition and the outcome on a data sheet, together with some information about the subject and the situation (sex, estimated age, dress, social class, place, day, time, and any statement made by the subject). The experimenters were not blind to the experimental conditions, but they were not told the experimental hypotheses.

In all, 84 subjects were tested, with about ten in each of the cells of a $2 \times 2 \times 2$ design comprising sex of experimenter, cost, and utility. The dependent variable was whether or not the subject claimed the money. The subjects included 49 males and 35 females, 54 of whom were judged to be aged 40 or less and 30 older; 27 dressed casually (e.g. jeans, anorak) and 57 more smartly; and 21 judged to be lower class on the basis of speech, 45 judged to be middle or upper class, and 18 judged to be students.

RESULTS

Thirty-one of the 84 subjects (36.9 percent) dishonestly claimed the money. An analysis of variance was carried out to compare the dependent variable of financial dishonesty with the independent variables of utility, cost, and sex of experimenter (see Kidd and Berkowitz, 1976, for a discussion of analysis of variance with dichotomous measures). The main effects of cost ($F = 3.94$, df $= 1/76$, $p = .05$) and sex of experimenter ($F = 4.21$, df $= 1/76$, $p = .04$) were statistically significant. Nearly twice as many of those in the low cost condition (46.5 percent as opposed to 26.8 percent in the high cost condition) falsely claimed the money, and nearly twice as many of those tested by a male experimenter (47.5 percent as opposed to 27.3 percent with a female experimenter). In contrast, the manipulation of utility had no effect on dishonesty (35.6 percent of those in the low utility condition being dishonest, in comparison with 38.5 percent of those in the high utility condition). There was also a significant interaction between cost and sex of experimenter ($F = 9.77$, df $= 1/76$, $p = .003$) and a near-significant interaction between cost and utility ($F = 3.50$, df $= 1/76$, $p = .06$). The cost manipulation affected dishonesty only with the male experimenter and not with the female experimenter; similarly, the cost manipulation affected dishonesty only in the high utility condition and not in the low utility condition. Alternatively, it could be said that high utility produced high dishonesty in the low cost condition, but that high utility produced low dishonesty in the high cost condition.

Dishonesty showed no signs of being related to any characteristics of the subject. Males were slightly, but not significantly, below average in their dishonesty rate (32.7 percent), as were those over 40 (33.3 percent), those dressed casually (29.6 percent) and those judged to be lower class (33.3 percent). Furthermore, none of these characteristics was significantly related to any of the three independent variables of utility, cost, and sex of experimenter. This shows that the random allocation was successful and that the above results cannot be explained away on the basis of different subject populations in the different conditions.

DISCUSSION

The results of this experiment do not wholly support the SEU theory. In agreement with the theory, decreasing the cost of the act resulted in the expected increase in dishonesty but only with the male experimenter. In trying to explain this, it might perhaps be suggested that the costs of falsely claiming money from the young female were higher than from the young male and that, in the case of the young female, the experimental manipulation of costs did not succeed in reducing them significantly. Contrary to the theory, increasing the utility of the act did not result in the expected, uniform increase in dishonesty. However, increased utility did seem to be associated with increased dishonesty at the low cost level, but associated with decreased dishonesty at the high cost level. Contrary to the theory, cost and utility did not have additive effects. It may be that cost and utility were not independent in this experiment and that an increase in the value of the money which could be falsely claimed simultaneously resulted in a disproportionate increase in the cost of claiming it.

Objectively, the behavior of the subjects in the present experiment was dishonest, in that they were claiming money which did not belong to them; subjectively, however, it is possible that some of them really did believe that the money was theirs. In our opinion, the number of subjects who genuinely believed this was extremely small. According to the experimenters' notes, most of those who claimed the money did so with alacrity and with no hesitation, often appearing very pleased and thanking the experimenter. Some seemed insincere in saying that the coin was theirs, and some showed signs of guilt: being flustered or hurrying away afterwards. Some tried to justify their acceptance of the coin by saying 'I often drop money' or 'I must have a hole in my pocket', although one said more frankly 'You never know your luck'. In contrast, many of those who refused the coin hesitated, checked bags or pockets, nearly accepted the money or accepted it and then gave it back. Although we had no measure of reaction time, it seemed from the experimenters' notes that the decision to refuse the coin took longer than the decision to accept it. One fairly typical refuser nearly accepted the coin, then said it was unlikely to be hers, since she did not see how it could have fallen, then said 'I'd take it if I thought it were mine, but why don't you have it?' A few were certain that the coin was not theirs, saying that they had not brought any money with them or that they had not had any 10p (or 50p) coins. Two refusers were annoyed or rude, and one engaged the experimenter in a discussion about the honesty of taking coins from people when you knew that they did not belong to you. As far as we can tell, no subject thought that the request was anything other than genuine, although one initially thought that it was a joke. Some others initially misunderstood what the experimenter was saying, thinking for example that he wanted them to give change. There was some evidence in the experimenters' notes that subjects had correctly perceived whether the coin were a 10p or a 50p piece and no evidence of mistakes on this score.

The experimenter effects found in Study 2 were difficult to explain, and it was unfortunate that the experimental design made it impossible to keep the experimenters blind to the conditions. It was therefore decided to investigate stealing using a nonreactive experimental paradigm (Webb, Campbell, Schwartz, and Sechrest, 1966) in which the experimenter was blind to the conditions.

STUDY 3

Studies 3 and 4 were carried out by David P. Farrington and Barry J. Knight. The method used in both was the 'lost letter' technique, which was originally used by Merritt and Fowler (1948) to study dishonesty. They showed that letters left on the street and containing a lead slug which felt like a 50 cent piece were less likely to be returned unopened than letters merely containing a message. Simon and Gillen (1971) found that letters containing what appeared to be $10 or $1 bills, but which in fact contained play money, were less likely to be returned than other letters. No researcher seems to have used the lost letter technique with real money to measure stealing. Hornstein, Fisch, and Holmes (1968) and Hornstein (1970) left a wallet in an envelope on the street containing, among other things, $2 in cash. These experiments were designed to investigate the effect of social models on helping behavior, but in fact failure to return the letter constituted stealing; this was not true in later research on helping, directed by the same author (Hornstein, Masor, Sole and Heilman, 1971; Sole, Marton, and Hornstein, 1975), for each 'lost' letter contained a $2 money order of no value to the subject. Nor was stealing involved in other research on helping behavior using either the lost letter technique (e.g. Gross, 1975; Lowe and Ritchey, 1973) or a lost postcard technique (e.g. Deaux, 1973; Korte and Kerr, 1975); finally, stealing was not involved in the very extensive use of the lost letter technique to measure political and social attitudes (e.g. Georgoff, Hersker, and Murdick, 1972; Himes and Mason, 1974; Jacoby and Aranoff, 1971; Milgram, Mann, and Harter, 1965; Wicker, 1969; Zelnio and Gagnon, 1977).

METHOD

1. Design

One hundred stamped, addressed, apparently lost, unsealed letters, each containing a handwritten note and, in most cases, also a sum of money, were left on the streets of London, England and were picked up by members of the public. The experiment employed a $2 \times 2 \times 2$ between-subjects factorial design, with two levels of utility (low or high), two levels of cost (low or high), and two levels of the probability of an unpleasant outcome (low or high). Ten letters were dropped in each of the eight main conditions of the experiment, and ten letters in each of two control (no money) conditions. The 100 letters were made up in a random order by D.P.F., with the restriction that each of the ten conditions occurred once in each block of ten letters. The initials of the recipient on the letter indicated the order in which the letters were dropped and made it possible to link up letters received with letters dropped (cf. Forbes and Gromoll, 1971; Stotland, Berger, and Forsythe, 1970). The letters were dropped by B.J.K., who was blind to the condition of each.

2. Independent Variables

An attempt was made to manipulate the utility of stealing by varying the amount of money contained in the letter, either 20p (low utility) or £1.00 (high utility); an attempt was made to manipulate the cost of stealing by varying the content of the note. In the low cost condition, the intended recipient was the male secretary of a yachting association and the sender's address was in Cambridge, a city associated with wealth and privilege. The note indicated that the sender was enclosing money for a yachting magazine. In the high cost condition, the intended recipient was an old lady, and the sender's address was in Croydon, a town not particularly associated with wealth. The note indicated that the sender was refunding money from a Senior Citizens' outing to the recipient. It was thought that stealing in the low cost condition would be less unpleasant, because the victims were less deserving. The fact that the cost conditions differed in three ways meant that it would be difficult to isolate which of the differences was the more important, but the aim was to make these conditions as different in cost as possible. The probability of an unpleasant future outcome, detection by the police, was varied by the form in which the money came: either cash (low probability) or an uncrossed postal order (high probability); the cash consisted of either two 10p coins or two 50p coins. With a postal order, it is necessary to forge the signature of the intended recipient in order to obtain the money, and it is possible that someone doing this might be asked for identification and hence be detected.

3. Dependent Variable

The dependent variable was whether the letter and its contents were returned intact to the intended recipient (B.J.K.).

4. Control Conditions

One problem with the operational definition of stealing as failure to return a 'lost' letter containing money is that it makes it impossible to separate honesty and helpfulness. By definition, those who return the letter are displaying both, but it is not necessarily true that helpfulness and stealing are two sides of the same coin. It may be that whether or not the finder wishes to help the recipient (or the sender) is a factor influencing whether or not he returns the letter, and it may be that costs and utilities influence helpfulness in the same way that they influence stealing. The 20 control (no money) letters were intended to investigate helpfulness in the absence of dishonesty. Ten had a very similar note to that used in the low cost condition, and ten had a very similar note to that used in the high cost condition. The low cost control letter requested the recipient to send the next copy of the yachting magazine, and promised to pay for it on receipt. The high cost control letter told the recipient about the date of the forthcoming Senior Citizens' outing, and asked her to inform the sender if she were able to come.

An additional 20 letters, two in each condition, were made up and posted by the authors, during the same period and in the same areas in which letters were dropped. Before beginning the experiment, we were informed by the Post Office that their sorting machinery was likely to tear up envelopes containing coins; however, during pilot work, we discovered that this never happened when good quality paper and envelopes were used. All 20 of the letters we posted ourselves were safely delivered (cf. Gross, 1975), leading us to conclude that the nonreturn of letters could not be attributed to theft nor inefficiency by Post Office workers nor to the Post Office's sorting machinery. We did not at any stage inform the Post Office about the experiment. These 20 self-posted letters will not be mentioned further. It should be pointed out that the Post Office had experienced difficulty in delivering at least one letter, because key words from the address had been obliterated by someone standing on it. The letter was opened by Post Office workers and was delivered to the correct address repeated on the note inside.

5. Procedure

The 100 letters were dropped on 27 days during a six-month period. The maximum number of letters dropped on any one day was seven, and each letter was dropped in a different location in Central or South London or Croydon, in order to avoid arousing anyone's suspicions. It is surprising to us that previous experimenters using the lost letter technique have dropped so many letters in so few locations over such short periods, with no mention of suspiciousness or adverse publicity. The only hint of possible difficulty in the literature is provided by Hornstein et al. (1971), who dropped 175 letters on three days in two locations, noting that anyone who found two letters was eliminated from their sample. The letters in the present experiment were dropped on every day of the week and at all times from 10:30 A.M. to 11 P.M.

The place to drop each letter was chosen by the experimenter before taking the envelope out of his pocket. Sites were chosen where people usually walked, which were dry (so that the envelope could not be spoiled by the ink running), which contained a minimum of competing litter and which were well lit (after dark). The experimenter waited until no one was directly in front of him or directly behind him and checked that no one was looking straight at him from other directions. He then bent down as if to tie a shoelace, placed the letter (address upwards) between his feet, and then walked briskly on. The whole manoeuvre was completed in seconds, and on no occasion was there any evidence to suggest that he had been seen. The experimenter walked on until he was at least 25 m from the letter and then sat in his car or pretended to look in a shop window until someone picked up the letter. He then recorded on a data sheet some details about the place and time, and some personal and behavioral details about whoever picked up the letter (the subject). These ratings were made in accordance with rules laid down in a coding manual which had been prepared in advance of the field work and modified in the light of pilot work.

Although the experimenter was blind to the condition of the letter, he reported that he often could not help noticing whether or not the letter contained coins as he placed it on the ground. On the other hand, because he was primarily concerned with dropping the letter without being seen, he hardly ever noticed whether the letter was addressed to a male or a female (i.e. Mr. or Mrs.). In the five instances in which the letter was picked up or touched by someone and put back on the ground unopened, it was left there to be picked up by someone else who was then defined as the subject. The original finder was counted as a passer-by. In the one instance in which the subject picked up the letter, took out the contents and then threw away the envelope, this was counted as stealing. Apart from this case and the one case in which the subject was actually observed posting the letter, the experimenter was blind to the value of the dependent variable. We deliberately did not try to drop letters near postboxes (cf. Bouchard and Stuster, 1969), because of the danger of the experimenter's ratings being biased by his knowledge of the dependent variable. Letters were either returned immediately or not at all: they were postmarked on the same day or the next possible day, and, in almost all cases, they were posted in the same postal area in which they were dropped.

Surprisingly few problems arose in the experiment. Two subjects disappeared from the scene so quickly that the experimenter was unable to observe their behavior after picking up the letter. One letter was returned without the money it had originally contained (a £1 postal order in this instance), and this was counted as stealing; otherwise, letters were returned intact or not at all. One subject located the telephone number of the experimenter and called to tell him that she had found a letter belonging to him and was going to put it in a postbox. Six others wrote comments accompanying the returned letter which explained how they had come to find it. There is no evidence to suggest that any subject thought that the letter was anything other than genuine.

We have described the research procedure in some detail, because previous experimenters using the lost letter technique have given very little information about it. Most of the previous studies relied on teams of largely unsupervised graduate students as experimenters and, with the exception of Hornstein et al. (1968), did not record details of the people who picked up the letters. In using the lost letter technique to investigate stealing, it is essential to use a very small number of completely trustworthy people, closely involved in all stages of the research, as experimenters; otherwise, it might be difficult to distinguish stealing by subjects from stealing by experimenters.

RESULTS

Twenty-three of the 80 letters in the main experiment were stolen. An analysis of variance was carried out to compare the dependent variable of stealing with the independent variables of utility, cost, and probability. Lunney (1970) and D'Agostino (1971) have shown that analysis of variance with dichotomous data and equal numbers of observations in each cell yields valid conclusions about statistical significance. The main effects of cost (F = 7.22, df = 1/72, p = .009) and probability (F = 20.05, df = 1/72, p = .001) were statistically significant: more than twice as many of the letters in the low cost condition were stolen as in the high cost condition (40.0 percent of 40 as opposed to 17.5 percent of 40: $\chi^2(1) = 3.91$, p < .05); more than four times as many of the letters in the low probability condition were stolen as in the high probability condition (47.5 percent of 40 as opposed to 10.0 percent of 40: $\chi^2(1) = 11.96$, p < .001). In contrast, utility did not have a significant effect on stealing (32.5 percent of 40 in the high utility condition, as opposed to 25.0 percent of 40 in the low utility condition: $\chi^2(1) = 0.24$, N.S.).

In addition to their significant main effects, there was also a significant interaction between cost and probability (F = 15.06, df = 1/72, p = .001): cost had a dramatic effect on stealing in the low probability condition but not in the high probability condition. In the low probability condition, 75 percent of the 20 low cost letters were stolen, in comparison with 20 percent of the 20 high cost letters ($\chi^2(1) = 10.03$, p < .002); in the high probability condition, only 5 percent of the low cost letters were stolen, in comparison with 15 percent of the high cost letters, an insignificant difference. The nonreturn rates of the low cost control and high cost control conditions were identical (20 percent). This suggests that the cost manipulation did not affect helping behavior and that the rate of unhelpfulness or carelessness in not returning letters was about 20 percent. This increases our confidence that stealing rather than unhelpfulness or carelessness was occurring in the low cost-low probability condition and that the cost and probability manipulations were influencing stealing specifically. The nonreturn rate in the low cost-low probability condition was significantly greater than in the control conditions ($\chi^2(1) = 10.03$, p < .002).

Of the other variables measured in this experiment, the estimated age of the subject and his behavior after picking up the letter were the most significantly related to stealing: the likelihood of stealing decreased with increasing age of the subject (63.6 percent of 11 aged 20 or less; 27.7 percent of 47 aged 21–50; 13.6 percent of 22 aged 51 or more: $\chi^2(2) = 9.02$, p < .02), in agreement with the age patterns found in the official English *Criminal Statistics*. The subjects who put the letter in their pocket or handbag were more than twice as likely to steal as those who walked along holding it (48.1 percent of 27, as opposed to 19.6 percent of 51: $\chi^2(1) = 5.61$, p < .02); this suggests that in most cases the decision to steal was taken immediately after picking up the letter. On picking up the letter, the vast majority of subjects (82.3 percent) took out and inspected its contents, while a small minority either glanced inside the letter (8.9 percent) or did not look inside it at all (8.9 percent).

The fact that the experimental manipulations of cost and probability had such clear-cut effects shows that they were very powerful, in view of the many sources of variation which were controlled only by the random allocation. Milgram (1969) argued that there was so much uncontrolled variance in the lost letter technique that it could only be transcended by using very large numbers, between 100 and 200 letters per cell of the design. Some researchers have tried to reduce the variance by eliminating certain finders from their sample (e.g. children and blacks were eliminated by Hornstein et al., 1971). Our results would have been even more significant if we had done this; for example, there were only three thieves out of 20 in the high cost-high probability condition. One was also the only child aged ten or less in the sample, and another was also the only tramp in the sample, and he had previously searched through litter bins. In his field notes, the experimenter predicted correctly "I bet it (the letter) does not come back whatever the condition." The only thief in the low cost-high probability condition was one of the eight noncaucasians, as were two of the four thieves in the high cost-low probability condition.

DISCUSSION

In agreement with the predictions derived from the SEU theory, stealing from a 'lost' letter decreased with increasing cost of the act and with increasing probability of future detection by the police; contrary to the theory, stealing did not increase significantly with increasing utility of the act. This replicates the result of Farrington and Kidd (1977), who found no difference between 10p and 50p in inducing financial dishonesty. These findings could be taken to indicate that the theory needs revision and that utilities have less influence on stealing than costs. Another possibility is that these utility manipulations were too weak, so that for the majority of subjects in this experiment the difference between 20p and £1 was not sufficient to have a significant effect on stealing. The operational definitions of the independent variables used in this experiment were chosen in the hope that the difference between each 'low' condition and each 'high' condition would be sufficient to have a significant effect on the dependent variable of stealing, but it is very difficult to produce comparable variations in utility, cost, and probability. Study 4 was carried out to investigate whether utility would influence stealing when larger monetary amounts could be stolen.

STUDY 4

METHOD

Sixty stamped, addressed, apparently lost, unsealed letters were left on the streets of London, England and were picked up by members of the public. In most respects, Study 4 was very similar to Study 3, but only one independent variable (utility) was manipulated. Each letter contained either £1 (low utility) or £5 (high utility) in cash or no money, and there were 20 letters in each condition. The note indicated that the female recipient had won a prize in the Senior Citizens' draw, so all the letters corresponded roughly to the low probability-high cost condition of Study 3. As in Study 3, 15 other letters were posted by the experimenters (five in each condition) and all were delivered by the Post Office.

RESULTS

The nonreturn rate increased significantly with the amount of money in the letter, from 5 percent in the no money condition to 25 percent in the low utility condition and 45 percent in the high utility condition (N = 20 in all cases; $\chi^2(2) = 8.69$, p < .025). In other words, stealing did increase with utility when larger amounts of money were involved.

As in Study 3, stealing in the money conditions decreased significantly with the estimated age of the subject: more than half (57.9 percent) of the 19 subjects aged 25 or less stole, in comparison with only 14.3 percent of the remainder ($\chi^2(1) = 6.53$, p < .025); furthermore, again as in Study 3, stealing was significantly related to behavior after picking up the letter. Seven of the nine subjects who put the letter in pockets or handbags stole, in comparison with only 22.6 percent of the 31 who walked along holding it (Fisher exact p = .004).

CONCLUSIONS

Taken together, these four studies suggest that the SEU theory can be used to explain stealing. The first study, using subjective measures and a correlational design, showed that the subjective probability of stealing increased with the SEU of stealing; the other three studies used behavioral measures and experimental designs. The second and third showed that stealing decreased with increasing cost (negative utility) of the act, and the third also showed that stealing decreased with increasing probability of a future, unpleasant outcome. These studies did not show that stealing increased with increasing (positive) utility of the act, but it seemed likely that the utility manipulations used in them were too weak. The fourth study confirmed this in finding that stealing increased with increasing utility when larger monetary amounts were involved.

The third and fourth studies also demonstrated that stealing was related to the age of the subject and to his behavior after picking up the letter. It might be suggested that cost, utility, probability, and age all influence the decision to steal, which in turn influences behavior after picking up the letter and stealing. This seems the most plausible causal chain. The fact that age was related to stealing suggests that the SEU theory needs to be extended to include individual factors, as well as situational ones. It is also plausible to state the theory probabilistically rather than deterministically, given the unpredictability of human behavior. The central postulate of the modified theory would then be that the probability of stealing depends partly on the individual factor of age and partly on the situational factors of costs, utilities, and probabilities.

This research raises ethical issues, partly because the subjects were not fully informed about its true aims and partly because they were given opportunities to steal; however, the requirement that subjects should give their informed consent would make it impossible to obtain behavioral measures of stealing. The subjects did not suffer in any way as a result of participating in the research, and it would not be realistic to argue that stealing in this research without being detected might encourage someone to embark on a life of crime. The subjects were not encouraged to steal but were merely given opportunities to do so, which could not have been dramatically different from others which had befallen them. While we are very concerned about ethical issues, we would like to argue that the social benefits of this kind of research in advancing our knowledge about stealing outweigh the ethical costs.

REFERENCES

Becker, G. M., and McClintock, C. G. Value: Behavioral decision theory. *Annual Review of Psychology* **18**: 239–286 (1967).

Bickman, L. The effect of social status on the honesty of others. *Journal of Social Psychology* **85**: 87–92 (1971).

Bouchard, T. J., and Stuster, J. The lost-letter technique: Predicting elections. *Psychological Reports* **25**: 231–234 (1969).

Brock, T. C., and Del Giudice, C. Stealing and temporal orientation. *Journal of Abnormal and Social Psychology* **66**: 91–94 (1963).

Burton, R. V., Allinsmith, W., and Maccoby, E. E. Resistance to temptation in relation to sex of child, sex of experimenter, and withdrawal of attention. *Journal of Personality and Social Psychology* **3**: 253–258 (1966).

Campbell, D. T., and Stanley, J. C. *Experimental and Quasi-experimental Designs for Research*. Chicago: Rand McNally, 1966.

Chiricos, T. G., and Waldo, G. P. Punishment and crime: An examination of some empirical evidence. *Social Problems* **18**: 200–217 (1970).

Coe, W. C., Kobayashi, K., and Howard, M. L. An approach toward isolating factors that influence antisocial conduct in hypnosis. *International Journal of Clinical and Experimental Hypnosis* **20**: 118–131 (1972).

Cohen, J. *Psychological Probability*. London: Allen and Unwin, 1972.

D'Agostino, R. B. A second look at analysis of variance on dichotomous data. *Journal of Educational Measurement* **8**: 327–333 (1971).

Deaux, K. Anonymous altruism: Extending the lost letter technique. *Journal of Social Psychology* **92**: 61–66 (1973).

Deutscher, I. *What We Say/ What We Do*. Glenview: Scott Foresman, 1973.

Diener, E., Fraser, S. C., Beaman, A. L., and Kelem, R. T. Effects of deindividuation variables on stealing among Halloween trick-or-treaters. *Journal of Personality and Social Psychology* **33**:178–183 (1976).

Dmitruk, V. M. Incentive preference and resistance to temptation. *Child Development* **42**: 625–628 (1971).

Edwards, W. Behavioral decision theory. *Annual Review of Psychology* **12**: 473–498 (1961).

Farrington, D. P. Self-reports of deviant behavior: Predictive and stable? *Journal of Criminal Law and Criminology* **64**: 99–110 (1973).

Farrington, D. P., and Kidd, R. F. Is financial dishonesty a rational decision? *British Journal of Social and Clinical Psychology* **16**: 139–146 (1977).

Feldman, R. E. Response to compatriot and foreigner who seek assistance. *Journal of Personality and Social Psychology* **10**: 202–214 (1968).

Georgoff, D. M., Hersker, B. J., and Murdick, R. G. The lost-letter technique: A scaling experiment. *Public Opinion Quarterly* **36**: 114–119 (1972).

Gross, A. E. Generosity and legitimacy of a model as determinants of helpful behavior. *Representative Research in Social Psychology* **6**: 45–50 (1975).

Hartshorne, H., and May, M. A. *Studies in Deceit*. New York: Macmillan, 1928.

Heisler, G. Ways to deter law violators: Effects of levels of threat and vicarious punishment on cheating. *Journal of Consulting and Clinical Psychology* **42**: 577–582 (1974).

Hill, J. P., and Kochendorfer, R. A. Knowledge of peer success and risk of detection as determinants of cheating. *Developmental Psychology* **1**: 231–238 (1969).

Himes, S. H., and Mason, J. B. A note on unobtrusive attitude measurement: the lost letter technique. *Journal of the Market Research Society* **16**: 42–46 (1974).

Hood, R., and Sparks, R. *Key Issues in Criminology*. London: Weidenfeld and Nicolson, 1970.

Hornstein, H. A. The influence of social models on helping. In Macauley, J. and Berkowitz, L. (Eds.) *Altruism and Helping Behavior*. New York: Academic Press, 1970.

Hornstein, H. A., Fisch, E., and Holmes, M. Influence of a model's feeling about his behavior and his relevance as a comparison other on observers' helping behavior. *Journal of Personality and Social Psychology* 10: 222–226 (1968).

Hornstein, H. A., Masor, H. N., Sole, K., and Heilman, M. Effects of sentiment and completion of a helping act on observer helping: A case for socially mediated Zeigarnik effects. *Journal of Personality and Social Psychology* 17: 107–112 (1971).

Jacoby, J., and Aranoff, D. Political polling and the lost-letter technique. *Journal of Social Psychology* 83: 209–212 (1971).

Kidd, R. F., and Berkowitz, L. Effects of dissonance arousal on helpfulness. *Journal of Personality and Social Psychology* 33: 613–622 (1976).

Korte, C., and Kerr, N. Response to altruistic opportunities in urban and nonurban settings. *Journal of Social Psychology* 95: 183–184 (1975).

Lemert, E. M. *Human Deviance, Social Problems and Social Control* (2nd ed.) Englewood Cliffs: Prentice-Hall, 1972.

Logan, C. H. General deterrent effects of punishment. *Social Forces* 51: 64–73 (1972).

Lowe, R., and Ritchey, G. Relation of altruism to age, social class, and ethnic identity. *Psychological Reports* 33: 567–572 (1973).

Lunney, G. H. Using analysis of variance with a dichotomous dependent variable: An empirical study. *Journal of Educational Measurement* 7: 263–269 (1970).

Merritt, C. B., and Fowler, R. G. The pecuniary honesty of the public at large. *Journal of Abnormal and Social Psychology* 43: 90–93 (1948).

Milgram, S. Comment on 'A failure to validate the lost letter technique'. *Public Opinion Quarterly* 33: 263–264 (1969).

Milgram, S., Mann, L., and Harter, S. The lost-letter technique: A tool of social research. *Public Opinion Quarterly* 29: 437–438 (1965).

Mills, J. Changes in moral attitudes following temptation. *Journal of Personality* 26: 517–531 (1958).

Nisbett, R. E., and Wilson, T. D. Telling more than we can know: Verbal reports on mental processes. *Psychological Review* 84: 231–259 (1977).

Penner, L. A., Summers, L. S., Brookmire, D. A., and Dertke, M. C. The lost dollar: Situational and personality determinants of a pro- and anti-social behavior. *Journal of Personality* 44: 274–293 (1976).

Phillips, L., and Votey, H. L. An economic analysis of the deterrent effect of law enforcement on criminal activity. *Journal of Criminal Law, Criminology and Police Science* 63: 330–342 (1972).

Piliavin, I. M., Vadum, A. C., and Hardyck, J. A. Delinquency, personal costs and parental treatment: A test of a reward-cost model of juvenile criminality. *Journal of Criminal Law, Criminology and Police Science* 60: 165–172 (1969).

Rapoport, A., and Wallsten, T. S. Individual decision behavior. *Annual Review of Psychology* 23: 131–176 (1972).

Robinson, W. S. Ecological correlations and the behavior of individuals. *American Sociological Review* 15: 351–357 (1950).

Shaffer, D. R., Rogel, M., and Hendrick, C. Intervention in the library: The effect of increased responsibility on bystanders' willingness to prevent a theft. *Journal of Applied Social Psychology* 5: 303–319 (1975).

Short, J. F., and Strodtbeck, F. L. *Group Process and Gang Delinquency.* Chicago: University of Chicago Press, 1965.

Simon, W. E., and Gillen, M. J. Return rates of 'lost' letters as a function of whether the letter is stamped and amount of money apparently in the letter. *Psychological Reports* 29: 141–142 (1971).

Slovic, P., Fischhoff, B., and Lichtenstein, S. Behavioral decision theory. *Annual Review of Psychology* 28: 1–39 (1977).

Sole, K., Marton, J., and Hornstein, H. A. Opinion similarity and helping: Three field experiments investigating the bases of promotive tension. *Journal of Experimental Social Psychology* 11: 1–13 (1975).

Tittle, C. R. Crime rates and legal sanctions. *Social Problems* 16: 409–423 (1969).

Tittle, C. R., and Rowe, A. R. Moral appeal, sanction threat and deviance: An experimental test. *Social Problems* 20: 488–498 (1973).

Trasler, G. B. Criminal behaviour. In Eysenck, H. J. (Ed.) *Handbook of Abnormal Psychology* (2nd ed.) London: Pitman, 1973.

Vitro, F. T., and Schoer, L. A. The effects of probability of test success, test importance and risk of detection on the incidence of cheating. *Journal of School Psychology* 10: 86–93 (1972).

Waldo, G. P., and Chiricos, T. G. Perceived penal sanction and self-reported criminality: A neglected approach to deterrence research. *Social Problems* 19: 522–540 (1972).

Webb, E. J., Campbell, D. T., Schwartz, R. D., and Sechrest, L. *Unobtrusive Measures: Nonreactive Research in the Social Sciences.* Chicago: Rand McNally, 1966.

West, D. J., and Farrington, D. P. *The Delinquent Way of Life.* London: Heinemann, 1977.

White, G. M. Immediate and deferred effects of model observation and guided and unguided rehearsal on donating and stealing. *Journal of Personality and Social Psychology* 21: 139–148 (1972).

Wicker, A. W. A failure to validate the lost-letter technique. *Public Opinion Quarterly* 33: 260–262 (1969).

Willcock, H. D. *Deterrents and Incentives to Crime among Boys and Young Men Aged 15–21 years.* London: Office of Population Censuses and Surveys, 1974.

Zelnio, R. N., and Gagnon, J. P. The viability of the lost letter technique. *Journal of Psychology* 95: 51–53 (1977).

3

Attributions in the Criminal Justice Process: Concepts and Empirical Illustrations

Daniel Perlman

Undoubtedly intellectual endeavors go through periods of growth and decline. During the past decade, both psychological approaches to legal issues and attribution theory have flourished. The growth of the psychology-law interface has been noted by June Tapp (1976) in her excellent *Annual Review* article. Tapp documented this growth in terms of conferences, grants, publications, the activities of professional associations, and the establishment of educational programs. Attribution theory has enjoyed an equally prosperous period: Bibliographies compiled by Clyde Hendrick and his associates in 1974, 1975, and 1976 (see Capasso, Hendrick, Rahal, and Coleman, 1977) showed attribution theory to be the most frequent topic of articles published in social psychology journals. Numerous books and monographs have also appeared (Shaver, 1975; Harvey, Ickes, and Kidd, 1976; Jones, Kanouse, Kelley, Nisbett, Valins, and Weiner, 1972; Harvey and Smith, 1977). Given the importance of the social area to the psychology-law interface, it is not surprising that efforts

This chapter was prepared while the author was enjoying a Canada Council funded sabbatical at UCLA. The paper evolved, in part, out of the author's association with Dr. Andrew Nesdale. Dr. Nesdale's contributions are gratefully acknowledged.

are now being made to study legal processes from an attributional perspective.

The purpose of the present chapter is to provide illustrations of the importance of attribution theory for understanding criminal justice processes. The chapter has three major sections. The first section sets forth the attributional perspective. Current attributional views stem largely from Heider's (1958) classic theoretical statement as elaborated upon by Jones and Davis (1965) and by Harold Kelley (1967, 1971, 1972, 1973). In selecting attribution theory concepts and postulates for presentation, particular attention was paid to key concepts in this intellectual tradition— especially key concepts in this tradition relevant to understanding criminal justice phenomena. The second section of the chapter reviews attribution theory studies of relevance to the criminal justice process. Given that the body of empirical literature is still relatively small, an excessive winnowing wasn't necessary. Studies illustrating the concepts introduced in the first section of the chapter were given preference. A few studies were excluded because I considered them methodologically or conceptually flawed. Research on attributions for rape (see Calhoun, Selby, and Warring, 1976) and accidents (see Vidmar and Crinklaw, 1974) was largely ignored, as it is only of peripheral relevance. The final section of the chapter contains reflections on the state of the literature. It focuses on advantages of the attributional approach and current trends in this area.

THE ATTRIBUTIONAL PERSPECTIVE

Attribution theorists are particularly concerned with how people explain the causes of behavior. For instance, in one recent attributional study (Kidder and Cohn, 1979) field workers talked with people about the high rate of crime in their neighborhoods. Here are some of the explanations people gave:

> "The judge lets 'em off too easy."
> "You see more and more young people getting into stealing . . . They have lots of time on their hands. Nothin to do. [Their] parents don't care enough."
> "I'd say the main reasons for our [crime] problems are a) the projects . . . b) the lack of employment, and c) welfare."
> "I think it's those drugs that are causing all this . . . you just don't know what they might make a person do."

According to Heider (1958) people tend to attribute acts to environmental factors, such as those just cited, or to internal properties inherent in the actor. Internal explanations focus on the actor's personality traits or "dispositions"; thus, a person holding a dispositional viewpoint might explain a purse snatching by saying "The offender was an immoral teen-ager."

In addition to this internal-external dimension in attributions, Weiner (1974) and others believe our explanations of behavior can be classified along a stable-unstable dimension. Stable causes are more enduring; unstable causes are more temporary. The difference in stable versus unstable attributions can be illustrated by the statements: "He got in a fight because he is an aggressive person" versus "He got in a fight because he was in a bad mood." Naturally, any given attribution can be classified on both dimensions simultaneously; thus, there are four major types of attributions: internal, stable; internal, unstable; external, stable; and external, unstable. (While other ways of classifying people's attributions have been suggested, the internal-external and stable-unstable distinctions are the most important, best documented dimensions at present.)

The process of making causal attributions can logically be divided into two component steps: In the first step, *causal assignment*, the observer must decide whether the behavior was caused by environmental or dispositional factors; then, if the observer attributes causality to the actor's attributes, the observer can then go on to make *dispositional inferences*. That is, the observer can decide which specific dispositions were important.

In the next subsections of this chapter, these two foci will be considered sequentially. The first sub-section on causal assignment will draw primarily on Kelley's insights and the second, on dispositional inferences, will feature Jones and Davis' (1965) "theory of correspondent inferences." Naturally, in actually trying to reach attributional conclusions, people often shift back and forth between issues of causal assignments and issues of dispositional inferences. Indeed, Jones and McGillis (1976) have recently provided a synthesis of the theorizing on these two component steps. They conclude that Kelley's postulates share a basic correspondence with those offered by Jones and Davis. Further references to these similarities will be made after considering each of these traditions separately.

Causal Assignment

Covariation Principles

Kelley (1973) distinguished two different cases faced by observers making causal assignments: In the first case (Kelley, 1971, 1972 in Jones et al., 1972), the attributor has information from multiple observations; in the second case (see Kelley, 1971, 1972 in Jones et al., 1972), the attributor has information from only a single observation. In the case of having multiple observations, the attributor relies heavily on the covariation principle in causal assignment. According to this principle, "an effect is attributed to the one of its possible causes with which, over time, it covaries" (Kelley, 1973; p. 108). To make a causal attribution, the observer naively employs J. S. Mills' method of difference: The act (or effect) is attributed to the conditions present when the act occurs and absent when the act does not occur. To determine this, the observer attends to variations in the act over entities (or stimulus situations), people, and time. Attribution to environmental factors is common, given the following conditions: 1) *high distinctiveness*—the actor responds differently to this stimulus situation than other stimulus situations; 2) *high consensus*—other people respond in the same way to the stimulus situation; and 3) *high consistency*—the actor responds to the stimulus presented in different modalities and on different occasions in the same way. Attribution to the person is common, given: 1) *low distinctiveness*—the actor responds to other stimulus situations in the same way; 2) *low consensus*—other people react differently to the stimulus situation; and 3) *high consistency*—the actor responds to the situation on different occasions in the same way. A number of studies (i.e., MacArthur, 1972) have provided empirical support for these tendencies.

Consider the example of Ted driving through a stop sign. Suppose: Ted never drives through other stop signs (high distinctiveness); most other people drive through this particular stop sign (high consensus); and Ted almost always drives through this particular sign (high consistency). Then observers would typically attribute Ted's behavior to environmental factors. If Ted drives through most other stop signs, other people typically don't drive through this particular sign, and Ted consistently drives through this sign, observers would undoubtedly attribute the behavior to something about Ted, himself; that is, they would assign an internal, dispositional cause.

The notion of consensus is generally related to legal arguments about what the "reasonable man" would do in a given situation. That all reasonable men would have acted similarly in the situation is a legal grounds for excusing an individual's behavior. Deciding how the reasonable man would act in a given situation is similar to judging what acts would be high in consensus.

Configuration Principles

Kelley (1971, 1972, 1973) has developed additional principles of causal attribution for cases where the attributor has information from only a single observation. In such situations, the attributor relies more heavily on the configuration of available evidence. Usually, in such situations, the attributor has observed similar effects in the past. He has some notions about what factors are necessary, and how various factors combine to result in a particular kind of effect. Kelley calls these notions causal schemata. Kelley discusses, among others, two important and basic causal schemata which attributors use. The first is the pattern of multiple *necessary* causes. Given this schema, the occurrence of an act implies that two (or more) causal factors were necessarily present. Supported by data from his study with Cunningham (Cunningham and Kelley, 1975), Kelley (1973; p. 117) argued "extreme effects are referred to the multiple necessary cause schema for their interpretation."

The second pattern is the pattern of multiple *sufficient* causes. According to this pattern, an act (or effect) can occur: 1) when *either* of two causes is strongly present; or 2) when *both* causes are present in moderate strength. In discussing the multiple sufficient cause schema, Kelley articulated the discounting and augmentation principles. According to the discounting principle, "The role of a given cause in producing a given effect is discounted if other possible causes are also present" (Kelley, 1973; p. 113). According to the augmentation principle, the presence of a force impeding an action serves to strengthen the attribution of the act to other possible causes.

The Principle of Actor-Observer Bias

In addition to Kelley's theorizing, another principle concerning causal assignment merits attention. Jones and Nisbett (see Jones and Nisbett, 1971 in Jones et al 1972) have argued that an *actor-observer bias* exists in attributions. Actors are more apt to attribute their behavior to external causes while observers are more apt to attribute their behavior to internal causes. This principle has an important implication for the criminal justice process. Defendants are apt to attribute their acts to external causes which might excuse their offenses. Judges and jurors are more apt to attribute the same acts to something about the person himself.

The Theory of Correspondent Inferences

Let us assume our hypothetical observer has decided that an actor's behavior was caused by internal factors. At this point, in addition to using Kelley's theory, Jones' and Davis' (1965) analysis also becomes important. They were concerned with how observers analyze the effects of acts to make inferences about the actor's underlying intentions and personal dispositions. They identified four factors that influence the strength and confidence with which dispositional inferences are made; the four factors are: social desirability, common effects, hedonic relevance, and personalism. Jones and Davis theorized as follows: First, acts which are low in *social desirability* (e.g., extreme and/or out-of-role) indicate more about the actor's dispositions than socially desirable acts; second, when an actor can choose among several courses of action, the unique, *"noncommon"* consequences of the chosen alternative are the most indicative of the actor's dispositions; third, acts which are high in *hedonic relevance*—that is, acts with positive or negative consequences for the perceiver—are more indicative of the actor's intentions than acts which are low in hedonic relevance. Finally, acts high in *personalism*—that is, acts seen as directed toward the perceiver him/herself—are more indicative of the actor's intentions than acts low in personalism.

As mentioned earlier, a basic correspondence exists between many of the postulates offered by Kelley and those offered by Jones and Davis; for instance, Jones' and Davis' notion of social desirability is akin to Kelley's concept of high consensus. Both notions imply that less information is gained about the actor from a response that is common or widespread among people. Similarly, the discounting/augmentation principles and the postulates concerning common effects both indicate that our attributions are influenced by knowing about the entire set of forces (or rewards) influencing the actor.

Jones and McGillis (1976) have argued that many of the classic attribution postulates offered both by Kelley and by Jones and Davis can be recast into a probability-type language. When we develop strong expectancies about a situation or group of people (category-based expectancies), these expectancies decrease the certainty of our dispositional inferences about a specific individual. However, when we develop strong expectancies about an individual's behavior via consistency, noncommon effects and the like, these so-called target-based expectancies increase our confidence in our dispositional inferences.

EMPIRICAL DEMONSTRATIONS OF THE ATTRIBUTIONAL APPROACH

For the attribution theorist interested in criminal justice processes, an obvious, central concern is the question: How are attributions related to the punishment offenders receive? Intuitively, it seems reasonable that behavior attributed to internal, stable causes would be punished more than behavior attributed to external or unstable causes. If true, then factors enhancing internal attributions should also enhance punishment.

There are now a small, but growing, number of studies which test the viability of an attributional approach to criminal justice phenomenon.

A logical way of presenting legally relevant research is to start with studies in which the investigators were directly concerned with causal assignment; then, studies concerned with the antecedents of causal assignment and/or correspondent inferences will be reviewed. Finally, a few well-established findings from outside the attribution literature will be presented. The purpose of considering this final set of studies is to illustrate how an attribution perspective is compatible with and might help to further explain existing evidence about the punishment of offenders.

Studies of Causal Assignment

Experimental Evidence

Carroll and Payne (1977a) directly manipulated causal assignments. They had college students and parole experts judge a series of different crime reports. Each report consisted of two short statements describing the crime and the defendant's circumstances. The descriptions were manipulated so that information suggesting an internal or external, stable or variable cause of each crime was presented. As predicted from an attributional analysis, students recommended longer prison terms for crimes with internal and stable causes than for crimes with external and variable causes. Among parole experts, the results were in the same direction, but they weren't statistically significant; however, the small (N = 24) sample size in this study may have undermined the power of the statistical analyses, and parole experts may have been reluctant to make strong recommendations on the basis of the scanty information contained in the case histories. Thus, further research with parole officers was warranted.

Naturalistic Evidence

In a follow-up study which largely surmounted such problems, Carroll (1978) got participating officials to complete questionnaires at the end of Pennsylvania parole board release hearings (N = 272). The parole officers were asked open-ended questions on the causes of the convict's crime and the reasons for his (or her) criminal record. These reasons were coded using the internal-external and stable-unstable dimensions. Officers were most likely to recommend parole if they attributed the offender's criminal history to unstable, external causes such as the offender being out of work. In general, officers were more sympathetic to convicts whose criminal histories they attributed to unstable rather than stable causes;

however, again in this study, the statistical main effect for the internal-external dimension was nonsignificant.

Additional Evidence

Although internality had little effect on parole recommendations, this dimension is undoubtedly important in other phases of the criminal justice process. Shaw and his associates (Shaw and Sulzer, 1964; Shaw and Reitan, 1969) provide one line of support for this contention. Shaw presented his subjects, who included lawyers and policemen, with descriptions of several events. The set of events was constructed to reflect different, successively more stringent criteria of the main character's personal responsibility for the situation's outcome. At the most basic level, association, personal responsibility was manifest with the main character merely being present when the incident occurred. At the next level, commission, the individual was responsible, in that his actions caused the outcome, even though he did not foresee the consequences of his behavior. At the third level, foreseeability, the individual was responsible in the sense of having been able to foresee the outcome of his actions, even if specific, undesired outcomes were not part of the goals for which the main character was striving. At the fourth level, intentionality, the individual was responsible for the outcome of the situation in the sense of foreseeing and seeking the consequences of his actions. As predicted, the higher the level of personal responsibility for negative acts, the more strongly subjects recommended punishing the person described in the scenario.

Another line of relevant evidence shows that people respond differently to others who are in difficulty depending on whether their problems were due to personal or environmental causes. For instance, Reed and Reed (1973) found that people attributing criminality to dispositional causes are more intent on avoiding social interactions with criminals than those attributing criminality to other causes. Similarly, in a laboratory analog study, Sawatsky and Perlman[1] found that subjects reacted more aggressively toward a poorly performing confederate when the confederate's performance was due to internal rather than external factors.

To sum up this review of work related to causal assignment, it appears that causes (i.e., internal-external; stable-unstable) of the offender's behavior do influence the reactions and punishment the offender receives. The general tendency, as expected from an attributional perspective, is for offenses associated with internal, stable causes to be treated more harshly.

Studies Involving the Antecedents
of Causal Assignment

Having seen the importance of causal assignment itself, we can go one step further back in the process. Do factors that promote internal, stable attributions also promote more severe reactions to offenders? Since apparently no criminal justice research has focused primarily on distinctiveness, this subsection will start with a review of work relevant to Kelley's two other major factors—consensus and consistency, then research on actor-observer bias and the severity of an act's consequences will be presented. Evidence for additional attributional principles will be integrated throughout this review.

Consensus

Carroll and Payne (1976) demonstrated the importance of consensus and hedonic relevance in the judgment of criminal acts. They had subjects rate 20 crimes on several characteristics; two of these characteristics were the frequency of the occurrence of the crime and the respondents' fear the crime might be perpetrated against themselves. These ratings served respectively as operational definitions for consensus and hedonic relevance. Consistent with an attributional model, acts rated as low in consensus and high in hedonic relevance were rated as more "criminal."

In another series of pertinent studies, Feldman and Rosen (1978) had college students recommend a sentence for a robbery defendant who either acted alone or with another person. From an attributional perspective, when many people commit a crime together, an observer can say that a given offender's action reflects either high consensus and/or group pressure as an external causal factor. Given either causal perception, an attribution theorist would expect what was found: a defendant who acted alone was rated as more responsible and given a longer sentence than a defendant who acted with an accomplice. In a follow-up archival study of actual cases tried in the State of Virginia, the investigators obtained comparable results.

Consistency

Judges and juries often have information about the defendant's previous record. From an attributional perspective, a person who commits a similar crime several times is probably manifesting both high consistency and low distinctiveness in his behavior. Given such an attributional pattern for an act rarely committed by other people, the behavior should be attributed to the offender's personal dispositions. Research by Lussier, Perlman, and Breen (1977) supports this viewpoint. Subjects read case histories of drug offenders and then made attributions about the causes of the offender's behavior. The acts of repeated (as opposed to first time) offenders were attributed more to the person himself; not surprisingly, subjects recommended more severe punishment for such offenders. Simulations (Doob and Kirshenbaum, 1972), analyses of actual cases (Hagan, 1974; Kalven and Zeisel, 1966), and research on bail setting (Ebbesen and Konečni, 1975) further support this finding: A defendant with previous criminal convictions stands a much greater chance of: having his bail set high, being found guilty, and of receiving a long sentence than does a defendant with no such history.

Naturally, theoretical purists might debate whether a history of frequent criminal offenses is precisely equivalent to high consistency as defined by Kelley. For instance, consider a criminal who has committed several grocery store thefts. This doesn't necessarily guarantee that his behavior manifests high consistency. If his behavior did show high consistency, every time he entered a small grocery store, he would be expected to perpetrate a crime. Despite such technical points, a record of frequent crimes undoubtedly does engender the general impression of high consistency and perhaps low distinctiveness in the offender's behavior. Given this caveat, these studies provide a noteworthy measure of support for the attributional perspective.

Ubiquitous Watergate: Actor-Observer Biases

The importance of actor-observer biases has been demonstrated in a study (West, Gunn, and Chernicky, 1975) designed as analogous to Watergate. Two groups of college students served as the actors and observers in this controversial study. The actors were approached by a "local private investigator" to help illegally enter an advertising agency. The prospective accomplices were told that the agency was maintaining a dual set of records to defraud the government out of several million tax dollars annually. The object of the burglary was to microfilm the records, not to steal anything. Some actors were offered $2,000 to participate, other actors in a control condition were offered nothing. The experiment was terminated after the subject agreed or refused to participate in the burglary. Subjects were debriefed, and the reasons for their decision concerning participation in the crime were obtained. Observers received a booklet describing in great detail the attempt to involve the actors in the crime. Half of the observers were asked to explain the reason why an actor agreed with this request; the other observers were asked why an actor disagreed.

Jones' and Nisbett's (1971) postulate concerning actor-observer differences was clearly supported. Decisions about participating in this crime were more strongly attributed to internal factors by observers than by actors. Furthermore, both observers and actors more strongly attributed the decision to internal, dispositional causes when the actor agreed to participate in the crime. This is consistent with Jones' and Davis' (1965) postulate that out of role, socially undesirable behavior enhances dispositional attributions.

Finally, the enticement method interacted with the actor's decision in determining attributions: When actors agreed to participate in the crime, the offer of $2,000 diminished dispositional attributions; when actors refused to participate in the crime, the offer of $2,000 enhanced dispositional attributions. In other words, the presence of an external cause served to minimize dispositional attributions for behavior facilitated by the external cause, but the presence of the external cause served to enhance dispositional attributions for behavior impeded by the external cause. Thus, these data are consistent with Kelley's (1973) discounting and augmentation principles.

Severity of an Act's Consequences

Rosen and Jerdee (1974) tested how the severity of an act's consequences influence attributions and recommended punishment. Rosen's and Jerdee's main hypothesis was derived from Kelley's (1973; pp. 117–118) discussion of extreme effects in causal schema involving compensatory causes and additive affects. This causal schema involves the following inferences: 1) an effect can occur if either internal or external causes are strongly facilitative; and 2) the strength of the facilitative causes is related to magnitude of the act's effects. In this discussion, Kelley implies a non-zero-sum quality to attributions. Kelley (1973; p. 118) also endorsed the prediction that as the outcomes of an act become more severe, the observer has an increasing tendency to attribute responsibility to the person.

Rosen and Jerdee (1974) tested this prediction using business students as subjects. Each subject considered four separate cases involving an infraction of company rules. Some subjects were told the infraction resulted in a mild consequence; others were told it resulted in a severe consequence. For instance, in one case an employee borrowed a company car under false pretenses. While using the car, the employee was involved in an accident described either as very minor or as entirely demolishing the car. As predicted, severe consequences led to greater attribution of personal responsibility; furthermore, subjects recommended that more severe discipline be administered in the cases involving severe outcomes.

Attributional Interpretations of Established Findings

Besides considering studies which directly test attributional concepts, another way of evaluating the value of the attributional approach is to ask: How well does it fit in with and/or explain established facts? An extensive treatment of this topic is beyond the scope of the present chapter; however, I have selected three established findings to discuss for illustrative purposes. These findings are that: a) people tend to be more lenient toward people they like; b) authoritarians tend to assign more severe punishments; and c) liberals tend to assign less severe punishments. The first finding, reported by Landy and Aronson (1969) and others (e.g., Reynolds and Sanders, 1975), can be succinctly explained in terms of fundamental attributional ideas. As already noted, observers tend to attribute the acts of disliked others to dispositional forces and the acts of liked others to environmental forces. Given the general tendency to be more lenient in the punishment of externally determined acts, it follows that people should recommend more lenient treatment of people they like.

That highly authoritarian subjects tend to assign more severe punishments than less authoritarian subjects (Berg and Vidmar, 1975; Centers, Shomer, and Rodrigues, 1970; Boehm, 1968) is a second generalization amenable to an attributional interpretation. Again, this may reflect a greater tendency among high authoritarians than among low authoritarians to emphasize the internal, dispositional causes of a defendant's behavior. Several studies support this interpretation: Berg and Vidmar (1975) found that high authoritarians recalled more evidence about a defendant's character, while low authoritarians recalled more evidence about situational aspects of the crime; similarly, Centers, Shomer, and Rodrigues (1970) found that people who believed dispositional factors are the main cause of delinquency scored high on authoritarianism. And finally, Boehm (1968; p. 746) commented that in simulating jurors "The authoritarians seemed prone to using subjective impressions of the character of the persons involved in the case . . . the anti-authoritarians tended to use the same kind of impressionistic evidence to conclude that even if the defendant were guilty as charged, it was not his fault but society's."

A general tendency among ideological liberals to be more lenient (see Nagel, 1962) may also involve attributional processes. As is frequently noted (see Miller, 1973), conservatives are more apt than liberals to attribute criminal behavior to enduring dispositions of the actor; furthermore, drawing on a concept studied by Brickman, Ryan, and Wortman (1975), conservatives may employ shorter causal chains. Causes have causes. Conservatives may stop with immediate, dispositional factors as an explanation of a criminal act; liberals may continue beyond immediate dispositional factors and further attribute these factors to external causes.

CONCLUDING REFLECTIONS

Rationale for an Attributional Approach

What are the advantages of an *attribution* theory approach to legal phenomena? First, the classic concerns of attribution theorists have been close in nature to the concerns of legal decision makers. Others beside the present author have noted this similarity of interests; for instance, Hendrick and Shaffer (1975; p. 316) commented that Hart's and Honore's (1959) classic *Causation in the Law* discusses "in great detail . . . what social psychologists call causal attributions." Given the notion of discretion, legal decision-makers naturally have an interest in the causes of an offender's actions. Attribution theory uniquely provides an understanding of causal inferences and the consequences that such inferences may have in the criminal justice processes.

It is worth underscoring, in this regard, that attributional thoughts are salient in the minds of criminal justice decision-makers. This was nicely demonstrated in research by Carroll and Payne (1977b): They asked parole officers to "think out loud" while preparing case recommendations for parole board hearings. These thoughts were then classified into several categories, such as information-seeking requests, judgments about the severity of the crime, etc. Of the statements coded, attributions were the single most common category of thoughts: Over twenty percent of all coded statements fell into this category.

Advocating the use of attribution theory does not necessarily mean it is the only (or even the best) psychological theory for guiding criminal justice research and practice. Like most psychological variables, attributional concepts account for only a small proportion of the variability in human behavior, but, this is an important proportion of the variance, given that attributions are salient for decision-makers and that offenders often give causal explanations as a line of defense for their criminal behavior. Furthermore, attribution theory has the advantage that it can be used in conjunction with a number of other theoretical models, such as information processing (Carroll and Payne, 1976), group dynamics (Davis, Bray, and Holt, 1977), and equity theory (Kidd and Utne, 1978) being employed in the psychology-law interface.

Current Trends in the Attributional Approach

In conclusion, a few trends in attributionally inspired legal research are worth noting: First, attribution theory is being applied to an ever widening set of legal phenomena; for instance, in addition to sentencing and parole studies, attribution research is being done on such topics as: The interaction of policemen with citizens (Rozelle and Baxter, 1975), the credibility of different styles of courtroom testimony (Lind and O'Barr, in press), and crime prevention efforts (Kidder and Cohn, 1979).

Second, based on the accumulating body of work, the attribution theory approach to criminal justice processes is becoming more refined (i.e., more elaborated, specific, revised in the light of new evidence, etc.). Similarly, within the general framework of attribution theory, differences in emphases are becoming apparent (see Fontaine and Emily, 1978); for instance, some theorists stress the logical aspects of the attribution process, while others stress ego-serving, often illogical aspects of the attribution process.

A third trend in attributional research is the effort being made to capture the attribution process as it occurs. Carroll and Payne (1977b) have developed a technique for having parole decision-makers verbalize their thoughts into a tape recorder while making actual case decisions. Fontaine and Emily (1978) have developed a similar procedure for analyzing attributional comments made by judges during trials. These techniques have the potential for producing exciting new results. They are also important for they signal a trend toward research being done in natural settings on individual cases. Given more such research, and, perhaps simply more outspoken champions of the approach, I anticipate psychologists giving lawyers attributionally inspired advice on specific cases in the near future.

REFERENCES

Berg, K. S., and Vidmar, N. Authoritarianism and recall of evidence about criminal behavior. *Journal of Research in Personality* **9**:147–157 (1975).

Boehm, V. Mr. Prejudice, Miss Sympathy, and the authoritarian personality. *Wisconsin Law Review* 734–750 (1968).

Brickman, P., Ryan, K., Wortman, C. B. Causal chains: Attributions of responsibility as a function of immediate and prior causes. *Journal of Personality and Social Psychology* **32**:1060–1067 (1975).

Calhoun, L. G., Selby, J. W., and Warring, L. J. Social perception of the victim's causal role in rape: An exploratory examination of four factors. *Human Relations* **29**:517–526 (1976).

Capasso, D. R., Hendrick, C., Rahal, L., and Coleman, J. Bibliography of journal articles in personality and social psychology: 1976. *Personality and Social Psychology Bulletin* **3**:307–325 (1977).

Carroll, J. S. Causal attributions in expert parole decisions. *Journal of Personality and Social Psychology*, **36**:1501–1511 (1978).

Carroll, J. S. Crime, the criminal, and the system: Causal attributions in parole decisions. In I. H. Frieze, D. Bar-Tal, and J. S. Carroll (Eds.), *Attribution Theory: Applications to Social Problems*. San Francisco: Jossey-Bass, 1979.

Carroll, J. S., and Payne, J. W. The psychology of the parole decision process: A joint application of attribution theory and information processing psychology. In J. S. Carroll and J. W. Payne (Eds.), *Cognition and Social Behavior*. Hillsdale, N.J.: Erlbaum, 1976.

Carroll, J. S., and Payne, J. W. Crime seriousness, recidivism risk, and causal attributions in judgments of prison term by students and experts. *Journal of Applied Psychology* **62**:595–602 1977 (a).

Carroll, J. S., and Payne, J. W. Judgments about crime and the criminal: A model and a method for investigating parole decisions. In B. D. Sales (Ed.), *Perspectives in Law and Psychology. Vol. 1: The Criminal Justice System*. New York: Plenum, 1977 (b).

Centers, R., Shomer, R. W., and Rodrigues, A. A field experiment in interpersonal persuasion using authoritative influence. *Journal of Personality* **38**:392–403 (1970).

Cunningham, J. D., and Kelley, H. H. Causal attributions for interpersonal events of varying magnitudes. *Journal of Personality* **43**:74–93 (1975)

Davis, J. H., Bray, R. M., and Holt, R. W. The empirical study of social decision processes in justice. In J. L. Tapp and F. J. Levine (Eds.), *Law, Justice and the Individual in Society*. New York: Holt, Rinehart and Winston, 1977.

Doob, A. N., and Kirshenbaum, H. M. Some empirical evidence on the effect of S.12 of the Canada Evidence Act on an accused. *Criminal Law Quarterly* **15**:88–96 (1972).

Ebbesen, E. B., and Konečni, V. J. Decision-making and information integration in the court: The setting of bail. *Journal of Personality and Social Psychology* **32**:805–821 (1975).

Feldman, R. S., and Rosen, F. P. Diffusion of responsibility in crime, punishment, and other adversity. *Law and Human Behavior* **4**:313–322 (1978).

Fontaine, G. and Emily, C. Causal attribution and judicial discretion: A look at the verbal behavior of municipal court judges. *Law and Human Behavior* **4**:323–337 (1978).

Hagen, J. Extra-legal attributes and criminal sentencing: An assessment of a sociological viewpoint. *Law and Society Review* **8**:357–384 (1974).

Hart, H. L., and Honore, A. M. *Causation in the Law*. Oxford: University Press, 1959.

Harvey, J. H., Ickes, W. J., and Kidd, R. F. *New Directions in Attribution Research* (Vol. 1). Hillsdale, N.J.: Lawrence Erlbaum, 1976.

Harvey, J. H., and Smith, W. P. *Social Psychology: An Attributional Approach*. St. Louis, Missouri: Mosby, 1977.

Heider, F. *The Psychology of Interpersonal Relations*. New York: Wiley, 1958.

Hendrick, C., and Shaffer, D. R. Murder: Effects of number of killers and victim mutilation on simulated jurors' judgments. *Bulletin of the Psychonomic Society* **6:**313–316 (1975).

Jones, E. E., and Davis, K. E. From acts to dispositions. In L. Berkowitz (Ed.), *Advances in Experimental Social Psychology* (Vol. 2). New York: Academic Press, 1965.

Jones, E. E., Kanouse, D. E., Kelley, H. H., Nisbett, R. E., Valins, S.; and Weiner, B. *Attribution: Perceiving the Causes of Behavior*. Morristown, N.J.: General Learning Press, 1972.

Jones, E. E., and McGillis, D. Correspondent inferences and the attribution cube: A comparative reappraisal. In J. H. Harvey, W. I. Ickes, and R. F. Kidd (Eds.). *New Directions in Attribution Research* (Vol. 1). Hillsdale, New Jersey: Lawrence Erlbaum, 1976.

Jones, E. E., and Nisbett, R. E. *The actor and the observer: Divergent perceptions of the causes of behavior*. Morristown, N.J.: General Learning Press, 1971.

Kalven, H., Jr., and Zeisel, H. *The American Jury*. Boston: Little Brown, 1966.

Kelley, H. H. Attribution theory in social psychology. In D. Levine (Ed.), *Nebraska Symposium on Motivation* (Vol. 15). Lincoln: University of Nebraska Press, 1967.

Kelley, H. H. *Attribution in Social Interaction*. Morristown, N.J.: General Learning Press, 1971.

Kelley, H. H. *Causal Schemata and the Attribution Process*. Morristown, N.J.: General Learning Press, 1972.

Kelley, H. H. The processes of causal attribution. *American Psychologist* **28:**107–128 (1973).

Kidd, R. F., and Utne, M. K. Reactions to inequity: A prospective on the role of attributions. *Law and Human Behavior* **4:**301–312 (1978).

Kidder, L. H., and Cohn, E. S. Personal theories about the causes of crime: An attributional analysis of crime prevention efforts. In I. H. Frieze, D. Bar-Tal, and J. S. Carroll (Eds.), *Attribution theory: Applications to Social Problems*. San Francisco: Jossey-Bass, 1979.

Landy, D., and Aronson, E. The influence of the character of the criminal and his victim on the decisions of simulated jurors. *Journal of Experimental Social Psychology* **5:**141–152 (1969).

Lind, E. A., and O'Barr, W. M. The social significance of speech in the courtroom. In H. Giles and R. St. Clair (Eds.), *Language and Social Psychology*. Oxford, England: Blackwell, in press.

Lussier, R. J., Perlman, D., and Breen, L. J. Causal attributions, attitude similarity and the punishment of drug offenders. *British Journal of Addiction* **72**:353–364 (1977).

McArthur, L. A. The how and what of why? Some determinants and consequences of causal attribution. *Journal of Personality and Social Psychology* **22**:171–193 (1972).

Miller, W. Ideology and criminal justice policy: Some current issues. *Journal of Criminal Law and Criminology* **64**:141–162 (1973).

Nagel, S. S. Judicial backgrounds and criminal cases. *Journal of Criminal Law, Criminology, and Police Science* **53**:333–339 (1962).

Reed, J., and Reed, R. Status, images, and consequences: Once a criminal always a criminal. *Sociology and Social Research* **57**:460–471 (1973).

Reynolds, D. E., and Sanders, M. S. Effect of defendant attractiveness, age, and injury on severity of sentence given by simulated jurors. *Journal of Social Psychology* **96**:149–150 (1975).

Rosen, B., and Jerdee, T. H. Factors influencing disciplinary judgments. *Journal of Applied Psychology* **59**:327–331 (1974).

Rozelle, R. M., and Baxter, J. C. Impression formation and danger recognition in experienced police officers. *Journal of Social Psychology* **96**:53–63 (1975).

Shaver, K. G. *An Introduction to Attribution Processes*. Cambridge, Mass.: Winthrop, 1975.

Shaw, M. E., and Reitan, H. T. Attribution of responsibility as a basis for sanctioning behavior. *British Journal of Social and Clinical Psychology* **8**:217–226 (1969).

Shaw, M. E., and Sulzer, J. L. An empirical test of Heider's levels in attribution of responsibility. *Journal of Abnormal and Social Psychology* **69**:39–46 (1964).

Tapp, J. L. Psychology and the law: An overture. *Annual Review of Psychology*, **27**:359–404 (1976).

Vidmar, N., and Crinklaw, L. Attributing responsibility for an accident: A methodological and conceptual critique. *Canadian Journal of Behavioural Science* **6**:112–130 (1974).

Weiner, B. (Ed.). *Achievement Motivation and Attribution Theory*. Morristown, N.J.: General Learning Press, 1974.

West, S. G., Gunn, S. P., and Chernicky, P. Ubiquitous Watergate: An attributional analysis. *Journal of Personality and Social Psychology* **32**:55–65 (1975).

FOOTNOTE TO CHAPTER 3

[1] Sawatsky, T. J., and Perlman, D. "An attributional analysis of aggressive reactions to punishment." Paper presented at the meeting of the Canadian Psychological Association, Quebec City, June, 1975.

4

Judgments of Recidivism Risk: The Use of Base-Rate Information in Parole Decisions

John S. Carroll

Accurate assessment of the risk which an offender poses to society is a necessary basis for attempts to isolate "dangerous" persons. As stated by Morris and Hawkins (1970):

> The policeman, the prosecutor, the jury, the judge, the probation officer preparing a presentence report, the clinician in the diagnostic and classification center, the correctional officer planning the inmate's treatment and custody, the parole board and the parole officer—all, like it or not, must make predictions about the possible social dangerousness of the offender they confront (p. 185).

Dealing with offenders on the basis of risk is of growing importance in the criminal justice system. As the crime problem becomes more evident, and, as resources for dealing with crime become strained, it is increas-

I would like to thank the Pennsylvania Board of Probation and Parole for providing use of parole case files, and the experts who acted as subjects in Study 2. Gail Naturale helped with Studies 1 and 2, Shirley Tucker and Jeanne Halpin helped with Study 3. Support for this research was provided by National Science Foundation Grant SOC75-18061 to the author and John W. Payne.

ingly necessary that the criminal justice system set priorities among the techniques available for crime control. Treatment models purporting to change offenders have mostly failed to demonstrate substantial results (e.g., Martinson, 1974); support for the deterrent effects of punishment, particularly increased sentence length, has been eroding, as research reveals a complex set of contested findings (Antunes and Hunt, 1973; Zimring and Hawkins, 1973). Increasingly, expert opinion and correctional practice is shifting toward models based upon just deserts and incapacitation of high risk offenders (e.g., Wilkins, 1976; Wilson, 1975). However, the past several years have seen progressively stronger criticisms of the ability of criminal justice decision makers to accurately evaluate risk or dangerousness (e.g., Kastenmeier and Eglit, 1973); for example, Hakeem (1961) found that experts were no better than students at predicting parole violations and both groups were worse than chance. Because prediction is central to many goals of the criminal justice system, recommendations have been made that statistical methods be employed to improve the assessment of risk (Gottfredson, 1967, 1975; National Advisory Commission on Criminal Justice Standards and Goals, 1973). The purpose of this chapter is to examine some psychological principles underlying the prediction of recidivism, with particular reference to the problem of incorporating statistical prediction aids in parole decisions.

CLINICAL AND STATISTICAL APPROACHES TO PREDICTION

The prediction of recidivism can draw upon two kinds of information. First, predictions can be based on the evaluator's knowledge of the specific case. The fine details and complex patterns of events and characteristics can be examined through the application of expert knowledge, experienced intuition, and personal one-to-one interactions. These are all part of a clinical approach to analyzing the unique case. In contrast, the second source of predictions examines several, easily measured characteristics of the offender (e.g., prior record, age) and relates them to the statistically assembled postrelease outcomes of other offenders sharing those characteristics; this is the statistical, or actuarial, approach. Glaser (1964) poses the issue when he states that "parole boards face the problem of how to integrate intimate knowledge of characteristics of a particular prisoner with general knowledge about broad categories of offenders" (p. 289).

Beginning with Meehl (1954), research spanning over two decades has addressed the relative efficacy of clinical and statistical approaches. The findings of a very large number of studies are surprisingly uniform: The statistical approach is as good or better at predicting future behavior than the clinical approach (e.g., reviews by Sawyer, 1966; Goldberg, 1968, 1970). Sawyer reports 45 studies comparing various ways of making clinical and statistical judgments. Criminal recidivism was the predicted characteristic in six of these studies, of which four concluded that statistical methods were superior to clinical methods and the other two concluded that they were as good.

The question of what happens when statistical prediction devices are made available, along with clinical information, to be incorporated by the decision maker in a generally clinical approach has also been addressed. Beginning with Cronbach (1955) and Meehl and Rosen (1955), research has challenged whether people can properly utilize this statistical information; for example, Sawyer (1966) reported three studies in which the availability of statistical predictions, along with other clinical data, did not improve prediction.

In a series of ingenious studies, Kahneman and Tversky (1973) showed how information about the base rates, or frequencies of some characteristic in the population, is largely ignored when case-specific information is present. In one experiment, subjects were asked to judge the probability that a very brief personality description allegedly sampled at random from a group of 100 professionals—engineers and lawyers—belonged to an engineer rather than to a lawyer. The descriptions were selected to be neutral for discriminating these occupations. One group of subjects was told that the descriptions had been drawn from a set consisting of 30 engineers and 70 lawyers; another group was told that the set had 70 engineers and 30 lawyers. Subjects under the two base-rate conditions produced essentially the same probability judgments, apparently basing their judgments on the degree to which the descriptions were similar to their stereotypes of lawyers and engineers. They did this even though they readily admitted that the brief descriptions were of little value for the decision. Kahneman and Tversky called this "perhaps one of the most significant departures of intuition from the normative theory of prediction" (p. 243).

Similar findings regarding the overdependence on case-specific information and neglect of base rates have been observed in a variety of situations (e.g., Lyon and Slovic, 1975; Meehl and Rosen, 1955; Nisbett, Borgida, Crandall, and Reed, 1976). Nisbett et al. provide an example of how compelling and concrete case-specific information is when compared with base rates:

Let us suppose that you wish to buy a new car and have decided that on grounds of economy and longevity you want to purchase one of those solid, stalwart, middle class Swedish cars—either a Volvo or a Saab. As a prudent and sensible buyer, you go to Consumer Reports, which informs you that the consensus of their experts is that the Volvo is mechanically superior, and the consensus of the readership is that the Volvo has the better repair record. Armed with this information, you decide to go and strike a bargain with the Volvo dealer before the week is out. In the interim, however, you go to a cocktail party where you announce this intention to an acquaintance. He reacts with disbelief and alarm: "A Volvo! You've got to be kidding. My brother-in-law had a Volvo. First, that fancy fuel injection computer thing went out. 250 bucks. Next he started having trouble with the rear end. Had to replace it. Then the transmission and the clutch. Finally sold it in three years for junk" (p. 129).

Logically, this specific case adds one more car to the thousands of Volvos and Saabs which were investigated by Consumer Reports. Yet psychologically, the impact far exceeds its statistical value.

Although statistical prediction devices have been available to parole decision makers for over forty years, little use has been made of them. Hoffman and Goldstein (1973) did find some effect of experience tables in simulated parole decisions by experts. However, they urged that "the empirical data should be interpreted extremely cautiously in that it suggests rather than confirms the various relationships" (p. 244). There is a genuine distaste for statistical prediction devices based on a variety of reasons: a) the view that the decisions are intrinsically individualized; b) the fact that statistical predictions cannot be right every time (this acknowledgment and estimates of the frequency of error may make decision makers feel more responsible for the mistakes, although, in relative terms, they are fewer than those made by clinical approaches); and c) the view (probably valid) that some important case factors will not be considered in the statistical prediction (Kastenmeier and Eglit, 1973, p. 505). To these reasons we should add: d) uneasiness over stating some reasons for decisions that are not part of the statistical predictions (e.g., public opinion, personal impressions, and private attitudes); and e) concern over loss of status or even loss of job in competition with statistical formulas. Kastenmeier and Eglit (1973) draw the pessimistic conclusion that:

> Even should increasingly refined prediction devices be developed, scientific clarity is still going to be adulterated by elements of imprecision and individualization at the juncture where the computer's role ends and the individual decision maker's role begins. (p. 505)

The single most ambitious use of statistical prediction devices took a different approach to aiding the decision maker. The United States Board of Parole is now using a two-dimensional system to "structure and control discretion—thus strengthening equity (fairness)—without eliminating it"

(Gottfredson, Hoffman, Sigler, and Wilkins, 1975; p. 41). A rating of offense severity and a statistical prediction based on 11 simple facts about the offender are used to determine guidelines for time served. For example, a "moderate severity" crime with "fair" probability of successful outcome (prediction) would have guidelines of 20–24 months of imprisonment. If the parole decision maker makes a recommendation outside the "discretion range" of the guidelines, he must provide extra justification. By relating statistical risk predictions directly to time served for each case, thereby avoiding subjective risk judgments that could dilute the predictions, decisions have been made more uniform and do conform to the statistical predictions (Genego, Goldberger, and Jackson, 1975; p. 869). Genego et al. discuss the legal issues involved in these guidelines. This approach, however, avoids the question of whether statistical prediction devices can be used by decision makers in ways other than to supercede their own risk judgments.

If the utility of statistical prediction devices is accepted, the question becomes how best to incorporate statistical and clinical approaches to prediction. The three studies which follow were conducted to examine what happens when different types of risk information are presented along with clinical information to decision makers who must make predictions of recidivism. These studies are part of an ongoing research project whose goals are: a) to gain an understanding of how decision makers predict recidivism; b) to determine under what conditions decision makers do utilize statistical information in risk judgments; and c) to prescribe how parole decision makers might best be made aware of statistical information in order to improve the accuracy of their risk assessments. The present discussion focuses most closely upon the second of these goals.

STUDY 1: NO USE OF STATISTICAL INFORMATION

The first study (Carroll, 1977) presented statistical information along with clinical information to decision makers who made predictions of recidivism. The first purpose of the study was to determine whether substantial use would be made of statistical information; the second purpose was to determine whether use of statistical information would depend on the *type* of statistical information presented. If some types of statistical information are used more than others, there would be two important implications: a) knowledge would be gained about the strategies decision makers use to deal with statistical information; and b) easier-to-use instances could make up the initial part of training experiences directed toward improving decision makers' strategies for reasoning with statistical information; these strategies could later be transferred to more difficult tasks.

The study presented 112 criminology student subjects with base-rate information about a population of 100 offenders, supposedly released two years before. The percentage of these offenders who committed a new crime during the two year post-release period was given, and subjects were asked to judge a sample of ten offenders, supposedly drawn from the population, and to predict (actually, postdict) whether or not each offender had committed a new crime. Each parolee was described briefly but realistically with information of the sort desired in parole hearings (cf. Wilkins, Gottfredson, Robison, and Sadowsky, 1973). The following is an example:

> Mr. Scott and two accomplices were convicted of conspiracy to commit burglary of a private home. He was sentenced to one to three years and has served one. He is 28 years old and married. He has had four previous convictions for burglary, larceny, and receiving stolen goods and was on probation at the time of the offense. His institutional adjustment has been good. He works in the music department as an instrument repairman and has had no misconducts. He is of average intelligence and has experimented with drugs but has no addiction or use of narcotics. He has been involved in counseling and displays considerably more maturity than before incarceration. He has been able to find employment as a musician in the past.

The information in each description was drawn from real cases but altered and recombined to give case descriptions which subjectively would be given a 50 percent chance of committing a new crime.

The base rates were presented in the introductory material, before any cases were examined. Subjects were told that we had examined the case files of the 100 parolees and had found that "(X) percent of the group of 100 offenders had committed another crime in the two years since release, while (100-X) percent had not committed another crime." Variations in the (X) percent and (100-X) percent constituted part of the experimental manipulations discussed below. Subjects were informed that the purpose of the study was to see whether accurate predictions could be made about future crimes of offenders released from prison, and that both experts and nonexperts would be asked to predict future crimes from brief descriptions of these case files, supposedly summarized by "Case Specialists from the Parole Board." They were then told that they would see ten descriptions picked by chance from the 100 available; that different subjects would see different cases; and that they should indicate whether each offender "did or did not commit another crime in the two years after release from prison.'' They could go back to reread descriptions if they wished, and it was again emphasized that these were real cases with known outcomes.

Three pairs of base-rate conditions were used. In all cases, subjects judged ten offenders drawn from a population of 100 offenders. In the first pair of conditions, either 75 or 25 percent of the population of offenders had committed a new crime. In the second pair, either 70 or 30 percent had committed a new crime. These pairs of conditions differ in that the second pair, while less extreme, is translatable into an exact seven-three split of the sample cases. This allows subjects to use abstract statistical information in a concrete way by reasoning that a fixed number of cases in the sample did recidivate. Subjects in a different kind of task used base-rate information to a substantial degree only when it was translatable in this way (Carroll and Siegler, 1977). In the third pair of conditions, either 75 or 25 percent of the offenders had committed a new crime, but two additional case histories were provided which included concrete outcomes (did or did not commit a new crime) congruent with the abstract base rates. This provides a concrete image of the link between the sample cases and other predicted behaviors. Nisbett et al. (1976) have shown in different setttings that concrete case histories strongly influenced prediction, while abstract base rates did not.

If high base rates for recidivism lead to predictions of more recidivists than low base rates for any types of base-rate information, it would show that subjects give some consistent weight to the base rates in making their judgments. Subjects do not have to ignore case-specific information nor give case-specific information less weight than base-rate information in order to exhibit an effect; they merely have to correctly perceive some relevance for the base rates. Only if they incorrectly perceive the case-specific information as almost perfectly valid should they fail to regress their judgments toward the population base rates.

The results were clear and compelling. Subjects in the high base-rate conditions predicted that 50 percent of the cases had actually recidivated, while subjects in the low base-rate conditions predicted that 49 percent had recidivated. This difference is thoroughly insignificant. No differences were found among the types of base rates. Subjects were also asked how they had made their predictions after they had completed the ten cases. Only one subject in the entire study even mentioned the base-rate information; thus, it is apparent that no appreciable use was made of the base-rate information. This was true despite the fact that the base-rate information was presented under very favorable conditions, including: high validity because outcomes were known, no time demands, small numbers, concrete examples in some conditions, and translatable base rates in some conditions.

At the end of the study, subjects were asked to predict the percent chance of recidivism of a case drawn from the 100 cases about which no clinical information was given. In this situation, subjects did utilize the base-rate information to a significant degree. This is consistent with work by Kahneman and Tversky (1973), showing that subjects know and understand the base-rate information, but that the presence of clinically-oriented information induces a purely clinical strategy of prediction. Apparently, the brief case descriptions, while sparse in comparison to the lengthy reports usually available to parole decision makers and selected to be neutral for prediction, were subjectively compelling enough to negate any strategy employing the base-rate information. Because our goals involve the behavior of expert parole decision makers, not simply criminology students (who will, however, operate in various capacities in the criminal justice system), we turned to the question of how the experts were dealing with risk information. This is reported in the next section.

STUDY 2: EXPERTS DO USE PREVIOUS RISK JUDGMENTS

Through our work with the Pennsylvania Board of Probation and Parole (e.g., Carroll, 1979; Carroll and Payne, 1977), we had copies of 210 Case Summaries of parole applicants. These summaries are two-page documents presenting important case information extracted from extensive case files by a Case Analyst; the Case Analyst also includes his judgments and recommendations on the Case Summary. The Case Summary is a major document used by the Hearing Examiner in making his recommendation which the Board nearly always ratifies

Examining these Case Summaries, we found that explicit risk statements appeared in 35 percent of them; examples would be, "Prognosis for success on parole is poor," and "A good parole risk." A total of 62 percent of the Case Summaries discussed risk in some fashion. Thus, the Case Analyst presents non-statistical predictions of risk in these documents which the Hearing Examiner will read. A simple question is whether this type of risk information does affect judgments about parole applicants. Study 2 was designed to systematically vary the presence of explicit risk statements in Case Summaries evaluated by experts. Nine expert decision makers from the Pennsylvania Parole system were asked to evaluate a set of Case Summaries on a one-page questionnaire. They were told that this was a pilot version of a post-decision questionnaire to be used in later research (which was true) and asked to provide comments about the questionnaire, as well as to make the requested judgments.

Twelve actual Case Summaries were selected from the 210 previously examined in order to represent the frequencies of crimes appearing in parole hearings and to be moderate subjective risks as evaluated on a simple scale by my research assistant and me. Three explicit risk statements were removed from the cases; eight explicit risk statements were taken verbatim from other cases: four favorable statements indicating a "good" or "above average" prognosis and four unfavorable statements indicating a "poor" or "questionable" prognosis. These eight risk statements were introduced into the Case Summaries in the place where they naturally occur: the Case Analyst's evaluation. For each subject, four cases had favorable risk statements, four had unfavorable risk statements, and four had no risk statements. The combination of cases and risk statements was varied across subjects using a repeated measurements Latin Square design (Lee, 1975; pp. 223–231).

As shown in Figure 4.1, experts' risk judgments were indeed in accord with the manipulated presence of explicit risk statements by the Case Analyst $[F(2,12) = 12.50, p < .001]$. The experts' recommendations for parole were also significantly better for "good" risks $[F(2,12) = 4.39, p < .05]$ and appeared to be similarly affected, but not significantly $[F(2,12) = 2.77, p < .11]$, in judgments of what the Case Analyst had recommended.

These results reiterate the importance of risk judgments in the parole decision. Furthermore, experts are quite sensitive to the risk information provided in another person's (clinical) judgment. Thus, the experts are not stubbornly pursuing their own risk analysis, disregarding all but their own knowledge, but are utilizing at least some outside information. The question now emerges: What is it that distinguishes this study, wherein experts use prior clinical judgments in making predictions, from Study 1, wherein students failed to use statistical information in similar judgments? Four hypotheses are readily available in answer to the above question: a) Expertise—experts will use information that students will not; b) Source—information from another evaluator will be used but not information from a statistical device; c) Form—information given verbally ("a good risk") will be used but not information given numerically ("70 percent chance"); and d) Reasoning—information provided with the case description will be used but not information provided about a group of case descriptions; the latter requires the inference that because the group is a good risk and the case is a group member the case is, therefore, a good risk. Study 3 was designed to investigate these hypotheses.

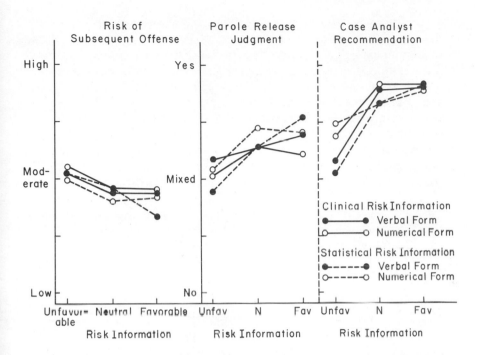

Figure 4.1. Experts' judgments about parole cases with verbal clinical risk information present.

STUDY 3: STUDENTS DO USE STATISTICAL RISK INFORMATION

Study 3 employed the same 12 Case Summaries as did Study 2. Seventy-two student subjects were drawn from the same criminology courses that had provided subjects the previous year for Study 1. The basic conception of this study was similar to Study 2; however, risk statements were provided in either verbal form or as a numerical percentage and alleged to come either from the Case Analyst or from a computerized statistical risk prediction device.

Thirty-six subjects received risk information embedded in the Case Analyst's evaluation, as in Study 2. For each subject: a) two cases had favorable verbal risk statements indicating a ''good'' or ''above average'' prognosis; b) two cases had favorable numerical risk statements indicating a 70, 75, or 80 percent chance of successful parole; c) two cases had unfavorable verbal risk statements indicating a ''poor'' or ''below average'' prognosis; d) two cases had unfavorable numerical risk statements indicating a 30, 35, or 40 percent chance of successful parole; and e) four cases had no explicit risk statements, two each associated with verbal and numerical form for ease of analysis. The wording of risk statements varied enough to avoid suspicion, using words like "chance," "risk," "prognosis," "remaining crime-free," and "success on parole." The combination of cases and risk statements was varied across subjects using a repeated-measurements Latin Square (Lee, 1975; pp. 223–231).

The remaining 36 subjects received risk information in a separate category of the Case Summary labeled "Statistical Risk Prediction." In the introduction to the task, these subjects had read that the

> "Statistical Risk Prediction" is assigned to the offender by a computer which used 11 characteristics of this offender (such as the crime, past record, age, marital status, parole plan, etc.) to compute a risk score. These 11 characteristics each has some statistical relationship to recidivism (new crimes) among past groups of parolees.

Half of these subjects always saw four favorable verbal risk statements and four unfavorable verbal risk statements (these were identical to those placed in the Case Analyst's evaluations) and four neutral risk statements indicating a "moderate" or "average" chance of success on parole. The remaining subjects evaluated the 12 Case Summaries with 12 numerical risk statements: four favorable and four unfavorable, identical to those used previously, and four neutral stating a 50, 55, or 60 percent chance of success. Thus, these 36 subjects either received all verbal or all numerical predictions for all cases in order to maintain a consistent cover story. The design was a repeated measurements Latin Square, crossed by the Form (verbal vs. numerical) variable (Lee, 1975; pp. 231–246).

Judgments were made on a subset of seven questions from the lengthy questionnaire used in Study 2. The three crucial measures were the subjects' assessment of the risk of a subsequent offense (recidivism), their recommendation for parole release, and their assessment of what the Case Analyst's recommendation had been. As shown in Figure 4.2, there was a consistent pattern of results indicating use of the risk information in all conditions.

In evaluations of risk, subjects receiving risk information from the Case Analyst exhibited a significant effect for risk $[F(2,150) = 3.13, p < .05]$. Individual contrasts comparing the favorable vs. unfavorable risk information for verbal and numerical forms showed a significant effect for these together $[t(150) = 2.20, p < .05]$ and non-significant trends for verbal information $[t(150) = 1.50, p < .15]$ or numerical information

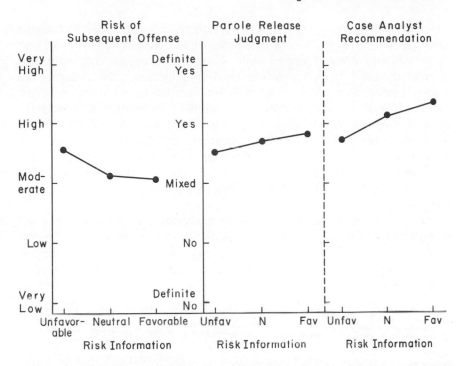

Figure 4.2. Students' judgments about parole cases with verbal or numerical, clinical or statistical risk information present.

$[t(150) = 1.62, p < .15]$ when examined alone. It is apparent from Figure 4.2 that cases receiving no explicit risk information did not differ from those receiving favorable risk information.

Subjects receiving risk information from the computer also exhibited a significant effect for risk $[F(2,60) = 3.32, p < .05]$. Individual contrasts showed the favorable risk information to produce lower risk ratings than the unfavorable information, for verbal and numerical forms together $[t(60) = 2.55, p < .05]$ and for verbal information alone $[t(60) = 2.60, p < .05]$, with a non-significant trend for numerical information alone $[t(60) = 1.59, p < .15]$. It is interesting to note that the effect of verbal information from the computer (verbal base-rate information) seems substantially larger than the effect of the other conditions, although this cannot be definitively demonstrated with post-hoc statistical tests. Only in the case of these verbal base rates is there an effect of favorable vs. neutral risk information. In other conditions, a 75 percent chance of success on parole is not distinguished from a 55 percent chance of success, although both differ from a 35 percent chance. Thus, subjects may be utilizing risk information in a categorical and concrete way, classifying cases into a very few categories which exhibit an uneven relationship with percent chance of success. Alternatively, subjects may be conservative about predicting favorable risk levels but may find the computer verbal statement to be uniquely compelling evidence for some (as yet unknown) reason.

Subjects' recommendations for release on parole follow a pattern similar to risk judgments, as they should if they are indeed based upon a risk assessment. The differences among risk information conditions is significant for the statistical information $[F(2,60) = 16.11, p < .001]$ and marginally significant for the clinical information $[F(2,150) = 2.88, p < .10]$. Individual contrasts between favorable and unfavorable risk information again showed verbal statistical information to have the greatest impact $[t(60) = 5.02, p < .001]$, followed by numerical statistical information $[t(60) = 2.56, p < .05]$, verbal clinical information $[t(150) = 1.65, p < .10]$, and numerical clinical information $[t(150) = 1.44, p < .20]$. As shown in Figure 4.2, only the verbal information from the statistical risk prediction produced an apparent difference in willingness to parole between neutral or moderate risk information and favorable risk information.

Subjects' assessments of what the Case Analyst's recommendation had been also showed the effects of the risk information. When the risk information originated in judgments made by the Case Analyst, subjects predictably felt this to be part of the Case Analyst's recommendation $[F(2,150) = 30.56, p < .001]$. Individual contrasts showed this to be the case for verbal information $[t(150) = 5.63, p < .001]$ and numerical information $[t(150) = 3.98, p < .001]$. When the risk information came from a statistical prediction device, there was less tendency to view this as fully representative of the Case Analyst's own view $[F(2,60) = 11.19, p < .001]$, although this tendency was stronger when the prediction was reported verbally $[t(60) = 3.75, p < .001]$ than numerically $[t(60) = 1.77, p < .10]$. As shown in Figure 4.2, this measure also reveals the equivalence between favorable and neutral information.

DISCUSSION

The results of Study 3 lead to one inescapable conclusion: risk information was used despite variations in source (clinician vs. computer) and form (verbal vs. numerical) and use of student subjects. Thus, three of the hypotheses originally stated have been unsupported, leaving the sole premise that associating risk information *with each case* is the critical difference between Study 1 and Study 3.

Two further hypotheses can be ruled out by additional data in Study 3. It is possible that the effects of risk information in Study 3 are very small (half the size of the effects in Study 2) and could not be detected were it not for the sophisticated design and multilevel dependent variables. This argument would propose that the relatively unsophisticated measures in Study 1 simply failed to detect a small, but real effect.

Although we cannot complexify the measures in Study 1, we can simplify those in Study 3. Risk of subsequent offense can be made something like a yes/no recidivism prediction by recoding into high risk (moderate and above) and low risk (below moderate). Collapsing across all conditions, except risk information, each subject evaluated a set of crimes with unfavorable, neutral, and favorable risk information. Across all subjects, 72 percent of the unfavorable risk cases were rated as a high risk of recidivism, as compared to 66 percent of neutral cases and 63 percent of favorable cases. The difference between unfavorable and favorable cases is significant $[\chi^2(1) = 5.34, p < .05]$; thus, it is readily apparent that the risk information in Study 3 produced large, visible, significant effects, whereas Study 1 produced no appreciable effects at all.

It is also possible that subjects learned to use the risk information during the study as they observed variations in risk information across the 12 cases they examined. In contrast, subjects in Study 1 had no variations in base rates to attract their attention or suggest the covariation of base rates and subjective risk (cf. Kelley, 1967). We can address this issue by looking at only the first case examined by each subject in Study 3. For this case, there was no opportunity to learn about the differences in risk information across cases.

Collapsing across all conditions except risk information, there were 29 subjects receiving unfavorable risk information in their first case (on any of 12 different crimes), and 79 percent of them rated the case as a high risk of recidivism; in contrast, 63 percent of 19 subjects receiving favorable risk statements did so, and 79 percent of 24 neutral subjects did so. The difference between unfavorable and favorable risk of 79–63 percent appears very much like the 72–63 percent effect present in the entire data, although not significant by itself $[\chi^2(1) = 1.52, n.s.]$. Using the complete multicategory dependent variable as shown in Figure 4.2, the means for unfavorable and favorable risk information would fall almost perfectly in place with the data from the entire study and be closer to a significant difference $[t(46) = 1.62, p < .15]$; thus, we have quite clear evidence that subjects were able to respond immediately to the risk information on even the first case.

The principal difference between instances in which risk information is utilized and those in which it is not has now emerged: the Reasoning

Hypothesis. Subjects in Study 1 were presented with the information that a group of parolees had a known recidivism rate and that each case they examined was drawn from this group. They apparently failed to complete the syllogism by saying, "therefore, each case has an expected risk of recidivism equal to that of the group." Some subjects in Study 1 were able to complete the syllogism when later asked to predict the outcome of a case from the group with no case-specific information. Yet, despite the significant difference between high and low base-rate conditions, only 14 percent of subjects gave the correct answer by repeating the base rate.

Clearly, then, the reasoning process involved is difficult and not immediately obvious to subjects. The completion of this reasoning process, accomplished in Study 3 by simply assigning a risk level to the individual case, does result in use of the risk information. This is in marked contrast to an extensive literature indicating only slight use of risk information.

These results are consistent with very recent work showing that base–rate information will be used if a *causal connection* is apparent between the characteristic about which the base rates are given and the events to be predicted (Tversky and Kahneman, in press). Thus, whereas in Study 1 the base rates do not cause recidivism (they are diagnostic rather than causal), in Study 3 subjects can understand high risk in a parole applicant as causing recidivism.

These results do not show, however, whether the use of base-rate information is in any way optimal. The shift in judgments observable in Figure 4.2 is quite small—it is possible to argue that subjects use the information but to an insufficient degree. Unfavorable risk information indicating roughly 60–70 percent chance of new crime, differs considerably from favorable risk information indicating 20–30 percent chance of new crime. Yet, as previously demonstrated, subjects judged 72 percent of cases with unfavorable risk statements to be high risk, but 63 percent of cases with favorable risk statements to be high risk; thus, subjects are altering their judgments considerably less than what *could* be "optimal" (we had no measures of optimality in this study).

In particular, the results of Study 3 suggest that subjects are not responsive to favorable risk information, treating it as roughly equivalent to neutral or no explicit risk information. Although one could explain such an effect for verbal information as a poor choice of labels, this cannot explain the relationship between numerical risk statements of 35–55–75 percent and subjective risk evaluations which only distinguish 35 percent from the two latter values. Furthermore, the same verbal risk statements *were* capable of establishing three distinct levels of risk when subjects believed that the statements represented a statistical risk prediction. This is evidence that the use of base–rate information is not a simple matter of whether or not it is used nor how much weight is assigned to it in judgment; rather, there may be marked differences in the use of a base rate depending upon whether it is favorable or unfavorable, and a verbally-stated statistical prediction may be the most effective means of transmitting risk information.

It is interesting to note that the major current use of prediction devices in parole decisions (Gottfredson et al., 1975) has adopted exactly this format—statistical risk categories labelled "fair," "poor," and so forth. This may be one reason why the approach has had some measure of success and acceptance. In this vein, it is interesting to compare parts of the results of Study 3, where risk information was provided verbally for our student subjects by the Case Analyst, with the results in Study 2, which gave nearly identical information to experts. The pattern of results is quite similar, even reproducing the similarity between favorable and neutral conditions. However, students are considerably different in overall level of their judgments and less affected by the risk manipulation. Students rate risk lower than do the experts, yet are less willing to parole, and even report the Case Analyst as having been less willing to parole. The differences among risk information conditions are much less for students than for experts in judgments of risk and release, although about equal in evaluating what the Case Analyst had said; thus, experts appear considerably more sensitive to explicit risk information than do students.

SUMMARY AND IMPLICATIONS

Our initial review of the literature on clinical judgment portrayed decision makers as obtusely subjective, unable to profit from "scientific" evidence. Study 1 provided support for this view, in that criminology students made no distinction in risk evaluations between parolees from a group with a known high rate of recidivism and those from a group with a low rate. However, Studies 2 and 3 demonstrated that experts and students can use risk information if it is provided with the individual case, regardless of whether it is stated verbally or numerically or appears to come from an expert's clinical judgments or from a computer's statistical formulas. However, the use of explicit risk statements appears quantitatively different along several dimensions: 1) experts are more sensitive to risk statements than students; 2) neutral and favorable risk statements are distinguished less (if at all) than either is distinguished from unfavorable risk statements—decision makers look for bad comments; and 3) verbally-stated statistical risk predictions seem more influential than either numerically-stated or clinically-derived risk statements, particularly in being the only instance in which favorable and neutral risk statements were appreciably distinguished.

The principal implication of these results is that more research is essential. We clearly do not know how risk information is used, only that it is used sometimes and not at other times. Improvement of this aspect of parole decision making, or clinical judgment in general, must rest on a better conception of the human judgment process. As yet, our knowledge of the differences between expert and layperson and our understanding of the strategies employed in prediction tasks are at an initial stage.

In practical terms, the research reviewed in this chapter demonstrates that risk information, provided to decision makers in a clinical setting, can affect judgment in appropriate ways. We can suggest that people do not have to be forced into using statistical information, but the degree to which it is then used may be less than optimal, especially for non-experts. Finally, the format currently in use for prediction devices in the Federal system, a set of verbal categories in which to present statistical risk predictions, appears to be the most effective presentational mode currently available. It is hoped that continuing research will improve the ability of parole decision makers to reach their goals of effective decision making.

REFERENCES

Antunes, G., and Hunt, A. L. The impact of certainty and severity of punishment on levels of crime in American states: An extended analysis. *Journal of Criminal Law and Criminology* **64**:486–493 (1973).

Carroll, J. S. Judgments of recidivism risk: Conflicts between clinical strategies and base-rate information. *Law and Human Behavior* **1**:191–198 (1977).

Carroll, J. S. Judgments made by parole boards. In I. H. Frieze, D. Bar-Tal, and J. S. Carroll (Eds.), *New Approaches to Social Problems: Applications of Attribution Theory*. San Francisco: Jossey-Bass, 1979.

Carroll, J. S., and Payne, J. W. Crime seriousness, recidivism risk, and causal attributions in judgments of prison term by students and experts. *Journal of Applied Psychology* **62**:595–602 (1977).

Carroll, J. S., and Siegler, R. S. Strategies for the use of base-rate information. *Organizational Behavior and Human Performance* **19**:392–402 (1977).

Cronbach, L. Factors affecting scores on "understanding of others" and "assumed similarity." *Psychological Bulletin* **52**:177–194 (1955).

Genego, W. J., Goldberger, P. D., and Jackson, V. C. Parole release decision making and the sentencing process. *Yale Law Journal* **84**(4):810–902 (1975).

Glaser, D. *The Effectiveness of a Prison and Parole System*. New York: Bobbs-Merrill, 1964.

Goldberg, L. R. Simple models or simple processes? Some research on clinical judgments. *American Psychologist* **23**:483–496 (1968).

Goldberg, L. R. Man vs. model of man: A rationale, plus some evidence for a method of improving on clinical inferences. *Psychological Bulletin* **73**:422–432 (1970).

Gottfredson, D. M. Assessment and prediction methods in crime and delinquency. In *Task Force Report: Juvenile Delinquency and Youth Crime*. Washington, D.C.: U.S. Government Printing Office, pp. 171–187 (1967).

Gottfredson, D. M. (Ed.) *Decision-Making in the Criminal Justice System: Reviews and Essays*. Washington, D.C.: U.S. Government Printing Office, DHEW No. ADM75-238 (1975).

Gottfredson, D. M., Hoffman, P. B., Sigler, M. H., and Wilkins, L. T. Making paroling policy explicit. *Crime and Delinquency* **21**:34–44 (1975).

Hakeem, M. Prediction of parole outcomes from summaries of case histories. *Journal of Criminology, Criminal Law, and Police Science* **52**:145–150 (1961).

Hoffman, P. B., and Goldstein, H. M. Do experience tables matter? *Journal of Criminal Law and Criminology* **64**:339–347 (1973).

Kahneman, D., and Tversky, A. On the psychology of prediction. *Psychological Review* **80**:237–251 (1973).

Kastenmeier, R., and Eglit, H. Parole release decision-making: Rehabilitation, expertise, and the demise of mythology. *American University Law Review* **22**:477–525 (1973).

Kelley, H. H. Attribution theory in social psychology. In D. Levine (Ed.) *Nebraska Symposium on Motivation*. Lincoln: Univ. Nebraska, 1967.

Lee, W. *Experimental Design and Analysis*. San Francisco: W. H. Freeman, 1975.

Lyon, D., and Slovic, P. On the tendency to ignore base rates when estimating probabilities. *Oregon Research Institute Research Bulletin*, 15, 1:1975.

Martinson, R. What works?—questions and answers about prison reform, *The Public Interest*, 1974, 35:22–54.

Meehl, P. E. *Clinical versus Statistical Prediction*. Minneapolis: University of Minnesota, 1954.

Meehl, P. E., and Rosen, A. Antecedent probability and the efficacy of psychometric signs, patterns, or cutting scores. *Psychological Bulletin* **52**:194–216 (1955).

Morris, N., and Hawkins, G. *The Honest Politician's Guide to Crime Control*. Chicago: University of Chicago, 1970.

National Advisory Committee on Criminal Justice Standards and Goals, *Task Force Report: Corrections*. Washington, D.C.: U.S. Government Printing Office, 1973.

Nisbett, R. E., Borgida, E., Crandall, R., and Reed, H. Popular induction: Information is not necessarily informative. In J. S. Carroll and J. W. Payne (Eds.), *Cognition and Social Behavior*. Hillsdale, N.J.: Erlbaum, 1976.

Sawyer, J. Measurement and prediction, clinical and statistical. *Psychological Bulletin* **66**:178–200 (1966).

Tversky, A., and Kahneman, D. Causal schemata in judgments under uncertainty.

In M. Fishbein (Ed.), *Progress in Social Psychology*. Hillsdale, N.J.: Erlbaum, in press.

Wilkins, L. T. Equity and republican justice. *Annals of the American Academy of Political and Social Science* **423**:152–162 (1976).

Wilkins, L. T., Gottfredson, D. M., Robison, J. O., and Sadowsky, A. Information selection and use in parole decision-making. Supplemental Report Five. National Council on Crime and Delinquency Research Center, Davis, California, 1973.

Wilson, J. Q. *Thinking about Crime*. New York: Basic Books, 1975.

Zimring, F. E., and Hawkins, G. *Deterrence: The Legal Threat in Crime Control*. Chicago: University of Chicago, 1973.

5

Prison or Mental Hospital: Factors Affecting the Processing of Persons Suspected of Being "Mentally Disordered Sex Offenders"

Vladimir J. Konečni, Erin Maria Mulcahy, and
Ebbe B. Ebbesen

The California Mentally Disordered Sex Offender (MDSO) Program is an example of the "rehabilitation through cure" approach to offenders that appear in some way "abnormal" or psychologically "maladjusted." More generally, the program is a reflection of the view that punishment should fit the offender, not the crime. The MDSO Programs in California and other states essentially make it possible for offenders convicted of any crime to be committed to the Department of Health and sent to a mental hospital for care and treatment for an indefinite period, instead of being sentenced under the applicable penal code provisions, if they are found to be "mentally disordered sex offenders." It is important to note that for a person to be suspected of being an MDSO, it is sufficient for him [1] to have engaged in abnormal sexual activities or offenses in the course of committing the offense for which he is eventually convicted, even though the conviction may be for a nonsexual offense (cf. Dix, 1976).[2] The legal definition of MDSO reads as follows:

> [A] "mentally disordered sex offender" [is] any person, who by reason of mental defect, disease, or disorder, is predisposed to the commission of sexual offenses to such a degree that he is dangerous to the health and safety of others. Wherever the term "sexual psychopath" is used in any code, such term shall be construed to refer to and mean a "mentally disordered sex offender" (West's Annotated California Welfare and Institutions Code §6300).

MDSO programs are interesting, not only as examples of the differential processing of offenders on the basis of somewhat vague criteria (indeed, such programs have been criticized for a variety of other reasons, as noted, for example, by Dix, 1976; p. 233), but also with regard to the general issue of the diagnosis and prediction of "dangerousness" (e.g., Cocozza and Steadman, 1974; Kozol, Boucher, and Garofalo, 1972).

This chapter describes an effort to develop a rudimentary causal model dealing with the disposition of persons suspected of being MDSOs. The project is an example of the application of our general theoretical and methodological approach to judicial decision-making in a specific and circumscribed problem area. Therefore, before describing the details of the present project, it is necessary to outline first the main features of the more general approach.[3]

GENERAL THEORETICAL AND METHODOLOGICAL CONSIDERATIONS

The criminal justice system is often represented as having a structure that fully constrains the processing of a "case" in an objective and codified manner. An alternative view is that of a system which brings together a number of decision-making participants or "actors" (e.g., the felon, the beat patrolman, the district and defense attorneys, the jurors, the judge, the probation and parole officers, etc.) or classes of such participants. To a large extent, the pool of information available to each participant at various points in time, and especially the various participants' respective decision rules, are not specified by law. The law merely codifies the gross consequences of certain decisions and the general direction and temporal aspects of information flow. In short, we view the criminal justice system as a network of interconnected decision-makers who have discretionary powers and whose actions influence one another. Each participant is seen as a decision-maker who must get information from several different sources, combine the different kinds of information according to some rule (whether implicit or explicit) and reach a decision. The decisions of a given class of participants often serve to influence the decisions of other participants. For example, in an earlier study (Ebbesen and Konečni, 1975), we discovered that in bail review hearings in San Diego county judges set bail by giving a large weight to the district attorney's recommendation (in dollars) who, in turn, based his recommendation largely on the severity of the crime; in other words, the judges' decisions seemed to be affected to a large extent by the decisions of the district attorneys.

Also, a decision made by one participant at one point in time often influences the decision of another participant many months later: In a study of sentencing of adult felons in San Diego county (Ebbesen and Konečni, 1976), it was found that the defendants' status with regard to being released on own recognizance vs. being released on bail vs. being kept in the cutody of the sheriff during the period prior to the plea-of-guilty or trial influenced, to a considerable extent, the eventual sentence (straight probation vs. probation with time in the custody of the sheriff vs. prison), even controlling factors such as the severity of the crime and prior record; thus, it could be argued that the bail decision made by one judge (or, rather, by the district attorney) influenced the sentencing decision made by another judge many months later. This example (many more could be given) supports our previously made suggestion that the criminal justice system can be profitably regarded as a network of interconnected decision-makers whose actions (decisions) influence one another. [Our work on sentencing is described in greater detail in Konečni and Ebbesen (in press—a) and Ebbesen and Konečni (1978). Our general approach is described in more detail in Konečni and Ebbesen (in press b), Konečni and Ebbesen (1978), and Ebbesen and Konečni (in press).]

To understand the criminal justice system from the perspective described above requires that: a) the exact types of information available to each class of participants at each point in time be identified; b) the decision rules (i.e., the ways in which the different bits of information are weighted) be discovered for each class of participants and, potentially, for individual participants; and c) the interpersonal influence channels, both "overt" (i.e., specified by law) and "covert" (i.e., informally developed in the actual day-to-day administration of the law), be traced. The types of information available to each participant, as well as the communication channels between the participants, can be discovered by carefully observing the system. However, in order to discover the decision rules used by various classes of participants, it is necessary to analyze statistically the covariation between the information available to the participants and the actual decisions that they reach. Once the communication channels and decision rules of various classes of participants are determined, it would essentially be possible to trace the operation of the entire system and predict with reasonable accuracy—possibly as early as the time of arrest—what the final disposition would be. The network of influence and communication channels, in combination with the decision rules at each "node" of the network, provide what amounts to a metatheory about the operation of the system under study. Such an empirically derived theory can be used to predict the behavior of both the entire system and each class of participants within the system.

In order to reach the objectives described above, we have undertaken an extensive data-gathering project in the various criminal justice agencies in San Diego county. Among the participants whose decision-making we have intensively studied so far have been police officers, district attorneys, defense attorneys, judges, and probation officers. Some of these results will be reported in the various chapters of Konečni and Ebbesen (in press—c). The MDSO project is thus only a small part of the ongoing, large-scale research activity.

Before turning to the details of this project, some additional considerations should be mentioned. Our theoretical/methodological orientation does not attempt to provide a "mediational" explanation for the decision rules used by the participants in the legal system. In other words, we do not attempt to explain, for example, a probation officer's decision-making behavior by postulating the operation of attributional processes, cognitive dissonance, or any other process currently in theoretical vogue. We do not question the *possibility* of generating "mediational" explanations for the decisions under study but merely doubt that they *add* anything to the ability to predict and understand the future behavior of the participants in the real legal system. The feeling of understanding that often accompanies such attempts to impose currently popular constructs on various kinds of social behavior may be illusory. Our past research suggests that there is a very weak relationship between the popularity of certain social-psychological constructs (e.g., "self-presentation," "attribution error," and so on) and their importance in terms of the *percent of variance for which they account* in the real-world decisions of participants in the legal system. Therefore, what we do is try to provide a descriptive (and usually quantitative) account of the covariation between the types of information presented to a participant and his/her decisions. It is clear that such an approach requires the collection of data in the actual settings in which legal decisions are being made daily. Such information cannot be obtained by laboratory studies of the decision-making behavior of undergraduates responding to fictitious, quasi-legal accounts of improbable cases on dependent measures or dimensions that have little or no resemblance to those used by the participants in the real system (undergraduates, for example, often "sentence" fictitious "people" to prison on a scale from 0 to 25 years). Also, whereas the claim that a given laboratory study "has to do" with some aspects of the legal system gives the appearance of "applied importance" to that study, such a claim provides little in the way of a true understanding of the actual system's operation. The only way to reach the latter is to study the system *in vivo*. The generality of any laboratory finding is an *empirical* issue which can be established only by studying the system to which one hopes to generalize. Therefore, to the extent that one's goals are to understand the actual system and possibly feed information back to the participants, it would seem more reasonable to *begin* by studying the real-world system and then go back to the laboratory to study the specifics (given ample time, funds, and human resources), rather than *vice versa*. Given that funds, time, and manpower are typically in limited supply, it is reasonable to question the current practice where it seems that close to 95 percent of social psychologists' efforts are devoted to the study of jury decision-making, when it is well known that in many jurisdictions less than 2 percent of all arrested felons eventually have a jury trial; instead, over 85 percent of those who are convicted are convicted because the defendant has pleaded guilty to a charge! (Such considerations are, of course, given further weight when one considers the enormous problems of generalization from the simulated-jury studies even to the decision-making of real juries.)

Finally, we think that despite our reluctance to rely on social-psychological theoretical constructs, our approach is relevant not only to the psychology of law but also to social psychology. First, the information and the decisions being analyzed are the products of an intact and inherently interesting *social* organization; second, a major aspect of this entire system is that many decisions are the results, at least in part, of *social influence* (as, for example, when a defense and a district attorney attempt to influence each other in the course of plea bargaining, or when a defense attorney attempts to influence his client to plead guilty to X in order to obtain Y). Thus, the results of the research might provide information about the way in which bargaining and social influence processes actually take place in an obviously important social setting.

PROCESSING OF PERSONS SUSPECTED OF BEING MDSOs

A brief description of the legal/administrative apparatus used in the processing of persons suspected of being MDSOs might be helpful. Certain details of the description that follows are peculiar to San Diego county;

however, the general procedure is common to all counties in California. If there are reasons to suspect the defendant of being an MDSO, the defendant is first interviewed by psychiatrists. This interview always takes place after the plea or verdict of guilty and always prior to sentencing. In San Diego county, during the period in which the present study was being carried out (October, 1976 to June, 1977) the same three psychiatrists, appointed by the court, typically interviewed all suspected MDSOs in interviews ranging from 10 to 30 minutes in duration and taking place typically two to four days prior to the sentencing hearing. The defendant's complete file up to that time is available to the psychiatrists prior to and at the time of the interview. Notable in this file is the probation officer's report containing detailed information concerning the offense, plea bargaining, social factors, prior record, etc. This report thus contains information that would be found in the reports of non-MDSO cases. (More information on the contents of this report is provided below.) Questions asked by the psychiatrists in the interview are fairly routine, starting with the inevitable "Do you know why you are here?", then attempting to probe, in a cursory manner, into the early shaping of the defendant's current "psychodynamics" (e.g., "Has anyone ever told you, or do you remember, that when you were young you set fires to things or wetted the bed?"), probing into the defendant's more recent sexual and/or marital history (e.g., "How was your sex life with your wife?"), but focusing mostly on the circumstances of the abnormal sexual behavior that took place around the time of the offense for which the defendant was convicted. The defendant's answers are typically taken in shorthand by one of the psychiatrists. Following the interview, the psychiatrists file separate or joint reports (depending on whether they had individual or joint interviews with the offender; joint interviews/reports are more typical). These reports are filed with the court.

The next step is a hearing in "psychiatric court." In San Diego county, psychiatric cases are processed within a single department of the Superior Court, and thus, during the period of the study, a single judge dealt with all persons suspected of being MDSOs. At the hearing, all three psychiatrists are typically present and available for cross-examination or judicial consultations. In the course of the hearing, they typically do not read from their reports. After the district attorney has read the report's diagnosis and recommendation, the report is entered into the record. If during the hearing a question arises about the recommendation or some other aspect of the report, the defense attorney or the judge or the district attorney can address a question to the psychiatrists; the psychiatrists never offer information during the hearing without being asked to do so. The MDSO hearings usually last five–ten minutes. If the defense disagrees with the psychiatric diagnosis and/or recommendation, a defense psychiatrist and character witnesses may be called in and then the hearing is much longer (20–60 minutes); however, in over 90 percent of the cases, no defense psychiatrist is present nor is there opposition by the defense to the court-appointed psychiatrists' recommendation.

The psychiatrists' report filed with the court is typically one–two (single-spaced) pages in length. The letter may contain information about the defendant's appearance, prior record, past sexual experience, a description of the offense, and other information sometimes taken verbatim from the probation officer's report. The report invariably ends with a diagnosis (e.g., female paedophilia) and a statement that the defendant either is or is not an MDSO.

At the hearing, the judge may find that the defendant is indeed an MDSO or the defendant may be remanded (that is, judged not to be an MDSO and sent back to another department of the Superior Court for sentencing) or the case may be continued, pending more psychiatric information. If the defendant is found to be an MDSO, in San Diego county he is always sent to Patton State Hospital for indefinite commitment; if, on the other hand, the defendant is found not to be an MDSO, he is sentenced (in another department) under the applicable penal code provisions for the offense to which he has pleaded guilty or of which he has been found guilty. During the period of the study, California still had the indeterminate sentencing system; therefore, a defendant could be given either probation or probation with time in the custody of the sheriff or an indeterminate prison sentence specified by the penal code.

After commitment in Patton State Hospital, the defendant is returned to the trial court. He is then given either: a) not less than five years' probation; or b) is sentenced under the applicable penal code provision for the original conviction. The court's action generally depends on the recommendation that accompanies the defendant's release from Patton State Hospital. What is known as an A recommendation indicates that the defendant is not any longer a danger to the community and that although he may not be fully "cured," he is unlikely to profit from further treatment. A B recommendation, on the other hand, indicates that the defendant is unlikely to profit from further treatment but continues to be a danger to the community. Typically, if the release is accompanied by an A recommendation, the defendant is given five years' probation and released into the community; on the other hand, in cases with the B recommendation, the court either sentences the defendant under the applicable provisions or indefinitely commits him (to the Department of

Health or the Department of Corrections), implying that the court believes that the defendant continues to be dangerous and must be kept out of the community.

THE PRESENT PROJECT

General Considerations

We have already indicated our preference for studying the legal system *in vivo* and specified in some detail the reasons for such a preference. This is not to say, however, that we do not acknowledge a variety of problems often associated with research in the real world. Apart from the usually mentioned issues, there are additional problems with doing naturalistic research in the legal system. Some of these problems are uniquely associated with using observation as a research method.[4] When the archival-analysis approach is used, other problems arise and, in the case of the legal system, they often go beyond those often associated with this method (e.g., miscoding, selective coding, selective placement of information in the files, etc.). Namely, in studying the legal system, the issue of *access* to data is paramount, because so much of the information is not in the public domain and special permissions to carry out the research have to be obtained. Such permissions are often difficult to obtain even when the noble motives and competence of the researchers can be easily documented, and when elaborate procedures for preserving the anonymity of all concerned are devised; there is typically no standardized procedure for obtaining permission and therefore the decision is often at the discretion of one or another individual in the agency in question. Some of the reasons for the often observed reluctance to allow access to the data can be traced to a genuine concern for due process and the preservation of anonymity of the defendants; sometimes, the reasons can be traced to what seem like petty but are, in fact, insurmountable economic problems, such as shortages of resources, space, or personnel. (Do the clerks have the time to retrieve the files in addition to their other duties? Are there spare desks in the office for the researchers to use since the files cannot be taken out?) However, much of the reluctance is clearly due to the defensiveness and secretiveness that so often characterize large organizations and bureaucracies. These points, of course, should not be taken for more than they are—our subjective impressions and observations that are difficult to document. However, we think that these remarks might find a sympathetic ear or two among our colleagues in legal psychology, many of whom must have experienced similar difficulties.

One purpose of the above remarks was to draw the attention of our present and future colleagues to the importance of describing the *reality* of the research process—an issue that is often glossed over; indeed, we feel that in legal psychology, in particular, an important aspect of graduate-student training ought to be the learning of skills (administrative, interpersonal, etc.) that would increase the probability of obtaining adequate access to elusive data (cf. Deutsch, 1975; p. 264).

Another purpose of the above remarks was to provide the reasons for certain obvious methodological limitations of the present project. Namely, only one person coded both the probation officers' reports and the letters which the psychiatrists filed with the court—the two main sources of data in the project. We hasten to add that, in this project, we met with extreme cooperativeness on the part of both the judge and the psychiatrists involved; nevertheless, for various administrative and interpersonal reasons, the permission was obtained for only one person to perform the coding.

Another obvious problem lies in the mentioned fact that the same judge and three psychiatrists dealt with all the cases during the period studied. Therefore, it is uncertain to what extent our results are generalizable either to other jurisdictions or to future MDSO-related decisions in San Diego county (following the eventual personnel changes). At least the latter problem could certainly not be remedied by us: Such is the way in which MDSOs are processed in San Diego county at this particular time. We hoped nevertheless that the research would be a useful first step in investigating the processing of MDSOs in a relatively large jurisdiction within a State that has perhaps the most developed MDSO program in the nation.

Method

Because of the project's preliminary nature, early on we decided to code only the information available from written documents (psychiatrists' letter, probation officers' report); thus, neither the contents of the psychiatric interview, nor the hearing in front of the judge were coded (although we attended many of these in order to acquaint ourselves in an informal way with their content). The next step in the research process was the definition of criterion variables (i.e., the participants' *decisions*). The project was concerned with the following three decisions: 1) The psychiatrists' diagnosis (eight categories, see Appendix 2); 2) the psychiatrists' classification of the defendant (MDSO vs. non-MDSO); and 3) the judge's ruling [MDSO (Patton) vs. non-MDSO (remanded) vs. continuance]. We were interested in which information contained in the mentioned written documents was strongly associated with ("predicted") these three sequential decisions. A related issue of interest was the association of certain diagnoses with the MDSO vs. non-MDSO classification of the defendant and, of course, the relationship between diagnoses and classification, respectively and the judge's ruling.

The next step was to define the "predictors" and develop the coding instruments. In line with our earlier research, a relatively large number of predictors of the various decisions was isolated; these predictors were to be coded either from the probation officer's report or from the psychiatrists' letter [5] and were to be as close as possible to the categories and dimensions used by the participants in the system being studied. In other words, we tried to minimize the extent of the "translation" from the categories used in the system to higher-level, abstract concepts or categories more common in social-psychological theories (this is evident in Appendices 1 and 2 which present our coding instruments). The reasons for this approach are simple: First, the research was preliminary and few guidelines, if any, existed as to the important predictors, optimal level of abstractness of the predictors, etc.; second, we were not aware of any reasonable theory or metatheory to guide us in the process of translation from concrete to abstract coding categories.

An additional decision was to use a modified content-analysis approach. More specifically, we identified parts (content *areas*) of the written documents to be used as predictors but ignored the specific, actual content. Thus, instead of the coding being based, for example, on the actual words and sentences in the documents (or the degree of extremity of the meaning), it consisted of recording the number of typewritten lines devoted to a discussion of a particular issue ("predictor"). This procedure was adopted in part because we felt that it was an adequate first step and, more importantly, because we had only one coder. Namely, we felt that the effect of unintentional coder bias could be minimized by having this person simply locate the predictor and count the number of lines devoted to it, rather than engage in far less reliable qualitative analyses (e.g., determining the "weight" of certain phrases, etc.). Moreover, we did code the general direction (positive vs. negative) of the comments in certain predictor areas. For example, in coding the number of lines devoted in the psychiatrists' letter to the defendant's description of the offense, negative and positive feelings about the offense (i.e., remorse vs. no remorse) were separately coded. Finally, for certain categories such as prior record (as described in the probation officer's report), the number of lines devoted to the description of prior record was in fact completely redundant with the number of prior convictions (i.e., one line per conviction).

Because of our interest in identifying predictors in those sections of the probation report in which the defendant was directly quoted (e.g., the reasons the defendant gave for committing the crime), these parts of the report were coded in a somewhat different way. As can be seen in Appendix 1, we were interested in the extent to which the defendant appeared to admit having committed the crime (as judged by the coder on a 10-point scale), how the defendant "explained" his behavior, and what extenuating circumstances, if any, he mentioned. In particular, the coder listed both "short-term" factors that were "external" to the defendant, not "under his control" (e.g., peer pressure) and long-term external factors (e.g., chronic unemployment). In addition, the coder listed "internal" factors (where the "locus of causality" for the behavior is seen as being within the defendant), again both short-term ones (e.g., being drunk or in pain) and long-term ones (e.g., drug addiction, alcohol, having long-term emotional problems).

Whereas the proponents of attribution theory might argue that these variables (internal vs. external locus of control; short-term vs. long-term factors) are derived from a general attribution-theory perspective, in our opinion this would simply mean claiming undue credit for age-old folk wisdom (or lack of it) that has, more importantly, been incorporated into almost all penal codes. That is to say, we know of no legal codex, ancient or modern, which does not take into account the causes and circumstances of the crime (into which the above-listed factors clearly translate). Be that as it may, whether such factors are considered "attributional" neither increases nor decreases, from our point of view, the inherent interest of treating them as predictors of the criterion decisions we studied.

Many of the predictions were similar to those in the coding instrument that we used in our studies of sentencing. However, we should emphasize that whereas in those studies many coders were used and estimates of coder reliability were obtained, in the present project we had no way of ascertaining or eliminating possible coder bias and related methodological problems.

The project was carried out during the period from October of 1976 to June of 1977. A total of 113 cases, all involving male defendants suspected of being MDSOs, was coded; this represented almost the total MDSO caseload in San Diego county during the duration of this study.

RESULTS

An essential first step is to examine the relationship between the three principal decisions, Psychiatric Diagnosis X Psychiatric MDSO vs. non-MDSO Classification X Judge's Verdict (Patton State Hospital vs. Remand vs. Continuance). These results are presented in Table 5.1.

Upon examining the breakdown of cases within individual decisions,

Table 5.1. Breakdown of the sample in terms of psychiatric and judicial decisions.

			Psychiatric Diagnosis							
Psychiatric Classification	Judge's Verdict	No Label	Homo-sexuality	Female Paedo-philia	Male Paedo-philia	Anti-social Persona-lity	Sexual devia-tion	Female & Male Paedo-philia	Schizo-phrenia	Total
MDSO	Patton	0	1	2	1	2	16	2	2	26
	Remand	0	0	0	0	1	0	0	0	1
	Continuance	0	2	0	0	0	5	2	0	9
		0	3	2	1	3	21	4	2	36
non-MDSO	Patton	0	0	0	0	0	0	0	0	0
	Remand	33	1	3	0	30	9	1	0	77
	Continuance	0	0	0	0	0	0	0	0	0
		33	1	3	0	30	9	1	0	77
	Total	33	4	5	1	33	30	5	2	113

Note—In many cases a defendant received more than one diagnostic label. The data in this table are based on the *first* in a string of labels.

one finds, for Psychiatric Diagnosis, that 33 cases (29 percent) had no diagnostic label attached to them; another 33 received the label "antisocial personality;" another approximate one-third was labeled "sexual deviation" (30 cases, 27 percent); and the remaining 17 cases (15 percent) received a variety of labels, including homosexuality, paedophilia, and schizophrenia. With regard to the Psychiatric Classification, 36 cases (32 percent) were classified as MDSOs, whereas the remaining approximate two-thirds were judged to be non-MDSOs. Finally, with regard to the Judge's Verdict, 26 cases (23 percent) were sent to Patton; 78 cases (69 percent) were remanded back to the original trial department; and the remaining nine cases (8 percent) were continued pending further psychiatric information.

When the three decisions are examined jointly, a very simple pattern emerges. In virtually all of the 66 cases (58 percent of the sample) in which the diagnosis was either "antisocial personality" or no diagnostic label was attached, the defendant both a) received the non-MDSO classification by the psychiatrists *and* b) was subsequently remanded back to the trial department by the judge; only two of these 66 cases were sent to Patton State Hospital.

The only other diagnostic category with a sizable number of cases was "sexual deviation" (see Table 5.1). In this category, there was an MDSO vs. non-MDSO split of some magnitude (21 of the 30 "sexual deviants," 70 percent, were classified as MDSOs; the remaining nine cases were classified as non-MDSOs). However, whereas the great majority of the "sexual deviants" who had been classified by the psychiatrists as MDSOs were sent by the judge to Patton (16 of 21, 76 percent; the remaining five cases were continued), none of those who had been classified as non-MDSO were sent there—every single one was remanded to the trial department (the relevant $\chi^2 = 29.50, df = 2, p < .001$). From this example, it would appear that when a psychiatric diagnosis does not entirely reduplicate the MDSO vs. non-MDSO classification, the judge's decision is nevertheless highly predictable from the psychiatric classification. In fact, it can be seen from Table 5.1 that of a total of 36 cases classified as MDSO, only one was remanded; of the 77 cases classified as non-MDSO, every single one was (the relevant $\chi^2 = 108.45, df = 2, p < .001$).

Some additional remarks are in order regarding diagnostic categories. As a footnote to Table 5.1 points out, in many cases a defendant received more than one diagnostic label; the diagnostic categorization presented in Table 5.1 is based on the *first* label in cases where there was a string of labels. Upon examining this issue more closely, one finds that among the non-MDSOs, a sizable majority (64 of 77, 83 percent) received only one label (typically "antisocial personality") or no label at all. Among the

MDSOs, on the other hand, only 25 percent of the cases (nine of 36) had only one label; all the rest had two labels (26 of 36, 72 percent), with the exception of one man who had three ($\chi^2 = 36.73$, $df = 2$, $p < .001$).

When one examines the number of diagnostic labels attached to "sexual deviants," an interesting finding emerges. Among the cases in which "sexual deviation" was the first label (30 cases; see Table 5.1), all of the 21 cases classified as MDSOs received two diagnostic labels; in contrast, among the 9 non-MDSO "sexual deviation" cases, there was an even split between those who received only one label (4 cases) and those who received two (five cases; the relevant $\chi^2 = 10.77$, $df = 2$, $p < .01$). However, a different picture is obtained when one examines the 15 cases (see Table 5.1) which had homosexuality (four cases), female paedophilia (five), male paedophilia (one), and female-and-male paedophilia (five) as the first label—in other words, cases which had a more specific sexual-deviation label as the first label (rather than "sexual deviation" itself). For these 15 cases, the results are exactly opposite: All five non-MDSO cases had two labels and eight out of ten MDSO cases had only one label ($\chi^2 = 11.42$, $df = 2$, $p < .01$). In other words, a person diagnosed as "sexual deviation; female paedophilia" is highly likely to be classified as an MDSO and thus be sent by the judge to Patton State Hospital. In contrast, a person diagnosed, for example, as "male paedophilia; schizophrenia" is likely to be classified as a non-MDSO and subsequently remanded, despite the fact that the first label is an example of sexual deviation.

Several early conclusions could be drawn from the data we have presented so far (these conclusions will be elaborated in the Discussion section). First, it would seem that the judge exercised very little discretion in these cases; in fact, he appeared to be little more than a rubber stamp for the psychiatric recommendation; in short, the judge's removal from the decision-making chain would have little effect on the processing of MDSO cases. [6]

A related preliminary conclusion that can be drawn on the basis of the above data is that a relatively simple "model" can describe the processing of cases from the point in time when the diagnosis is given to the time when the verdict is reached by the judge. Certain kinds of diagnostic labels used by the psychiatrists reliably predict whether they will classify the offender as an MDSO (although there is some "noise" when "sexual deviation" is the first diagnostic label attached), and this classification almost perfectly predicts whether the judge will send the offender to Patton or remand him to the trial court. In other words, once the diagnosis and, especially, the MDSO/non-MDSO classification has been reached, the manner in which the offender will spend the next few years of his life has also been determined.

The remainder of the Results section will be devoted to a quantitative elaboration of the causal model. Several groups of analyses were carried out, including attempts to predict: a) the psychiatric diagnostic label from the contents of the probation officer's report; b) the MDSO/non-MDSO classification from the probation officer's report; c) the judge's verdict from the probation officer's report; d) the psychiatric diagnostic label from the contents, length, etc., of the letter prepared by the psychiatrists for the judge; e) the MDSO/non-MDSO classification from the psychiatrists' letter; and f) the judge's verdict from the psychiatrists' letter. Because of the almost perfect agreement between the MDSO/non-MDSO classification and the judge's verdict, analyses c) and f) were redundant with analyses b) and e), respectively, and the former two will, therefore, not be discussed any further. In addition, because only three of the diagnostic categories (no label, "antisocial personality," and "sexual deviation") had a large number of cases, and because in only one of these categories ("sexual deviation") there was a sizable split in terms of the MDSO/non-MDSO classification, analyses that used the psychiatric diagnosis as the criterion [a) and d) above] typically produced results and led to conclusions that were similar to those reached by analyses that used the MDSO/non-MDSO classification as the criterion [b) and e) above]. For this reason, the results concerning the psychiatric diagnosis and those concerning the MDSO/non-MDSO classification are not reported separately but rather in a mixed sequence. Analyses that used predictors from the probation officer's report are reported first, followed by analyses that used predictors from the psychiatric letter; only relationships that were statistically significant at least at the .05 level are reported and discussed. Finally, statistical tests and tables are provided only for the most important results.

Predictors from the Defendant's File (Including the Probation Officer's Report)

Statistical analyses revealed that only a few aspects of the probation officer's report were useful predictors of either the psychiatric diagnosis or of the MDSO/non-MDSO classification. It was found that probation officers provide longer descriptions of the offenses committed by those people who eventually become classified as MDSOs by the psychiatrists. For example, of the 36 MDSOs, only one had his offense described by the probation officer in less than 25 lines, whereas 18 had their offenses described in over 50 lines of text. In contrast, of the 77 people who were eventually classified as non-MDSOs, 28 had their offenses described in under 25 lines and only nine in over 50 lines. In addition, in the MDSO cases, in comparison to the non-MDSO ones, the probation officers' summary evaluation and discussion of prior record were both significantly longer; there was significantly more discussion of the negative aspects raised in the various letters written to the judge about the defendant by the people in the community; and there was significantly less discussion of the offender's "intention to improve" (all of the above effects were significant at the .01 level). As it turned out, however, all of the above factors were also statistically related to what we think is the major predictor of both the psychiatric diagnosis and MDSO/non-MDSO classification, *prior convictions of the defendant for sexual offenses.*

Table 5.2 presents the breakdown of the sample in terms of the psychiatric diagnosis, MDSO/non-MDSO classification, and prior convictions for sexual offenses. As can be seen from this table, and more clearly from Tables 5.3 and 5.4 for the three most frequently used diagnostic labels only (no label, "antisocial personality," and "sexual deviation"), the label "sexual deviation" is significantly more frequently associated with prior convictions for sexual offenses than are no-label and "antisocial-personality" categories ($\chi^2 = 12.21, df = 4, p < .05$; see Table 5.3). Similarly, people who ended up being classified as MDSOs were significantly more likely to have prior convictions for sexual offenses than were those eventually classified as non-MDSOs ($\chi^2 = 32.38, df = 2, p < .01$; see Table 5.4). When one considers the 30 cases with the "sexual deviation" label (the only category with a substantial MDSO/non-MDSO split), every single one of the nine cases who were eventually classified as non-MDSOs had no prior convictions for sexual offenses; in contrast, of the 21 "sexual deviation" cases who were eventually classified as MDSOs, 17 (18 percent) had at least one prior conviction for a sexual offense (see Table 5.2). In summary, the diagnosis "sexual deviation" is largely dependent on prior convictions for sexual offenses and very rarely leads to the MDSO classification unless there is a record of prior convictions for sexual offenses.

Tables 5.5, 5.6, and 5.7 illustrate the fact that prior *sex-related* criminal record, rather than overall prior record, is the critical factor. Table 5.5 presents the breakdown of the sample in terms of the psychiatric diagnosis, MDSO/non-MDSO classification, and *all* prior convictions (both for sexual and non-sexual offenses). The major difference between the results presented in this table and the data in Table 5.2 is in the nine "sexual deviation" cases which were eventually classified as MDSOs. From Table 5.5, one sees that four of these nine cases had a prior criminal

Table 5.2. Breakdown of the sample in terms of psychiatric diagnosis, MDSO/non-MDSO classification, and prior convictions for sexual offenses.

Psychiatric Classification	Number of prior sex-related convictions	Psychiatric Diagnosis							
		No Label	Homo-sexuality	Female Paedo-philia	Male Paedo-philia	Anti-social Person-ality	Sexual devia-tion	Female and Male Paedo-philia	Schizo-phrenia
MDSO	0	0	1	1	0	1	4	0	1
	1–4	0	2	0	1	2	12	2	1
	5 and over	0	0	1	0	0	5	2	0
non-MDSO	0	27	1	2	0	24	9	1	0
	1–4	4	0	0	0	4	0	0	0
	5 and over	2	0	1	0	2	0	0	0

113

Table 5.3. Association of psychiatric diagnosis with prior convictions for sexual offenses (for the three most frequent diagnostic categories only).

Number of prior sex-related convictions	Psychiatric Diagnosis		
	No Label	Antisocial Personality	Sexual Deviation
0	27	25	13
1–4	4	6	12
5 and over	2	2	5
			96

Table 5.4. Association of MDSO/non-MDSO classification with prior convictions for sexual offenses (for the three most frequent diagnostic categories only).

Number of prior sex-related convictions	Classification	
	MDSO	non-MDSO
0	5	60
1–4	14	8
5 and over	5	4
		96

record but were nevertheless judged to be non-MDSOs (Table 5.2 shows that none of these cases, however, had prior convictions for *sexual* offenses). In other words, the relationship between overall prior record and the psychiatric diagnosis and classification is not as strong as the relationship discussed above between prior convictions for sexual offenses and the psychiatric diagnosis and classification.

The above conclusion is further substantiated by the data in Tables 5.6 and 5.7. The data in Table 5.6 show that although the proportion of "sexual deviation" cases with some criminal record is relatively greater (in comparison to the proportion of "sexual deviation" cases with some prior sex-related convictions in Table 5.3, which leads to a χ^2 of 15.61 for the data in Table 5.6, as opposed to a χ^2 of 12.21 for the data in Table 5.3), the data presented in Table 5.7 show that it is only the *non*-MDSOs who had the proportionately greater number of overall prior convictions (in comparison to the proportion of non-MDSOs with prior sexual-related convictions in Table 5.4, which leads to a χ^2 of 22.86 for the data in Table 5.7, as opposed to a χ^2 of 32.38 for the data in Table 5.4).

The argument that prior sex-related criminal record is the key predictor

Table 5.5. Breakdown of the sample in terms of psychiatric diagnosis, MDSO/non-MDSO classification, and all prior convictions (for sexual and non-sexual offenses).

Psychiatric Diagnosis

Psychiatric Classification	Number of prior convictions	No Label	Homo-sexuality	Female Paedo-philia	Male Paedo-philia	Anti-social Person-ality	Sexual devia-tion	Female & Male Paedo-philia	Schizo-phrenia
MDSO	0	0	0	0	0	0	4	0	0
	1–4	0	3	0	1	3	12	2	2
	5 and over	0	0	2	0	0	5	2	0
non-MDSO	0	25	1	2	0	22	5	1	0
	1–4	5	0	0	0	6	4	0	0
	5 and over	3	0	1	0	2	0	0	0

113

Table 5.6. Association of psychiatric diagnosis with prior convictions (for sexual and non-sexual offenses) for the three most frequent diagnostic categories only.

| *Number of prior convictions* | Psychiatric Diagnosis | | |
	No Label	Antisocial Personality	Sexual Deviation
0	25	22	9
1–4	5	9	16
5 and over	3	2	5

96

Table 5.7. Association of MDSO/non-MDSO classifications with prior convictions (for sexual and non-sexual offenses) for the three most frequent diagnostic categories only.

| *Number of prior convictions* | Classification | |
	MDSO	non-MDSO
0	4	52
1–4	15	15
5 and over	5	5

96

of the psychiatric diagnosis and classification is further strengthened by the fact that this factor is strongly associated with each of the five significant variables from the probation officer's report that were discussed earlier (i.e., length of the description of the offense, length of the evaluation, length of the discussion of the prior record, etc.). Tables 5.8 and 5.9

Table 5.8. Association of prior sex-related criminal record and length of probation officers' descriptions of the offense (for 30 "sexual deviation" cases only).

| *Prior convictions for sexual crimes* | Length of description of offense (number of lines in the P.O. report) | | |
	0–25	26–50	50 and over
NO	2	9	2
YES	0	7	10

30

Table 5.9. Association of prior sex-related criminal record and length of probation officers' references to negative aspects of personal letters sent to the judge concerning the defendant.

		Length of negative references to letters (number of lines in the P.O. report)		
Prior convictions for sexual offenses		0–1	2–4	5 and over
	NO	11	2	0
	YES	6	6	5
				30

illustrate this point for two of the mentioned variables (taking into account the 30 "sexual deviation" cases only). From Table 5.8, it is clear that the probation officers' descriptions of the offense tend to be significantly longer for people with prior sex-related criminal records ($\chi^2 = 7.18$, $df = 2$, $p < .05$). Table 5.9 shows that probation officers tend to make significantly more references to the negative aspects of personal letters sent to the judge concerning the defendant when it is a question of people with prior convictions for sexual offenses ($\chi^2 = 8.08$, $df = 2$, $p < .05$).

Predictors from the Psychiatrists' Letter

The fact that prior sex-related criminal record is a strong predictor of the psychiatric diagnosis and classification is particularly important because this kind of information about the defendant is available very early in the processing of a case, in fact, before the defendant has ever committed the offense under consideration. In other words, a meaningful prediction about the outcome of a case can, generally speaking, be made long before the probation officer's interview with the defendant and the filing of the probation officer's report and, especially, before the court psychiatrists' interview with the defendant and the hearing before the judge. In a sense, strong predictors that occur very early in the sequence of events—such as prior sex-related criminal record—almost eliminate the need for information that becomes available at stages that are temporally far closer to the final verdict in the processing of a case but is nevertheless highly correlated with the earlier information. For example, coding the hearing before the judge would seem to have little utility for the purpose of prediction, given that the judge very closely follows the psychiatric MDSO/non-MDSO recommendation made several days earlier. Similarly, if the psychiatric diagnosis and recommendation can be reliably predicted on the basis of information available even before the commission of the offense, the content of the psychiatric interview with the defendant assumes a secondary importance at best.[7]

In view of these considerations, the predictors isolated from the second of the two written documents coded for each case in the present project—the psychiatrists' letter—are somewhat less important than was originally expected, because the information from the letter is available only concurrently, rather than before, the diagnosis and the MDSO/non-MDSO classification (which are typed at the end of the letter). Nevertheless, some of the results of our content analysis of psychiatrists' letters are intriguing, regardless of these letters' predictive utility. More specifically, Table 5.10 presents a summary of the way in which psychiatrists' letters that conclude with a non-MDSO classification differ in form and content from the letters that conclude with an MDSO classification.

Psychiatrists' letters which concluded with an MDSO recommendation were significantly longer than were letters that concluded with a non-MDSO recommendation. Although the two groups of letters, leading to different recommendations, did not differ from each other in terms of the amount of space devoted to a relatively large number of predictors that we examined, in most cases in which a significant difference was found, it was in the direction of the MDSO letter containing a longer discussion of the factor under consideration than did the non-MDSO letter.

Table 5.10. Formal aspects of the psychiatrists' letters as a function of the MDSO/non-MDSO classification.

Letters that conclude with an MDSO classification devote more space to a discussion of:	Letters that conclude with a non-MDSO classification devote more space to a discussion of:
1. Defendant's physical appearance 2. Family history 3. Childhood experiences 4. Negative aspects of prior life-style 5. Past sexual experiences of defendant 6. Prior sex-related criminal record 7. Negative aspects of current status 8. Arrest report 9. Results of psychological assessment (from the P.O. report) 10. Psychological interpretation of offense 11. Feelings of indifference toward offense 12. Various outside sources of information (defense psychiatrist, relatives, district attorney, police, victims, etc.) 13. Negative future prospects	1. Positive aspects of letter from employer 2. Positive aspects of current status (employment, marriage)

Note: All effects are statistically significant at least at .05.

An examination of the entries in Table 5.10 reveals a relatively coherent pattern. In the case of people whom they intended to classify as MDSOs, the psychiatrists dealt significantly more with "psychodynamic" issues (e.g., childhood experiences, family history, results of psychological assessment, and psychological interpretation of offense) and with the sexual aspects of the defendant's offense, prior crimes, and general life-style (e.g., past sexual experiences of the defendant, prior sex-related criminal record, etc.). In general, there was a considerable tendency to impute negative habits, intentions, and motives to the defendant classified as an MDSO and to evaluate his prior life-style, current status, and future prospects negatively (e.g., negative aspects of prior life-style, negative aspects of current status, negative future prospects, feelings of indifference towards the offense, defendant's physical appearance). There was also a tendency to directly quote more, and generally rely more on, the evidence from a variety of outside sources (e.g., arrest report, results of psychological assessment, information from the defense psychiatrists, victims, etc.). It almost appears as if the psychiatrists perceived a greater need to substantiate their MDSO than their non-MDSO classifications, presumably either because the psychiatrists believed that the MDSO classification is more controversial, or because they thought that such a classification would have more severe consequences for the defendant (for example, in terms of the duration and quality of incarceration). This issue will be raised again in the Discussion section.

Predictors Derived from the Defendant's Description of the Offense and His Stated Reasons for His Behavior

As was previously mentioned, in certain sections of the probation report the defendant was directly quoted. This fact made possible an examination of the extent to which offenders who differed in terms of the psychiatric diagnosis and classification also differed in terms of a) admission to have committed the crime, and b) explanations for the behavior (including extenuating circumstances). As it happened, no differences were obtained for the "admit-guilt" factor; therefore, the remaining discussion will be limited to the reasons which the defendants gave for committing the crime.

Table 5.11 presents the percentage of people in each of the three most frequently used psychiatric diagnostic categories who listed at least one reason for their offense that could be classified in one of the four following classes of reasons: External Short-Term, External Long-Term, Internal Short-Term and Internal Long-Term (also see Appendix 1). Overall, short-term reasons were given significantly more often than long-term

Table 5.11. Percent of offenders in the three most frequently used diagnostic categories who gave external/internal, short-term/long-term reasons for their offense.

			Psychiatric Diagnosis		
			None	Antisocial Personality	Sexual Deviation
Reasons for the offense	External	Short-term	40	48	44
		Long-term	10	6	23
	Internal	Short-term	28	36	57
		Long-term	20	30	52

Note: See Appendix 1 for the complete list of reasons within each of the four classes (e.g., "external short-term").

reasons and this difference was particularly pronounced for external factors. Looking at the sample as a whole, short-term external factors were about equally likely to be listed as were short-term internal factors; the least used category of reasons was the long-term external factors. More interestingly, people subsequently diagnosed as "sexual deviants" were significantly more likely than the no-label and "antisocial-personality" people to list at least one classifiable reason for their crime. As can be seen from Table 5.11, this difference was mainly due to the "sexual deviants" significantly greater propensity to list internal factors, both long-term and short-term.

When one examines the actual reasons listed within the four classes of reasons by people with different diagnostic labels, the following findings are obtained. With regard to the *external short-term* reasons, both the no-label and the "antisocial-personality" people gave almost exclusively the "just happened" and "the situation presented itself" reasons, whereas the "sexual deviants" tended to use a greater variety of reasons, including "outside pressure," "just happened," "family problems," and "the situation presented itself" (see Appendix 1). Whereas both the no-label and the "antisocial-personality" people very rarely listed any *external long-term* factors, the "sexual deviants," when they used reasons from this category, tended to list "social pressures" and "chronic family problems." For *internal short-term* reasons, the no-label people listed exclusively the "was drunk" and "was on drugs" reasons, whereas the "antisocial-personality" people listed exclusively the "was drunk" and "was out of control" reasons but seldom cited the influence of drugs. "Sexual deviants," on the other hand, tended to give a large variety of reasons including "was drunk," "was confused," "was angry," and "heard a voice." Finally, for *internal long-term* factors, the no-label people cited exclusively alcoholism and drug addiction, whereas both the "antisocial-personality" and "sexual deviation" people used a variety of categories, except that the sexual deviants were especially likely to mention long-term emotional problems.

With regard to the relationship between psychiatric classification (MDSO/ non-MDSO) and the use of various classes of reasons, it was found that people who were eventually classified as MDSOs did not differ from the non-MDSOs in the use of either short-term or long-term external factors. About 30 percent of the people in each group gave the "it just happened" and "the situation presented itself" external short-term reasons (few people in either group gave external long-term reasons). For internal short-term factors, the non-MDSOs gave exclusively "was drunk" (18 percent) and "was on drugs" (10 percent) reasons; in contrast, the MDSOs gave a variety of internal short-term reasons, including "was confused" (17 percent), "was angry" (14 percent), "was on drugs" (9 percent), "was drunk" (3 percent), "was out of control" (8 percent), and "a voice commanded me" (8 percent). Finally, for internal long-term factors, the non-MDSOs gave almost exclusively chronic alcoholism and drug addiction as reasons, whereas the MDSOs gave most frequently "chronic emotional problems" (15 percent) and "loneliness" (8 percent) as reasons for the offense; interestingly enough, only 5 percent gave "sex life dissatisfaction" as a reason.

In summary, people who were eventually diagnosed as "sexual deviants" (and were therefore more likely than people with other diagnostic labels to be classified as MDSOs) tended to give a greater number and a greater variety of reasons for their offense. The variety was manifested both in terms of the number of classes of reasons used and in terms of the kinds of reasons given within classes. The most frequent reasons given were internal in nature and within this class were equally likely to be short-term and long-term, including reasons such as "chronic emotional problems" (the most frequently given reason), "was confused," "was angry," etc.; alcoholism, drug addiction, and sexual dissatisfaction were infrequently given as reasons.

DISCUSSION

Our results allow the formulation—at this point still tentative—of a causal model of the processing of persons suspected of being mentally disordered sex offenders in San Diego county. Perhaps the most remarkable thing about the emerging model is that it is quite simple. Of the hundreds of individual predictors and their interactions that we examined, only very few reached the statistically significant level of association with the criterion variables. Perhaps this should not have come as a surprise, because we have repeatedly found in our work on other legal decisions (e.g., bail-setting, sentencing, etc.) that simple models, consisting of few factors (some of which are often extralegal) account for a large proportion of the variance in the criterion decisions. Thus, it would seem that despite the protestations that "every case is different," that "the complexity of cases and decisions defies the possibility of scientific analysis," that "every participant in the system has a unique contribution to make and is not replaceable by an equation," etc., which we have so often heard from judges and other participants in the legal system, the decisions in this system are just as predictable by a simple model as are those in other domains that have been mapped by logical/quantitative analyses. It also seems to us that the outcome of our projects, including the present one, justifies the type of data we collect and the overall methodological and metatheoretical approach.

Let us briefly summarize the main characteristics of the emerging model. If a person suspected of being an MDSO (because of the type of offense committed or the circumstances under which it was committed) has no prior sex-related criminal record, he is very likely to be diagnosed by the psychiatrists as having an "antisocial personality" or to be given no diagnostic label at all. In either case, the probability is high that the psychiatrists will classify him as a non-MDSO, following which he will almost automatically be remanded to the trial court by the judge.[8] If, on the other hand, a person suspected of being an MDSO has a prior sex-related criminal record, he is likely to be diagnosed as a "sexual deviant" and almost certainly receive another, more specific, sex-related diagnostic label, after which the chances are very high that he will be classified as an MDSO and then almost automatically be sent to Patton State Hospital by the judge. The importance of prior sex-related criminal record is underscored by the fact that all of the individuals in the sample who had been diagnosed as "sexual deviants," but who had no prior convictions for sexual offenses, were classified as non-MDSOs and therefore remanded to the trial court by the judge, rather than sent to Patton State Hospital.

The probation report and the psychiatrists' letter for people who are eventually diagnosed as "sexual deviants" and classified as MDSOs are somewhat different from the documents for people who are not thus diagnosed and classified. In the case of MDSOs, the probation officers tend to write longer overall evaluations, longer descriptions of the offense and of prior record, and to be more negative, by referring more frequently to the negative aspects of personal letters concerning the defendant and to the lack of the defendant's intention to improve. These MDSO/non-MDSO differences in the length and content of the probation officers' reports are echoed in the letters written by the psychiatrists. As summarized in Table 5.10, the MDSO letters tend to be longer, more negative, more "psychological" in tone (including a good deal of jargon), and with more apparent intent to substantiate the recommendation by reference to other sources (e.g., police officers, victims, results of the formal psychological assessment).

Nevertheless, it may well be that the differences in the length, content, and emphasis of the probation officers' reports and psychiatrists' letters for the MDSO and non-MDSO cases—interesting as they are from several points of view—are quite irrelevant to the basic underlying causal sequence. After all, the processing of persons suspected of being MDSOs can be summarized by the following simple causal sequence: a) prior sex-related criminal record leads to b) the psychiatric diagnosis and classification as "sexual deviation" and MDSO, respectively, resulting almost automatically in c) the judge's verdict that the defendant be sent to Patton State Hospital. In this view, differences in the content of probation reports and psychiatrists' letters merely serve to: justify an already formed conclusion based on prior sex-related criminal record; give the appearance of complexity to the processing of MDSOs; and smooth out the rough edges of the causal sequence.

As we pointed out in the Results section, the fact that the information concerning the main predictor—prior sex-related criminal record—temporally precedes the commission of the offense under consideration makes prediction of the final disposition particularly easy. This fact and the simplicity of the causal model outlined above lead us to two straightforward, though at this point still tentative, conclusions: a) as far as MDSO processing is concerned, the judge may serve as little more than a rubber stamp for the psychiatric diagnosis and MDSO/non-MDSO classification; b) the psychiatric diagnosis and classification (which, as we have seen, are largely redundant with each other) to a very high extent eventually depend on a factor known well before the compilation of the probation report (with its costly and time-consuming investigations, interviews, and paper-shuffling) and, especially, before the relatively lengthy (and therefore costly) interview which the court psychiatrists have with the offender. Indeed, to the extent that psychiatrists are basing their recommendations on such an easily observed and agreed upon factor as prior sex-related criminal record, their usefulness in the processing of persons suspected of being MDSOs would appear to be rather limited.

Of course, none of the above in any way implies "foul play" on the part of the judges and other participants in the system when they claim that every case is different, that a scientific/quantitative analysis of their decisions is impossible and that, generally, they are indispensable. In part, such statements may stem from a lack of understanding of the methods of behavioral science. Besides, a judge may well subjectively *believe* that he is responding to various multi-faceted and complex aspects of the case (e.g., each type of information from the probation report and psychiatrists' letter, the various behaviors of the defendant during the hearing, etc.) and combining these many bits of information in a complex, configural manner that is aided by his judicial training, experience, skill, and wisdom. Similarly, the psychiatrists may well *believe* that their diagnostic and classification decisions are based on the information in the probation officer's report and the answers to their questions that the defendant gives in the interview. Finally, the probation officer may *believe* that his recommendation and evaluation could not be made without a great deal of footwork and the collection of information from a variety of sources. However, the complexity of these people's thoughts and cognitive operations at various points in the decision-making process, as well as their beliefs about the "true" causes of their behavior, should not be uncritically accepted as representing the real causal sequence. As we have seen, a rather different model emerges when an outside observer of the participants' behavior systematically examines the covariation between the participants' decisions and the information available to them at each point in the decision-making process. It would be a relatively simple matter for the participants in the system to achieve the same goal by keeping data on themselves, but this idea is not generally regarded with favor in legal circles. For such an idea to gain acceptance, one would need a dramatic change in the curricula of law schools and the adoption of a different world view and view of science on the part of legal practitioners.

It seems to us that the operation of the legal system could be made more effective, faster, simpler, and certainly far less costly. To do so, the system would have to give up its obsession with ritual procedures and antiquated views of "human nature;" with rules and hearings that are a self-serving show for the public, rather than necessary for furthering justice; with spreading the responsibility across many participants for what are claimed to be complex—but in reality emerge as very simple—decisions, while at the same time, the participants in the system attempt to promote their status and insure that the operation of the system is not subject to public or scientific inquiry. Such concerns could be profitably replaced by a concern for the discovery of the *de facto* causes of legal decisions, for base-rates, for appropriate data collection, for internal checks, and for the application of modern behavioral science, in general.

By examining what actually determines legal decisions (as opposed to what the participants *think* determines them), a quantitative approach can achieve two additional, important goals: a) a system that is more *fair,* in the sense that similar crimes, committed under similar circumstances, by similar people, with a similar prior record would, in fact, be punished similarly, rather than subject to "noise" introduced into the system by the differences among judges and other practitioners in views, values, and assumptions; and b) a system that is more *just,* in a sense that it would be possible to determine whether particular legal decisions indeed reflect the kinds of factors that both the participants in the system and, especially, the public feel these decisions *should* reflect (unlike the present situation, where the participants and the public may be under the impression that a particular factor is being taken into account when it, in fact, is not). Thus, a quantitative approach does not impose values on the legal system and the public; rather, it may help determine whether legal decisions do actually reflect certain factors and general values that the participants in the system and the public find desirable.

Despite some of the criticisms expressed earlier in this section, the emerging model of the processing of persons suspected of being MDSOs does appear, from several points of view, to be reasonable. In the first place, it seems intuitively acceptable for prior sex-related criminal record to be a major determinant of MDSO classification, especially given the laws presently on the books; second, unlike our work on bail-setting, sentencing, and other legal decisions, the present project has revealed few, if any, *extralegal* determinants of the processing of MDSOs. Moreover, it could be argued that the psychiatrists must be doing something right in their diagnosis and classification when one considers the fact that "sexual deviants" and MDSOs do give different explanations for their behavior than do the non-MDSOs and that the types of explanation they predominantly give (internal long-term factors, such as chronic emotional problems) seem congruent with the eventual psychiatric diagnosis and classification. However, this last point can be interpreted in several different ways. For example, since the psychiatrists' decisions occur after and with a full knowledge of the offenders' attributions, one could argue that the psychiatrists are merely following the offenders' own "recommendation," rather than reaching an independent judgment. One version of this interpretation would be that the offenders' attributions determine the psychiatrists' classification and that this causal factor is independent of prior, sex-related criminal record. Another version of the same general interpretation is that the attributions are not a causal factor, independent of prior, sex-related criminal record, because the offenders—being themselves fully aware of their prior, sex-related criminal record—merely relate what they think would be the causes of the behavior of a person with such a record. Finally, it is possible that the offenders' attributions—whether or not they influence the psychiatrists and whether or not they are a causal factor, independent of prior sex-related criminal record—find their way into the probation report only because probation officers feel that these attributions fit the picture of an offender with a prior, sex-related criminal record. In fact, it is possible that the probation officers intentionally (or unintentionally) *elicit* different explanations for the offense from offenders with, as opposed to those without, a prior, sex-related criminal record. In this last version, the prior, sex-related criminal record of the offender again emerges as the sole causal factor, in that it causes the probation officers to elicit certain kinds of explanations from the offenders and to quote these in the reports.

In summary, while the issue remains unresolved as to whether the offenders' stated explanations for their behavior: a) *validate* the psychiatrists' diagnosis and classification; b) *cause* the diagnosis and classification independently of prior, sex-related criminal record; or c) are merely an *irrelevant consequence* of prior, sex-related criminal record, the points made earlier in the Discussion section should not obscure the fact that the causal sequence that we suggest underlies the current processing of MDSOs contains intuitively acceptable and no extralegal factors.

The reasons for two other aspects of the psychiatrists' behavior remain unclear. The first of these is the finding that almost all of the cases that had a very specific sexual-deviation label, such as "male paedophilia" (as opposed to the general "sexual deviation" label) as the first label and a non-sexual-deviation label, such as "schizophrenia," as the second label were eventually classified as non-MDSOs. This was in contrast to cases where the first label was "sexual deviation" and the second label was some specific sexual-deviation label, such as "male paedophilia," most of which were classified as MDSOs. It is almost as if the non-sexual-deviation second label offset the effect of the first label with regard to the MDSO classification; however, the small number of cases involved precludes a more conclusive analysis of this issue.

The second issue concerns the psychiatrists' previously discussed apparent motivation to substantiate MDSO classifications to a greater extent than the non-MDSO ones, and generally to be far more negative in their descriptions of MDSOs' personality, habits, life-style, past and present behavior, and future prospects. As we mentioned earlier, one possible reason for this behavior on the part of the psychiatrists may be that they regard the MDSO classification as technically more controversial or challengeable; another possibility is that the psychiatrists believe that the consequences for the defendant would be far more severe in the case of

MDSO classification and that therefore the classification has to be better justified. Regardless of whether either of these two alternatives is correct, it is of considerable interest to examine briefly what happens to people classified as MDSOs and therefore sent to Patton State Hospital. Fortunately, some information concerning this issue is available in an article by Dix (1976).

By the time of Dix's study (summer of 1974), none of the 30 MDSOs committed in 1967 to the State hospital (Atascadero State Hospital in Dix's case) were still hospitalized. Dix discovered that none had been retained longer than two years and approximately one-half had been discharged within one year. Only six out of 30 were returned with a *B* recommendation (i.e., the defendant is unlikely to profit from further treatment but continues to be a danger to the community), and, moreover, these cases remained in the hospital for a very short period of time, certainly much shorter than the remaining 24 cases that had been returned with an *A* recommendation (i.e., the defendant is not any longer a danger to the community). The 24 cases returned with the *A* recommendation, none of which—to emphasize this point again—remained in the hospital over two years, were typically not sentenced under the applicable penal code provisions following their release from the hospital but were instead immediately released into the community with a five-year probation term. Dix then proceeded to compare the treatment of these 30 MDSOs to persons who had been processed through alternative programs (i.e., originally classified as non-MDSOs and remanded to the trial court to be sentenced under the applicable penal code provisions). On the basis of the data in his Tables V, VI, and VII (pp. 239–240), Dix justifiably concludes that "many offenders who were processed as MDSOs would have been institutionalized significantly longer, had they been sentenced to imprisonment under the penal code provision" (p. 238). Thus, to the extent that any aspect of the psychiatrists' behavior is governed by the belief that the MDSO classification leads to more severe consequences for the defendant, this would mean that they were relying on a belief not based on facts. People classified as MDSOs are returned to the community after a shorter period of time than those classified as non-MDSOs (at least in California); moreover, it is highly likely that their treatment in the hospital is preferable from several points of view to the treatment that they would receive in jail or prison. It would be highly interesting to find out whether judges, psychiatrists, defense attorneys, and, above all, the defendants themselves are aware of these facts, and whether their behavior is governed by them.

Ironically, on the basis of Dix's findings and those in the present project, the following bit of advice could be given to persons suspected of being MDSOs regarding the optimal defense strategy. After committing and being arrested for an offense of the type that would likely lead to the suspicion that the defendant were an MDSO, he should (unless, of course, he already has a prior, sex-related criminal record) get himself released on bail and quickly commit additional sex-related crimes. Such behavior would presumably sufficiently impress the psychiatrists and the judge to classify the defendant, after he has been convicted, as an MDSO and to send him to the hospital, from which he would have a 50 percent chance of emerging within a year.

One final point is in order, concerning the validity of the proposed model of MDSO processing. As is the case with other legal decisions that we have examined, it is highly likely that the model is the least applicable for the most "visible" cases: These cases receive a lot of publicity and are characterized by other extraneous factors which make them atypical along many dimensions. It is, therefore, important to realize that our intention was to develop a model that successfully deals with the "run-of-the-mill," everyday cases that never reach even the back sections of local papers and yet are, because of their sheer frequency, perhaps more important in the long run than the "special" cases.

One such special case that recently received a great deal of publicity was that of the renowned film director, Roman Polanski. The reasons for the fact that our model almost certainly would not apply to this case should be obvious when one contrasts the characteristics of a modal, obscure MDSO case with the following features of the Polanski case: [9] a) a deluge of provocative newspaper headlines about the case; b) the judge (Laurence T. Rittenband) held press conferences about the case, gave interviews to popular magazines, such as *People*, and made numerous public announcements, including statements that Mr. Polanski did not belong in this country, that his sentence would be shorter if he agreed to be deported, etc.; c) the judge, on one hand, received highly favorable descriptions of Mr. Polanski's character from well-known Hollywood producers and actors and, on the other hand, received a flood of mail from "concerned citizens" of the "I hate Polanski and people like him" variety; d) the judge received requests from multi-millionaires, such as the film producer Dino De Laurentis, to let Polanski finish a film in Tahiti; e) the newspapers tried to outguess each other on a daily basis about Mr. Polanski's whereabouts and published accounts about his having been seen in Germany, etc.; f) the crime for which Mr. Polanski was convicted, "unlawful sexual intercourse" (Section 264 of the State of California Penal Code; this offense used to be known as "statutory rape"), is not considered a crime in thirteen States of the Union, and only 44 people were convicted of this crime in 1976 in all of Los Angeles County; g) Mr. Polanski had no prior criminal record, sex-related or otherwise, the prosecutrix was described by the judge as a "not . . . inexperienced and unsophisticated girl," and yet Mr. Polanski was suspected of being an MDSO and sent to the Chino facility for a diagnostic study to be done on him.

In a sense, the Polanski case illustrates not only why it would be unreasonable to expect our model to be applicable to "special" cases, but also raises more general questions about the sometimes arbitrary nature of MDSO classification and processing. Finally, it highlights the role of the media in misinforming the public about the operation of the legal system. By being exposed only to sensationalist accounts of Perry-Mason-type cases, the public gets an entirely distorted picture of how modal cases are handled. Hopefully, the present chapter corrects this biased view by providing a more accurate description of MDSO processing.

REFERENCES

Cocozza, J. J., and Steadman, H. J. Some refinements in the measurement and prediction of dangerous behavior. *American Journal of Psychiatry* **131**:1012–1014 (1974).

Deutsch, M. Graduate training of the problem-oriented social psychologist. In M. Deutsch and H. A. Hornstein, *Applying Social Psychology: Implications for Research, Practice, and Training.* Hillsdale, N.J.: Lawrence Erlbaum Associates, 1975.

Dix, G. E. Differential processing of abnormal sex offenders: Utilization of California's Mentally Disordered Sex Offender Program. *Journal of Criminal Law and Criminology* **67**:233–243 (1976).

Ebbesen, E. B., and Konečni, V. J. Decision making and information integration in the courts: The setting of bail. *Journal of Personality and Social Psychology* 32:805–821 (1975).

Ebbesen, E. B., and Konečni, V. J. Fairness in sentencing: Severity of crime and judicial decision making. Paper presented in a symposium entitled "Seriousness of crime and severity of punishment" held at the 84th Annual Convention of the American Psychological Association, Washington, D.C., September, 1976.

Ebbesen, E. B., and Konečni, V. J. Factors affecting sentencing of adult felons. To appear in B. D. Sales (Ed.), *Perspectives in Law and Psychology (Vol. II): The Jury, Judicial, and Trial Processes.* New York: Plenum Press, 1978 (in preparation).

Ebbesen, E. B., and Konečni, V. J. Social psychology and law: Theoretical considerations. In V. J. Konečni and E. B. Ebbesen (Eds.), *Social-Psychological Analysis of Legal Processes.* San Francisco: W. H. Freeman and Co., in press.

Konečni, V. J., and Ebbesen, E. B. A critical analysis of method and theory in psychological approaches to legal decisions. To appear in B. D. Sales (Ed.), *Perspectives in Law and Psychology (Vol. II): The Jury, Judicial, and Trial Processes.* New York: Plenum Press, 1978 (in preparation).

Konečni, V. J., and Ebbesen, E. B. Sentencing felons. In V. J. Konečni and E. B.

Ebbesen (Eds.), *Social-Psychological Analysis of Legal Processes*. San Francisco: W. H. Freeman and Co., in press—a.

Konečni, V. J., and Ebbesen, E. B. Choice of research problems and methodology in the psychology of law. In V. J. Konečni and E. B. Ebbesen (Eds.), *Social-Psychological Analysis of Legal Processes*. San Francisco: W. H. Freeman and Co., in press—b.

Konecni, V. J., and Ebbesen, E. B. (Eds.), *Social-Psychological Analysis of Legal Processes*. San Francisco: W. H. Freeman and Co., in press—c.

Kozol, H. L.; Boucher, R. J.; and Garofalo, R. F. The diagnosis and treatment of dangerousness. *Crime and Delinquency* **18**:371–392 (1972).

APPENDIX 1.

The coding instrument and levels of variables used in the statistical and computer analyses for the DEFENDANT'S FILE (available to the psychiatrists and the judge).

Date: ——————————— Court: ——————————— MH#: ———————————
Judge: ——————————— D.A. ——————————— Examining psychiatrists:
1. ———————————
2. ———————————
3. ———————————

Number of lines devoted to describing the following categories:

1. PROBATION OFFICER'S REPORT: # of pages: (1–3=1, 4–5=2, 6–up=3)
   a. custody data: (0–1=1, 2–2, 3–up=3)
   b. related court date: (0–3=1, 4–6=2, 7–up=3)
   c. plea-bargain: (0–3=1, 4–6=2, 7–up=3)
   d. offense described: (0–25=1, 26–50=2, 51–up=3)
   e. defendant's statement: (0–25=1, 26–50=2, 50–up=3)
   f. prior record: (0-1, 1–4=2, 5–up=3)
   g. social factors: (0–10=1, 11–20=2, 21–up=3)
   h. probation adjustment: (0–5=1, 6–10=2, 11–up=3)
   i. additional information: (0–15=1, 16–30=2, 31–up=3)
   j. evaluation: (0–12=1, 13–20=2, 21–up=3)
   k. recommendation: (0–5=1, 6–10=2, 11–up=3)
2. COMPLAINT: actual # of pages
   actual # of copies
   # of lines: (0–5=1, 6–15=2, 16–up=3)
   charges: (0–3=1, 4–6=2, 7–10=3, 11–14=4, 15–up=5)
3. DOCKET: actual # of pages
   actual # of copies
   # of lines: (1–5=1, 6–10=2, 11–up=3)
4. RECEIPT ON TRANSFER: # of copies: (0–1=1, 2–3=2, 4–up=3)
   # of lines: (1–5=1, 6–15=2, 16–up=3)
5. INFORMATION: actual # of pages
   actual # of copies
   # of lines: (0–20=1, 21–40=2, 41–up=3)
   a. charges: (0–1=1, 2–4=2, 5–up=3)
   b. victim's state: b. (0–5=1, 6–10=2, 11–up=3)
   c. police report: (0–5=1, 6–10=2, 11–up=3)

6. CHANGE OF PLEA FORM: (0–4=1, 5–8=2, 9–up=3)
7. ORDER ADJOURNING PROCEEDINGS AND CERTIFYING ALLEGED MDSO FOR EXAM AND HEARING:
   actual # of copies
8. PERSONAL LETTERS ABOUT THE DEFENDANT: [total] (0–5=1, 6–10=2, 11–up=3)
   a. positive: (0–3=1, 4–7=2, 8–up=3)
   b. negative: (0–1=1, 2–4=2, 5–up=3)

NOTE FOR CODERS: If info is available and it is *objective* then write "obj" next to scale or in appropriate slot.

9. DEFENDANT'S STATEMENT AND/OR INTERVIEW INFORMATION (information in quotes or "the defendant said that . . .")
   a. Is section filled out? 0=NO, 1=YES
   b. To what degree does the defendant admit having committed the crime(s)? (for each charge if appropriate)

(0–33mm=1, 34–67mm=2, 68–100mm=3)

Admits |--| Denies
Completely | | Completely

   c. How does the defendant "explain" his behavior? Were there any extenuating circumstances?
      1) External factors not under the defendant's control: *Short-Term*
         (i)   none
         (ii) outside pressure
         (iii) "it just happened"
         (iv) situation presented itself
         (v)   family problems
      2) External factors not under the defendant's control: *Long-Term*
         (i)   none
         (ii) chronic social pressure (subculture)
         (iii) chronic family problems
      3) Internal factors not under the defendant's control: *Short-Term*
         (i)   none
         (ii) drunk
         (iii) on drugs
         (iv) confused
         (v)   angry
         (vi) out of control, on an impulse
         (vii) auditory hallucination ("heard a voice")
      4) Internal factors not under the defendant's control: *Long-Term*
         (i)   none
         (ii)   drug addiction
         (iii) alcoholism
         (iv)   addiction and alcoholism
         (v)   sex-life dissatisfaction
         (vi)   homosexuality
         (vii) loneliness
         (viii) frequent auditory hallucinations ("voices")
         (ix)   chronic emotional problems

APPENDIX 2.

The coding instrument and levels of variables used in the statistical and computer analyses for the PSYCHIATRISTS' LETTER (available to the judge).

Date: _____ Court #: _____ MH#: _____
Judge: _____ D.A. _____ Examining psychiatrists:
1. _____
2. _____
3. _____

Number of lines devoted to describing the following categories.

1. DEFENDANT'S APPEARANCE: [total] (0=0, 1=1, 2–up=2)
   a. physical: [bodily] (0=0, 1=1, 2–up=2)
   b. subjective impression: [dressed, groomed] (0=0, 1=1, 2–up=2)
2. DEFENDANT'S DESCRIPTION OF OFFENSE: [total] (1–15=1, 16–30=2, 31–up=3)
   a. details: [planning, procedure] (0–15=1, 16–30=2, 31=up=3)
   b. feelings about offense: [total] (1–2=1, 3–4=2, 5–up=3)
      1) negative [remorse] (0–1=1, 2–3=2, 4–up=3)
      2) positive [no remorse] (0–1=1, 1=2, 2=3)
      3) indifferent: (0–2=1, 3–4=2, 5–up=3)
      4) admits guilt: (0–1=1, 2–4=2, 5–up=3)
3. PRIOR RECORD: [total] (0–5=1, 6–10=2, 11–15=3, 16–20=4, 21–25=5, 26–up=6)
   a. criminal: (0=1,1–4=2, 5–up=3)
   b. MDSO-related: (0=1, 1–4=2, 5–up=3)
4. PRIOR LIFE STYLE: (0=1, 2–3=2, 4–up=3)
   a. negative: (0=1, 1–3=2, 4–up=3)
   b. positive: (0=1, 1–3=2, 4–up=3)
5. PAST SEXUAL EXPERIENCE OF DEFENDANT: [total] (0–2=1, 3–5=2, 6–up=3)
   a. defendant offers info.: (0–1=1, 2–3=2, 3–up=3)
   b. defendant responds to psychiatrists' questions: (0–2=1, 3–6=2, 7–up=3)
      1) childhood: (0–1=1, 2–3=2, 4–up=3)
      2) adulthood: (0–2=1, 3–4=2, 5–up=3)
6. CURRENT STATUS OF DEFENDANT: [job, school, etc.; total] (0–2=1, 3–4=2, 5–up=3)
   positive [stable, etc.] (0=1, 1–2=2, 3–up=3)
   negative [unstable . . .] (0–1=1, 2–3=2, 4–up=3)
7. FUTURE STATUS OF DEFENDANT: [total] (0=1, 1=2, 2–up=3)
   a. defendant's desires for future: (0=1, 1=2, 2–up=3)
   b. probation officer's evaluation of future prospects: (0=1, 1=2, 2–up=3)
8. PROBATION OFFICER'S REPORT INFORMATION: [taken directly from report total] (0–15=1, 16–30=2 31–up=3)
   a. description of offense: (0–15=1, 16–30=2, 31–up=3)
   b. psychological assessment: (0=1, 1=2, 2–up=3)
   c. physical description: (0=1, 1=2, 2–up=3)
   d. family history: (0=1, 1=2, 2–up=3)
   e. Probation Officer's recommendation: (0=1, 1=2, 2–up=3)
9. PSYCHIATRISTS' EVALUATION OF OFFENSE: [total] (0=1, 1–20=2, 21–up=3)
   a. interpretive statements [interprets acts psychologically] (0=1, 1–20=2, 21–up=3)
   b. offers new information about offense (0=1, 1–4=2, 5–up=3)
   c. implies "force" (0=1, 2–4=2, 5–up=3)
   d. implies drug-related factors (0=1, 1–4=2, 5–up=3)
10. OTHER SOURCES OF INFORMATION: [total] (0=1, 1–10=2, 11–up=3)
   a. defense psychiatrist's report (0=1, 1–10=2, 11–up=3)
      1) positive (0=1, 1=2, 2–up=3)
      2) negative (0=1, 1=2, 2–up=3)
   b. police reports (0=1, 1–10=2, 11–up=3)

        1) positive (0=1, 1=2, 2–up=3)
        2) negative (0=1, 1=2, 2–up=3)
    c. District Attorney's file (0=1, 1–10=2, 11–up=3)
        1) positive (0=1, 1=2, 2–up=3)
        2) negative (0=1, 1=2, 2–up=3)
    d. victim's statement (0=1, 1–10=2, 12–up=3)
        1) positive (0=1, 1=2, 2–up=3)
        2) negative (0=1, 1=2, 2–up=3)
    e. defendant's employer (0=1, 1–10=2, 11–up=3)
        1) positive (0=1, 1=2, 2–up=3)
        2) negative (0=1, 1=2, 2–up=3)
    f. defendant's relatives (0=1, 1–10=2, 11–up=3)
        1) positive (0=1, 1=2, 2–up=3)
        2) negative (0=1, 1=2, 2–up=3)
11. PSYCHIATRISTS' DIAGNOSIS AND RECOMMENDATION: [total]
    a. diagnosis [number of labels]
        labels: 1. none
                2. homosexuality
                3. female paedophilia
                4. male paedophilia
                5. antisocial personality
                6. sexual deviation
                7. female & male paedophilia
                8. schizophrenia
    b. recommendation [actual number of lines]
        classification: 1. non-MDSO
                     2. MDSO
12. JUDGE'S SUBSEQUENT DECISION
    1. Remand
    2. Patton State Hospital
    3. Continuance

FOOTNOTES TO CHAPTER 5

[1]Throughout this paper, we refer to people suspected of being MDSOs as men. This is not sexist usage but reflects the curious fact that an enormous proportion of what are these days considered "sex crimes" (and MDSO activities) are carried out by men

[2]As an example, in California in 1976 (according to the State of California Bureau of Criminal Statistics), over 15 percent of the felons classified as MDSOs were eventually convicted of non-sexual offenses, such as burglary, robbery, and assault.

[3]Dix (1976) recently published a very valuable article examining the California MDSO program; however, he focused mostly on what subsequently happens to people originally found to be MDSOs (duration of confinement, recidivism, etc.). In contrast, one of the major aspects of our work is the attempt to identify predictors of the MDSO/non-MDSO decision within a more general causal-analysis framework. In addition, Dix looked at relatively few factors and drew conclusions in an informal manner rather than on the basis of statistical analyses of the data.

[4]Observation was one of several methods we used in our studies of sentencing (Ebbesen and Konecni, 1978; Konecni and Ebbesen, in press—a). It was used to record the events in the sentencing hearing (who spoke, how long, what about, after whom, etc.), as well as to code variables, such as the defendant's appearance, attractiveness, articulateness, etc. We might note that none of the latter, defendant-associated variables were useful predictors of the sentence. This is instructive when one considers that "attractiveness of the defendant" is one of the favorite variables used in social-psychological laboratory experiments on various aspects of the legal process.

[5]It should be noted that the probation officer's recommendation at the conclusion of the report was *not* treated as a predictor. This may appear odd, given the great value of the probation officer's recommendation as a predictor of the *sentence* (in non-MDSO adult-

felony cases). However, in MDSO cases, probation officers typically do not openly suggest either a diagnostic label or the MDSO/non-MDSO classification; instead, they conclude the reports by some variation of the following (in a paedophilia case): "If the court finds that X. is not an MDSO, then I nevertheless respectfully recommend that a condition of probation be that X. must not be in the company of minors below age Y."

[6]One could plausibly argue that the psychiatrists' recommendations are such as they are because the psychiatrists correctly anticipate what the judge would do anyway and are also for some reason motivated to maximize agreement with the judge. A similar argument can be raised in the case of sentencing decisions (e.g., Ebbesen and Konečni, 1978; Konečni and Ebbesen, in press—a), where a high agreement between the probation officers' recommendations and the judges' sentencing decisions has been observed. In the case of sentencing, however, auxiliary data that were available suggested relatively strongly that of the various possible causal models, the correct one was that which proposed that the probation officers' recommendations were "causing" the judges' sentences. Unfortunately, in the present case, such auxiliary data were not available. Nevertheless, the psychiatrists' (assumed or real) far greater expertise in diagnosing and prognosticating "mental disease," coupled with the fact that their recommendations temporally precede the judge's verdicts, leads one to the tentative conclusion that the judge's behavior is "caused" by the psychiatric recommendation, rather than vice versa. This issue is, of course, quite separate from the question of the causes of the psychiatric recommendation itself, which, therefore, also indirectly influence the judge's verdict.

[7]It should be noted that the proposed model is concerned with the operation of the *system* and not with the actual steps taken by individual decision makers in reaching their decisions. For example, our model does not deal with the judge's thought content and processes nor with the documents and information he *actually* scans prior to reaching the decision. The judge may well look only at the psychiatrists' letter and not even attend to documents that contain information about the defendant's prior convictions for sex crimes. That prior sex-related criminal record predicts the judge's verdict so accurately is presumably a consequence of the fact that to whatever information the judge attends and is influenced by (for example, in the psychiatrists' letter), is highly correlated with prior, sex-related criminal record. Therefore, we are not able to specify the extent to which the predictive accuracy of our model would be changed by removing some of the information currently at the judge's disposal. For example, some might argue that the costly psychiatric interviews (and thus the psychiatrists' letters) could be painlessly eliminated from the MDSO-processing system, because the information about the defendant's prior, sex-related criminal record is quite sufficient for accurate prediction. Such a step could, however, potentially decrease the accuracy of the model if the judge—in the absence of the psychiatrists' letter—began to attend to, and be influenced by, *other information* and documents in the file that are *less well correlated* with the prior, sex-related criminal record. In fact, removal or addition of *any* of the sources of information currently available to the judge, whether they be presently correlated with the final MDSO classification or not, might well alter the operation of the system. Needless to say, such a change in the causal sequence could easily be detected by a project similar to the present one, and the judge could be advised accordingly. He would then have the choice of adjusting his decisions, so that they would be more similar to those before the elimination of psychiatric interviews by, for example, attending directly to information about the defendant's prior, sex-related criminal record.

[8]One might ask how a person ever acquires a sex-related prior record. One plausible answer is that when an overwhelming amount of evidence exists concerning the role of the defendant's sexual abnormality in his criminal actions (in terms of the number of charges, counts, or the type of activity in which the defendant engaged), he receives a sexual deviation label and is classified as an MDSO, even in the absence of prior convictions for sexual offenses. In our sample, there were four such cases (see Table 5).

[9]Most of our information comes from personal communications on February 24 and March 2, 1978 with attorney Douglas Dalton (of the Los Angeles law firm of Hodge and Dalton) and from a brief (No. A334 139, "Statement of disqualification for cause of judge"), which attorney Dalton filed on behalf of Mr. Polanski. We would like to thank attorney Dalton for giving us a copy of the brief and other information and to gratefully acknowledge his cooperation in this matter.

II
APPROACHES TO IMPROVING THE LEGAL PROCESS AND SYSTEM

6

Juveniles' Comprehension of Miranda Warnings

Thomas Grisso and Sam Manoogian

Present due process protections in the taking of confessions during police interrogation derive from now famous *Miranda v. Arizona* (1966), the case of an adult murder suspect. Miranda contended that his confession, which was used to incriminate him, was given under conditions which should not have allowed the confession to be admitted as evidence. The Supreme Court's opinion in the case detailed the procedures and conditions which must be met for a confession to be construed as valid—that is, to be admitted as evidence in court. Among these conditions are the necessity of warning the suspect of the privilege against self-incrimination (the right to silence and the use of confessions in court) and the right to counsel (before and during interrogation and the availability of free counsel). Soon after, this information was embodied in the four "*Miranda* warnings," now widely associated with police arrest; these include informing the suspect of the right to remain silent; that anything the suspect says may be used against him or her in court; that he or she can consult an attorney before interrogation and may have an attorney present at the time of

The project of which this study is a part was supported by research grant MH–27849 to the first author from the Center for Studies of Crime and Delinquency, National Institute of Mental Health. Initial stages in test development and research design were supported by student dissertation grant 76N1–99–0067 to the second author from the Law Enforcement Assistance Administration. The St. Louis County Juvenile Court is gratefully acknowledged for its cooperation as a research site. The interpretations and conclusions in this report do not necessarily represent those of NIMH or the Juvenile Court. Professionals in law or psychology who assisted in various ways were Corinne Goodman, Eugene Kissling, David Munz, Paul Piersma, and Carolyn Pomicter. Special thanks are due to three research assistants: Robert Neems, Ronald Peal, and Linda Vierling.

interrogation; and that the suspect may have an attorney appointed by the court, if he or she cannot afford one. Interrogation may not proceed if these rights are not waived. Furthermore, the Court said that the suspect must have waived the rights knowingly, intelligently, and voluntarily in order for a subsequent confession to be valid.

Juvenile Waiver and Confessions

Soon after the *Miranda* decision, the court in *In re Gault* (1967) held that juveniles were to be accorded the protections and rights in *Miranda* but left open the question of these privileges during pretrial procedures. Despite this uncertainty, most states soon interpreted *Gault* as extending the *Miranda* ruling to apply to interrogation of juveniles prior to trial. In addition, all states that have addressed the issue have ruled that the mere fact that the suspect is a child is not seen as invalidating an otherwise competent (knowing, intelligent, and voluntary) waiver of rights by the child (Davis, 1975). Arguments for parental consent for a juvenile's waiver have received no support since their rejection in *People v. Lara* (1967).

Very little is known about the specific impact which the aforementioned rulings have had upon the interrogation of juveniles and the use of confessions after waiver. In the only systematic study in this area (Grisso and Pomicter, 1977), police interrogation occurred in 75 percent of a large, random sample of felony referrals to a metropolitan juvenile court during three years. Approximately 20–25 percent of the interrogations involved juveniles who were 14 years of age or younger. Furthermore, juveniles provided information to police (beyond information about their own identity) in about 90 percent of the interrogations. Unfortunately, the study offered no clear indication of the nature of the information provided by juveniles after waiver, its use in court in an incriminating fashion, or its admissibility. But the results clearly indicate that pretrial interrogation to seek potentially self-incriminating information from juvenile felony suspects is more the rule than the exception and that it is not confined to cases involving older juveniles. Furthermore, the high frequency of waiver suggests that self-incrimination could have occurred in most of these cases.

The potential importance of juveniles' confessions is especially apparent when it is considered that all states allow for procedures whereby certain juveniles may be tried in criminal courts as adults and, if convicted, may be subjected to the harsher punishments generally reserved for adult offenders. A juvenile's confession prior to transfer to a criminal court may, under certain circumstances, be admitted as evidence in the criminal court trial. Furthermore, there is a clear trend toward standards within the juvenile justice system itself which emphasize punishment, determinant sentencing, and consequences which fit the seriousness of the crime (Institute of Judicial Administration/American Bar Association, 1977 a,b). Given such policy changes, juveniles' confessions can assume an importance parallel to those in adult criminal cases, even when the case remains within the jurisdiction of the juvenile court.

Validity of Waiver by Juveniles

The legal standard for determining the admissibility of a juvenile's confession in court generally is the same as that for adults: That is, waiver is viewed as valid, or effective, if it has been provided intelligently, knowingly, and voluntarily. But considerations of the lesser maturity of juveniles, concern for their protection, and the vagueness of the general standard have resulted in special attention to the effectiveness of waiver by juveniles.

There have been two broad approaches to dealing with the question of validity of waiver by juveniles: One has been an argument for a blanket exclusion of juvenile confessions on the grounds that juveniles, as a class, are not sufficiently mature to satisfy the standard. The legal argument will not be detailed here, since recent case law offers no acceptance of a blanket exclusion. For example, in *In the Interest of Thompson* (1976), the court noted: "It is apparent that courts, required to deal pragmatically with an ever-mounting crime wave in which minors play a disproportionate role, have considered society's self-preservation interest in rejecting a blanket exclusion for juvenile confessions" (P 5) (See also *Cotton v. United States*, 1971; *United States v. Ramsey*, 1973.) The court's concern in this regard can be expected to continue for some time.

The second and more enduring approach was provided by the California Supreme Court (*People v. Lara*, 1967), which developed a "totality of circumstances" doctrine to test the purported waiver by a juvenile. Most courts now employ this doctrine, often referring to further refinements in *West v. United States* (1968). In *West*, the court provided a list of circumstances which were to be considered; basically they were of two kinds: 1) characteristics of the juvenile, such as age, intelligence, and amount of prior experience with police and courts; and 2) several circumstances of the interrogation, such as the length of interrogation and care with which due process was applied.[1] Neither the court in *West* nor subsequent decisions have provided clear guidelines regarding how such circumstances are to be applied when deciding the validity of waiver by a juvenile. Nevertheless, the list of circumstances in *West* has served to structure judicial decision-making in that the circumstances direct attention to two classes of variables: One class is more or less external to the juvenile; that is, were the environmental circumstances, the procedures employed, and existing protections sufficient to *allow* a valid waiver to be made? The second class of variables involve characteristics of the juvenile him/ herself, addressing the competence of the juvenile to make an intelligent, knowing, and voluntary waiver of rights. While it is acknowledged that judicial decision-making must often involve consideration of interactions between competency variables and procedural variables, the dichotomy is useful conceptually. For example, the presence of a clear deficiency on the part of the juvenile might by itself permit a decision to invalidate a waiver (and exclude the confession), even when procedural elements have been satisfactory by normal standards.

CONCEPTUALIZING COMPETENCE TO WAIVE RIGHTS

The remainder of the chapter will focus on the question of juveniles' competence to waive rights, recognizing that competence includes only one class of variables to be weighed in judicial decisions regarding the validity of waiver by juveniles. We will look briefly at competence variables which have been noted in case law and then provide a conceptualization of competence to waive rights which guided an empirical study to be reported in this chapter.

Variables Noted in Case Law

A review of the many cases since 1968 which have involved rulings on juvenile waiver reveals considerable variability in the application of circumstances in *West*. (For detailed analyses and summaries of cases from 1968 to 1976, see Davis, 1975–77 and National Juvenile Law Center, 1977.) Frequently courts have commented on the variables or circumstances which were weighed, but their conclusions fail to specify how these circumstances were weighed and which of them were viewed as critical to the conclusion. Thus judicial assumptions regarding any single variable—e.g., age—as an index of competence are difficult to discern from a review of case law. Generally, most cases have involved juveniles of age 14 or younger. Courts' comments regarding competence and the fact that waiver was ruled valid in some of these cases but not in others indicate that presumption of competence is rebuttable below age 14.

When intelligence has been considered, IQ scores in the retarded or borderline range have been most common in those cases in which confessions were invalidated. When IQ scores are in the 80's, however, courts generally have decided that juveniles could understand the substance of the *Miranda* warnings, even though they might have some difficulty with certain words in the warnings (for example, see *In the Interest of Stiff*, 1975). Juveniles' degrees of past experience with courts or police have occasionally been used as a variable to be weighed when determining whether or not a juvenile is capable of a valid waiver; little or no past experience has sometimes been used to suggest increased susceptibility to intimidation, while a greater amount of experience has sometimes been viewed as suggesting a probable understanding of rights in spite of lower intelligence.

Some cases have involved expert testimony by psychologists in an attempt to determine whether the juveniles in question had the capacity to comprehend the *Miranda* warnings, and occasionally attorneys have attempted to demonstrate their juvenile client's lack of comprehension during direct examination in trial. For example:

Q: What are rights? A: Something you're supposed to do with. Q: Rights are when you're supposed to do right? A: Yes sir (*In the Interest of Holifield*, 1975, p. 472–473).

In summary, recent cases have not produced standard guidelines or clear criteria for judging the competence of juveniles in relation to the validity of waiver, but courts have manifested an awareness of the necessity of weighing variables which bear upon the issue of juveniles' competence, and certain variables (age, intelligence, experience with police) have been cited with some regularity. Not surprisingly, empirical relationships between these variables and the legal standard (knowingly, voluntarily, and intelligently) have not been studied.[2]

Definition of Competence to Waive Rights

The first step in testing such relationships would involve the translation of the legal standard into concepts which are amenable to psychological study and which are consistent with the intended meaning of the legal standard. Case law does not provide the necessary, conceptual definition of the "knowing, intelligent, and voluntary" standard; therefore, in preparation for our examination of competence to waive rights, lawyers and psychologists worked together to arrive at consensual views regarding a conceptualization which would specify the areas of inquiry needed in an empirical study of competence.[3] The primary areas of inquiry which emerged were: 1) cognitive capacity; 2) belief or expectancy; and 3) personality variables.

The first area of inquiry, cognitive capacity to make a competent waiver of rights, was further defined as one's ability: a) to comprehend the standard *Miranda* rights warnings; and b) to understand the intended function and significance of those rights in the context of interrogation. The second area, expectancy, refers to an individual's beliefs regarding the consequences for oneself, given the decision to waive rights or to assert one's rights as provided in *Miranda* warnings; that is, one might understand the *intended* significance and protections afforded by the rights (as noted under ''cognitive capacity'') but might believe that the *actual* consequences of waiver or assertion of rights do not correspond with the more formal intentions or promises. The third area includes personality variables which, in interaction with various interrogation circumstances, might invalidate a waiver of rights (e.g., an extremely fearful and dependent youth faced with implicitly or explicitly coercive conditions).

The remainder of this chapter offers the major results from a study of juveniles' abilities to understand the *Miranda* rights warnings. It will be noted that such understanding is conceptualized as only part of the cognitive capacity component, and competence to waive rights is viewed as requiring more than cognitive capacity alone. Therefore, while a deficiency in understanding of *Miranda* warnings would suggest incompetence to waive rights, adequate understanding of the warnings might not necessarily signify competence.

THE STUDY

The primary objectives of the study were to assess comprehension of *Miranda* warnings and to examine the relationships between degree of comprehension and a range of demographic and offense history variables in a sample of juveniles with court contact. Of special interest was the development of age-related and IQ-related norms for *Miranda* comprehension in this population, employing several criterion measures of *Miranda* comprehension.

Definition of Understanding Miranda Rights

Three measures of comprehension of *Miranda* warnings were developed. Each measure employed a different response format: 1) subject's paraphrase of the four *Miranda* warnings; 2) subject's definitions of critical words in the *Miranda* warnings; and 3) subject's ability to identify simply-worded, preconstructed sentences as being accurate or inaccurate interpretations of the various *Miranda* warnings (''true-false''). The use of multiple measures was intended to allow for cross-validation of results and to provide for more adequate interpretations of results by employing several modes of subject response.

The paraphrase measure, entitled Comprehension of Miranda Rights (CMR), employs a reading of the four standard *Miranda* warnings and, after each one, requires the subject to say "in your own words" what it is that the warning says. Criteria for adequate and inadequate responses were developed by collecting sample responses from juveniles, classifying the responses by content and allowing lawyers to judge the adequacy of the various classes of responses; in other words, consensus of a range of experts in juvenile law (including a national panel) was the criterion for the development of the scoring system. An example of the scoring system is provided in Table 6.1, showing the scoring criteria for the first *Miranda* item in the CMR. Responses on each statement are scored two for adequate, one for questionable, and zero for inadequate, according to scoring standards in the manual for CMR administration and scoring.[4] Five separate tests of interscorer reliability yielded Pearson r coefficients between scorer pairs of .91–.95 for CMR sum scores and .86–.95 for each of the four items (*Miranda* warning statements) in the measure.

Administration includes reading a *Miranda* warning statement to the subject who has been given a card on which the warning is printed. The subject is asked to tell what the warning says "in your own words." When a subject's initial response is of questionable adequacy, as defined in the Manual, the examiner employs standardized inquiry to allow clarification by the subject or discovery of any further understanding. (For an example of standard inquiry, see Table 6.1.) The procedure then continues through each of the remaining three warning statements.

Special efforts were made to develop administration procedures and scoring criteria which would not penalize persons who might be less verbally sophisticated or who might use nonstandard English. For example, in addition to attempts at clarification provided within the aforementioned standardized inquiry, examiners sought from subjects their definitions of any slang words which might produce confusion in scoring (e.g., "bad," which in current usage by adolescents sometimes means "good"). They questioned certain conventional phrases which might conceal inadequate understanding (e.g., "plead the fifth") but generally accepted without question certain colloquialisms which have nearly universal meaning among adolescents (e.g., "fuzz"). In addition, examples of two-point responses in the manual included some sample responses which met the essential criteria, while employing simply worded, brief paraphrases, some of which were grammatically imperfect.

The vocabulary measure, entitled Comprehension of *Miranda* Vocabulary (CMV), employed six words from the standard *Miranda* warn-

Table 6.1. Scoring criteria for CMR item I. ("You do not have to make a statement and have the right to remain silent.")

---

2 Points

General: The idea that one does not have to say anything to the police, answer any question, and/or make any formal or informal statements.

A. A paraphrase regarding one's choice or implied choice of whether or not to talk, without explanation.

    Examples: You do not have to say a word to police or anyone (implied choice)—you do not have to say anything to anyone, but if you want to you can—you don't have to say anything.

B. Only the idea that one has a choice regarding whether or not to talk is essential. But if a description or consequences associated with legal rights is given, it must be accurate.

    Examples: You don't have to say anything, and if you don't it will not be held against you in court—you don't have to answer any questions, because it can be used against you (might hurt your case, be incriminating, etc.)

1 Point

A. Choice or implied choice is present, but rationale for the right is erroneous, illogical, or inaccurate.

    Examples: You don't have to talk if you don't want to, because you might not have done it (because the police might not want you to) (because your parents might get mad.)

B. The idea that it is better not to say anything under any circumstances.

    Examples: I think I should keep quiet—it means don't talk to the police—I would say it's best to say nothing—it means you better keep your mouth shut.

C. The idea that one can refuse not only to say anything, but also to do anything.

    Examples: You don't have to do nothing you don't want to do—they can't make you do a thing.

0 Point

A. Stated lack of understanding.

    Examples: I don't know—it doesn't mean anything at all to me.

B. The idea that you must remain silent and do not have the right or choice to talk if you want to.

    Examples: You got to be quiet—you must speak quietly.

C. The idea that you have to talk, stated generally or under certain circumstances; or that if you do not talk, it will go against you either with police or in court.

    Examples: It means you don't have to talk unless you're guilty—you don't have to make statements but you have to tell them what they want to know.

Table 6.1 (continued)

Standardized inquiry for CMR I

Examinee's Initial Response	Inquiry
If any of the following phrases occur verbatim: —make a statement —have the right —remain silent	What does _____ mean?
That it is best not to talk.	Tell me what the sentence says in your own words, not what you think a person should do.
That one does not have to *do* anything they do not want to do.	What do you mean by "not do anything"?

In addition, examiners may attempt clarification of verbal confusions or slang which make the meaning of the response unclear. Questions which are permissible are:
What do you mean by _____?
Can you tell me more about that?
Can you explain that again?

ings which seemed to manifest the greatest variability in responses during exploratory discussions with juveniles about definitions of many words in the warnings. The words in the CMV are: entitled, right, attorney, interrogation, appoint, and consult. Procedures for developing scoring criteria were similar to those described for the CMR measure. Interscorer reliability between scorer pairs was .96–.98 for CMV sum scores and .87–.96 for various single vocabulary words.

The nature, development, and use of the third measure, CMR-True/False, will be described later, since it is best understood in the context of a methodological issue which will receive considerable attention in the description of results.

Subjects

During an eleven-month period, 431 juveniles participated in the study. The sample included 359 juveniles in St. Louis County Juvenile Court detention, 39 juveniles at a boys school, and 33 juveniles at a boys town; ages ranged from 11–16 (mean = 14.5), with 20 percent of the sample younger than age 14; 55 percent were male, 27 percent were black, and 30 percent were of lower-middle and lower socioeconomic status (based on U.S. Census tract information on median income and median education in tract of residence). Mean number of prior court referrals (arrests) was 3.38, and 33 percent of the sample had at least one felony arrest in their court record. IQ scores ranged from 46 to 132 (mean = 88.12, standard deviation =16.16); eleven percent of the sample obtained IQ scores of 70 or below. The court would not allow the testing of any juvenile who was being admitted to detention on an alleged felony charge. In addition, we chose not to test juveniles before they had resided in detention for at least 24 hours, in order to allow initial emotional reactions to detention to subside. These two restrictions allowed for a testable pool of about one-third of the detention admissions, nearly all of whom are included in the study sample.

Our objectives did not require a sample with demographic proportions similar to those of the total detention population, since all data was to be analyzed separately for each demographic group; but it was important that for each demographic variable, each variable class occurring in the nontested portion of the population should be represented sufficiently in the tested sample. A comparison between the tested and nontested samples during a four-month period revealed that for every demographic and offense variable in the study, every variable class in the nontested group was represented in the tested group in numbers sufficient for planned data analysis. In addition, no differences were found between the two samples in proportions of subjects in each age, socioeconomic class, or in any offense history class (e.g., subjects with two or more past felonies constituted 24 and 22 percent of the tested and nontested samples, respectively). The tested sample included a somewhat smaller percentage of blacks (25 percent; nontested = 36 percent) and greater percentage of females (45 percent; nontested = 35 percent); neither difference was statistically significant. Finally, there were no significant differences between age groups with regard to IQ scores, race proportions, sex proportions, or socioeconomic status.

Procedures

Procedures were designed to provide confidentiality and to maximize the likelihood that participation by subjects was voluntary and nonstressful. All subjects were tested between 24 and 72 hours after admission to detention or, at the nondetention settings, from 1–18 months after admission. Each subject was seen individually by research assistants under conditions clearly described to subjects as research and having no bearing upon their future in detention or with the court. These conditions are quite different from those in which juveniles normally would be asked to consider their rights as expressed in *Miranda* warnings. Thus it was anticipated that the results might reflect a higher level of comprehension than that of which juveniles would be capable under the more stressful conditions of actual interrogation procedures. Tests administered were the Comprehension of Miranda Rights (CMR) measure and Comprehension of Miranda Vocabulary (CMV) (about 100 subjects also received the CMR–TF, as will be described later) and three subtests from the WISC–R (Similarities, Vocabulary, Block Design) with which IQ scores were prorated. Demographic and offense history data were obtained from the court's computer storage of juveniles' records.

Results and Discussion

The CMR's four items (standard *Miranda* warnings) are scored two (adequate), one (questionable or partial understanding), or zero (inadequate), for a range of scores of 0–8. Of the total sample, 20 percent obtained perfect (eight points) scores and 45 percent obtained no zero credits on any of the four *Miranda* warnings. The panel of legal experts who assisted in the development of scoring criteria viewed two-point criteria as necessary to demonstrate understanding sufficient to contribute to valid waiver and zero credit to represent clear failure to understand the warning in question. Employing these standards, either four-fifths of the sample (with less than perfect scores), or slightly more than one-half of the sample (with one or more zero credits), are conceptualized as deficient in critical understanding of the warnings. (In the remainder of this chapter, the more liberal standard of "no zero credits on any item" will be employed to define adequate comprehension. To employ "perfect score" as the standard would require the assumption that one-point responses signify inadequate comprehension, while in fact such scores sometimes are obtained when the subject's response is not clearly wrong but is insufficient to conclude that full understanding exists. The use of the more liberal standard reduces the likelihood of erroneously "penalizing" subjects on the basis of such responses.)

The two warnings producing the greatest percentage of inadequate responses, 24 and 45 percent of the sample, respectively, were those indicating that statements which the suspect makes "can and will be used against you in a court of law," and that the suspect has a right to consult an attorney before and during interrogation. For the first of these, the most common misinterpretation was that failure to maintain appropriate demeanor (e.g., swearing at the police) might result in negative consequences. While this belief might be realistic, it ignores the critical meaning concerning self-incrimination. As for the warning regarding the right to legal counsel, many subjects believed that this applied only to future court hearings; others believed that the warning offered them the help of a social worker. A relatively small percentage of the sample provided inadequate interpretations of the warnings regarding the right to remain silent and the availability of free legal counsel (9 and 5 percent respectively).

On the CMV, only 36 percent of the subjects obtained no zero credits on any of the six vocabulary words. Zero credit was obtained most frequently on the words "interrogation" (59 percent) and "consult" (28 percent); both of these words appear in the *Miranda* warning which, on the CMR, produced the greatest percentage of inadequate responses ("You have the right to consult an attorney before interrogation—"). Only 6–9 percent of the sample provided inadequate responses on the other four vocabulary words in the CMV, including the word "right." But partial or questionable understanding of the word "right" was especially frequent (64 percent) compared to other words; that is, many subjects interpreted a right as something one is "allowed to do," but did not express a notion of entitlement or protection of the privilege.

CMR sum scores were more substantially correlated with CMV sum scores ($r = .67$) than was either CMR or CMV with IQ score (CMR and IQ, .47; CMV and IQ, .59); thus similar abilities or knowledge seem to contribute to performances on both *Miranda* measures, a fact which is not surprising, given their similarity in content. Furthermore, their relationships to IQ score suggest that some aspects of the content of the *Miranda* measures render performances which are not solely a consequence of general intellectual performance.

Age and Intelligence. Table 6.2 presents CMR means and standard deviations for various ages and IQ classifications, as well as the percent-

Table 6.2. CMR means for age and race by IQ classifications, and percentage with no zeros on any CMR items (in parentheses).

Variable	IQ Classification					Total
	70 or less	71–80	81–90	91–100	101+	
Age						
10/11	— *	2.00 (00)	3.50 (00)	4.66 (33)	— *	3.75 (12)
12	1.50 (00)	2.80 (20)	— *	5.33 (00)	5.75 (30)	4.66 (27)
13	3.40 (00)	5.00 (25)	5.58 (41)	6.57 (50)	6.15 (38)	5.64 (35)
14	2.92 (14)	5.39 (34)	6.00 (40)	6.41 (58)	7.10 (70)	5.84 (46)
15	4.38 (23)	5.56 (39)	6.10 (41)	6.51 (58)	6.69 (69)	6.04 (49)
16	4.30 (30)	5.69 (28)	6.17 (51)	6.29 (54)	7.45 (81)	6.11 (47)
Total	3.70 (19)	5.29 (31)	5.97 (42)	6.34 (53)	6.88 (65)	5.86 (45)
						s.d. = 1.85
Race						
White	4.86 (26)	5.65 (40)	6.10 (43)	6.36 (53)	6.92 (65)	6.26 (51)
Black	3.15 (15)	4.75 (18)	5.62 (38)	6.25 (50)	6.20 (60)	4.74 (28)

* Insufficient number of subjects.

age of subjects in each group obtaining no zero credits on any *Miranda* warnings. Both age and IQ were positively and significantly related to CMR scores (age: $F = 4.57$, $p < .001$; IQ: $F = 35.66$, $p < .001$) and to CMV scores (age: $F = 12.01$, $p < .001$; IQ: $F = 63.41$, $p < .001$). But the correlation between age and CMR scores ($r = .19$) was far less than the correlation between IQ and CMR scores ($r = .47$). (Similarly, $r = .32$ for age and CMV, and $r = .59$ for IQ and CMV.) In a multiple regression analysis, a greater proportion of the variance in CMR scores (25 percent) was associated with IQ than with any other single variable.

The relatively low correlation between CMR scores and age might be attributable to several factors, the first of which is the considerable amount of variance which IQ contributes to CMR scores at each age. This can be seen in Figure 6.1, where CMR scores are described graphically by age for each of four IQ classifications.

Figure 6.1 demonstrates a second reason for the low CMR-age correlation: Within each IQ classification (excluding IQ of 70 or below), CMR means are very similar from one age group to the next, after about age 14; that is, a "plateau" in CMR performance is reached by that age, so that the relationship between CMR and age exists only at ages 13 and below. This finding is consistent with the age curve usually found for the development of general intellectual abilities (Wechsler, 1955). But the result does not necessarily suggest that older age groups in the sample have attained an "adult level" of comprehension. Since certain abilities involving the use of verbal concepts and abstractions are known to continue to increase in age groups well into adulthood (Wechsler, 1955; Jones and Conrad, 1933), the plateau in this adolescent sample might represent some temporary developmental stage which is still deficient in terms of adult levels of comprehension.[5]

As a third explanation for the plateaus one might question whether they are due to certain properties of the measure itself. For example, as more subjects at higher age levels obtain perfect (eight point) scores, one might anticipate a ceiling for age-group CMR means. The plateaus in Figure 6.1 are, however, seen to occur for subjects in the low IQ classifications (71–80, 70 and below), even though only a very small percentage of these subjects obtained perfect CMR scores. Finally, the relatively low age-CMR correlation cannot be attributed to differences between ages in the distribution of IQ scores in this sample, since such differences were not statistically significant.

Offense History. Several courts have assumed that juveniles with more frequent police contacts are most sophisticated in their knowledge of *Miranda* rights. We found no relationship between CMR scores and several indexes of amount of prior experience with police (number of prior court referrals, felony referrals, misdemeanor referrals, "status offense"

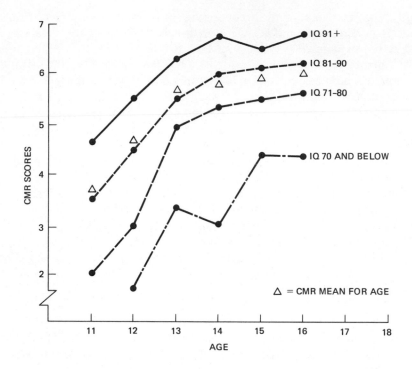

Figure 6.1. CMR mean scores by age within IQ classifications

referrals, detention admissions). One statistically significant (p < .03) interaction effect was found in a two-way analysis of variance of CMR scores by race and number of prior court referrals (arrests). Specifically, whites with more referrals tended to have higher CMR scores than did other whites, but blacks with more referrals tended to have *lower* CMR scores than did other blacks. The effect is consistent with our discovery of an unexplained negative relationship between number of prior referrals and IQ for blacks; this relationship was not found in the white sample. Whatever the reason, the results suggest that for those black subjects with high arrest rates, their increased amount of experience with police apparently did not compensate for difficulties in CMR performance which were assumed to be related to low intellectual ability.

Race. Black subjects obtained a significantly lower CMR mean than did white subjects (black: mean = 4.74, s.d. = 2.30; white: mean = 6.26, s.d. = 1.46; F = 64.84, p < .001); the correlation between CMR scores and race was .36. The interpretation of this relationship requires an examination of relationships between race and other variables employed in the study. Blacks obtained an IQ mean significantly below that of whites, race and IQ being correlated at .42; therefore, partial correlation analysis in which IQ was controlled reduced the correlation between race and CMR scores to .20, a level which may not seem remarkable but which (in our opinion) should not be dismissed. For example, in a three-way analysis of variance of CMR scores by age, race, and IQ, the amount of variance attributable to race was statistically significant (p < .001).

To discover the source of the CMR-race relationship, we first examined CMR means by race for various classes of IQ. Table 6.2 demonstrates that the CMR-race difference is derived primarily from CMR mean differences between blacks and whites in the two lowest IQ classifications. CMR means were then examined by race, IQ, and socioeconomic classification (although tests of significance were not possible, due to low frequencies in some cells). Generally, CMR means were nearly identical for blacks and whites of comparable IQ in the two higher socioeconomic categories in the study, but for subjects in the two lower socioeconomic classes, CMR means for blacks were from one to two CMR points below those of whites at matched IQ levels. In contrast, CMR means for lower socioeconomic, white subjects were very similar to those of whites in higher socio-economic groups at matched IQ levels.

Various studies (e.g., Entwisle, 1968) point to linguistic differences between black and white children, especially in lower socioeconomic classes, and to the effects of such differences on performance in verbal tasks (Williams and Rivers, 1976). Given this information, either or both of two factors could account for the CMR-race relationship. First, some black subjects may have had special difficulty in expressing what they knew or expressed their knowledge in ways which made scoring more difficult, given the verbal expressive requirements and scoring system of our measurement of *Miranda* comprehension; this explanation would view the difference potentially as an artifact of the method of measurement. Second, some black subjects may have had special difficulty understanding the words and phrases of the warnings, such words or sentence construction being more foreign to their own linguistic background; this explanation would suggest poorer comprehension of the standard *Miranda* warnings by such subjects, possibly for reasons apart from intellectual capacity.

To examine the weight of the first explanation, the Comprehension of Miranda Rights/True-False (TF) measure was developed. For each of the four standard *Miranda* warnings, three short and simply-worded interpretations of a warning were developed, each being either an accurate or inaccurate restatement of the *Miranda* warning to which it was related. Each of the 12 items was presented orally and in print simultaneously, along with the standard *Miranda* warning to which it was related. Subjects were asked merely to indicate whether the true-false item "said the same thing" as the *Miranda* warning in question. Since the procedure required merely a "yes or no" response, differences between subjects in verbal expressive ability or style and consequent scoring errors were virtually eliminated.

The TF measure was administered to the final 105 subjects in the main study sample, all of whom received the CMR as well. The demographic composition of this subsample was similar to that of the total study sample. Correlation coefficients between TF scores and age were similar to those between CMR scores and age (age and: CMR, $r = .24$; TF, $r = .21$); the correlation between CMR and TF was not low ($r = .55$). For the sample of 105 subjects, correlations between CMR and IQ (.50), CMR and race (.34), and CMR and race with IQ controlled statistically (.19) were nearly identical to those in the total sample of 431 subjects.

If the verbal expressive requirement of the CMR was selectively disadvantaging to some black subjects, then: 1) the CMR-race relationship should be greater than the TF-race relationship; and 2) the IQ-race correlation should be more similar to the CMR-race correlation than to the TF-race correlation (since both the CMR and the intelligence test required verbal expression). Differences between these correlations were in the directions anticipated (race and: TF, .27; CMR, .34; IQ, .38), but the expected differences between the TF-race correlation and the other two were relatively small. The difference between the TF-race and CMR-race correlations did not change substantially when controlled for IQ scores (with IQ controlled, race and: TF, .14; CMR, .19). Thus, while the results suggested a small but significant black-white difference in CMR response even when differences in intelligence test performance were controlled, the difference did not appear to be related substantially to the verbal expressive requirements of the CMR. Therefore, the second explanation offered earlier is more tenable; that is, the relatively formal, "legalistic" words or phrasing in the standard *Miranda* warnings may be more foreign to lower-class, black juveniles than to whites in general or to middle-class blacks, because of differences between these groups in their cultural or linguistic backgrounds. If true, this would suggest diminished competence of this group (but not necessarily diminished intellectual capacity) in understanding the warnings.

A third explanation, however, would suggest that the lower CMR scores for the black subjects in question were a result of interpersonal and motivational, rather than verbal-cognitive, factors. All examiners were white, and past research regarding the testing of black juveniles by white examiners suggests the possibility of impairment of test performance under such conditions (La Crosse, 1965; Kennedy and Vega, 1965). This explanation would be consistent with most of the aforementioned findings, but a CMR-race relationship remained when CMR scores were controlled statistically for IQ scores. Any motivational factors would be expected to influence performance on the intelligence test, as well as on the CMR and therefore to nullify the CMR-race relationship when IQ was controlled.

Other variables. No significant difference in CMR scores was found between males and females. While socioeconomic status was related to CMR scores ($r = -.27$), the correlation was reduced to insignificance (partial $r = .04$) when controlled for IQ and race. Finally, since most of the subjects were tested within 24–72 hours after admission to detention, one might question the degree to which the emotional impact of confinement influenced CMR scores. To examine this possibility, the CMR scores of 73 juveniles who were residing in relatively open settings (a boys town and a boys school) were compared to a subsample of juveniles tested in detention. Detention subjects were selected from the detention sample, so that each nondetention subject was matched with a detention subject on the variables of age, race, IQ, socioeconomic status, and number of prior court referrals. The CMR scores of boys school subjects were not significantly different from those of matched detention subjects, but the scores of the boys town subjects were significantly lower (p < .04) than those of matched detention subjects. These results suggest that the testing conditions in detention did not produce lower scores than would be expected under less restricting conditions. These results do not necessarily ensure the CMR means in the present study are representative of those which would be obtained (or represent a level of comprehension to be found) in circumstances of actual arrest and interrogation procedures with similar juveniles; that is, the present results probably reflect comprehension under relatively facilitative conditions, and comprehension may be impaired (relative to the present results) in more stressful situations.

IMPLICATIONS

A major value of the results lies in their potential as empirical guidelines to assist courts and policy-makers when weighing various circumstances bearing upon the capacity of juveniles to waive rights. Most court cases in which the validity of waiver by juveniles has been considered have involved juveniles below age 14. This is consistent with the assumption in common law rule that children below age 14 are not presumed to be responsible for criminal acts (Schultz and Cohen, 1976) and is consistent with past research which documents a deceleration of age-related increments in the development of general mental abilities beyond ages 14 or 15 (Wechsler, 1955). Consistent with these assumptions, the present data offer compelling reason to believe that juveniles below age 13 are not likely to comprehend the *Miranda* warnings sufficiently to make an informed waiver of their rights. But *if* the traditional presumption of competence at age 14 and above is accepted, the present data offer no compelling reason to exclude 13 year olds from this presumption (at least in terms of capacity to understand the warnings), since their performance in this study was not remarkably different from that of juveniles ages 14–16.

A more critical implication, however, is that age alone is quite limited in its effectiveness as a guide for weighing the ability of juveniles to understand the *Miranda* warnings, especially at ages 13–16. Subjects within any given age group demonstrated a wide range of intellectual functioning and CMR performance. Past developmental research (Piaget, 1965; Kohlberg, 1969; Tapp and Levine, 1974; Loevinger, 1976) has documented the considerable variance in cognitive and other developmental characteristics of children at any given age in this age range. The present results extend these findings in the applied context of comprehending *Miranda* warnings. Special caution is suggested in cases where juveniles of ages 13–16 obtain IQ scores below 80; for example, for juveniles of ages 15 and 16, with IQ scores of 70 or below, mean CMR scores were below the CMR mean for all 12 year olds and were nearly one standard deviation below the CMR mean for the total sample. Only about one in five subjects in this older, but less intelligent, subsample obtained no zero credits on the *Miranda* items, compared to four in five of the 16 year olds with IQ scores in the average range.

Some courts have assumed that juveniles with more prior experience with police will have a better understanding of *Miranda* warnings. This assumption is based on the simplistic view that more exposure to a set of information leads to learning. But one can argue that the emotionally arousing conditions under which juveniles are exposed to the *Miranda* warnings during arrest might inhibit or impair incidental learning of the rights warnings. The negative effects of anxiety upon the learning of verbal material have been researched and documented extensively (Sarason, 1960; Spence and Spence, 1966). In this light, it is not surprising that the present study discovered no direct relationship between the amount of prior experience with police and *Miranda* comprehension. The study employed multiple indexes of the amount of prior experience and included a juvenile sample with a very wide range of prior arrests in terms of number and type and was conducted in a metropolitan area where interrogation of juveniles (usually including a reading of *Miranda* warnings) occurred in 75 percent of arrests for felony charges. Thus the study is viewed as providing an adequate test of the "experience hypothesis." It may be true that certain juveniles become quite sophisticated in their knowledge of rights through experience, but the proportion of juveniles that does not "benefit" in this way through experience, and the proportion that apparently understands the *Miranda* warnings without extensive police contact, produced results suggesting that little weight should be placed on prior experience with police as a guideline.

We have found no court cases in which race or subcultural background has been noted as a variable which was weighed in decisions about juveniles' comprehension of *Miranda* warnings. Clear warnings have been issued by psychological studies (Williams and Rivers, 1976) that when many black children are provided information input in standard English, they are being asked to perform a transformation of the information which is not necessary for most white children. That is, these black children may have learned and retained various facts in the context of their own linguistic background (other than standard English), so that standard English cues do not facilitate the retrieval or recall of the information sought. In the context of the present study, some black juveniles might be capable of understanding their rights if informed of them in a linguistic style more similar to their own but will not adequately process the incoming language stimuli when they are not familiar. The data in the present study, regarding poorer CMR performance for lower socioeconomic blacks than whites, are consistent with this view. The guideline suggested by the results is that race should be weighed as a factor suggesting poorer comprehension for blacks, when IQ scores are below 80 and/or when lower socioeconomic status applies.

In contrast to the usefulness of the results for the formulation of general guidelines, the data in Table 6.2 cannot be employed to predict or postdict comprehension of *Miranda* warnings in individual cases. An examination of percentage figures in most of the age-IQ classes indicates that the probability of error would be considerable when concluding that any given subject within a class did or did not obtain zero credit on some item in the CMR.[6] Moreover, the data indicate that except for older juveniles in the average IQ range, understanding of the *Miranda* warnings for juveniles as a group is at best a 50-50 proposition. These results are not an effective argument for blanket exclusion of juvenile waiver or confession, because of the compelling need for the state to employ confessions in some cases in the interest of protecting society. What the results might underscore, however, is our responsibility for advocating the protection of juveniles in custody, including effective availability of legal counsel at the pretrial stage.[7]

As noted earlier, the focus of the present study (understanding of

Miranda warnings) is but one component in a broader concept of competence to waive rights, which itself includes only some of the circumstances to be weighed in deciding upon the validity of waiver by a juvenile. Understanding the *Miranda* warnings is best viewed as a minimum requirement in the absence of which a meaningful waiver is doubtful, but general conclusions regarding juveniles' competence to waive rights must await the results of studies regarding other aspects of competence. For example, one study now underway assesses juveniles' abilities to understand the function of rights in interrogation. Another examines the reasoning which juveniles employ when making decisions regarding the waiver or assertion of *Miranda* rights, especially as this reasoning relates to children's level of ego development. The results of those studies could support or modify the recommendations offered in this chapter.

REFERENCES

Cotton v. United States, 446 F.2d 107 (1971).

Davis, S. *Rights of Juveniles.* New York: Clark Boardman, 1975 (Supplements, 1976, 1977).

Entwisle, D. Subcultural differences in children's language development. *International Journal of Psychology* 3:13–22 (1968).

Ferguson, A., and Douglas, A. A study of juvenile waiver. *San Diego Law Review* 7:39 (1970).

Grisso, J. T., and Pomicter, C. Interrogation of juveniles: an empirical study of procedures, safeguards, and rights waiver. *Law and Human Behavior,* 1977, 1, 321–342.

In re Gault, 387 U.S. 1 (1967).

In the Interest of Holifield, 319 So.2d 471 (1975).

In the Interest of Stiff, 336 N.E.2d 619 (1975).

In the Interest of Thompson, 241 N.W.2d 2 (1976).

Institute of Judicial Administration/American Bar Association. *Juvenile Justice Standards Project: Standards Relating to Dispositions.* Tentative draft, 1977 (a).

Institute of Judicial Administration/American Bar Association. *Juvenile Justice Standards Project: Standards Relating to Juvenile Delinquency and Sanctions.* Tentative draft, 1977 (b).

Keith-Speigel, P. Children's rights as participants in research. In G. Koocher (Ed.), *Children's Rights and the Mental Health Professions,* pp. 53–81. New York: Wiley, 1976.

Kennedy, W., and Vega, M. Negro children's performance on a discrimination task as a function of examiner race and verbal incentive. *Journal of Personality and Social Psychology* 2:839–843 (1965).

Kohlberg, L. Stage and sequence: the cognitive-developmental approach to socialization. In D. Goslin (Ed.), *Handbook of Socialization Theory and Research,* pp. 347–480. Chicago: Rand McNally, 1969.

LaCrosse, L. Race of examiner: effects on the Stanford-Binet with adolescents. *Journal of Social Psychology* **64** (1965).

Loevinger, J. *Ego development: Conceptions and Theories.* San Francisco: Jossey-Bass, 1976.

Miranda v. Arizona, 384 U.S. 436 (1966).

National Juvenile Law Center. *Law and Tactics in Juvenile Cases.* St. Louis: NJLC, 1977 (third edition).

People v. Lara, 432 P.2d 202 (1967)

Piaget, J. *The Moral Judgment of the Child.* New York: Free Press, 1965.

Sarason, I. Empirical findings and theoretical problems in the use of anxiety scales. *Psychological Bulletin* **57**:403–415 (1960).

Schultz, J., and Cohen, F. Isolationism in juvenile court jurisprudence. In M. Rosenheim (Ed.), *Pursuing Justice for the Child.* Chicago: University of Chicago Press, 1976.

Spence, J., and Spence, K. The motivational components of manifest anxiety: drive and drive stimuli. In C. Speilberger (Ed.), *Anxiety and Behavior,* pp. 291–326. New York: Academic Press, 1966.

State v. Melanson, 259 So.2d 609 (1972).

Tapp, J., and Levine, F. Legal socialization: strategies for an ethical legality. *Stanford Law Review* **27**:1–72 (1974).

Theriault v. State, 223 N.W.2d 850 (1974).

United States v. Ramsey, 367 F.Supp. 1307 (1973).

Wechsler, D. *The Measurement and Appraisal of Adult Intelligence.* Baltimore: Williams and Wilkins, 1955.

West v. United States, 399 F.2d 467 (1968).

Williams, R., and Rivers, W. The effects of language on the test performances of black children. In G. Koocher (Ed.) *Children's Rights and the Mental Health Professions,* pp. 205–218. New York: Wiley, 1976.

FOOTNOTES TO CHAPTER 6

[1]Many states have specified by statute that juveniles must have the benefit of advice from a parent/guardian at the time of rights waiver, and some courts have included the absence of parents as a relevant circumstance to be weighed. But where parents' presence has not been required by statute, most courts have held strictly to the "totality of circumstances" test in ruling that the absence of a parent/guardian at interrogation does not necessarily invalidate juvenile waiver or confession (e.g., *State v. Melanson,* 1972; *Theriault v. State,* 1974). In any event, it is questionable whether the presence of parents/guardian necessarily ensures the protections which that procedural safeguard is intended to provide, given the emotional state of many parents at the time of their child's arrest (National Juvenile Law Center, 1977) or the attitudes of some parents regarding their child's welfare (Keith-Speigel, 1976). In one recent study (Grisso and Pomicter, 1977), an increase in frequency of cases in which parents were present at juveniles' interrogations produced no change in the frequency with which juveniles waived rights.

[2]Only one empirical study was found to be directly relevant. Ferguson and Douglas (1970) investigated the abilities of 46 juveniles (in public schools and training schools) to describe

"what you understand your rights to be," after each subject was taken individually and without explanation to a room where the investigators formally read the *Miranda* rights warnings. Scoring criteria were not specified in the report, no tests of statistical significance were employed, and methodological difficulties severely limit the conclusions. Nevertheless, a general increase in adequacy of responses was suggested with increased age (in the limited range of ages 14–16 in this study).

[3]For developing the conceptualization, the authors (psychologists) met with lawyers in a series of "brainstorming" sessions, with individual work assignments carried out by each member prior to and following each session and dictated by the needs arising in the sessions. Lawyers involved in the conceptualization sessions were staff members of the National Juvenile Law Center of St. Louis. Attorneys from local juvenile courts also reviewed the initial conceptualizations and contributed suggestions leading to further modifications. The same lawyers participated in the development of scoring criteria in a phase of the process to be discussed later. Then the conceptualizations and scoring criteria were submitted for review and recommendations to five attorneys in five separate geographic areas of the country. Among them were attorneys in legal aid agencies providing defense services to juveniles and attorneys involved in the drafting of legislation of juvenile codes. Finally, their suggestions were incorporated into the conceptualizations and scoring criteria and reviewed again by the local panel.

[4]Grisso, J. T., and Manoogian, S. *Comprehension of Miranda Rights: Manual for Administration and Scoring*. Unpublished, St. Louis University, 1977.

[5]A study now underway investigates Miranda comprehension in an adult sample and will provide data with which to address this question.

[6]In a multiple regression analysis, the combined power of the five subject variables in this study which had the greatest relationships to CMR scores accounted for 33 percent of the total variance in CMR scores.

[7]One state (West Virginia) has established that juveniles must be represented by legal counsel at adjudicatory hearings, but no state yet requires legal counsel for juveniles during interrogations.

7

Reducing Juror Bias: An Experimental Approach

Martin F. Kaplan and Cynthia Schersching

INTRODUCTION

The past decade has seen the widening application of experimental strategies commonly found in attitude change and person perception paradigms to the study of courtroom judgments. In a parallel vein, though lagging behind empirical findings, theoretical models of person perception are being applied to the real-world problem of jury decision making. These include reinforcement (Mitchell and Byrne, 1973), attribution (Thibaut and Walker, 1975), equity (Walster and Walster, 1975) and information integration (Kaplan, 1977a; Kaplan and Kemmerick, 1974) models of social cognition. However, application of theoretical models of judgment to a particular real-world realm is an empty exercise, unless the application can suggest answers to problems indigenous to that realm (or, in the absence of conclusive answers, the model should pose meaningful questions). This chapter will outline information integration theory (Anderson, 1974; Kaplan, 1975), describe its conceptual and methodological relevance to judge and juror judgment, and illustrate its utility by reporting several studies.

The studies reported here were supported by Grant #MH23516 from the Center for Study of Crime and Delinquency, National Institute of Mental Health, awarded to the first author. We are indebted to Gwen Kemmerick and Sharon Krupa who assisted in the experiments, and to Luann Zanzola for permission to cite her unpublished Master's Thesis. We are also grateful to Professor Karl Sorg and the administration of the Lewis University College of Law for their assistance and use of their facilities for the trial enactment.

INFORMATION INTEGRATION THEORY

Conceptually, information integration theory (IIT) begins with the straightforward assertion that judgment is based on an integration of relevant information about the judged object. While any belief about an object may convey information along several dimensions (for example, a person's appearance may give information about his/her trustworthiness, likableness, attractiveness, or whatever), judgment is based on the information value for the particular judgment dimension. This value may be represented quantitatively as a *scale value* which gives its position on the dimension of judgment. For example, a defendant's sexy appearance may possess high scale value for judgment of likableness, but low scale value for judging innocence of a charge of prostitution (see Sigall and Ostrove, 1975, for a convincing demonstration of this point). Perhaps the prime assumption behind IIT is that any action or attribute of an object may carry information for judgment in the form of scale value on the judgment dimension. Information also has weight, or importance for the judgment. For example, greater weight is given to information which is more reliable, consistent, and highly correlated with the criterion. The last reflects the extent to which information is "diagnostic," or informative, with regard to the judgment to be made.

In understanding any judgment, an essential task is to identify and decompose the informational determinants of the response. Since for some judgments this may be a near impossible task (e.g., consider the enormous array of information in a typical trial), the identification of components might best proceed on a molar level, so that instead of dealing with each piece of evidence or testimony as the unit of analysis, we may aggregate the individual items into the three major categories of admissible evidence (Wigmore, 1929): ability, motive, and opportunity; thus, the sizable array of evidence in a criminal trial may be represented by molar scale values reflecting the defendant's *ability* to commit the act, his *motive* or *mens rea,* and his *opportunity.* For each component, individual items of evidence would contribute to the respective scale value for guilt appearance.

IIT searches for a "cognitive algebra" to describe the integration of informational components. It is asked: what algebraic rules capture the policy of judges in combining the weighted scale values of components? This is the second process in judgment: the integration process. Consequently, the next step in an integration inquiry is to co-vary several levels of the salient components in order to discover the weighting strategies and algebraic rules governing judgment formation. It is often instructive to also vary situational constraints which act upon weight parameters, such as witness prestige, testimony credibility, consistency, and redundancy. While IIT need not be tied to a particular algebra, weighted average models have proven most general in social judgments (Anderson, 1974; Kaplan, 1975). The beauty of a policy-capturing rule, whereby values are *effectively* weighted by their *relative* importance (as in such a model) is that both linear and nonlinear data can be easily handled (Kaplan, 1975). In turn, the particular integration rule, whether averaging or multiplying (as in culpability = motive x opportunity), has practical implications as a means of enhancing or inhibiting effects of given factors, as we shall soon see.

JUROR BIAS AND JUDGMENT

Let us start with the very broad premise that judgments of any sort are based on three classes of determinants:

1. *Information about the judged object.* In a trial this could consist of evidential testimony, which possesses scale value for guiltiness, as well as weight. Factors such as witness credibility, logical consistency, and so on, would affect the latter.
2. *Situational demands.* Here would be included deliberation effects, legal restrictions, time demands, needs of society, and peer (other juror) pressures.
3. *Personality of the decision maker.* The juror's pretrial biases, whether specific to the defendant or general toward all accused persons, and whether relatively permanent (*trait* characteristics) or transient (*state* characteristics) enter here.

This chapter considers the effects of biases from an information integration standpoint. Tradition dictates that juror bias is an evil which should be avoided, or at least voided in its effects. The *Voir Dire* is an attempt to eliminate jurors with biases specific to the issue or defendant. But it is only partially successful: First, we don't always know the questions to ask because specific biases that may be detrimental (or favorable) to a particular defendant are unknown; second, we can't always be sure that the prospective juror is answering the questions factually or honestly as jurors may not always be aware of their biases or may deliberately hide them; third, there are limitations to the number and causes of dismissals of jurors; finally, there is a more general bias of leniency/stringency which may go undetected, while we are looking for more specific responses to the case or issue.

It is clear that biases in jurors cannot be completely avoided. To do so would require seeking value-less or perhaps lobotomized persons. Knowing that biases are unavoidable when dealing with human judges and jurors, some studies have sought to identify the biasing characteristics of jurors (e.g., Lipsitt and Strodtbeck, 1967) or judges (e.g., Nagel, 1969) and others have even tried to systematically select jurors for their pro-defendant biases (e.g., Schulman, J.; Shaver, P.; Colman, R.; Emrich, B.; and Christie, R., 1973), but the selection of jurors for their favorable biases is not altogether desirable. It flies in the face of the doctrine of trial by a representative group of one's peers and gives the advantage to defendants with celebrated causes or the finances to enlist social scientists to study the backgrounds of prospective jurors. Moreover, since the strength of the evidence for or against the defendant has not been system-atically controlled in cases where jurors have been "scientifically" selected, we don't even know whether selection procedures were worth the effort (see Berk, Hennessy, and Swan, 1977, for a detailed critique). It would seem to better serve the cause of justice and to be more realistic, as well, to study instead how biases affect judgments and how their impact may be minimized.

Observation in natural settings and experimentation in controlled sur-roundings both produce evidence that bias does enter into both real and hypothetical judgments. Surveys of functioning courtrooms show wide differences between judges in acquittal rates (Simon and Oster, 1973), rates of granting probation (Simon and Oster, 1973), and severity of sen-tencing (Gaudet, 1938; Kalven and Zeisel, 1966) in criminal trials. Simi-larly, individual differences in judges' backgrounds, political and social attitudes, and other demographic characteristics have been related to decisions in civil cases (Nagel, 1969; Pritchett, 1948). Politically and so-cially conservative judges tend to be prosecution prone in criminal cases and favor businesses in regulation cases. Studies of experimental juries show that jurors who favor capital punishment, assign more punitive sen-tences, and those who are more prone to convict are also more authoritar-ian, dogmatic, and conservative (Boehm, 1968; Crosson, 1968; Hatton, Snortum, and Oskamp, 1971; Jurow, 1971; Mitchell and Byrne, 1973; Nemeth and Sosis, 1973; Thayer, 1970). Biases *do* affect judgment; the interesting question is how to reduce their effect in any particular case.

Several types of biases may be identified. For example, biases may be specific to the defendant (e.g., racial prejudice), or issue (e.g., right-to-work laws), or may be general (e.g., leniency/harshness or conviction-proneness). In addition, biases may be enduring and stable *trait* disposi-tions in the juror (e.g., harshness) or relatively transient, situational *states* in the individual (e.g., a rotten mood caused by indigestion or a cold). In integration theory, biases of any of these sorts affect the *initial impres-sion,* or the response to the judged object in the absence of information. Like information, initial impression has a scale value and weight for the judgment and is integrated into the total response, along with information value and weight. A leniency bias, for example, would have a low scale value for guilt, and an objective or unbiased juror would be one who applies little weight to his/her initial impression.

To return to our question, the effect of juror bias would be reduced if the effective weight of the initial impression is reduced. This could be accomplished by two general strategies: First, one might reduce weight directly by instructing jurors to ignore their predispositions and attend only to the evidence. Such instructions are traditional, yet we see biases continuing to operate; indeed, such attempts to remove biases instilled by ascribing undesirable characteristics to hypothetical defendants are either totally ineffective (Kaplan and Kemmerick, 1974) or are successful only for jurors low in authoritarianism (Mitchell and Byrne, 1972). The second means suggested by integration theory is *indirect:* If information and initial impression values are integrated by a weighted averaging rule, an increase in the weight of any component (e.g., information *or* initial impression) will decrease the *effective* weight of the other. So, if the values derived from testimonial evidence are made more salient for judgment, the effect of bias should be reduced. Four experiments are instructive. In the first two, subjects were identified as either harsh or lenient in their conviction and punishment tendencies by means of an established attitude scale. These stable tendencies may be labeled *trait* dispositions. In the remaining two, situational conditions were manipulated to produce transient *state* dispositions in subjects similar to those often found in courtroom proceedings.

PERSONAL (TRAIT) BIASES

The Experiments

In both experiments, subjects were drawn from a population of introductory psychology students at Northern Illinois University who had volunteered for the experiments to earn extra course credit. Only students who were registered voters (and therefore likely to be called for jury duty) were asked to serve. On the basis of scores on the *Attitude Toward Punishment of Criminals Scale* (Wang and Thurstone, as cited in Shaw and Wright, 1967), subjects with either harsh or lenient biases were selected. Scores on this scale reflect one's punitive tendency toward transgressors of the law and correlated highly with the Authoritarianism scale in this sample.

The first experiment varied the guilt appearance of the defendant, instructions regarding the importance of the evidence, and, of course, the subject's predispositional biases. Subjects read one-page summaries of each of eight different traffic felony cases, with the charges covering a range of seriousness. Half the cases were contrived to present a mild appearance of defendant guilt and half a mild appearance of innocence; that is, on a 21 point scale (0–20) of guilt appearance, the former cases had obtained a mean rating of 15.2 and the latter cases a mean rating of 4.7 in a normative sample. Guilt and innocent appearing versions of each of the eight cases had been constructed, and, by means of a Latin Square stimulus design, the particular case and level of guilt appearance was rotated. Consequently, each version of each case appeared equally across the entire design, while any one subject saw only one version of all eight cases.

Prior to judging the trials, subjects rated four practice cases which served as anchors for the dependant rating measures. All four were photocopied directly from summaries in the *California Law Reports:* Two were cases of obvious guilt, and two were of clear innocence. Following the instructions subjects rated the defendant's guilt (0 = definitely innocent, 20 = definitely guilty) and were then asked to assume that he or she had been found guilty and to recommend severity of punishment within the statutes (one = minimum, seven = maximum) for each experimental case.

The weight of evidence was varied by remarks about evidential reliability inserted into the instructions for judging the experimental cases. Reliable condition subjects were told that the case summaries, like the practice cases, had been prepared by a respected judge known for his ability to prepare accurate summaries and that both defense and prosecution had attested to the accuracy of the representation. In contrast, Unreliable condition subjects were told that the summaries, unlike the practice cases, were the work of an inept clerk, who was no longer employed, and that both lawyers had raised questions regarding the accuracy of some segments. The "inaccurate" segments were not identified, and subjects were asked to "do their best" with the evidence at hand. Control subjects were not informed of the source. In summary, subjects judged defendant culpability in cases contrived to be either high or low in guilt appearance and were given either reason to doubt or to trust the evidence; control subjects were given no instruction either way. Twenty-four harsh and 24 lenient subjects served in each reliability condition; subjects were equally divided among the sexes.

The results are rather straightforward and are displayed in Figure 7.1. We include here only the data for guilt ratings, since punishment ratings closely paralleled these findings. Harsh subjects were more stringent in their judgments, and they maintained this stringency across both levels of

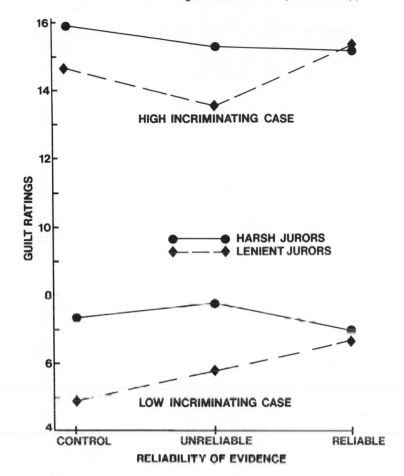

Figure 7.1. Guilt ratings as a function of juror bias, evidential incrimination value, and evidential reliability.

evidential incrimination value. Statistically, this effect for bias is shown by the significant main effect ($F(1, 138) = 10.95, p < .001$) and the lack of an interaction between bias and trial guilt appearance ($F(1, 138) = 1.18$). While biasing effects were consistent across trials, instructions stressing the reliability of evidence did reduce bias; this is shown in the convergence of the curves for harsh and lenient subjects. Regardless of whether the evidence gave a predominant appearance of guilt or innocence, both subjects with harsh or lenient prejudgmental biases gave essentially the same response when the evidence was characterized as trustworthy and uncontested. This lack of biasing sharply contrasts with the bias apparent when nothing is said about the evidence, or when evidence is contested and potentially inaccurate. The interaction between instructions and bias is statistically significant ($F(2, 138) = 3.73, p < .05$).

Experiment 2 posed a situation closer to one which would be encountered in many trials. Whereas evidence in the first experiment gave a predominant appearance of guilt or innocence, subjects in the second experiment judged summaries of four cases contrived to be of mixed evidential value; that is, half the facts pointed toward guilt of a traffic felony and half toward innocence. Four such cases were judged. Though facts were opposed in guilt/innocence valence, care was taken so that they were not directly contradictory. As before, subjects first judged the anchoring practice cases, and then rated guilt and recommended punishment for the experimental cases. Twenty-four harsh and 24 lenient subjects participated; they were equally divided among the sexes. Half the subjects were told that the facts of the cases might not be entirely consistent, some facts might not be entirely correct, and one or the other attorney had raised questions regarding the accuracy of some facts in the course of each trial. The remaining subjects were told, that while there might be inconsistencies, both attorneys had agreed that the facts in the summary gave a true account of events and that they (the subjects) were to consider all facts as true and accurate.

The data are quite compatible with those of Experiment 1. Figure 7.2 shows a large effect for prejudgmental bias when evidence is characterized as argumentable, and a convergence of response when evidence is not contested. This reduction of biasing effect is reflected in the significant bias by instructions interaction ($F(1, 44) = 4.37, p < .05$).

One additional set of data is interesting. Subjects listed the individual items of evidence which they felt had most influenced their judgment. These items were coded by two independent scorers as either incriminating or exonerating in value (interscorer coefficient of agreement = .95). Table 7.1 gives the mean proportion of exonerating evidence for each group of 12 subjects. In a striking parallel to the guiltiness ratings, harsh and lenient subjects retrospectively cited about the same proportion of exonerating facts when told the summary was reliable, but lenient subjects cited less incriminating and more exonerating facts when the evidence was contested. A Chi-square analysis of number of exonerating facts produced overall significance ($X^2(3) = 5.1, p < .05$), as did the comparison between harsh and lenient subjects under contested evidence conditions ($X^2(1) = 3.93, p < .05$). The comparison of harsh and lenient subjects under reliable evidence conditions showed no difference. Thus,

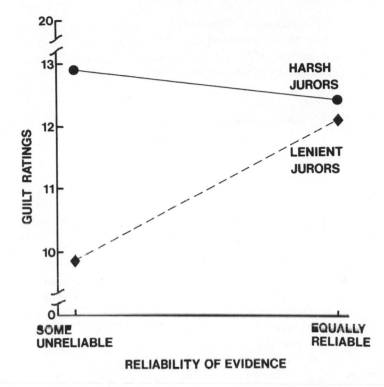

Figure 7.2. Guilt ratings as a function of juror bias and evidential reliability in cases of mixed evidential value.

lenient subjects told that some evidence is unreliable will discount evidence contrary to their evaluative bias. It would be premature, though, to suggest a causal sequence between retrospective reports of information utilized and subsequent judgments. We cannot tell at this point whether subjects first discounted evidence inconsistent with their biases and then reached a judgment based on the discounted weights, or first judged the defendant based on a heavily weighted initial impression and then retrospectively justified the judgment by citing supportive evidence.

The findings of both experiments bear on the integration rule describing the combination of bias and evidence. They suggest that the two are inversely weighted: Increasing the weight of one component (evidence) reduces the weight of the other (bias). While indirect, this appears to be an effective means of reducing the importance of "unwanted" components in the judgment process.

Table 7.1. Proportion of exonerating facts cited as influential in
the judgment of cases of mixed
incrimination value.

Evidence Characterization	Subject Bias	
	Harsh	Lenient
Reliable	.27 (16/59)	.30 (20/67)
Unreliable	.22 (15/69)	.42 (28/66)

Note: 12 subjects per cell

Implications

We have taken the position that decision makers, being human, will have some sort of bias in their approach to any judgment. The question is: What conditions are likely to enhance or to reduce the *effects* of bias on the judgment? The preceding experiments suggest that courtroom procedures which increase the contentiousness of available evidence will enhance effects of predispositional biases, while reductions in evidential unreliability will correspondingly reduce biasing effects. Unfortunately, traditional trial procedures, devised to serve the interests of justice, may simultaneously enhance bias. We see at least two dilemmas posed by our results.

Our Anglo-American justice system is predicated upon the adversary principle. Parties in conflict are represented by attorneys presenting evidenciary materials each in their own interest before decision makers. The decision maker depends on opposing counsels to develop the case. This system presupposes that truth will emerge as each advocate selectively presents information to the court (Freedman, 1970). To strengthen their respective positions, lawyers often attempt to discredit the other's argument by presenting conflicting evidence, cross-examination, and destroying the credibility of witnesses or testimony. These strategies often yield contradictory, or at least inconsistent, information and, in the process, cast doubt on both the witness and testimony. The decision maker, most often unskilled and quite naive in matters of legal importance, is faced with a problem: The facts on which to draw conclusions and base decisions are questionable. As one cannot clearly extract the truth from conflicting claims, and doubt is cast on evidence presented by both sides, the general weight of this information is reduced. It appears to be the nature of the judgment process that as the weight of information components is reduced, the weight of predispositional bias is increased.

The inquisitorial system, common in continental Europe, offers an alternative judicial approach (Ploscowe, 1935). Here the presentation of evidence to the court depends upon a skilled fact finder acting independently of partisan interests. The inquisitor searches out factual evidence pertinent to the case in a presumably impartial manner. A major difference, then, between adversary and inquisitorial systems is that attacks on information credibility are lacking in the latter. Since the evidence itself is no longer the focus of dispute, the effects of bias should be reduced. Thibaut, Walker, and their colleagues have conducted an extensive series of experiments comparing the two systems. As we would suspect, the inquisitorial approach results in evidence which is less contentious and more homogeneous than evidence derived from adversary methods (Lind, Thibaut, and Walker, 1973); if our goal is to increase the weight of testimony, the inquisitorial approach appears advantageous. Adversary presentation, though, is "preferred"; impartial observers sense that it appears more fair (Thibaut; Walker; La Tour; and Houlden, 1974). Too, Thibaut, Walker, and Lind (1972) claim it lessens the likelihood of order effects, since jurors will be alerted to keep an open mind when expecting opposing views. However, perceived fairness is really irrelevant to the question, and order effects can be effectively averted by careful instructions from the bench to withhold judgment until all the evidence has been presented. The unanswered questions are whether either system can elicit the relevant evidence in a trial, and whether a given manner of presenting evidence lessens bias effects. On this score, there are no direct data, although inquisitorial presentation does result in more extreme beliefs in guilt (Thibaut, et al., 1972). If bias is generally more neutral in value than the evidence presented to a jury, greater response extremity would signal less reliance on predispositional bias under inquisitorial rule.

The dilemma, then, is whether to give full rein to a system of civil and criminal trial which gives an appearance of fairness and protection of the accused while enhancing the manifestation of bias in the decision maker. Perhaps this dilemma can be eased by greater use of pretrial conference techniques (see Walker and Thibaut, 1971, for some examples and suggestions) to sift through potential evidence and testimony and reduce argumentation during the trial proper.

The second dilemma is posed by the pattern of bias-reduction shown in both experiments. Traditionally the Anglo-American justice system has deliberately favored the accused (Ploscowe, 1935). Indeed, conviction is not possible until jurors determine, beyond a reasonable doubt, the defendant's culpability. The dilemma surrounds the finding that jurors biased in favor of leniency reduced their bias more than did subjects predisposed to more severe punishments. This is contrary to the principle best expressed by Blackstone's (1769/1962, p. 420) admonition that "it is better that ten guilty persons escape than one innocent suffer." If bias is to influence decision making, lenient biases are preferred. It remains, then, to reduce bias without seriously damaging the rights of the defendant to a client-centered defense and to do so for both harsh and lenient jurors. This is a problem with which legal scholars and empiricists will have to deal.

SITUATIONALLY INDUCED (STATE) BIASES

The preceding studies dealt with residual or personalistic biases in jurors, (created by past experience, toilet-training or whatever). Biases may also be instilled by conditions in the courtroom or immediately prior to trial, though they will not generally produce lasting effects. Uncomfortable conditions, obnoxious behavior by defendants or attorneys, lapse of health in the juror, or even an argument with the milkman are but a few examples of the conditions which can affect the mood, and potentially, the judgment of a juror. More systematically, pretrial publicity relating to the case at trial can predispose one towards a biased judgment. The conceptual treatment of such temporary but potent influences is the same as with trait biases. These situationally induced biases affect the scale value and weight of the juror's initial impression. It follows that measures which increase the import of evidence in forming the judgment should consequently decrease the effective weight of temporarily biasing conditions. We assume, once again, a weighted average model of the judgment formation process, whereby the contributions of initial impression and of evidence sum to unity, so that an increase in the importance of one *de facto* decreases the importance of the other. In the previously described experiments we manipulated the importance of trial evidence via its contentiousness and unreliability. In the following experiments, we followed instead the tack that evidence would contribute more to judgment after it is discussed and thought about in the course of deliberation among jurors.

The Experiments

In a mock-jury setting, we investigated the effects of courtroom behavior of the attorneys and judges. Eight trials were conducted in a setting closely resembling a typical courtroom. Each jury consisted of 12 jurors who were paid volunteers from the community surrounding Glen Ellyn, Illinois, and were eligible for jury duty. Jurors had responded to newspaper advertisements and notices in public areas (e.g., supermarkets) asking for people to participate in a study of the jury process. Each juror was paid $5. Roughly two-thirds of participating jurors were female, and jurors represented a diversity of occupations and ages (mean age = 35).

Two basic trials were contrived: Both concerned a case of attempted manslaughter in which the defendant was accused of stabbing the victim with broken glass during a tavern argument. Evidential facts for both trials were taken from a contrived trial reported by Walker, Thibaut, and Andreoli (1972). These facts were then constituted into two trial transcripts: One was designed to give the defendant a moderate appearance of guilt, the other was designed to give the defendant a moderate appearance of innocence. Mean normative ratings of guilt appearance on a 21 point guilt scale were 15.85 and 7.15, respectively (Kaplan, 1977b). Four versions of each trial were enacted, one for each of the eight juries. In all versions, the trial facts elicited from witnesses (who were portrayed by graduate students) were the same—the difference lay in the conduct of the officers of the court.

One version of each trial was run on a "straight" basis—these were 15 minute control trials. The other three enacted versions were designed to prolong proceedings to 50 minutes, annoy the jurors, and, in general, create bad feelings. The second version was prolonged due to the obnoxious, repetitive, and argumentative behavior of the defense attorney, who was portrayed by an advanced law student. Although he did not elicit any more facts than in the control version, the defense counsel established the same facts repetitively by asking redundant questions of the witnesses; he expressed his annoyance with witnesses; and he made many unnecessary and irrelevant inquiries, in addition to obnoxious asides. All this was done in a highly dramatic manner in the best tradition of television lawyers. In the third version of each basic trial, the same behavior was practiced by the prosecutor who was also an advanced law student. The final version had the judge (played by an older law student) creating delays and ill-feeling by interrupting the trial at numerous points to ask the actors to speak up, have the attorneys approach the bench for unnecessary conferences, go out for coffee, phone calls, etc. In this version, the experimenter also helped frustrate by interrupting several times to administer to a balky tape recorder or to check his trial notes. Jurors had been told in advance that an actual trial was being reenacted but in truncated form and that it should take only 15 minutes. They had been warned, though, to allot two hours for their appointment, since they might have to wait for other trials to be completed; however, all trials began "on time," so that jurors had a reasonable expectation that they would be done shortly after the beginning of the trial.

To summarize the experiment, eight juries of 12 members each observed an enacted trial which was designed to give an appearance of either guilt or innocence to the defendant and in which annoyance and unnecessary delay were created by either the defense attorney, prosecutor, judge (and experimenter), or not at all. After the trial concluded, jurors individually rated the defendant's guilt (0 = definitely not guilty, 20 = definitely guilty). To ensure involvement, jurors had been told before the trial that this was a reenactment of a real trial which had lasted several weeks and that we were trying to see whether presenting shorter versions, with only a portion of the testimony, would lead to the same verdicts as in the actual trial. Jurors appeared to take their task seriously and were very determined to behave as a real jury, so that they could match the original jury.

After indicating their preliminary ratings, jurors deliberated for 10 minutes and then again individually rated the defendant's guilt. This was followed by a debriefing, where they were asked for their response to the trial and the actions of the principals; after this, the purpose of the experiment was thoroughly explained. During debriefing, jurors spontaneously expressed annoyance with the source of the delay in the six delayed trials. Results are displayed in Figure 7.3. Note first the effect of courtroom behavior on predeliberation judgments. Greatest guilt was attributed to the defendant when his attorney was the source of annoyance, and least guilt was assigned where the prosecutor was offensive or where annoying conditions were lacking (i.e., the control trials). The condition where the "neutral parties"—the judge and experimenter—were at fault for annoyance fell between these extremes in guilt ratings. Analysis of variance of predeliberation ratings yielded a main effect for trial conditions ($F(3,88) = 6.04$, $p < .01$). Moreover, the ordering of trial conditions was identical for both guilt and innocent appearing trials; the interaction between trial conditions and trial guilt appearance was negligible ($F(3,88) = .07$).

We draw three conclusions from the predeliberation ratings: First, obnoxious and annoying behavior in the courtroom does affect the judgments of individual jurors; specifically, it biases judgment towards the guilty end of the spectrum. Second, the impact of a juror's negative state on judgment of the defendant is mediated by the extent of the connection between the source of the state and the defendant. The effect of biasing conditions was greatest for the source most associated with the defendant (his lawyer) and nonexistent for the source directly dissociated with him (the prosecutor). Ill-feelings resulting from the behavior of a person neutral to the defendant's case (the judge) led to a moderate impact of bias. Third, the differential effects of sources of annoyance were identical for

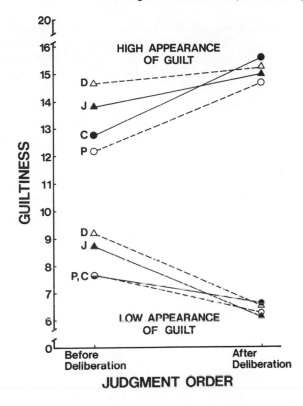

Figure 7.3. Guilt ratings as a function of courtroom behavior of attorneys and judge. (Note: The four sets of curves represent the different sources of annoyance: D = Defense attorney, J = Judge and experimenter, P = Prosecutor, C = Control (no annoyance).)

guilt-appearing and innocent-appearing trials. This agrees with the findings reported earlier for trait biases. Thus, the notion that biasing effects, whether state or trait in origin, are general across levels of defendant guilt is strengthened.

Now consider the judgments by individuals after deliberation. The biasing effects of courtroom conditions virtually disappear. This observation is supported by the significant interaction between trial conditions and pre/postdeliberation ratings (F(3, 88) = 6.2, p < .01). While this might be taken as evidence that the negative state dissipated in the course of deliberation and that jurors were no longer biased during the second vote, we believe otherwise. First, content analyses of the taped deliberation revealed very few references to lawyer or judge behavior (10 statements over all 8 trials referred to courtroom behavior, compared to 204 separate references to testimonial evidence); thus, deliberation allowed little "venting" of feelings. Second, jurors in all six delayed trials spontaneously expressed strong feelings about lawyer's and judge's actions during debriefing. The data suggest instead that jurors still harbored negative feelings after deliberation; that is, they still possessed biased initial impressions, but the effective weight of these biases had been reduced, due to an increase in weight of evidence. The distinction, as with personalistic biases, is between *possessing* a bias and *using* it in judgment. Perhaps this distinction ought to be applied to Broeder's (1966) finding that surveyed jurors express strong reactions to lawyer's behavior. Here, after deliberating the facts of the case, jurors were less prone to apply their reactions to judgment.

The courtroom behavior of principal actors in a trial is, of course, but one example of the many extralegal factors that may temporarily affect predispositional biases. Another source commonly encountered in our judicial system is pretrial publicity (PTP). Spurred on by the decisions in Irwin v. Dowd (366 U.S. 717, 1961) and Sheppard v. Maxwell (384 U.S. 333, 1966), there has been great alarm over the potential effects of prejudicial pretrial publicity. Indeed, in Justice Frankfurter's words in the former decision:

"Not a term passes without the court being importuned to review convictions, had in states throughout the country, in which substantial claims are made that a jury trial had been distorted because of inflammatory newspaper accounts . . . exerting pressures upon potential jurors before trial. . . ."

But, curtailing the public reporting of events prior to trial in the hopes of securing a "fair" trial (as is the case in England) would spark a confrontation between the First and Sixth Amendments to the Constitution. This is the Free Press/Fair Trial issue with which the law and the media are struggling (see, e.g., Winters, 1971, for a representative example). Without getting into the constitutional ramifications, it is important for behavioral scientists to determine empirically whether PTP *does* affect post-trial judgment, and whether effects may be mollified without abridging the principle of a free press. In this respect, Justice Frankfurter complained in Stroble v. California (343 U.S. 181, 1952):

"Science with all its advances has not given us instruments for determining when the impact of such newspaper exploitations has spent itself or whether the powerful impression . . . can be dissipated in the mind of the average juror by the tame and often pedestrian proceedings in Court."

In our model PTP would be seen as affecting the initial impression, and the generalizations derived from state and trait biases should apply for PTP; that is, conditions which enhance the weight of trial evidence should reduce the "powerful impression" of "newspaper exploitations." And they do: In an unpublished study, Zanzola (1978) provided subjects with one of three newspaper accounts of the attempted manslaughter case described earlier. One account was favorable to the defendant; it described his stable family life, and his claims that he was provoked and acted in self-defense. The second account gave only the bare facts of the case (i.e., a man was stabbed with glass during an argument), while the third was unfavorable towards the defendant, citing his previous criminal record, his admission to stabbing the victim, and the district attorney's certainty of his guilt. After reading the newspaper accounts, the subjects indicated the extent of their beliefs in the defendant's guilt and then listened to a tape of one of the two enacted trials. Half the subjects heard the trial in which the evidence gave an appearance of guilt, and the remainder heard the innocent-appearing trial. They then rated his guilt, discussed the trial in juries of 12, and once more rated guilt.

As Justice Frankfurter observed, PTP strongly affected prejudgments of the defendant's guilt before subjects heard the trial; that is, PTP evoked biases in *both* directions. In addition to the obvious *negative* effect of the unfavorable newspaper account, the favorable account led to a greater belief in the defendant's innocence compared to the neutral story. However, similar to Simon (1966), the effects of PTP markedly diminished after the trial and were no longer significant, either in ratings before ($p < .26$) or after ($p < .10$) deliberation. In addition, content analyses of deliberations revealed no references to PTP in any of the 12 juries.

It appears, then, that merely presenting the facts of the case substantially reduces the importance of PTP-induced biases. Though we might have expected deliberation to further reduce biasing effects, this was not so; possibly bias reduction had already reached its optimum before deliberation. These results are suggestive. Until we can produce conditions in the laboratory under which PTP bias is *not* reduced after witnessing a trial, we cannot be sure what it is about participating in a trial that affects the weight of PTP. On the basis of the experiments on trait biases, we can speculate that the "impact of newspaper exploitations" will be enhanced by conditions which cloud the credibility of evidence presented at trial and will be "dissipated in the mind of the average juror" when evidence is informative, credible, and generally uncontested.

Implications

Bias can be produced by a variety of conditions; these conditions exist both before and during trial, and temporarily affect the juror's way of judging the case at hand. Here we have looked at the behavior of principals in the courtroom drama and at pretrial publicity, but certainly the list could be extended to include other mood affecting agents, perhaps even indigestion or—not to overlook *positive* biases—a good meal, pleasant music, and satisfying lovemaking before the trial. These diverse influences have in common the status of extralegal factors; they do not constitute evidence fairly presented in court. Happily, justice is not so fragile as the existence of prejudgmental biases might suggest. The key lies in enhancing the attention paid to relevant evidence, and in maintaining its credibility and weight in the judgment equation. It appears that deliberation by juries acts as one safeguard in emphasizing the trial evidence to the exclusion of pretrial impressions (see Kaplan, 1977 a,b and Kaplan and Miller, 1977, for more on this theme).

CONCLUSIONS

The Sixth Amendment provides that ". . . the accused shall enjoy the right to a speedy and public trial by *impartial* jury" (emphasis ours). In other words, questions are to be decided solely on the basis of evidence presented in court. However, few doubt that impartiality is often violated in practice; in fact, we have suggested that truly impartial jurors are rare. Minimization of biasing *effects* is within our reach.

We have considered biases as stemming from two sources. *Trait* biases represent long term dispositions to judge others in lenient or stringent ways. Though we have limited our inquiry to generalized tendencies, these may also be specific to certain groups of litigants or to certain issues. Situational conditions may induce temporary *states* in jurors, a second form of bias. Prejudgmental beliefs in guilt or innocence due to bias are not, strictly speaking, removed in the course of a trial; rather, their *effects* on judgment may be reduced or set aside. The reported experiments show that reducing the contentiousness of evidence presented in court, or increasing awareness of the evidence in the course of deliberation, serves to curtail biasing effects. We may speculate more broadly that any technique which increases the amount of information effectively taken into account in judgment formation would lessen bias. Juror's recall of evidence, for example, could be enhanced with the use of videotape and note-taking (see Kaplan and Miller, 1977, for an illustration of the effect of memory factors on jury decisions).

These findings are meaningful in the context of the information integration model in which both initial impression, or the response prior to apprehending relevant information, and the information itself possess scale values and weights for the judgment dimension. Biases affect the value of the initial impression, and, in turn, the initial impression and information values are averaged, each weighted by its relative importance. This model suggested that the impact of bias could be reduced indirectly by increasing the impact of relevant information, as indeed we found.

In our legal tradition, juror bias has a rather curious role. As is evident in the Sixth Amendment, the juror ideally should approach the trial with a "blank mind." But this requirement of impartiality is of fairly recent vintage: Juries were originally composed of people with prior knowledge of the facts of the case (and therefore with pretrial biases). It was not until the sixteenth century that litigants would offer evidence to a jury who then weighed its truth or falsity. Thus, the juror's role as expert on the case eventually shifted to one who decides. Even then it was required that jurors be chosen from the locality of the litigation, so that the facts of the case could be decided in the context of local customs. Therein was born the tradition of the jury as the "conscience of the community": People who decide with an eye to local and community mores. The historical conflict between impartiality and recognition of local customs is reflected today in two different legal traditions. One tradition mandates that the jury act as the judge of the facts in the case, obeying the strict "letter of the law" as interpreted by the judge (see, for example, Sparf and Hansen v. United States, 156 U.S. 51, 1895). This tradition stresses objectivity and adherence to the law and allows little variance from case to case. Thus this tradition requires a "blank mind" on the part of triers of fact. The other tradition, currently followed, requires that the jury act as "conscience of the community" (Brooks and Doob, 1975), applying the current mores and values of the community to each individual case. Allowing the jury greater discretionary powers permits flexibility in administering the law to individual circumstances (Curtis, 1952) and enables the law to keep pace with changing societal views and tastes (Howe, 1939; Wigmore, 1929). Proponents of the latter tradition suggest that lay juries are better able to apply prevailing and shared standards to judgment than are judges acting solely under the law. Such a milieu in all probability enhances the manifestation of extralegal factors in decisions of guilt and, even more so, in punishment and in damage awards. And so, we find ourselves in a perplexing state: The juror is formally charged with judging a case solely on the evidence presented in court, while at the same time, is expected to apply community standards to the administration of the law, a form of bias in itself. In short, *some* biases, in the "conscience of the community" tradition, are not only permissible but are expected, if they represent the communal spirit of the times.

In the broad sense, the jury is not only a legal institution, but a political and social body as well (DeTocqueville, 1956). Perhaps this explains why there remains such an interest in its workings, even though trial by jury accounts for such a small proportion of the disposition of cases in the justice system (Kalven and Zeisel, 1966). Perhaps too this suggests the need to more clearly and systematically distinguish between socially desirable and undesirable biases in jurors and judges.

REFERENCES

Anderson, N. H. Information integration theory: A brief survey. In D. Krantz, R. Atkinson, R. D. Luce, and P. Suppes (Eds.), *Contemporary Developments in Mathematical Psychology* (Vol. 2). San Francisco: Freeman, 1974.

Berk, R. A., Hennessy, M., and Swan, J. The vagaries and vulgarities of "Scientific" jury selection: A methodological evaluation. *Evaluation Quarterly* **1**:143–157 (1977).

Blackstone, W. *Commentaries on the Laws of England of Public Wrongs.* Boston: Beacon Press, 1962. (Originally published, 1769.)

Boehm, V. R. Mr. Prejudice, Miss Sympathy, and the authoritarian personality: An application of psychological measuring techniques to the problem of jury bias. *Wisconsin Law Review* 734–750 (1968).

Broeder, D. W. The impact of the lawyers: An informal appraisal. *Valparaiso University Law Review* **1**:40–76 (1966).

Brooks, W. N., and Doob, A. N. Justice and the jury. *Journal of Social Issues* **31**(3):171–182 (1975).

Crosson, R. F. An investigation into certain personality variables among capital trial jurors. *Proceedings of the 76th Annual Convention of the American Psychological Association,* pp. 371–372 (1968).

Curtis, C. P. The trial judge and the jury. *Vanderbilt Law Review* **5**:150–166 (1952).

DeTocqueville, A. *Democracy in America.* New York: New American Library, 1956.

Freedman, M. H. Professional responsibility of the civil practitioner: Teaching legal ethics in the contracts course. In D. T. Weckstein (Ed.), *Education in the Professional Responsibilities of the Lawyer.* Charlottesville, VA: University Press of Virginia, 1970.

Gaudet, F. G. Individual differences in the sentencing tendencies of judges. *Archives of Psychology* **32**:5; 9–26; 29–42; 55 (1938).

Hatton, D. E.; Snortum, J. R.; and Oskamp, S. The effects of biasing information and dogmatism upon witness testimony. *Psychonomic Science* **23**:425–427 (1971).

Howe, M. de W. Juries as judges in criminal cases. *Harvard Law Review* **52**:582–616 (1939).

Jurow, G. New data on the effect of a "death qualified" jury on the guilt determination process. *Harvard Law Review* **84**:567–611 (1971).

Kalven, H., Jr., and Zeisel, H. *The American Jury*. Boston: Little, Brown, 1966.

Kaplan, M. F. Information integration in social judgment: Interaction of judge and informational components. In M. F. Kaplan and S. Schwartz (Eds.) *Human Judgment and Decision Processes*. New York: Academic Press, 1975.

Kaplan, M. F. Judgments by juries. In M. F. Kaplan and S. Schwartz (Eds.) *Human Judgment and Decision Processes in Applied Settings*. New York: Academic Press (1977a).

Kaplan, M. F. Discussion polarization effects in a modified jury decision paradigm: Informational influences. *Sociometry* **40**:262–271 (1977b).

Kaplan, M. F., and Kemmerick, G. D. Juror judgment as information integration: Combining evidential and nonevidential information. *Journal of Personality and Social Psychology* **30**:493–499 (1974).

Kaplan, M. F., and Miller, C. E. Judgments and group discussion: Effect of presentation and memory factors on polarization. *Sociometry* **40**:337–343 (1977).

Lind, E. A., Thibaut, J., and Walker, L. Discovery and presentation of evidence in adversary and non-adversary proceedings. *Michigan Law Review* **71**(6):1129–1144 (1973).

Lipsitt, P. D., and Strodtbeck, F. L. Defensiveness in decision making as a function of sex-role identification. *Journal of Personality and Social Psychology* **6**:10–15 (1967).

Mitchell, H. E., and Byrne, D. *Minimizing the Influence of Irrelevant Factors in the Courtroom: The Defendant's Character, Judge's Instructions, and Authoritarianism*. Paper presented at the meeting of the Midwestern Psychological Association, Cleveland; May, 1972.

Mitchell, H. E., and Byrne, D. The defendant's dilemma: Effects of jurors' attitudes and authoritarianism. *Journal of Personality and Social Psychology* **25**:123–129 (1973).

Nagel, S. S. *The Legal Process from a Behavioral Perspective*. Homewood, Illinois: Dorsey, 1969.

Nemeth, C., and Sosis, R. A simulated jury: Characteristics of the defendant and the jurors. *Journal of Social Psychology* **90**:221–229 (1973).

Ploscowe, M. The development of present-day criminal procedures in Europe and America. *Harvard Law Review* **48**:433–473 (1935).

Pritchett, C. H. *The Roosevelt Court*. New York: MacMillan, 1948.

Schulman, J., Shaver, P., Colman, R., Emrich, B., and Christie, R. Recipe for a jury. *Psychology Today* **6**(12):37–44; 77–84 (1973).

Shaw, M. E., and Wright, J. M. *Scales for the Measurement of Attitudes*. New York: McGraw-Hill, 1967.

Sigall, H., and Ostrove, N. Beautiful but dangerous: Effects of offender attractiveness and nature of the crime on juridic judgment. *Journal of Personality and Social Psychology* **31**:410–414 (1975).

Simon, R. Murder, juries, and the press. *Trans-Action* **3**(4):40–42 (1966).

Simon, R., and Oster, P. R. Inside justice. *Chicago Sun Times,* pp. 4; 20, September 23, 1973.

Thayer, R. E. Attitude and personality differences between potential jurors who could return a death verdict and those who could not. *Proceedings of the 78th Annual Convention of the American Psychological Association,* pp. 445–446, 1970.

Thibaut, J., and Walker, L. *Procedural Justice: A Psychological Analysis.* Hillsdale, New Jersey: Lawrence Erlbaum Associates, 1975.

Thibaut, J.; Walker, L.; LaTour, S.; and Houlden, P. Procedural justice as fairness. *Stanford Law Review* 26:1271–1289 (1974).

Thibaut, J.; Walker, L.; and Lind, E. A. Adversary presentation and bias in legal decisionmaking. *Harvard Law Review* 86:386–401 (1972).

Walker, L., and Thibaut, J. An experimental examination of pretrial conference techniques, *Minnesota Law Review* 55(6):1113–1137 (1971).

Walker, L.; Thibaut, J.; and Andreoli, V. Order of presentation at trial. *The Yale Law Journal* 82:216–226 (1972).

Walster, E., and Walster, G. W. Equity and social justice. *Journal of Social Issues* 31:21–44 (1975).

Wigmore, J. A programme for the trial of jury trial. *Journal of the American Judicature Society* 12:166–170 (1929).

Winters, G. R. (Ed.). *Fair Trial—Free Press.* Chicago: American Judicature Society, 1971.

Zanzola, L. The role of pretrial publicity in the trial process and jury deliberations. Unpublished master's thesis, Northern Illinois University, 1978.

8

Evidentiary Reform
of Rape Laws:
A Psycholegal Approach

Eugene Borgida

Over the past several years, a considerable amount of attention has been focused on the fact that a rape victim is often twice victimized—as a victim of sexual assault and as a victim when she testifies in court. The common law rules of evidence in rape cases, which typically facilitate unrestricted admission of testimony about the victim's prior sexual history with third persons (i.e., persons other than the defendant), have particularly come under attack for contributing to this situation. As a result, various legislative reforms have been enacted, and a number of states have recently revised their evidentiary rules concerning the admissibility of the victim's prior sexual history with persons other than the accused assailant.

The research reported in this chapter was supported in part by a National Institute of Mental Health Research Grant No. 1 R01 MH30724-01 and by a faculty research grant from the Graduate School of the University of Minnesota to the author. The author would like to acknowledge the cooperation of Judge Donald Barbeau, Fourth Judicial District Court in Minneapolis; Jack Provo, District Court Administrator and his colleague, Dennis Chamberlin, in obtaining the sample of jurors for the research discussed in this chapter. The author would also like to acknowledge the helpful ideas and suggestions of Graeme Bush and Marilyn Steere, the assistance of Myrina Pettman, Marilyn Steere, and Brian Flakne during data collection, and Sherry Resler, Catherine Ludden, Phyllis Oksner, and Alan Tomkins in the analysis phase. Graeme Bush, Mark Snyder, and Anthony N. Doob commented on an earlier version of this chapter.

The rationale behind such reforms is basically twofold: first, by excluding evidence of the victim's prior sexual history, the victim is less likely to be subjected to humiliation and abasement in court. Legal reformers have not only expressed concern about unjust acquittals resulting from the admission of prior sexual history testimony (and, conversely, the difficulty of obtaining convictions in rape cases), but also concern that the admissibility of such testimony inhibits a victim's willingness to prosecute because of the strong possibility of exposure to humiliating and irrelevant cross-examination. The reforms, in this respect, are meant to alleviate the extent to which a victim is "on trial" along with the accused assailant. Second, the reforms should shield potentially irrelevant, prejudicial testimony from being heard by the jury. The admissibility of such evidence, according to the reformist position, is highly prejudicial and non-probative. Restricting its admissibility presumably will, therefore, reduce juror prejudice and, in turn, improve the rate of convictions in rape cases.

The purpose of the present chapter is to examine the psycholegal assumptions underlying these recent evidentiary reforms in rape laws. First, the chapter briefly discusses the peculiar legal status of rape and the most controversial aspect of the evidentiary reforms—the admissibility of third party prior sexual history evidence. The reformist assumption that the admission of such evidence has a prejudicial effect on juror fact-finding is then discussed in the context of related experimental research in social psychology and law, as well as research on human judgment processes. The final section of the chapter presents the results of an exploratory study which examined some of the psycholegal assumptions about the impact of third party prior sexual history testimony in a rape case. The research specifically addresses a) whether the current types of legal reform seem to eliminate or reduce the prejudice which purportedly inheres in the common law rules of evidence; b) the extent to which empanelled adult jurors properly (i.e., without prejudice) utilize prior sexual history evidence in an individual judgment context; and c) the extent to which the different types of reform interact with the varying degrees of perceived victim consent that characterize rape cases and affect their outcome.

THE LAW OF RAPE [1]

In an analysis of the peculiar legal status of rape, Berger (1977) argues that rape is unique as a sex-specific crime. In rape cases, for example, the law goes beyond the protections offered defendants accused of other crimes and has constructed evidentiary rules that essentially protect men from irresponsible or fabricated accusations by women (LeGrand, 1973; Berger, 1977). One of the most obvious legal anomalies is the corroboration rule, which requires evidence other than the victim's testimony to convict a defendant charged with rape.[2] Although the corroboration rule has been dropped in all but a few states, there is no similar rule in other areas of criminal law.

Another practice peculiar to rape law is the judge's cautionary instruction to the jury. The jury is advised that a rape charge is easily made and difficult to disprove and that the testimony of a woman must be examined with caution.[3] In addition, judges often add their own opinions of the woman's credibility either directly or by innuendo (Mathiasen, 1974; Robin, 1977). Both the corroboration rule and the cautionary instruction, then, place a special burden on the credibility of the woman as a prosecuting witness which is not placed on such witnesses in other crimes.

The most controversial aspect of the law of rape is, however, the admissibility of evidence regarding the prior sexual history of the victim. Evidence of this nature is usually assumed to be relevant to the issue of consent. In fact, non-consent, in addition to the fact of sexual penetration, is perhaps the most basic element of the crime of rape, which is traditionally defined as an act of sexual intercourse forcibly accomplished by a man with a woman not his wife, without her consent and against her will (cf. Harris, 1976). There indeed are rape cases where consent is not an issue,[4] but proof of non-consent is usually regarded as absolutely crucial to the prosecution's case.[5]

Controversy particularly surrounds the question of whether evidence of the victim's prior sexual history is probative of consent. There is general agreement that evidence of the victim's past sexual behavior with the defendant is relevant and should be admitted. It is also generally agreed that the prosecutrix's sexual contact with another man is relevant to show the probable source of semen, pregnancy, or disease which might otherwise be attributed to the defendant (Berger, 1977).[6] Under common law rules of evidence, however, courts have admitted evidence of the victim's prior sexual history with third parties for a variety of other reasons.

Two major reasons are commonly cited. First, the defense has been allowed to introduce evidence of the victim's unchaste character in order to impeach her credibility as a prosecuting witness. The assumption behind this rather archaic notion is that a woman's sexual behavior is directly related to her credibility. If that were so, then one might expect that such testimony would also be admissible in any trial in which a woman serves as a witness (Note, Valparaiso Law Review, 1976). General evidence of immorality is, however, not permitted to impeach the credibility of a witness in any other area of criminal law. The second reason for the use of prior sexual history is that the defense should be allowed to introduce evidence of the victim's prior sexual history in order to show likelihood of consent in the particular case. The assumption behind this rule is that a woman who has consented to various sexual advances in the past is more likely to have consented to the sexual encounter in question than is a chaste woman (Eisenbud, 1975). The weight of legal commentary in recent years, however, is highly critical of such an assumption. When evidence of a victim's reputation for promiscuity is, for example, admitted for the purpose of proving the probability of consent, despite uncontradicted evidence of physical abuse and medical evidence of forcible rape, the argument is made that the prejudicial effect of such evidence outweighs its minimal probative value (Note, Valparaiso Law Review, 1976). The fact that a woman has engaged in sexual relations with one man or with many simply does not prove that she consented to the act in issue [7] (Berger, 1977; Mathiasen, 1974; Harris, 1976).

Traditional common law rules of evidence have been strenuously criticized on the grounds that they distort the fact-finding process in a manner prejudicial to the rape victim and that they often tend to result in the acquittal of rape defendants who are guilty. Rather than carefully weighing evidence against a standard of "reasonable doubt" to determine the guilt or innocence of the accused, jurors may be moved by inflammatory prior sexual history evidence to blame the victim and thus to acquit the defendant. Moreover, the introduction of prior sexual history contributes to the trauma already experienced by a rape victim and has the effect of discouraging rape prosecutions. The overall effect is that the victim rather than the rapist bears the social cost of the crime. Efforts to shift the burden of the social cost of rape onto the rapist have resulted in widespread proposals for change in state and federal rules of evidence. All of the reforms restrict, to a greater or lesser degree, the evidence which may be introduced about a rape victim's prior sexual history. These reforms are discussed in the next section.

EVIDENTIARY REFORMS AND THE ADMISSIBILITY
OF PRIOR SEXUAL HISTORY

Legislative response to criticism of existing laws has been dramatic in the past few years. Forty states have enacted "rape shield" reform statutes which limit, to varying degrees, the admissibility of the victim's prior sexual history with persons other than the defendant. Although the reforms make several other interesting changes in the common law, the discussion will focus on the admissibility of third party prior sexual history evidence, because this is the area in which there is the most variety among the different reforms and about which there is the most controversy.

The laws governing the admission of prior sexual history with third parties may be divided into three categories based on the extent to which such evidence is excluded when consent is involved. Those states having no statutory exclusionary rule pertaining to prior sexual history evidence are designated as *Common Law* in Table 8.1. For these 11 states, admission of prior sexual history evidence is of course subject to the conventional rule governing the admission of any kind of evidence; i.e., it must be relevant, and any prejudicial effect it may have must not outweigh its probative value. In addition, trial court decisions as to the admissibility of such evidence in a Common Law state are guided by case law. Although theoretically that law could favor a strict exclusionary rule, the practical effect of such a ruling would be minimal, because discretion still rests in the hands of the trial judge. Thus, the Common Law category includes any state without an exclusionary statute and assumes the comparatively unlimited admissibility of prior sexual history evidence.

In contrast, both categories of reform statutes reflect the arguments put forth by critics of the traditional law of rape. The major difference between the reform statutes categorized in Table 8.1 is the amount of discretion which is left to the trial judge in determining the admissibility of the offered evidence. In the 21 states governed by a *Moderate Reform* exclusionary rule, prior sexual history evidence is generally excluded, unless a consent defense is raised, or unless the court determines the evidence to be material to a fact in issue.[8] The latter evidence must meet a statutory standard of relevance, such that its probative value is not substantially outweighed by the possibility of undue prejudice. Most Moderate Reform statutes provide for an *in-camera* hearing where the defendant presents his offer of proof supporting the admissibility of prior sexual history evidence and the prosecution may make rebuttal arguments. Laws of this type allow the trial judge considerable discretion in balancing the probative and prejudicial aspects of the evidence in question, but the effect of the statute is clearly to limit the admissibility of such evidence when compared to the Common Law. Furthermore, the Moderate Reform statutes provide for a recording of the trial court's findings and reasons for the ruling, which may then be reviewed on appeal for any abuse of discretion.

In contrast to this limited, discretionary mode of exclusion, 19 states have adopted statutes with a *Radical Reform* exclusionary rule that totally excludes third party prior sexual history when offered on the issue of consent (but not when pertaining to past sexual conduct with the defendant or establishing the source of semen, pregnancy, or disease). The Radical Reform statutes require complete exclusion of such evidence, because it is conclusively presumed to be irrelevant, overly prejudicial, and confusing to the jury by the creation of extraneous and collateral

Table 8.1. Classification of states' exclusionary rules per evidence of the victim's prior sexual history with persons other than the defendant when offered on the issue of the victim's consent.[a]

Common Law [b]	Moderate Reforms [c]	Radical Reforms [d]
1. Alabama	1. Alaska	1. California
2. Arizona	2. Colorado	2. Delaware
3. Arkansas	3. Florida	3. Indiana
4. Connecticut	4. Georgia	4. Louisiana
5. District of Columbia	5. Hawaii	5. Maryland
6. Illinois	6. Idaho	6. Massachusetts
7. Maine	7. Iowa	7. Michigan
8. Mississippi	8. Kentucky	8. Missouri
9. Rhode Island	9. Kansas	9. Montana
10. Utah	10. Minnesota	10. New Hampshire
11. Virginia	11. Nebraska	11. North Dakota
	12. Nevada	12. Ohio
	13. New Jersey	13. Oklahoma
	14. New Mexico	14. Oregon
	15. New York	15. Pennsylvania
	16. North Carolina	16. South Carolina
	17. South Dakota	17. Vermont
	18. Tennessee	18. West Virginia
	19. Texas	19. Wisconsin
	20. Washington	
	21. Wyoming	

[a] The statutory sections upon which this classification is based may be found as follows: Alaska Stat. §12.45.045 (Supp. 1977); Cal. Evid. Code §1103 (2) (a) (West Cum. Supp. 1977); Colo. Rev. Stat. §18–3–407 (Cum. Supp. 1976); Del. Code Ann. §3509 (Cum. Supp. 1976); Fla. Stat. Ann. §794.022 (2) (West 1976); Ga. Code Ann. §38.202.1 (Cum. Supp. 1977); Haw. Rev. Stat. §707–742 (Supp. 1976); Idaho Code §18–6105 (Cum. Supp. 1977); Ind. Code Ann. §35–1–32.5–1, –2 (Burns Cum. Supp. 1977); Iowa Code Ann. §782.4 (West Cum. Supp. 1977); Ky. Rev. Stat. §510.145 (Cum. Supp. 1976); Kan. Evid. Code §60–447a (1976); La. Code Crim. Proc. Ann. art. 15:529.1 §498 (West Cum. Supp. 1977); Md. Ann. Code art. 27 §461A (Cum. Supp. 1977); 1977 Mass. Adv. Legis. Serv. C. 110; Mich. Comp. Laws Ann. §750.520j (Cum. Supp. 1977); 1977 Minn. Sess. Law Serv. Rules Evid. 404(c) (West); 1977 Mo. Legis. Serv. Act 87 (Vernon); Mont. Rev. Code Ann. §94–5–503(5) (1977); Neb. Rev. Stat. §28–408.05 (Supp. 1975); 1977 Nev. Stat. Sec. 11, 12, 59th Sess. (Amends §§48.069, 50.090); N. H. Rev. Stat. Ann. §623–A: 6 (Supp. 1975); N. J. Stat. Ann. §2A: 84A–32.1 (West Supp. 1977); N. M. Stat. Ann. §40A–9–26 (Supp. 1975); N. Y. Crim. Proc. Law §60.42 (McKinney Cum. Supp. 1976–1977); N. D. Cent. Code §12.1–20–14 (Supp. 1977); 1977 N. C. Adv. Legis. Serv. C.851; Ohio Rev. Code Ann. §2907.02 (D) (Baldwin Supp. 1976); Okla. Stat. Ann. tit. 22 §750 (West Cum. Supp. 1977–78); Or. Rev. Stat. §163.475 (Supp. 1975); Pa. Stat. Ann. §3104 tit. 18, §3104 (Purdon Supp. 1977–78); S. C. Code §16–3–659.1(1) (Supp. Nov. 1977); S. D. Compiled Laws Ann. §23–44–16.1 (Supp. 1977); Tenn. Code Ann. §40.2445 (Cum. Supp. 1976); Tex. Penal Code Ann. tit. 5, §21.13 (Vernon Cum. Supp. 1977); Vt. Stat. Ann. tit. 13, §3255 (Supp. 1977); Wash. Rev. Code Ann. §9.79.150 (Supp. 1977); W. Va. Code §61–8B–12 (Supp. 1977); Wisc. Stat. Ann. §972.11 (2) (West Cum. Supp. 1977); Wyo. Stat. §6–63.12 (Interim Supp. 1977).

[b] Defined in terms of the *comparatively unlimited admissibility* of prior sexual history evidence when offered on the issue of consent.

[c] Defined in terms of *partial limitation* on the admissibility of prior sexual history when offered on the issue of consent.

[d] Defined in terms of *total exclusion* of prior sexual history evidence when offered on the issue of consent.

issues. Such statutes may expressly exclude prior sexual history offered to suggest consent or may simply omit consent from a list of permissible exceptions to the exclusionary rule.[9] The ultimate effect of the Radical Reform statutes is specifically to relieve the trial judge of virtually all discretion in determining the admissibility of third party prior sexual history evidence when offered on the issue of consent.

The assumption underlying both categories of reform statutes is essentially the same: The assumption that evidence of prior sexual history with a third party has a prejudicial effect on the outcome of the trial. Jurors will be inclined to give such testimony more weight than it deserves, or else they will be misled by the bias inherent in such evidence and decide the case on the basis of their disapproval of the victim's previous sexual conduct.[10] The Moderate Reforms' method of compensating for the assumed prejudicial effect is to place constraints on the admissibility of prior sexual history by prohibiting its admissibility, unless a judge determines that its probativeness outweighs its prejudicial effect. This limited admission of prior sexual history is justified on either one of two grounds: 1) the only evidence which will be admitted under these statutes is evidence which a jury will be able to evaluate properly; or 2) whatever prejudice remains must be tolerated, because of the greater probativeness of the evidence admissible by this standard.

Radical Reforms which make, however, the same general assumptions about the prejudicial effect of prior sexual history evidence, go further in terms of the weight that they give to the factor of prejudice. They conclusively presume that no evidence of prior sexual conduct with third parties can be evaluated properly by a jury. Its relevance and probativeness to the issue of consent is so attenuated, in all cases, to justify a blanket exclusion. Rather than balancing the interests of the rape victim and the rape defendant, as the Moderate Reforms attempt to do, the Radical Reforms shift the inequity of the Common Law from the victim to the defendant. Some legal scholars have in fact argued that the total exclusion of prior sexual history evidence under the Radical Reform statutes may, in certain circumstances, unconstitutionally infringe a rape defendant's due process right to mount a defense to the charges against him (cf. Herman, 1977).

PRIOR SEXUAL HISTORY AS A FORM OF EVIDENCE

As noted previously, central to the assumption underlying both reform categories is the notion that, as a form of evidence, prior sexual history will be regarded by jurors as informative about a victim's character and that such information will be over-weighted and represent a source of bias in the juror decision process. A number of studies in social psychology and law suggest indeed that evidence which evokes character may influence jurors (cf. Stephan, 1975). Evidence of "good" character or "bad" character, as conveyed by manipulating personal characteristics, such as perceived respectability of the victim or the defendant, has been shown to influence the fact-finding process in hypothetical rape cases (e.g., Feldman-Summers and Lindner, 1976; Frederick and Luginbuhl, 1976; Jones and Aronson, 1973). Evidence of prior criminal conviction, for example, which is suggestive of "bad" character, tends to increase the likelihood of criminal conviction, even when mock jurors are informed that such evidence should only be used to evaluate the credibility of the witness (Doob and Kirshenbaum, 1972; Hans and Doob, 1976; Kalven and Zeisel, 1966; Landy and Aronson, 1969). On the basis of a hypothetical rape case, Brooks, Doob, and Kirshenbaum (1975) showed that when a man was convicted of raping a woman with a history of prostitution ("bad" character), as opposed to a woman of chaste character, both male and female subjects felt that justice had not been done.

Recent research on human judgment processes also suggests that evidence of prior sexual history may be likely to prejudice the juror decision process. In terms of the decisions that we often have to make, as well as our attributions and predictions about others' behavior, it has been demonstrated that certain kinds of information are more influential than others (e.g., Bower, 1972; Nisbett, Borgida, Crandall, and Reed, 1976; Ross, 1977). Evidence that is specific and anecdotal in content (as evidence of prior sexual history can be) may be the sort of information that remains in thought longer and triggers more inferences because of its greater emotional interest and salience (e.g., Borgida and Nisbett, 1977). Specific, anecdotal information may also be more evocative of a person's character than, for example, reputational testimony about a person's character in the community which, in contrast, seems bland, anonymous, and generally uninformative. The assumption here, of course, is that it is easier to assess character and future behavior from specific examples than from more global evaluations.

In fact, the rules of evidence pertaining to character evidence make a very similar assumption about the informational value of general reputation testimony and specific acts testimony. It is recognized, for example, that general reputation testimony is the less interesting method of character proof for jurors to hear and perhaps the least informative about character, as well. Nevertheless, general reputation testimony is the preferred mode of proving character, primarily because such evidence is more stable and less subject to bias. In contrast, specific acts testimony is regarded as most informative and convincing about character. McCormick (1972), for example, notes the greater "pungency and persuasiveness" of specific acts testimony. Other legal scholars, however, have also argued that specific acts testimony "possesses the greatest capacity to arouse prejudice, to confuse, to surprise, and to consume time" (Rule 405, Advisory Committee Note, Federal Rules of Evidence for U.S. Courts and Magistrates, p. 29). Specific acts are too easy to fabricate or misconstrue and are difficult to verify or rebut, according to this view. There is concern, therefore, that jurors could lose sight of the evidentiary issues before them and instead be swayed by issues of character raised by the specific acts. Consequently, the Federal Rules of Evidence carefully restrict the admissibility of specific acts testimony, in order to minimize any potentially confusing or prejudicial considerations which might arise as a result of introducing such evidence.

In a recent experiment, Borgida (1976) tested this legal assumption about the potentially prejudicial impact of specific acts character testimony in relation to general reputation testimony. To the extent that jurors' intuitive assessments of character affect the fact-finding process, it was expected that specific acts testimony—as specific, anecdotal information—would be more suggestive of a person's character than general reputation testimony and would therefore have more influence on juror verdicts. Undergraduate subjects served as non-deliberating jurors for a videotaped enactment of an automobile negligence trial. As part of the trial, subjects were shown character testimony on behalf of the plaintiff in the case. All character testimony was substantially pro-plaintiff and favorably commented upon the plaintiff's "cautiousness" which, in an auto negligence case, presumably is the central character trait in issue. Control subjects were not exposed to character evidence. Character testimony was presented either in terms of specific acts of conduct or in terms of general reputation. Cross-cutting the type of character evidence, subjects either received a low or a high amount of character evidence.

Borgida (1976) found that an *in vivo* presentation of a high amount of specific acts testimony, as opposed to a low amount, had a damaging effect on individually rendered negligence verdicts. In order to clarify this effect, which resulted from increasing the amount of specific acts testimony, an analysis of subjects' open-ended personality sketches of the plaintiff was conducted. It generally was expected that a cautious characterization of the plaintiff would be correlated positively with pro-plaintiff verdicts; this was, in fact, the case ($r = .35, p < .01$). Hence, subjects who regarded the plaintiff as a cautious, prudent person tended to render verdicts which were more favorable to the plaintiff. Thus, research in social psychology and law tends to support the notion that evidence suggestive of a person's character may have prejudicial effects on juror and possibly jury verdicts (very few studies have, however, directly explored the latter possibility). Thus, an exploratory investigation was conducted to specifically test the generality of this finding and assess the impact of admitting prior sexual history evidence in rape cases.

TESTING THE VALIDITY OF THE RAPE REFORMS

A number of more specific questions about the recent reforms in evidentiary rules governing the admission of prior sexual history evidence can now be raised. With regard to the Moderate Reforms, for example, 1) does the admission of "sanitized" evidence increase the likelihood of conviction? and 2) how valid is the assumption that jurors, either on an individual basis or in the context of simulated jury deliberations, can properly (i.e., without prejudice) utilize such evidence? With regard to the Radical Reforms, 1) will such reforms obtain a higher conviction rate than the more Moderate Reforms, because no evidence of the victim's prior sexual history whatsoever is admissible? 2) do the Radical Reforms exclude evidence which is relevant and which could be assessed in a non-prejudicial manner by jurors? More generally, do both the Radical and the Moderate Reforms eliminate or reduce prejudice which the reforms assume inhere in the Common Law rules of evidence? And finally, to what extent do these different legal criteria (the Common Law vs. both reforms) governing the admissibility of prior sexual history interact with the varying degrees of implied victim consent, which characterize different rape cases?

This latter issue is particularly important in light of the substantive centrality of consent in the law of rape. Research on mock juror judgments in rape cases also suggests that implied consent is an important, though neglected variable (cf. Scroggs, 1976). Kalven and Zeisel (1966) found, for example, that jurors were less likely to convict the accused in criminal cases where there was some degree of victim precipitation. Indeed, research by Klemmack and Klemmack (1976) on the variables that affect whether or not various social situations are defined as rape provides support for the idea that situational scenarios or case fact patterns, irrespective of prior sexual history evidence, may be informative with respect to the inference of victim consent.[11] A random sample of female respondents in Tuscaloosa, Alabama was asked to evaluate seven situations in terms of the extent to which they believed a rape had occurred. According to the law of rape, forcible rape had occurred in each situation. The ratings revealed that for the three situations where implied consent was minimal, at least 75 percent of the respondents were certain that a rape had occurred. In contrast, however, for the two situations where victim consent was strongly implied (e.g., the man forces sexual relations after the dating couple had been necking, despite the woman's resistance), only 20 percent were certain that a rape had occurred; situations where implied consent was ambiguous were rated midway between the two other clusters. Thus, it may be the case that fact patterns which convey a high probability of victim precipitation or consent actually increase the likelihood that jurors will make use of the victim's character, whether or not evidence of prior sexual history with third parties is admitted. Inference of victim consent may, therefore, be as likely from the case fact pattern as from personal characteristics of the victim, such as prior sexual history, although the latter inference is more straightforward than the former. The assumption here, of course, is that, in the absence of specific information about character, situations and contexts per se may be sufficiently informative about a person's character and behavior (cf. Price, 1974; Price and Bouffard, 1974).

In order to directly examine the extent to which levels of implied victim consent in a fact pattern might interact with the evidentiary rules of a Common Law, Moderate Reform and Radical Reform jurisdiction, the author and two of his colleagues, Marilyn Steere and Phyllis Oksner, conducted an exploratory study. Over a three-month period, encompassing a new jury panel every two weeks, questionnaires were administered to a total of 180 male and female adult jurors serving their last day of jury duty with the Fourth Judicial District Court in Minneapolis. [12] In addition to providing personality and demographic information, each juror read the condensed case facts of a hypothetical rape trial involving a consent defense and was asked to render a non-deliberated verdict, as well as to rate the degree of victim consent.

Evidence of the victim's prior sexual history and varying degrees of implied victim consent were embedded within the set of case facts presented to each juror on the basis of a 3 x 3 between-subjects design, with 20 jurors randomly assigned to each condition. For each juror, the admissibility of prior sexual history in the rape trial description was governed either by evidentiary restrictions under the Common Law exclusionary rule (comparatively unlimited admissibility) or the Moderate Reform exclusionary rule (partial limitation on admissibility), or the Radical Reform exclusionary rule (total exclusion of such evidence). Because prior sexual history with third parties is inadmissible under the Radical Reform, the latter conditions, in effect, also served as no evidence control conditions. In addition to a different type of exclusionary rule, each juror either read a case fact pattern which conveyed a Low Probability of Victim Consent, an *Ambiguous Probability of Consent,* or a *High Probability of Consent.*

Pretest ratings of these case fact patterns by an independent sample of subjects corroborated this differential probability of consent. [13] Before reading the case fact summary, all jurors were instructed as follows:

> We are studying the process by which jurors make decisions. On the following pages, you will be presented with a case summary of a rape trial based on the actual trial transcript. You will be asked to make a number of judgments, and we therefore ask that you read the account carefully. Take as much time as you need in order to make your decision. The case summary contains all the essential facts of the case as originally presented in trial. Base your decision only on the case facts as given. If, for example, there is no mention of a weapon, assume that one was not used. In other words, you are to assume that all the evidence is before you as a juror, and you must render what you believe is an appropriate judgment. We realize that written summaries of such trials are not the same as sitting on the jury during the actual trial. Nevertheless, we ask that you approach this task seriously, just as you would, if you had been on the original jury.

The introductory scenario of the rape trial case summary presented to jurors in the nine experimental conditions was identical:

> The accusing party in this case was a medical technologist employed in a downtown medical laboratory. During the trial, she testified that on the evening in question she and a female co-worker worked late and then went out to dinner. They drove to a nearby restaurant in separate cars since they lived in different parts of the city. The two stayed at the restaurant for approximately an hour and then decided to leave because they both had to work the next day. On the way to the parking lot, the accusing party realized that she had left her purse in the restaurant. She explained her problem to the man who was sitting at the table that she had previously occupied and together they looked for her purse.

Jurors in the Low Probability of Consent conditions, however, next read that:

> Upon finding the purse, she thanked him and left the restaurant. As she approached her car in the parking lot she realized that he had followed her out of the restaurant. He caught up with her just as she reached her car, and he suggested that they go somewhere to have a drink. When she refused, he shoved her into the car where, despite her attempts to fight him off, he raped her and then fled the scene.

Jurors in the Ambiguous Probability of Consent conditions instead read:

Upon finding the purse, he asked her to stay and to have a drink with him. Relieved to have found her purse, she accepted his offer. After a drink and some casual conversation, the accusing party explained to him that she had to be at work early the next day. She thanked him for the drink and for his assistance in finding her purse and then excused herself from the table. As she approached her car in the parking lot, she realized that he had followed her out of the restaurant. He asked her for a ride home and she agreed. Following his directions, she then drove to his apartment building parking lot where, despite her attempts to fight him off, he raped her and then drove them back to the restaurant where he left in his own car.

And jurors in the High Probability of Consent conditions read the following after the introductory scenario:

Upon finding the purse, he asked her to stay and to have a drink with him. Grateful for his help in finding the purse, she accepted his offer. They had several drinks and after a couple of hours, the accusing party explained to him that she had to be at work early the next day. She thanked him for the drinks and offered him a ride home. He quickly agreed, and they walked out to her car in the parking lot. She then asked him to drive her car because she was not sure how to get to his apartment building from the restaurant. He then drove to his apartment building parking lot where despite her attempts to fight him off, he raped her and then persuaded her to drive him back to the restaurant, whereupon he left in his own car.

The case summary for each juror, regardless of experimental condition, then described the medical evidence introduced during the trial and stated the consent defense as follows:

Medical tests taken shortly after the alleged rape and introduced as evidence during the trial indicated the presence of semen in her vagina.

During the trial, the defendant testified that he did not rape the accusing party, that she appeared to display sexual interest in him while they were in the restaurant, and that she agreed to have sex with him in the car.

Finally, for jurors in the Common Law conditions, the case fact summary concluded with the following potentially admissible evidence about the victim's prior sexual history with third parties:

A witness for the defense, who had known the accusing party since college and had the opportunity to learn her reputation for chastity, testified that it was generally known that the accusing party had sex frequently with many different men, some of whom were strangers, and that once during a college fraternity party, she had sex with several men on the same evening.

On the other hand, for jurors in the Moderate Reform conditions, the case fact summary concluded with the following potentially admissible evidence about the victim's prior sexual history with third parties:

> A witness for the defense who had known the accusing party for several years and who had the opportunity to learn her reputation for chastity testified that it was generally known among her friends and acquaintances that she had frequently had sexual relations with men who had picked her up at a bar. [14]

Jurors in the Radical Reform conditions, consistent with the total exclusionary rule pertaining to prior sexual history with third parties, did not receive such evidence.

We generally expected main effects and a two-way interaction for Type of Exclusionary Rule and Probability of Consent on the primary dependent measures: juror certainty of defendant guilt and juror certainty of victim consent. It was expected, for example, that verdicts would reflect a greater likelihood of acquittal in the Common Law conditions than in the Radical Reform conditions. Consistent with the reformist assumption, admission of inflammatory and prejudicial prior sexual history was expected to result in higher acquittal rates, regardless of the degree of implied consent. The implication of victim consent should be particularly salient when inflammatory evidence of prior sexual history is combined with a fact pattern that per se is highly suggestive of victim consent.

Verdicts in the Moderate Reform conditions were not, however, expected to reflect uniformly higher acquittal rates. In Ambiguous Consent cases, for example, the discretionary limitation on the admissibility of prior sexual history might in effect resolve the ambiguity for jurors—though, it was expected, in a prejudicial manner. Rather than increasing the likelihood of conviction, as was the intent of the Moderate Reforms, such testimony may nevertheless increase the likelihood of acquittal. On the other hand, in the Low Probability Consent condition, where the implication of victim consent is lower according to pretest data, the introduction of prior sexual history was not expected to increase the likelihood of acquittal.

It should be noted that such predictions rest on the general expectation of an inverse relationship between defendant guilt and victim consent; that is, the more jurors infer victim consent from the case fact summary, the less likely they were expected to convict the defendant. Conversely, the less jurors infer victim consent, the greater the likelihood of conviction. Unlike cases that are tried under Common Law evidentiary rules, however, where the inference of victim consent is often exacerbated by inflammatory evidence of prior sexual history, the inference of victim consent should be somewhat, perhaps considerably, attenuated by the Moderate Reform rule.

Verdicts in the Radical Reform conditions, which exclude prior sexual history altogether, should reflect victim or defendant bias, depending on the degree of implied consent conveyed by the case fact pattern. In the Low Probability Consent condition, for example, where victim consent is not an issue, the greatest likelihood of conviction was expected. Presumably, jurors will not be able to infer victim consent when there is no prior sexual history evidence available and when the fact pattern itself suggests virtually nothing about the victim's character. In fact, we suspect that prosecutors regard such cases as very strong cases for the complainant (i.e., cases which have a high likelihood of resulting in conviction and which should therefore be prosecuted). It may be that the reportedly higher conviction rates for rape cases are partially attributable to the more likely prosecution of this kind of case. In contrast, we suspect that few prosecutors would bother bringing to trial a case which, in our terms, would be classified as a High Probability Consent case adjudicated under Common Law evidentiary rules (in fact, such cases are usually screened out by the police before they ever reach a prosecutor).

As shown in Figure 8.1, there was a significant main effect for Probability of Consent on certainty of defendant guilt, $F(2, 171) = 9.49, p = .001$. Individual contrasts showed that, as predicted, defendant guilt was more likely in the Low Probability Consent conditions compared with the Ambiguous Probability Consent conditions $[t(118) = -1.83, p < .07]$, but especially more likely when compared with the High Probability Consent conditions $[t(118) = -4.53, p < .0001]$.[15] For this dependent measure there was, however, only a trend effect for type of Exclusionary Rule $[F(2, 171) = 1.67, p = .19, ns]$. As is apparent from Figure 8.1, there was no interaction between Type of Exclusionary Rule and Probability of Consent.

Figure 8.2 shows a somewhat similar pattern of results for jurors' certainty ratings of perceived victim consent. As with certainty of defendant guilt, there was a significant main effect for Probability of Consent on certainty of perceived victim consent $[F(2, 171) = 3.40, p = .04]$. The pattern of individual contrasts was the same as for certainty of guilt. There was also a significant main effect for Type of Exclusionary Rule $[F(2, 171) = 8.79, p = .001]$, and, as expected, jurors were more certain about victim consent in the Common Law conditions than in the Radical Reform conditions $[t(118) = -2.39, p < .02]$. Interestingly, jurors perceived as much victim consent in the Moderate Reform conditions as in the Common Law conditions $[t(118) < 1, ns]$; again, there was no interaction between Type of Exclusionary Rule and Probability of Consent.

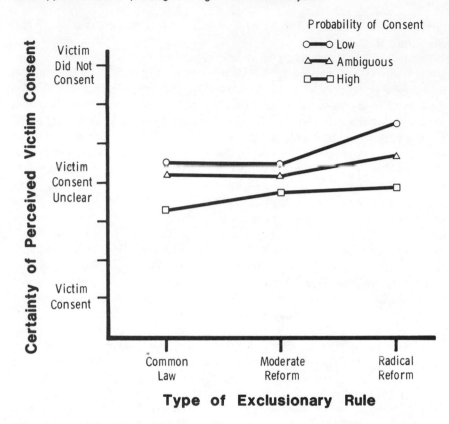

Figure 8.1. Mean juror verdicts as a function of type of exclusionary rule and probability of consent.

The impact of the rape reforms on the likelihood of conviction is, however, perhaps best understood in terms of the distribution of dichotomous juror verdicts displayed in Table 8.2. The overall distribution of dichotomous verdicts, as a function of Type of Exclusionary Rule and Probability of Consent, was highly significant [$\chi^2(8) = 26.67$, p = .0008]. Although this relationship was obtained for male jurors [$\chi^2(8) = 22.08$, p = .005], it was not significant for female jurors [$\chi^2(8) = 11.81$, p = .16, ns]. More important, however, across levels of Probability of Consent, the distribution of juror verdicts for Type of Exclusionary Rule varied significantly [$\chi^2(2) = 6.67$, p = .04]. Whereas the proportion of guilty verdicts was 33 percent for *both* Common Law and Moderate Reform conditions, the proportion of guilty verdicts increased to 53 percent under the Radical Reform exclusionary rule.[16]

Thus it appears to be the case that with a Radical Reform rule, which completely excludes evidence of the victim's prior sexual history with third parties, the likelihood of conviction is increased. It is also the case that with a Radical Reform rule, jurors are more likely to feel that they would have liked additional evidence in order to make a more informed decision. After rendering a verdict, each juror in the present research was asked to indicate whether there was "anything else you feel you would have liked to know about this case in order to make a better decision about it." Open-ended responses were then coded in terms of the frequency and type of evidentiary request.[17]

A 3x3 analysis of variance on the number of additional requests revealed a significant main effect for Type of Exclusionary Rule [F(2, 171)

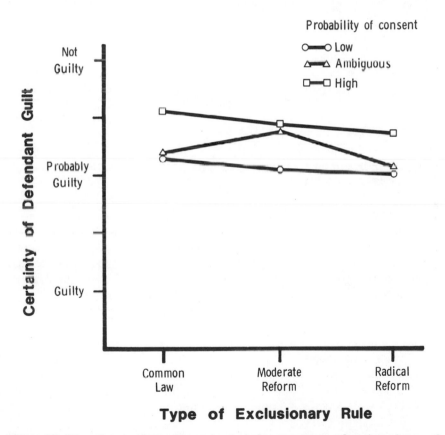

Figure 8.2. Mean juror ratings of perceived victim consent as a function of type of exclusionary rule and probability of consent.

Table 8.2. Dichotomous juror verdicts as a function of Type of Exclusionary Rule and Probability of Consent.[a]

	Common Law		Moderate Reform		Radical Reform	
	Guilty	Not Guilty	Guilty	Not Guilty	Guilty	Not Guilty
Low Probability of Consent	9	11	12	8	13	7
Ambiguous Probability of Consent	8	12	4	16	13	7
High Probability of Consent	3	17	4	16	6	14

[a]$\chi^2(8) = 26.67$, p = .0008

Note. There are eight degrees of freedom because the χ^2 analysis was performed on the distribution of guilty/not guilty verdicts across the nine experimental conditions.

= 7.64, p < .001]. Of the total number of such requests, 24 percent were made in the Common Law conditions, 33 percent in the Moderate Reform conditions, and 43 percent in the Radical Reform conditions. Of those jurors who did *not* request additional evidence, almost twice as many were in the Common Law conditions (47 percent) as in the Radical Reform conditions (26 percent); in other words, jurors in the Common Law conditions were more likely to feel that the evidence presented in the case was sufficient.

The question remains, however, as to whether jurors were more likely to request certain kinds of evidence, particularly in the Radical Reform conditions. Do jurors, for example, disproportionately request evidence of the victim's prior sexual history which was excluded under the Radical Reform rule? First, it should be noted that the most frequent request for additional evidence across Type of Exclusionary Rule was for a more detailed account of the interaction between the victim and the defendant on the night in question (e.g., exactly what the two said to one another, were either intoxicated at the time, etc.). The frequency of this request (23 percent of all requests in Common Law conditions, 22 percent in Moderate Reform conditions, and 26 percent in Radical Reform conditions) undoubtedly reflects the difficulty of deciding a case solely on the basis of a written fact summary.

The next most frequent request for additional evidence was indeed for character and prior sexual history information. Interestingly, regardless of the Type of Exclusionary Rule, jurors more frequently requested such evidence about the defendant than about the victim. As might be expected, this was especially the case in the Common Law conditions, where jurors were much more likely to request further information about the defendant's prior sexual history (21 percent) than about the victim's prior sexual history (2 percent). In the Common Law conditions jurors were, of course, already quite well-informed about the victim's prior sexual history. Jurors may have felt compelled to request comparable information about the defendant, in order to somehow correct for this evidentiary imbalance. In both the Moderate Reform and Radical Reform conditions, however, juror requests for evidence of the victim's prior sexual history and character were five times more frequent than in the Common Law conditions! Thus, not only do jurors in the Radical Reform conditions generally make more requests for additional evidence, but, as the reformist position assumes, they specifically tend to request evidence of the victim's prior sexual history which has been denied them under the Radical Reform rule and, to a lesser extent, under the Moderate Reform rule. In contrast, jurors in the Common Law conditions generally make fewer requests for additional evidence and specifically do not request evidence of the victim's prior sexual history, probably because such evidence is so readily available to them.

As shown in Table 8.2, the distribution of dichotomous verdicts is influenced by Probability of Consent, in addition to the Type of Exclusionary Rule. Across Type of Exclusionary Rule, for example, the distribution of verdicts for Probability of Consent varied significantly [$\chi^2(2) = 15.42$, p = .0004]. As predicted, the proportion of *guilty* verdicts decreased linearly from the Low Probability Consent conditions (57 percent) to the High Probability Consent conditions (22 percent). This trend was the same for male and female jurors; in fact, the correlation between juror certainty of a guilty verdict and perceived consent was −.72, p = .001. [18] Furthermore, it may be seen from Table 8.2 that, as predicted, the lowest conviction rate (15 percent) was obtained under the Common Law when the case fact pattern conveyed High Probability Consent, and it may also be seen that under the Radical Reform law, the lowest conviction rate (30 percent) occurred when the case fact pattern implied High Probability Consent.

In light of the central importance of perceived consent in rape cases, the distribution of dichotomous perceived consent judgments was also examined. Table 8.3 shows that this distribution was indeed significant [$\chi^2(8) = 24.11$, p = .002], though an analysis for sex differences revealed that the relationship is obtained only for male jurors [$\chi^2(8) = 16.89$, p = .03]. This sex difference is clarified upon further partitioning of the overall distribution. Whereas male jurors inferred victim consent regardless of the Type of Exclusionary Rule that was operative [$\chi^2(2)$ = 2.07, ns], female jurors were much *less* likely to infer victim consent, especially under the Radical Reform rule [$\chi^2(2)$ = 5.59, p = .06].[19] That males are more likely to infer victim consent has also been found in research on the social perception of rape victims (e.g., Calhoun, Selby, and Warring, 1976; Cann, Calhoun, and Selby, 1977; Selby, Calhoun, and Brock, 1977). The present research, however, demonstrates that this appears to be the case for male jurors, regardless of the Type of Exclusionary Rule involved. More importantly, though, the proportion of consent judgments displayed in Table 8.3 generally shows that only the Radical Reform rule suppresses the inference of victim consent [$\chi^2(2)$ = 7.03, p = .03] and that the proportion of consent judgments increased from the Low Probability Consent conditions (48 percent) to the High Probability Consent conditions (78 percent), as predicted [$\chi^2(2)$ = 11.63, p = .003].

Finally, the importance of perceived consent was further supported by the results of a least squares, stepwise multiple regression analysis (Nie, et al, 1975) which treated perceived consent, as well as several personality and demographic variables, as predictors of juror certainty of defendant guilt. The demographic predictors were juror age, income, and education. The personality measures were the *Just World Scale* (Rubin and Peplau, 1973, 1975) and a modified version of the *Rape Belief Scale* (Burt, 1978), Cronbach's Alpha = .71 and .55, respectively. Briefly, the Just World Scale was included in order to examine whether a juror who believed strongly in a just world would attribute more blame to a rape victim (i.e.,

Table 8.3. Dichotomous perceived consent judgments as a function of Type of Exclusionary Rule and Probability of Consent.[a]

	Common Law		Moderate Reform		Radical Reform	
	Consent	Non-Consent	Consent	Non-Consent	Consent	Non-Consent
Low Probability of Consent	10	10	13	7	6	14
Ambiguous Probability of Consent	13	7	16	4	9	11
High Probability of Consent	18	2	14	6	15	5

[a]$\chi^2(8)$ = 24.11, p = .002

Note. There are eight degrees of freedom because the χ^2 analysis was performed on the distribution of consent/non-consent judgments across the nine experimental conditions.

the victim somehow deserved her fate) and would therefore be more likely to render an acquittal verdict. The Rape Belief Scale was included in order to examine whether a juror whose belief system incorporated a high number of stereotypical beliefs about rape and sexual assault would be more acquittal prone. The results of the multiple regression analysis were rather striking: The R^2 for perceived consent was .51 [$F(1, 167) = 172.90$, $p < .0001$]. Neither of the personality measures nor any of the demographic variables increased the prediction equation's R^2 by even 1 percent!

CONCLUSIONS

Doob (1976) recently articulated two approaches to psychological research on evidentiary questions in legal contexts. The first approach involves research on a question of interest to the psychologist, which may or may not be of interest to the legal community. The major drawback of this approach is that the researcher most likely does not consider the law of evidence in the original formulation of the problem, thereby limiting the applicability of the findings that are obtained. The second approach to evidentiary questions does, however, consider the law and examines the psycholegal assumptions underlying that law. "The law of evidence and the courts that interpret it, make a lot of assumptions about the way in which a judge or jury will use evidence. The psychologist can try to find out whether these assumptions are reasonable" (Doob, 1976, p. 137). The advantage to this approach is that the evidentiary question is initially framed so that the results are more directly applicable to the legal system.

The analysis of psycholegal assumptions underlying the recent evidentiary reforms in rape laws presented in this chapter is clearly in line with Doob's (1976) second approach to evidentiary questions. Both categories of reform statutes assume, for example, that third party evidence of the victim's prior sexual history will have a prejudicial effect on the outcome of a rape trial. In particular, it is assumed that jurors are overly influenced by such evidence, in that they will be more prone to base their verdicts on judgments about the victim's previous sexual conduct with persons other than the defendant, rather than on judgments about the facts of the particular case. Results from the exploratory study reported in this chapter tend to suggest that only the Radical Reform exclusionary rule (which totally excludes third party prior sexual history evidence when consent is in issue) seems to reduce this prejudice. Relative to a Common Law standard, only the Radical Reform rule increased the proportion of guilty verdicts in a case where forcible rape indeed occurred. The Moderate

Reform rule, in contrast, had no more impact on the conviction rate than the Common Law exclusionary rule.

Similarly, the Radical Reform rule was most effective in reducing potentially prejudicial inferences about implied victim consent, although jurors in the Radical Reform conditions indicated that they would have liked more explicit evidence about the victim's prior sexual history and character. In contrast, jurors in the Moderate Reform conditions perceived as much victim consent as jurors in the Common Law conditions. That the Radical Reform rule seems to curtail the perception of victim consent is especially important in light of the strong, inverse relationship overall between victim consent and defendant guilt, as well as the finding that victim precipitation (cf. Feild, 1978) or perceived consent is the most reliable predictor of juror verdict.

There are nevertheless several evidentiary questions raised by the reforms that are unresolved by the data reported in this chapter. It would be difficult to argue, for example, that the present data address the truly important assumptions of the reformist position concerning how jurors or, for that matter, juries actually utilize third party prior sexual history evidence, and whether they could ever assess such evidence in a non-prejudicial way. Whereas the present data clarify the impact of different types of exclusionary rules on conviction rate, one would have to examine, for example, the content of simulated jury deliberations in order to know to what extent these effects were attributable to prejudicial utilization of prior sexual history evidence. Related to this question is, of course, the thorny problem of determining what exactly constitutes prejudicial utilization in the deliberation process and how jurors ought to process such evidence. A more ecologically valid jury deliberation research strategy (cf. Davis, Bray, and Holt, 1976; Gerbasi, Zuckerman, and Reis, 1977; Kessler, 1975), perhaps based on the design employed in the study reported herein, would provide data more pertinent to these questions.

Finally, further research would be necessary in order to explicate the constitutional status of the Radical Reform rule. The interesting question here is whether the defendant is denied due process of law by the exclusion of evidence, possibly relevant to the issue of consent, which could be evaluated by jurors in a non-prejudicial manner had it been admitted. Recent research in cognitive social psychology, as well as the exploratory study discussed in this chapter, tends to suggest that jurors would not be able to evaluate such evidence non-prejudicially. Should further jury deliberation research support this view, then a convincing argument could be made that the Radical Reforms more effectively vindicate the intent of the reform movement. If, however, the results of such research demonstrated that some of the excluded evidence could have been evaluated properly by jurors, then the argument could be made that the Moderate Reforms should be adopted in order to protect both the rape victim and the constitutional rights of the defendant.

REFERENCES

Berger, V. Man's trial, woman's tribulation: Rape cases in the courtroom. *Columbia Law Review* 77(1):1–101 (1977).

Borgida, E. "Character Testimony in the Law: What Kind of Evidence Is Informative?" Unpublished doctoral dissertation, University of Michigan, 1976.

Borgida, E., and Nisbett, R. E. The differential impact of abstract vs. concrete information on decisions. *Journal of Applied Social Psychology* 7(3):258–271 (1977).

Bower, G. H. Mental imagery and associative learning. In L. Gregg (Ed.), *Cognition in Learning and Memory*. New York: Wiley, 1972.

Burt, M. Attitudes Supportive of Rape in American Culture. Unpublished manuscript, Minnesota Center for Social Research, University of Minnesota. Testimony submitted to the U.S. House of Representatives Committee on Science and Technology, Subcommittee on Domestic and International Scientific Planning, Analysis, and Cooperation, January 3, 1978.

Calhoun, L. G., Selby, J. W., Warring, L. J. Social perception of the victim's causal role in rape: An exploratory examination of four factors. *Human Relations* 29(6):517–526 (1976).

Cann, A., Calhoun, L. G., and Selby, J W. "Sexual Experience as a Factor in Reactions to Rape Victims." Paper presented at the annual meeting of the American Psychological Association, 1977.

Davis, J. H., Bray, R. M., and Holt, R. W. The empirical study of social decision processes in juries. In J. Tapp and F. Levine (Eds.), *Law, Justice, and the Individual in Society: Psychological and Legal Issues*, 326–361. New York: Holt, Rinehart & Winston, 1976.

Doob, A. N. Evidence, procedure, and psychological research. In G. Bermant, C. Nemeth, and N. Vidmar (Eds.), *Psychology and the Law: Research Frontiers*, 135–147. Lexington, Massachusetts: Lexington Books, 1976.

Doob, A. N., and Kirshenbaum, H. M. Some empirical evidence on the effect of s. 12 of the Canada Evidence Act upon an accused. *Criminal Law Quarterly* 15(1):88–95 (1972).

Eisenbud, F. Limitations on the right to introduce evidence pertaining to the prior sexual history of the complaining witness in cases of forcible rape: Reflection of reality or denial of due process? *Hofstra Law Journal* 3:403–426 (1975).

Federal Rules of Evidence for U.S. Courts and Magistrates. St. Paul, Minnesota: West Publishing Co., 1975.

Feild, H. S. Attitudes toward rape: A comparative analysis of police, rapists, crisis counselors, and citizens. *Journal of Personality and Social Psychology* 36(2):156–179 (1978).

Feldman-Summers, S., and Lindner, K. Perceptions of victims and defendants in criminal assault cases. *Criminal Justice and Behavior* 3(2):135–149 (1976).

Frederick, J., and Luginbuhl, J. E. R. "The Accused Rapist: Influence of Penalty Options and Respectability." Paper presented at the annual meeting of the American Psychological Association, 1976.

Gerbasi, K. C., Zuckerman, M., and Reis, H. T. Justice needs a new blindfold: A review of mock jury research. *Psychological Bulletin* 84(2):323–345 (1977).

Hans, V. P., and Doob, A. N. S.12 of the Canada evidence act and the deliberation of simulated juries. *Criminal Law Quarterly* 18:235–253 (1976).

Harris, L. R. Towards a consent standard in the law of rape. *University of Chicago Law Review* 43:613–645 (1976).

Herman, L. What's wrong with the rape reform laws? *Victimology: An International Journal* 8–21 (Spring, 1977).

Jones, C., and Aronson, E. Attribution of fault to a rape victim as a function of respectability of the victim. *Journal of Personality and Social Psychology* 26:415–419 (1973).

Kalven, H., Jr., and Zeisel, H. *The American Jury*. Chicago: The University of Chicago Press, 1966.

Kessler, J. B. The social psychology of jury deliberations. In R. J. Simon (Ed.), *The Jury System in America: A Critical Overview*. Sage Criminal Justice System Annuals, Vol. IV. Beverly Hills, CA: Sage Publications, Inc., 1975.

Klemmack, S. H., and Klemmack, D. L. The social definition of rape. In M. J. Walker, and S. L. Brodsky (Eds.), *Sexual assault*. Lexington, Massachusetts: Lexington Books, 1976.

Landy, D., and Aronson, E. The influence of the character of the criminal and his victim on the decisions of simulated jurors. *Journal of Experimental Social Psychology* 5:141–152 (1969).

LeGrand, C. E. Rape and rape laws: Sexism in society and law. *California Law Review* 61: 919–941 (1973).

McCormick's Handbook of the Law of Evidence. Edited by E. Cleary. St. Paul, Minnesota: West Publishing Co., 1972.

Mathiasen, S. E. The rape victim: A victim of society and the law. *Willamette Law Journal* 11:36–55 (1974).

Nie, N. H., Hull, C. H., Jenkins, J. G., Steinbrenner, K., and Brent, D. H. *Statistical Package for the Social Sciences* (2nd ed.). New York: McGraw-Hill, 1975.

Nisbett, R. E., Borgida, E., Crandall, R., and Reed, H. Popular induction: Information is not always informative. In J. Carroll and J. Payne (Eds.), *Cognition and Social Behavior*. Potomac, Maryland: Erlbaum Associates, 1976.

Note. If she consented once, she consented again—a legal fallacy in forcible rape cases. *Valparaiso Law Review* 10:127–167 (1976).

Price, R. H. The taxonomic classification of behaviors and situations and the problem of behavior-environment congruence. *Human Relations* 27(6): 567–585 (1974).

Price, R. H., and Bouffard, D. L. Behavioral appropriateness and situational constraint as dimensions of social behavior. *Journal of Personality and Social Psychology* 30:579–586 (1974).

Robin, G. D. Forcible rape: Institutionalized sexism in the criminal justice system. *Crime and Delinquency* 136–153 (April, 1977).

Ross, L. The intuitive psychologist and his shortcomings: Distortions in the attribution process. In L. Berkowitz (Ed.), *Advances in Experimental Social Psychology*, Vol. 10. New York: Academic Press, 1977.

Rubin, Z., and Peplau, L. A. Belief in a just world and reactions to another's lot: A study of participants in the national draft lottery. *Journal of Social Issues* 29(4):73–93 (1973).

Rubin, Z., and Peplau, L. A. Who believes in a just world? *Journal of Social Issues* 31(3):65–89 (1975).

Scroggs, J. R. Penalties for rape as a function of victim provocativeness, damage, and resistance. *Journal of Applied Social Psychology* 6(4):360–368 (1976).

Selby, J. W., Calhoun, L. G., and Brock, T. A. Sex differences in the social perception of rape victims. *Personality and Social Psychology Bulletin* 3:412–415 (1977).

Stephan, C. Selective characteristics of jurors and litigants: Their influences on juries' verdicts. In R. J. Simon (Ed.), *The Jury System in America: A Critical Overview*. Sage Criminal Justice System Annuals, Vol. IV. Beverly Hills, CA: Sage Publications, 1975.

FOOTNOTES TO CHAPTER 8

[1]The "law of rape" is used here to refer not only to the definition of the crime, but also to the laws of evidence which govern proof in a rape trial. The criticism of the definitional principles of rape, while often quite perceptive, see Note, Recent Statutory Developments in the Definition of Forcible Rape, 61, Va. L. Rev. 1500 (1976), is not so widespread as criticism of the evidentiary principles governing proof, perhaps because the impact of these latter principles on the victim and upon the outcome of the prosecution is so much more obvious.

[2]The corroboration rule precludes a conviction for rape on the testimony of the victim alone without some other evidence which corroborates her testimony that she was raped. Many jurisdictions permit rather attenuated facts to serve as corroboration, and still others have abolished the requirement altogether. See Note, The Rape Corroboration Requirement: Repeal not Reform 81 Yale L. J. 1365 (1972); Note, Corroborating Changes of Rape, 67 Colum. L. Rev. 1137 (1967).

[3]As a result of recent court decisions, this instruction is no longer required in some jurisdictions. See 123 Cal. Rptr. 119, 538 P.2d 247, 252 (1975).

[4]In cases of statutory rape or in cases where the defense is that the event never occurred (fabrication defense) or where the defense claims that the defendant was not the assailant (mistaken identity defense) the issue of consent may never be raised.

[5]Much has been written about the need for some uniform standard of consent. Various criminal statutes use the phrases "against her will," "by force," and "without her consent" without clearly defining the standards to be met. In some jurisdictions, a woman who passively submits to a sexual assault has consented or at least has not been taken "against her will." Some courts have interpreted "by force" to mean that physical violence is an essential element of the crime; others have argued that resistance should be considered an essential element in addition to force and non-consent (Harris, 1976; LeGrand, 1973; Robin, 1977).

[6]There is one other circumstance in which the admission of evidence of the victim's unchastity is non-controversial. If the prosecution attempts affirmatively to prove that the complainant is a woman of chaste character, the defense may counter with character evidence tending to prove the opposite.

[7]Evidence of a person's prior conduct is generally inadmissible in contexts other than rape

prosecutions, when it is offered to show that the person acted similarly on another occasion. Such evidence is only admitted when it shows habitual, as opposed to isolated incidents of behavior, or where it reveals some peculiarity or characteristic which ties the person to the act performed.

[8]Evidence which is likely to be considered material to a fact in issue (other than consent) may refer to the complainant's sexual relations with another person on the day of the alleged rape to show source of semen, pregnancy, or disease.

[9]Statutes in the latter category state a general exclusion of evidence of the victim's prior sexual history and then list exceptions, such as past sexual conduct with the defendant to show the source of semen, pregnancy, or disease. If the list of exceptions does not include admission for the purpose of showing consent, the statute is classified in the Radical Reform category.

[10]Kalven and Zeisel, in their classic book on *The American Jury* (1966), attribute the gross judge-jury disagreement in the verdict in rape trials to the inability of jurors to avoid the second pitfall.

[11]Hitchhiking is a good example of this point. A Louis Harris survey of a national sample of 1,536 adult respondents recently reported that 79 percent of those polled believe that "any woman who hitchhikes alone can expect to run the risk of having a man driving a car try to have sex with her or even rape her" (*Minneapolis Star,* October 24, 1977, p. 8b). Judge Compton of the Second District Court of Appeal in California apparently shares this assumption that a female hitchhiker has sex and not a ride in mind. Although Compton and his colleagues later changed the inflammatory wording, they overturned the 1977 rape conviction of Clifford Hunt in a decision which strongly suggested that a woman who goes out alone and tries to hitch a ride is asking to be raped (*Washington Star,* November 10, 1977).

[12]The modal juror in the sample was a white (77.2 percent), married (54.4 percent), relatively young (39.5 percent of the jurors were less than thirty years old), high school graduate with some college (33.3 percent), whose yearly income from a non-professional occupation was between $15,000 and $19,999.

[13]The low probability implied consent fact pattern was rated as conveying low probability victim consent and was associated with a greater likelihood of conviction. The ambiguous implied consent fact pattern was rated as conveying ambiguous victim consent, and there was no significant correlation between implied consent and verdict. Finally, a high probability consent situation was rated as conveying high probability victim consent and was associated with a greater likelihood of acquittal. The range of scores on both the verdict and consent scales was, however, somewhat clustered around mid-scale, ranging from probably guilty of rape to probably not guilty. Similarly, pretest ratings of the likelihood of victim consent, given knowledge of either form of prior sexual history evidence, revealed scores that were clustered toward the "consent extremely likely" end of the scale.

[14]This particular example of prior sexual history evidence probably would be admissible under the Common Law, as well. Its admissibility under the Moderate Reform is, however, consistent with those Moderate Reform statutes (e.g., Minnesota) which might admit such inflammatory evidence on the basis of a "common plan, scheme, or design" criterion at the judge's discretion. "Common plan, scheme, or design" would justify the admission of testimony about a repetitive pattern of factual circumstances that was similar to the fact pattern in question. Thus, as the restricted range of pretest ratings suggests, the present operationalization of the Common Law and Moderate Reform categories represents a rather stringent test of the hypothesis.

[15]All p values for the contrasts are based on two-tailed tests.

[16]An identical proportion of guilty verdicts for Common Law and Moderate Reform conditions in this case only underscores the point made in footnote 15 that the present operationalization of Common Law and Moderate Reform indeed constitutes a rigorous test of the hypothesis.

[17]There were ten categories in this coding scheme: none (juror specifically requests no additional evidence); non-specific requests (e.g., "I need more information"); resistance evidence; dispositional information (e.g., appearance, demeanor, age, marital status, etc.); situational information (time, place); corroboration of act; nature of interaction between

victim and defendant (e.g., intoxication, threats, conversation); relationship between victim and defendant prior to the occasion in question; character of defendant and his prior sexual history; character of victim and her prior sexual history. Intercoder reliability, based on percentage agreement between two coders, was 87 percent.

[18]It could be argued that this zero order correlation between perceived consent and certainty of defendant guilt was artifactually inflated by the relationship between Probability of Consent as an independent variable and perceived consent as a dependent measure. A MANOVA (Nie, et al, 1975) was therefore conducted in order to control for the effects of Probability of Consent. The average within cell correlation between perceived consent and certainty of defendant guilt was nevertheless substantive ($r = -.68$).

[19]It appears that male jurors are much more willing to infer victim consent when the case involves a High Probability fact pattern. For males, the inference of consent increases from 55 percent in the Low Probability of Consent conditions to a striking 93 percent in the High Probability of Consent conditions [$\chi^2(2) = 11.48$, $p = .003$]; for female jurors, this trend is not even significant [$\chi^2(2) = 3.55$, $p = .17$, ns].

9

Neighborhood Justice Centers as Mechanisms for Dispute Resolution

Daniel McGillis

In a recent address to legal scholars, Sander (1976) noted that in considering dispute processing, adjudication is "the one process that so instinctively comes to the legal mind that I suspect if we asked a random group of law students how a particular dispute might be resolved, they would invariably say 'file a complaint in the appropriate court' " (p. 114–5). A similar response might be anticipated from many social scientists, and Abel (1977) has noted that social science scholarship often follows the lead of legal scholarship in this area and focuses upon the courts as mechanisms for dispute resolution. This observation is supported by recent reviews of psychological research on legal issues. Shaver, Gilbert, and Williams (1975) have noted the prevalence of jury research in psychology and point out that, "without diminishing the value of jury research, we contend that social psychology ought to address itself to other issues as well" (p. 472). Similarly, Tapp (1976) has highlighted the prevalence of jury research in her review of research on law and psychology in the *Annual Review of Psychology*. Tapp notes, "Among psychologists concerned with social behavior perhaps the oldest, best known, and continuous work has been in jury research" (p. 388).

This research was supported under contract number J–LEAA–030–76 awarded to Abt Associates, Cambridge, Massachusetts. Points of view or opinions stated in this document are those of the author and do not necessarily represent the official position or policies of the U.S. Department of Justice. A detailed report on the project was submitted to the Department of Justice with the title *Neighborhood Justice Centers: An Analysis of Potential Models,* and parts of this chapter are drawn from the Justice Department report.

The stress upon the courts in psychological research on dispute processing is understandable. The United States is known for its heavy reliance upon the courts, and Johnson, et al. (1977) estimate that approximately 5,000 new civil cases are initiated each year for every 100,000 Americans, in comparison to such rates as 307 per 100,000 population in Norway and 493 per 100,000 population in Finland (see Sarat and Grossman, 1975). Despite the prevalence of court actions, the vast bulk of disputes in the United States are processed more informally through such means as negotiation, conciliation, and mediation (Galanter, 1974). These processes are employed by citizens to settle disputes in the course of everyday life, and, more recently, governmental and private agencies have developed projects which provide services, such as conciliation, mediation, and arbitration as alternatives to court processing. This chapter will provide a discussion of the problems with court case processing, review available dispute processing techniques, cite major recommendations for new dispute processing forums, describe experimental Neighborhood Justice Center projects which process disputes by means of such techniques as mediation and arbitration, and suggest potential contributions of psychological research to the development of dispute resolution mechanisms.

CURRENT PROBLEMS IN AMERICAN COURT CASE PROCESSING

The heavy U.S. reliance on the courts for the resolution of disputes and concomitant difficulties experienced by the courts in handling their large caseloads has resulted in an extensive reexamination of the appropriate role of the courts in dispute processing. The courts' problems in case processing are strongly evidenced in the extreme delays typical in the processing of both criminal and civil cases. For example, personal injury cases often take over four years to process in such cities as Boston, Chicago, New York (the Bronx) and Philadelphia (Johnson et al. 1977), and many criminal cases also require extended periods of time.

Discussions of court problems in dispute processing typically stress: 1) *problems of delay,* such as those cited above; 2) *limited access to the courts,* due to the high costs resulting from legal fees, lost wages while attending court sessions, court fees, etc.; 3) *inefficiency due to high dismissal rates* (e.g., over 40% of cases involving felony charges were dismissed in the New York courts in 1971). This inefficiency results in high costs to society for the partial processing of cases, and 4) *logical limitations in the use of adjudication.* Fuller (1963, 1971) has argued persuasively that many cases are simply not suited to the decision making style of adjudication. Adjudication is best suited for issues which can be resolved by a yes-no or more-less decision. Many conflicts do not conveniently array themselves on such dimensions but are rather "polycentric", i.e., many centered; for example, a long-standing dispute between two neighbors might involve a very large number of real and imagined offenses committed by both parties. A current offense can only be understood in light of the prior relationships of the disputants, and forms of dispute processing, such as mediation and arbitration, lend themselves to the exploration of these relationships, and the development of a settlement which takes the reciprocal nature of the dispute into account. The winner-takes-all approach, or adjudication, is not well suited for such compromise settlements.

A recent study of criminal court processing in New York by the Vera Institute of Justice entitled *Felony Arrests: Their Prosecution and Disposition in New York City's Courts* highlights how many of these problems interact in the criminal courts. The authors point out:

> Because our society has not found adequate alternatives to arrest and adjudication in coping with interpersonal anger publicly expressed, we pay a price. The price includes large court caseloads, long delays in processing and, ultimately, high dismissal rates. These impose high financial costs on taxpayers and high personal costs on defendants and their families. The public pays in another way, too: The congestion and drain on resources caused by an excessive number of such cases in the courts weakens the ability of the criminal justice system to deal quickly and decisively with the "real" felons, who may be getting lost in the shuffle. The risk that they will be returned to the street increases, as does the danger to law-abiding citizens on whom they prey. (Vera Institute, 1977, p. xv.)

The Vera researchers note that in 56 percent of all felony arrests for crimes against the person, the victim had a prior relationship with the defendant. Eighty-seven percent of these cases, in turn, resulted in dismissals due to complainant noncooperation with the prosecution, compared to only 29 percent of the cases involving strangers. Complainants in such cases are simply not interested in having the defendant prosecuted once they have cooled off, and the Vera report strongly recommends the use of Neighborhood Justice Centers rather than the courts to process the vast majority of prior relationship cases. *Neighborhood justice centers* are defined by the American Bar Association Pound Conference Report (1977) as "facilities . . . designed to make available a variety of methods for processing disputes, including arbitration, mediation, referral to small claims courts, as well as referral to courts of general jurisdiction."

Many groups have joined in the debate regarding the court's role in dispute processing. The American Bar Association is investigating alternatives to current dispute resolution techniques and has established a Committee on the Resolution of Minor Disputes. This committee is extending the proposals of the National Conference on the Causes of Popular Dissatisfaction with the Administration of Justice (the Pound Conference), which was co-sponsored by the ABA, the Judicial Conference of the United States, and the Conference of Chief Justices. Among the issues being promoted by the ABA are the development of neighborhood justice centers, revitalization of small claims courts, and the increased use of compulsory arbitration in the processing of disputes. The House Judiciary Subcommittee on Courts, Civil Liberties and the Administration of Justice chaired by Robert Kastenmeier has recently held hearings to explore new proposals for the courts. Senator Edward M. Kennedy has submitted legislation (S.957) to provide 18 million dollars per year for research and the development of alternative dispute resolution projects. The U.S. Department of Justice has developed an Office for Improvements in the Administration of Justice which has as its mandate the development of new alternative procedures to court processing, as well as the improvement of current mechanisms, and the National Institute of Law Enforcement and Criminal Justice has funded several recent research studies on alternative dispute resolution mechanisms.

Chief Justice Burger has aptly summarized the spirit of the current reappraisal of the courts in noting, "It is time, therefore, to ask ourselves whether the tools of procedure, the methods of judicial process that developed slowly through the evolution of common law, and were fitted to a rural, agrarian society, are entirely suited, without change, to the complex, modern society of the late 20th and the 21st centuries."

OVERVIEW OF AVAILABLE DISPUTE PROCESSING TECHNIQUES

Societies tend to differ in their patterns of use of various dispute processing mechanisms. Some societies rely heavily upon the formal adjudication of disputes, while others strongly prefer informally negotiated or mediated settlements of disputes. Despite differences in preferences among the dispute processing mechanisms, virtually all societies provide their citizens with a range of options for action when confronted with a dispute.

Table 9.1 presents a summary of the range of U.S. dispute processing mechanisms. The options are divided into three primary categories: Category 1 includes unilateral actions on the part of a single disputant, such as inaction, active avoidance of the other disputant, and self-help to eliminate the perceived deficit caused by the dispute; category 2 includes dyadic options involving contacts between the disputing parties. Coercion is one form of dyadic option and has been defined by Koch, Sodergren, and Campbell (1976) as the threat or use of force whereby "one principal

Table 9.1. Dispute processing options.

1. Unilateral Actions on the Part of a Disputant
   A. Inaction
   B. Active Avoidance (move, terminate relationship, etc.)
   C. Self-Help

2. Dyadic Options—Contacts Between the Disputing Parties
   A. Coercion (threats and use of force)
   B. Negotiation

3. Third Party Resolution Techniques
   A. Conciliation (bringing parties together for negotiation)
   B. Mediation (structured communication, recommendations)
   C. Arbitration
   D. Fact-Finding
   E. Administrative Procedures
   F. Adjudication

imposes the outcome of a dispute and alone determines his concession, if any, to the opponent." Koch, et al. (1976) have discussed a number of cultures in which coercion appears to be the primary method of dispute resolution; the use of coercion presupposes that the disputant can credibly threaten or force the opponent into compliance. Many disputes escalate when one disputant unsuccessfully threatens the other disputant and in turn provokes a counter threat. This property of coercion makes it a particularly risky strategy, sowing the seeds of even greater disputes in the attempt to resolve the present dispute.

Negotiation on the other hand involves an attempt by the two disputing parties to arrive at a settlement by means of discussion and bilateral agreement. The disputants communicate their perceptions of the disputed issue to one another and, if possible, develop a settlement to the dispute that is satisfactory to both parties. Compromises are the essence of negotiation, and each party is expected to have an interest in arriving at a mutually acceptable resolution to the dispute. Galanter (1974) notes that negotiation is particularly likely to occur within relationships involving mutual dependence (e.g., husband-wife, purchaser-supplier, landlord-tenant, etc.), because "a capacity to sanction is built into the relationship." Relationships among more independent entities (e.g., businesses in a given industry, casual acquaintances, etc.) tend to require the development of sanction systems operated by third parties, because "the parties have little capacity to sanction the deviant directly." Negotiated settlements can pave the way for common perceptions of a given situation and hopefully forestall future disputes. This property tends to make negotiation superior to the various, unilateral dispute processing options cited earlier.

Category 3 includes the various third party intervention techniques. Conciliation involves a very limited role for the third party, whereby the party simply attempts to encourage negotiation among the disputing parties. This encouragement can involve the conciliator serving, for example, as a "go-between" in communications among the parties and providing a place for the negotiations to take place. Conciliation in its pure form is likely to be relatively rare, because conciliators are often likely to be asked for advice on settlement of the dispute or to offer advice spontaneously. This form of active assistance in structuring the communication or offering recommended settlements results in the conciliator becoming a mediator. Because of the close gradation between conciliation and mediation, many scholars (e.g., Sander, 1976; Galanter, 1975) have chosen to treat conciliation and mediation as roughly interchangeable tactics. The two processes are discussed separately here, because it is likely that at least in close-knit groups (families, clubs, etc.), a substantial amount of pure conciliation still occurs. An individual who is close to both parties in the dispute may not wish to risk alienating either party by becoming actively involved in the dispute and yet may work hard to ensure that negotiations occur. This facilitative role provides an interesting intermediate conflict resolution tactic between negotiation and mediation.

Mediation involves the active participation of the third party in the processing of a dispute. This participation can range from minor involvement, where an individual who is essentially a conciliator offers some advice to the disputants regarding a possible resolution, to highly structured interaction with the disputants. Some organizations which attempt to mediate disputes adhere to detailed procedures, whereby the two parties meet together and discuss their perceptions in turn, then leave the room while the mediators formulate a plan for further mediation, then return to the room separately to discuss the issues in individual caucuses and finally meet together again, hopefully to achieve a resolution of the matter at hand. By definition, mediators do not have the power to compel a resolution but must rely upon the mutual agreement of the disputants. Numerous projects have been developed across the country to provide mediational services to disputants. Some of these projects serve a broad spectrum of the population and mediate a wide range of matters; others serve a similar range of people but limit themselves to highly specific disputes (consumer projects, warranty programs); still others provide services to a limited spectrum of the population but on a wide range of matters (e.g., Chinese and Jewish community mediation boards); and some projects serve both a small group of people and deal with only a limited range of issues (e.g., institutional grievance programs).

In contrast to mediation, arbitration involves a third party decision regarding the matter in dispute. The decision is typically backed by sanctions and is thus termed "binding" arbitration, although "nonbinding" arbitration, where the arbitrator's decision is merely advisory, also occurs in some settings. Some dispute processing procedures treat arbitration as the method of last resort and precede arbitration efforts with informal resolution attempts and mediation hearings. Other projects which limit themselves to arbitration hearings incorporate mediation as the initial phase of the hearings. An attempt is made to have the disputants develop an agreement which can be converted into a binding arbitrator's award for the purposes of enforcement. If the mediation attempt fails, then the arbitrator is empowered to render a binding decision which imposes conditions upon the disputing parties. Disputants may become involved in arbitration through a number of means, including voluntary submission to arbitration, contractual agreement that all relevant disputes will be processed by arbitration, and compulsory arbitration as an adjunct to the courts. Numerous types of arbitration projects have been developed. Some of the projects are similar to the general mediational projects discussed earlier—processing a wide range of disputes for the general public—but using arbitration rather than mediation. Participation in these programs is voluntary. Other projects are attached to small claims courts and either request or compel civil disputants with claims within a given range to submit their disputes to arbitration. Many consumer projects employ arbitration as a last resort procedure, with participation generally being voluntary for the consumer and highly recommended or compelled for the merchant. Contractually based arbitration is common in business, either as part of labor management disputes or as part of contractual agreements between business firms.

Fact-finding involves a third party judgment of the merits of a dispute following an investigation of the matter in controversy. The fact-finder typically lacks coercive power to enforce a settlement to the dispute but often derives authority from his neutral position which lends persuasive power to his finding. Some fact-finding inquiries involve the conduct of hearings where the disputants can present their positions. These hearings differ from mediation in that the parties anticipate a judgment of the issues on the part of the fact-finder. Hearings in which both parties are simultaneously present to present their positions resemble nonbinding arbitration. Fact-finding inquiries often involve very limited contacts with the parties, however (e.g., phone conversations, letters, etc.), as in the case of newspaper action-lines, and these cases are very clearly distinguishable from the various forms of mediation and arbitration.

Administrative procedures are dispute processing techniques which are highly dependent upon judicial functioning and yet fall short of the full-dress adjudication of a dispute. These processes range from settlement arranged out of court by attorneys and yet closely oriented to the court process, to processes informally conducted by court officials (e.g., plea bargaining), to the routine forms of administrative processing of simple offenses, such as traffic violations. In addition, some recent reforms have attempted to alter standard adjudicatory procedures in some areas by either reducing the need for adjudication (e.g., decriminalization) or making adjudication simpler.

Adjudication conducted by a judge in a court of law is our most formal dispute resolving mechanism. The judge represents the state and possesses the coercive power associated with such a position. Elaborate rules and procedures strictly limit the types of information presented in court and the order in which information is presented. Many of the processes discussed earlier are similar to formal adjudication; for example, a fact-finder may proceed in a fashion similar to an adjudicator but will lack coercive power to enforce his recommended settlement. An arbitrator has coercive power but typically differs from a judicial adjudicator in that he is not a government salaried employee, often sits on a panel of two or more arbitrators, uses relatively informal procedures, rules of evidence, etc., and may focus in detail on the underlying relationship and attempt to mediate a settlement. Arbitrator's decisions may typically be appealed for a *trial de novo,* if the arbitration is compulsory. Participation in arbitration is often voluntary, either at the time of the dispute or by consent, when a contract is initially developed. Numerous courts in the United States adjudicate disputes, including the panoply of lower, upper, and appellate criminal courts, the various civil courts, juvenile courts, and courts with specialized jurisdictions, such as landlord-tenant courts.

MAJOR RECOMMENDATIONS FOR NEW DISPUTE PROCESSING FORUMS

Given the wide array of potential dispute processing mechanisms reviewed above, it is necessary to consider which techniques, or combinations of techniques, might best serve the needs of individual communities. Recent proposals have suggested widely differing forums for processing minor civil and criminal disputes. These proposals differ both in the services recommended and the degree of coercion of disputants considered appropriate. Danzig (1973) has proposed an essentially non-coercive forum; Fisher (1975) recommends a highly coercive forum; and Sander (1976) has suggested the development of programs using a variety of techniques intermediate in their level of coercion of disputants. Each of these proposals will be reviewed briefly, and further refinements recommended by the Pound Conference Task Force and the U.S. Department of Justice will be noted.

Minimal Coercion of Disputants—Danzig's Community Moots

Danzig (1973) has recommended the decentralization of dispute processing through the development of "community moots." These programs would be similar in many respects to the "tribal moots" common in Liberia and would stress the mediation and conciliation of disputes in informal settings. Danzig (1973) feels that many types of cases would be appropriate for this form of processing, including "family disputes, some marital issues (e.g., paternity, support, separation), juvenile delinquency, landlord-tenant relations, small torts and breaches of contract involving only community members, and misdemeanors affecting only community members." Danzig notes that many criminal cases are dismissed because disputants decide that they do not want to involve acquaintances in the criminal courts, and many civil proceedings are avoided because the parties are "too ignorant, fearful, or impoverished to turn to small claims courts, legal aid, or similar institutions." Community moots could reduce or eliminate these difficulties with traditional criminal and civil case processes.

Danzig (1973) stresses that community moot projects could vary, depending on community needs, but that a promising possibility would simply involve the employment of a counselor familiar with the neighborhood. The counselor could accept referrals from such sources as social agencies, the police, courts and individuals and schedule sessions convenient to the disputing parties (e.g., at the home of a disputant, if both parties agree to the location). At the moot sessions, the disputing parties and any individuals they brought with them could discuss the matter of controversy and attempt to arrive at a settlement with the assistance of the counselor. If a disputant refused to attend the session, the complainant would of course be free to proceed with normal court processing.

Danzig stresses that the counselor should not have coercive power, but rather the community itself can potentially bring pressure to bear upon disputants for maintaining agreements. This community impact upon the disputants would be maximized if a range of community members participated in the actual moot session. Danzig (1973) cites the example of a dispute between a teenage loiterer and a shopkeeper that might be effectively resolved to the benefit of the whole community by the presence at the moot of the teenager, his friends, the shopkeeper, his family and employees and other shopkeepers. Presumably, the counselor would insure that all parties were allowed to communicate their positions fully, and the discussion of the case at hand might serve to reduce tensions generally in the community rather than to increase them, as often occurs in court cases. Felstiner (1974) has criticized the notion of community moots as being virtually unworkable in a complex, atomistic society such as ours, and Danzig and Lowy (1975) have provided an interesting rejoinder to Felstiner's criticism. The newly developing San Francisco Community Board Program is similar, in many respects, to Danzig's community moot concept.

High Coercion of Disputants—Fisher's Community Courts

In contrast to Danzig's non-coercive model for a neighborhood justice program, Fisher (1975) recommends that "community courts" be provided by the legislature with exclusive jurisdiction over certain minor disputes and have the authority to impose sanctions when necessary. Fisher (1975) notes that Danzig's proposal for conciliation is admirable but unlikely to work unless the project has the credibility that comes with coercive power. A community court could function in relatively small communities, such as an apartment complex, and be composed of three to five community members elected periodically. Lawyers would be excluded from participating as judges because of their potential undue influence on the other judges on the panel. The elected judges would be required to "undergo minimal formal training" and could have an attorney as an advisor when legal questions arose. Sanctions which might be available to a community court could range from demands for restitution on the part of the guilty part, to "deprivations from enjoyment of certain community property," such as recreational facilities, to eviction from the community. The formal courts would be employed as the enforcement apparatus when necessary. Fisher stresses that the hearings should be open to the public and scheduled at convenient times. Disputants would be permitted the right of appeal to the formal courts, if abuses of due process were perceived by a disputant. In support of his proposal, Fisher (1975) cites the successful operations of various university, labor union, and prison disciplinary mechanisms, as well as various socialist programs, such as Soviet Comrades' Courts.

Little imagination is required to envision Fisher's community courts readily declining into the legendary forums often associated with Australian marsupials. Narrow community groups might find themselves quite capable of unfairly sanctioning individuals who deviate from them, and the recourse to court appeal for abuses by the community court might be available only in theory to poor, uninformed members of the community. Fisher's extrapolation from the highly limited settings of university and prison projects to the general society seem very strained, and the vast differences between the various socialist societies and American law and society make the socialist examples equally uncompelling.

An Intermediate Approach—Sander's Dispute Resolution Centers

Sander (1976) has recommended the development of programs which would include a range of dispute processing mechanisms. These *Dispute Resolution Centers* would be operated by the government and would screen cases into various processes or sequences of processes, including mediation, arbitration, and fact-finding. If necessary, cases would be referred to the courts for adjudication.

The dispute resolution centers would provide an intermediate option between the non-coercive community moots recommended by Danzig and the highly coercive community courts proposed by Fisher. The mediation services of the dispute resolution centers would presumably be similar to community moots in many respects but would differ in that the center would be a government agency with close ties to the courts and could also provide binding arbitration when mediation failed. These characteristics would be likely to make the dispute resolution center's mediation services a more credible option than those provided by the community moots. In Sander's model the courts would retain the power of adjudication and would not transfer this coercive authority to another forum, as in the case of Fisher's community courts. The binding arbitration services offered by the dispute resolution center would presumably be voluntary and would typically be offered only after attempts to mediate a dispute. If compulsory arbitration were employed, disputants would be provided with the privilege of a *trial de novo* to appeal the arbitration. The fact-finding services of the dispute resolution centers would provide a valuable supplement to the other dispute processing options and neither Danzig's nor Fisher's model include such a component.

The general mediation and arbitration projects illustrate how isolated components of the dispute resolution centers could operate. Mediation projects in Columbus and Miami are operated by the local prosecutors' offices and demonstrate the possibilities for running mediational programs in official justice agencies. New York and Rochester arbitration projects are sponsored by independent organizations but have close ties to their local courts. A dispute resolution center would presumably bring such programs under one roof with unitary sponsorship and supplement them with related dispute processing mechanisms such as ombudsman services.

Pound Task Force's Neighborhood Justice Centers

The National Conference on the Causes of Popular Dissatisfaction with the Administration of Justice (the Pound Conference) was held in 1976 under the joint sponsorship of the American Bar Association, the Judicial Conference of the United States, and the Conference of Chief Justices. President Walsh of the ABA subsequently appointed a Task Force to insure that the reforms discussed at the conference would be carefully considered. The Task Force was chaired by Griffin Bell and produced recommendations in its *Report of the Pound Conference Follow-up Task Force.*

A central recommendation was for the development of *neighborhood justice centers,* defined as facilities which would "make available a variety of methods for processing disputes, including arbitration, mediation, referral to small claims courts, and referral to courts of general jurisdiction." Both civil and criminal matters would be appropriate for such an alternative forum. The Task Force did not recommend a unitary model for such a forum but stressed the need for the flexible adaptation of such programs to local conditions. The aim of the Task Force recommendation was to "stimulate experimentation, evaluation, and widespread emulation of successful programs."

Neighborhood Justice Center Program of the Department of Justice

The U.S. Department of Justice has recently initiated a program to develop experimental neighborhood justice centers in three communities (Atlanta, Kansas City, and Los Angeles). The program was developed jointly by the National Institute of Law Enforcement and Criminal Justice, research arm of the Law Enforcement Assistance Administration, and by the newly formed Office for Improvements in the Administration of Justice, headed by Assistant Attorney General Daniel Meador. As in the case of the ABA recommendations, the Department of Justice acknowledges the need for individual communities to tailor programs in line with their local needs. The Department has recommended that the programs incorporate both mediation and arbitration, use community members as hearing officers, actively refer disputants to social service agencies and appropriate courts when necessary, and process both minor civil and criminal cases. The Department intends to encourage the independent development of similar projects by communities across the country. The neighborhood justice centers being developed by the Department of Justice come closest to being variants of the dispute resolution centers recommended by Sander (1976), in contrast to Danzig's community moots and Fisher's community courts.

Neighborhood justice centers can employ any of the non-adjudicatory third party dispute resolution techniques outlined in Table 9.1 and discussed in the preceding text. These approaches include: conciliation, mediation, arbitration, fact-finding, and the informal court oriented processing listed under "administrative procedures," where compromises are encouraged in light of impending adversary proceedings. Sander (1976) has recommended that the whole panoply of dispute processing mechanisms be housed together and that screening staff allocate incoming disputants to specific processes or sequences of processes (e.g., mediation followed by arbitration if necessary). This recommendation seems sound. Clearly, this type of thorough restructuring of the way in which we process disputes cannot be accomplished overnight. The Department of Justice's pilot projects, incorporating mediation and arbitration for the processing of disputes, will provide a valuable first step toward the development of a comprehensive and highly integrated dispute processing mechanism suitable to the widely varying types of disputes which occur in society.

Although the unilateral and dyadic approaches to dispute processing cited earlier are under the control of the individual disputants rather than third party forums, neighborhood justice centers can provide a valuable service in teaching disputants how to use these informal techniques for dispute processing. Many disputes could be successfully resolved without the need for third party intervention, if disputants first attempted to use constructive unilateral and dyadic approaches, such as careful consideration of whether the dispute is justified, attempts at negotiation, etc. Mediational sessions at the neighborhood justice centers can provide disputants with valuable experience in negotiating differences in order to arrive at a compromise. Neighborhood justice center staff should receive training in methods of educating disputants to resolve disputes independently. Hopefully, the centers could serve both to resolve immediate conflicts and also to teach citizens how to avoid the need for official third party intervention in the resolution of future conflicts.

CHARACTERISTICS OF CURRENT EXPERIMENTAL NEIGHBORHOOD JUSTICE CENTERS

A number of projects have been developed in recent years which are similar in many respects to the broad definition of neighborhood justice centers. These projects provide a forum for the resolution of minor disputes as an alternative to arrest or formal court action. In addition to arbitration, mediation, and referral to the courts, the projects often employ social work staff, make referrals to social service agencies, and conduct fact-finding and related functions. Virtually all of these projects are of very recent origin: The Columbus Night Prosecutor Program, the forebear of many of the current projects, was only established in 1971; similarly, the pioneering work of the American Arbitration Association and the Institute for Mediation and Conflict Resolution in applying labor-management conflict resolution techniques to citizen dispute resolution is a recent innovation.

As part of a study I conducted for the Department of Justice, a sample of dispute processing projects was selected which spanned the range of resolution techniques, referral sources, organizational affiliations, and mediation staff characteristics. These projects were studied in detail. Project selection was based on a review of the characteristics of a variety of projects across the country and discussions with leaders in the field of dispute resolution regarding the range of projects which might represent the currently available models.

The six projects selected for intensive review were:

A. The Boston Urban Court Project;
B. The Columbus Night Prosecutor Program;
D. The Miami Citizen Dispute Settlement Program;
D. The New York Institute for Mediation and Conflict Resolution Dispute Center;
E. The Rochester American Arbitration Association Community Dispute Services Project;
F. The San Francisco Community Board Program.

All of the projects were visited during May of 1977, except for the San Francisco project, which was still in the developmental phase at the time of the study and had not begun to process cases. Prior to project site visits, descriptive materials regarding the projects were requested from the project directors. Materials received included grant proposals, annual and quarterly reports, evaluative studies, media accounts of the projects' achievements, and concept papers. A project survey instrument was developed which included: questions regarding the nature and size of the community; project start-up including questions on initial development, grant processing, and early implementation; case criteria; referral sources; resolution techniques; hearing staff qualifications; follow-up procedures; project organization; staff training; costs; evaluation; and general recommendations of the project regarding models for neighborhood justice centers.

During the site visits, efforts were made to observe the various components of the project in operation. In many cases, representatives of the projects' referral sources were interviewed, visits were made to the local courts, prosecutors' offices, etc., to observe intake and screening practices, and, where permissible, mediation hearings were observed. Project directors and relevant staff members were interviewed at each project, and past project directors were contacted if they had recently been replaced by the current project director. In the case of the San Francisco project, the project director was interviewed during a site visit to the East Coast, and project materials were reviewed.

Neighborhood justice center projects can clearly vary on a wide range of dimensions from where they are located to how they acquire cases, to how they process appeals, etc. For the purposes of this paper, 12 major dimensions on which neighborhood justice centers can vary will be discussed. These dimensions comprise the most obvious, and probably the most significant, variables for characterizing specific neighborhood justice centers. The dimensions are:

1. the nature of the community served
2. the type of sponsoring agency
3. project office location
4. project case criteria
5. referral services
6. intake procedures
7. resolution techniques
8. project staff
9. hearing staff training
10. case follow-up procedures
11. project costs
12. evaluation

Table 9.2 presents a summary of the six sampled dispute processing projects in terms of these twelve dimensions. In addition, information is provided regarding the staff organizations, the models used in developing project structures and additional services provided by the projects.

In the subsections that follow, each of the major dimensions is discussed briefly in turn and an attempt is made to identify the advantages and disadvantages of the various options that are available on each dimension.

The Nature of the Community Served

Neighborhood justice centers can clearly be developed in many types of communities. The need for neighborhood justice centers is not likely to be constant in all areas, however. Both rural areas and small towns are likely to have many of the older dispute resolution mechanisms still intact. Churches, extended families, neighborhood police officers, and community organizations have traditionally served the function of assisting those associated with them in resolving minor disputes, and rural areas and small towns are likely to have these institutions at least partially in place. Barring research to the contrary, urban communities and their associated lower courts would seem to be in the greatest need of dispute processing projects.

Within urban areas, dispute centers have been developed in a variety of communities. A number of strategies are available for selecting a target population within a given community, including choosing countywide areas, citywide areas, subsections of a city, and specific institutions, such as housing projects, schools, etc. The size of the communities served in the six sites visited ranged from approximately 22,000 in San Francisco's first target community, to 200,000–300,000 in Boston, Rochester and Miami, to three million in New York City. Based on the data available, it would appear that the area served by the New York City project is too large and disparate to benefit from the community spirit in smaller areas. The experience of existing projects also points to the desirability of locating neighborhood justice centers in communities whose residents have shown an interest in group problem solving, and whose criminal justice agencies are receptive to court reform projects. An alternative to geographic service areas is to define a target community by demographic characteristics. Available census data would enable researchers to define these non-geographically based communities. In some sense, for example, subcultural groups form a "community" regardless of the location of their residences. However, substantial logistical difficulties are likely to occur in defining a project's target community solely in terms of demographic characteristics, due to the need to publicize the program to a widely dispersed "community" and to educate referral sources to supply only clients with specific characteristics. In addition to logistical difficulties, limiting the target community in this way can eliminate one of the strengths of a project. Numerous projects have found that they serve as a meeting ground for people with different ethnic, racial and socioeconomic characteristics. The Rochester project, for example, was founded by an interracial advisory board after the city experienced racial conflict during

Table 9.2. Major characteristics of the six sampled dispute processing projects.*

CITIES / FEATURES	Boston	Columbus	Miami	New York City	Rochester	San Francisco
Project Name	Boston Urban Court Project	Columbus Night Prosecutor Program	Miami Citizen Dispute Settlement Program	Institute for Mediation & Conflict Resolution Dispute Center	Rochester Community Dispute Services Project	Community Board Program
Start-up Date	9/75	11/71	5/75	6/75	7/73	In planning stages
Community Served Name	Dorchester District, Boston, Massachusetts	Franklin County, Ohio	Dade County, Florida	Manhattan and Bronx, New York	Monroe County, New York	Selected Sections of San Francisco
Population	Dorchester: 225,000	County: 833,249 Columbus: 540,025	County: 1,267,792 Miami: 334, 859	Manhattan: 1,539,233 Bronx: 1,471,701 Total: 3,010,934	County: 711,917 City of Rochester: 296,233	San Francisco: 715,674
Sponsoring Agency Name	Justice Resource Institute (non-profit)	City Attorney's Office, Columbus, Ohio (Contractor: Capital University Law School)	Administrative Office of the Courts	Institute for Mediation & Conflict Resolution (non-profit)	Rochester Regional Office of the American Arbitration Association (non-profit)	Community Board Program (non-profit)
Source of Funds	Law Enforcement Assistance Administration	Originally Law Enforcement Assistance Administration. Now city funded	Law Enforcement Assistance Administration	Law Enforcement Assistance Administration	Law Enforcement Assistance Administration	Foundation Funds

Location	Private storefront near the court	Prosecutor's office	Government building which also houses court & district attorney	Office building in Harlem, not near court	Downtown office building near the court		Likely to have offices in the neighborhoods
Case Criteria							
General Rationale	Generally ongoing relationships among disputants	Generally ongoing relationships among disputants and bad checks	Generally ongoing relationships among disputants	Generally ongoing relationships among disputants	Generally ongoing relationships among disputants		Generally ongoing relationships among disputants
Types of Cases	36% family disputes; 20% neighbor; 17% friends; 10% landlord/tenant; 17% miscellaneous	39% interpersonal disputes, 61% bad checks	Statistical data are not currently available. Many assaults, harassments, neighborhood problems, domestic problems	Statistical data are not currently available. Cases include both misdemeanors and felonies	Approximately 2/3 are interpersonal criminal matters, 14% city regulations, 5% bad checks & miscellaneous. May begin to process family court cases		Not available
Referral Sources					1975	1976	
Walk-ins	See Other	(to prosecutor)	20% approximately	6%	14%	18%	(likely to be high)
Police	2.2%		20% approximately	42%	—	1%	(likely to be high)
Prosecutor	See Bench	Most cases received through this office	60% approximately		6%	11%	
Clerk	33.4%			52%	66%	70%	
Bench	57.4% (including district attorney)	10-15% approx			11%		
Community Organizations	See Other				—	—	"Third party" referrals will be encouraged
Other	7%				2%	0%	

215

* Reprinted from McGillis and Mullen, *Neighborhood Justice Centers: An Analysis of Potential Models* (1977)

Table 9.2. Major characteristics of the six sampled dispute processing projects (continued).

CITIES / FEATURES	Boston	Columbus	Miami	New York City	Rochester	San Francisco
Screening/ Intake Procedures	Staff member attends morning arraignment sessions; staff also answer calls from bench. Interviews conducted at court or project office	Staff members of district attorney's office and intake staff of project refer disputants to project. Respondents are requested to appear at hearing or face possible charges	Intake staff are located at the project office & interview clients referred to the project from other criminal justice agencies	Cases are received from intake workers at summons court, criminal court, & police desk of district attorney's office	The project intake worker screens and refers cases at the clerk's office. Walk-in cases are screened at the project's office	Currently being developed
Resolution Techniques Type	Mediation	Mediation	Mediation	Mediation followed by imposed arbitration if mediation is unsuccessful. Only 5% of cases have required imposed arbitration	Mediation followed by imposed arbitration if necessary. In 1976 40% of cases heard required an imposed arbitration award.	Mediation
Enforceability of Resolutions	Court cases continued pending follow-up after mediation	Disputants are informed that case charges will be filed if case is not satisfactorily re-	Disputants are informed that case charges may be filed if case is not satisfactorily re-	Arbitration agreements are prepared at the end of all hearings and are enforceable in the civil	Arbitration agreements are prepared at the end of all hearings and are enforceable in the civil	Peer pressure

Resolution Techniques (continued)		solved. Respondents are occasionally placed on prosecutorial probation	solved	court	court	
Time Per Hearing	2 hours	30 minutes	30 minutes	2 hours	One hour and 45 minutes	Not available
Availability of Repeat Hearings	Rarely more than two	Rarely used	Very rare	Most case are completed in 1 session. Small number require two	Rarely used	Not available
Use of Written Resolutions	Yes	Rarely used	Yes	Yes. Resolutions are binding	Yes. Resolutions are binding	Yes (unsigned ones are planned)
Hearing Staff Qualifications and Training Type	Diverse group of community members	Law students	Professional mediators	Diverse group of community members	Diverse group of community members	Diverse group of community members
Form of Recruitment	Widespread advertising, group contact	Contacted by staff at Capital University Law School	Through community contacts	Contacts with community groups and agencies	Contacts with organizations	Widespread effort to contact. Community meetings
Number Used Per Session	2–3	1	1	1–3	1	5
Rate of Payment	$7.50 per night	$3.75 per hour	$8–10 per hour	$10 per session	$25 per case	Not determined yet (may be same as jurors)

Table 9.2. Major characteristics of the six sampled dispute processing projects (continued).

CITIES / FEATURES	Boston	Columbus	Miami	New York City	Rochester	San Francisco
Hearing Staff Qualifications and Training (continued) Training	40 hour training cycles originally conducted by IMCR and now by local staff	12 hours of training conducted by the Educational and Psychological Development Corporation	Discussions and co-mediation with experienced mediators	50 hours of training conducted by IMCR	40 hours of training conducted by AAA	2 day training cycles are planned
Follow-up Techniques Appeal/ Rehearing Availability	Yes, but rare	Rarely used. Disputants can return on new charges	Yes, but rare	Only if both parties agree. Parties can appeal under state law if they feel award was arrived at fraudulently	Yes, if both parties agree	Probably appeal to new board
Follow-up Contacts	Disputants are contacted two weeks after hearing and again three months later	Disputants are contacted 30 days after hearing to see if resolution is being maintained	No. Project plans follow-up in summer of 1977	Yes. 30–60 days post hearing to see if resolution is being maintained	Assist in maintaining resolution if contacted. No systematic recontact	Some follow-up planned
Case Preparation for District Attorney/ Court	No	Yes. Charging material is prepared and filed if necessary	Court is contacted regarding outcomes	No	No	No

218

Overall Costs and Unit Costs						
Annual Operating Budget	$105,268 ****	$43,000	$150,000	$170,000	$65,000 *	$167,500
Total Annual Referrals	350	6,429 ** (1976)	4,149 (1976)	3,433 ***	663 (1976)	Not available
Cost/Referral	$300	$6.69 plus in kind costs	$36.15	$78.65	$98.03	Not available
Total Annual Hearings	283	3,478 (1976)	2,166 (1976)	643 ***	457 (1976)	Not available
Cost/Hearing	$372	$12.36 plus in kind costs, approximately $20	$69.25	$416 (recently $270)	$142	Not available
Goal Achievement						
Total Annual Referrals	350	6,429 interpersonal disputes in 1976; 10,146 bad checks; total = 15,575	4,149 (1976)	3,433 extrapolated from 15–18 months through November, 1976	663 (in 1976)	Not available
Percentage Having Hearing	71%	54% of interpersonal disputes	54%	46% hearing scheduled, 19% held due to clients resolving disputes	69% (in 1976)	Not available
Percentage of Hearings Resulting in Resolutions	89% (i.e., written agreement)	Not Available	Project reports 97%	100%: 95% mediated, 5% arbitrated	100% due to arbitration provision. 60% mediated agreement; 40% arbitrated agreement	Not available

Table 9.2. Major characteristics of the six sampled dispute processing projects (continued).

CITIES / FEATURES	Boston	Columbus	Miami	New York City	Rochester	San Francisco
Goal Achievement (continued) Percentage of Failures to Uphold Resolutions	15%	10% (survey of 892 1976 cases)	Not Available	9% according to a follow-up	Unknown	Not available
Percentage of ''Resolved'' Cases Returning to Court	Unknown	2.2%	Not Available	Less than 1%	5% seek enforced agreement	Not available
Project Organization Total Number of Project Staff	4	Approximately 5 full-time equivalents	8	10	6	5½
Administrative	Supervisor	Coordinator, Director	Program Director, Administrative Officer	Executive Director, Center Director, Summons Court Supervisor, fiscal officer	Project Director, Coordinator, Tribunal Administrator	Project Director Program Manager
Intake	2 case coordinators	6 senior clerks, 6 clerks	3 intake counselors	Intake Coordinator, Intake Worker, Police Liaison	Intake Worker (partly by Tribunal Administrator)	2½ organizers
Social Service	Case coordinators provide referrals	6 social work graduate students	Social worker	Social worker		

Project Organization (continued) Mediation	Approximately 50	Approximately 30	Approximately 20	Approximately 50	Approximately 70	Will train approximately 50
Clerical	Administrative Assistant	None	1 secretary, 1 receptionist	Receptionist, Administrative Assistant	Administrative Assistant, Receptionist	Evaluator
Project Models	IMCR Dispute Center		Columbus Project Rochester Project	Rochester Project, Columbus Project, Jewish Conciliation Boards, Bronx Youth Project	Philadelphia Arbitration as an Alternative Project	Danzig's model of Community moots
Additional Services Provided	Disposition program/victim service component	Problem drinker's group, battered wives' group			Community Group Dispute Resolution, training programs	Community Group Dispute Resolution

NOTES:

   * Total budget is $126,723, including additional components (community group dispute resolution and community organizational training).

   ** Interpersonal disputes only—bad check cases add an additional 10,196 referrals but involve very little project case processing time.

   *** Extrapolated from aggregated data on initial 18 months of referrals through November 30, 1976.

   **** Based on portion of larger Urban Court Budget attributed to the mediation component; case figures are estimates for the corresponding years (6/77–6/78).

a major school reorganization. The Boston project has served a similar function of bringing together a community with a rapidly changing demographic makeup.

Type of Sponsoring Agency

The choice of a specific form of organizational sponsorship is likely to be influenced by a number of factors, including the types of cases desired, the specific stage of criminal justice processing seen as most appropriate for diversion into mediation, the availability of organizations willing and able to sponsor the project, and the degree of coercive authority desired by the project. The most basic decision to be made is whether the project is to be attached to a governmental agency or to be under private sponsorship. In comparision to public sponsorship, private sponsorship has the likely advantages of greater perception of project neutrality, less stigmatization of clients, greater accessibility to community input, and availability of organizational sponsors which are highly sophisticated in alternative forms of dispute resolution. Disadvantages of private sponsorship include possible greater difficulties in developing close relationships with referral sources, possible difficulties in maintaining long-term funding, and restrictions in the availability of coercive power, if such power is desired.

If public sponsorship is selected, the further choice of a specific agency is required. The primary advantage of police sponsorship is the ability to receive cases close to the time of the incident and before the system has expended considerable resources and perhaps stigmatized the defendant as well. Significant disadvantages in police sponsorship include the difficulties in receiving police officer referrals, as evidenced in the projects which were studied, and the potential hesitancy of many complainants to bring a personal dispute to the attention of the police. The prosecutor's control over charging places him in an advantageous position for diverting cases to an alternative dispute processing forum, while still maintaining the option to bring charges. Disadvantages of prosecutor sponsorship include the fact that cases reaching the prosecutor are likely to have already incurred system expenses if the police were involved substantially in the case, and minor disputes may never reach the prosecutor's office, due to citizen hesitancy to entangle an acquaintance in formal prosecution. A further problem with prosecutor sponsorship is the possibility of a presumptive bias in favor of the complainant being perceived by disputants. The primary advantage of court sponsorship is the close structural ties possible with criminal justice agencies, and the court's traditional image as a neutral forum. However, the problem of possible stigmatization of the defendant is likely to increase if the court serves not only as the sponsor but also as the primary referral source, since the defendant will typically have already been processed by both the prosecutor and the police before reaching the stage of referral from the clerk or the bench. The costs of this processing are a further disadvantage of referrals from the bench. Clearly, a great many factors will inevitably determine the choice of an organizational sponsor for a dispute processing project.

Project Office Location

To a large extent, the physical location of the project is closely related to the nature of its sponsoring agency. An independent location reinforces an image of neutrality, conveys a more relaxed informal atmosphere which may be conducive to dispute resolution, and, if the court or prosecutor is overburdened or understaffed, avoids pressures to become involved in routine case handling tasks. The advantages of an official location are also compelling: ease of access to referrals; immediate communications with court personnel; an atmosphere which reinforces the serious nature of the mediator's task; and greater opportunity to institutionalize project procedures into daily court routine. Given proper access and assuming that adequate official space is available, the issue of independent vs. official location presently appears to be an open question.

Case Criteria

A number of factors must be taken into account in devising case criteria, including: 1) the nature of the relationship among the clients; 2) the level of seriousness of the offense; 3) the role of civil vs. criminal matters; 4) the inclusion of domestic matters; and 5) the inclusion of matters that are essentially not amenable to mediation.

All of the projects reviewed have tended to place primary focus upon disputes occurring among individuals with an ongoing relationship of some sort, whether as relatives, landlord and tenant, employer and employee, neighbors, etc. A substantial consensus seems to exist that relationships of this sort are the most appropriate for minor dispute processing projects. Citizen dispute projects can deal with a wide range of offenses from minor grievances, which would normally never have surfaced to the attention of the criminal justice system, to serious felonies. Research is needed to determine the limits in the seriousness of offenses which are amenable to mediation. Some felony cases are currently being successfully mediated, but clearly in many felony cases, even among close acquaintances, mediation would seem extremely unsatisfactory to the complainant. In any event, most projects will no doubt want to perfect their skills in the processing of relatively minor disputes before moving on to more serious matters.

All of the projects which were studied process civil matters as well as criminal matters. The question of what limits to place on the size of civil matters referred for mediation is a difficult one. As Sander notes, "When one considers the lack of rational connection between amount in controversy and appropriate process," one can appreciate the problems that have occurred in trying to allocate cases by this rubric. A common thread tying together the various civil matters processed by the projects studied is the existence of an ongoing relationship between the disputants. Many civil matters among relatives, neighbors and acquaintances, such as failures to pay back debts or to deliver promised services can quickly become criminal matters. The confrontation with the acquaintance on the "civil" matter can often culminate in criminal action. A project's choice of whether to accept civil cases, and if so, what proportion of the caseload to devote to such cases, will be determined in part by the project's funding source, its sponsoring agency, etc. It should be noted that both of the projects sponsored by criminal justice agencies, Miami and Columbus, have still been willing to process civil cases when the cases seemed amenable to mediation. The degree to which projects process cases involving divorce issues, such as custody, visitation rights, support payments, etc. is dependent upon the project's relationship with the local court. If appropriate authority can be delegated to dispute processing projects, domestic legal matters seem to be quite well suited for their form of case processing.

Citizen dispute processing projects at times serve as a forum for the processing of non-mediational cases: for example, bad check cases make up 61 percent of the Columbus project's caseload. The cases are not mediated in the strict sense of the word. The issues at hand tend to be factual and very little of the give and take of the type characteristic of true mediation sessions is likely to occur. Furthermore, the complainants in these cases tend to be institutions, while the respondents are individual citizens. Projects will have to seriously consider the likely adverse impact on their image, especially among the underprivileged, resulting from processing such cases.

Referral Sources

The brief summary of "sponsoring agency" issues above also provides considerable information on the advantages and disadvantages of various referral sources. A continuum of referral sources is represented among the projects studied: beginning with San Francisco, which is the strongest preventive model and will primarily accept its referrals from the community and the police, the continuum includes primary referrals from the prosecutor's office in Columbus, the clerk's office in Rochester and finally the entire spectrum of court-based referral sources in Boston. Research is needed on the trade-offs involved in processing cases which would never have received substantial criminal justice system attention, versus devoting resources primarily to cases firmly caught up in the system. Sander (1976) discusses issues relating to the surfacing of cases which normally are not processed and states "whether that will be good (in terms of supplying a constructive outlet for suppressed anger and frustration), or whether it will simply waste scarce societal resources (by validating grievances that might otherwise have remained dormant) we do not know."

Given the multiplicity of goals inherent in the concept of neighborhood justice, the choice of referral strategy will be a reflection of a project's particular objectives, as well as the access routes permitted that project by official criminal justice agencies. However, a model which intervened at all stages in the pre-trial process from informal citizen complaints through arraignment may well represent a strategy that allows for the maximization of both citizen and criminal justice system needs for a non adjudicatory dispute resolution forum.

Intake Procedures

A number of issues are relevant to the construction of intake procedures. Projects differ substantially in the degree to which they actively pursue complainants. There are no doubt a number of reasons why complainants fail to proceed with case processing, either by not appearing at the project or appearing and then declining hearings, after referral. In many cases, clients may have successfully resolved their dispute, while in others attrition may indicate that complainants are wary of institutional attempts to solve their personal problems. Rigorous data are needed to determine the causes of case attrition at the various stages of case processing. If cases are actually being solved outside of the project, active pursuit of referred complainants would be an invasion of their right to solve their problems privately. If, on the other hand, case attrition is caused in large part by disaffection with institutions in general, conscientious efforts to encourage complainant participation in the project, such as phone contacts or personal contacts, may be in order.

A second issue involving project intake procedures is the choice of threatening respondents for non-appearance and non-participation in the project vs. requests for voluntary participation by the respondent. Projects using binding arbitration for resolving disputes rely on the voluntary participation of respondents. Some mediational projects do likewise, but others use threatening letters to compel respondents to appear for mediation with the complainant. The typical closing line in these letters is, "Failure to appear may result in the filing of criminal charges based on the above complaint." The value of these various approaches has to be researched. Preliminary examination of the available data from the projects inicates that voluntary compliance can at times produce low cooperation from respondents.

A third intake issue involves the use of cooling off periods prior to the conduct of hearings. A clerk's project using this procedure has experienced a high rate of case attrition, and the question arises as to whether the disputes are successfully resolved outside the project or, the complainant is simply disgusted with institutional treatment and sees the long delay prior to the hearing as evidence that the system has little to offer in the way of thoughtful and timely assistance to his problems.

A fourth issue is the use of signed agreements to participate in hearings. The arbitration projects, of necessity, use such a procedure, and one mediation project does likewise. Newly developed projects should consider the merits of this type of procedure as a way of enhancing the participants' perception that they are voluntarily entering into a serious attempt to resolve their differences with the opposing party.

Resolution Techniques

A wide variety of issues arises in the selection of resolution techniques and many combinations and sequences of techniques are possible. Most practitioners and theoreticians seem to agree that disputes should be first dealt with by mediation, even within a session that may terminate in an arbitrated decision. As part of the mediation attempt, an opportunity is typically provided for both parties to simply air their grievances, usually with the complainant speaking first. This phase of the mediational session closely approaches conciliation, where parties are simply given the opportunity to state their problems and possibly negotiate a solution on their own without third party assistance. If the conciliatory effort does not result in an agreement among the parties, then the mediator takes the role of a third party neutral and may ask questions to help clarify issues and identify areas of agreement and disagreement. Suggestions may be made regarding possible solutions and individual caucuses may be held with the complainant and the respondent in order to better determine the parties' "bottom line" positions on a settlement.

A number of projects which solely employ mediation attempt to work toward written agreements regarding the dispute. In Miami and Boston, both parties sign the agreement in cases where an agreement is reached, while in San Francisco unsigned, written agreements are anticipated. The Columbus project rejects the use of written agreements in most cases as providing the parties with an illusory unenforceable contract. Efforts by projects to increase the probability that agreements will be maintained include threats of prosecution in some projects and peer pressure in others. In arbitration, the hearing officers impose arbitration agreements upon disputants who fail to arrive at agreements during the mediational phase of the hearing. If disputants do arrive at a settlement, the agreement is converted an arbitrator's award for the sake of future enforcement. In these latter cases, the agreement includes only those points arrived at in the disputants' own resolution. Arbitrator's awards are enforceable in the civil courts, and the majority of states have "modern arbitration legislation" which provides the legal structure for the enforcement of the arbitrated agreements.

Sander has noted an interesting problem in the combined conduct of mediation followed by arbitration: the possibilities for true mediation may be constrained when the disputants know that the hearing officer will later have the power to impose an agreement. A further interesting question is the degree to which threats by some projects to file charges if resolutions are broken amount to *de facto* arbitration but with criminal, rather than civil, remedies as the enforcement device.

Numerous additional mechanisms are also available and appropriate for certain types of disputes, e.g., ombudsmen, fact-finders, and of course adjudicators. Research is needed to help with the decision of which technique or combination of techniques is most useful for the types of disputes likely to be processed by neighborhood justice centers. A sequential application of mediation and arbitration seems to have promise, and the Rochester project illustrates how one jurisdiction has combined these two approaches in a pre-warrant hearing project under the sponsorship of the clerk of the court and a privately sponsored arbitration project.

Project Staff

Table 9.2 presents an overview of the staff organizations of the six projects studied, including the total number of full-time staff, the number of mediation staff, and the titles of other staff categories, such as administrative, intake, social work, and clerical. As can be seen from Table 9.2, staff configurations vary widely among projects, with the Boston project having only four full-time staff, while the New York project has ten full-time staff members.

Citizen dispute processing projects which are currently in operation use a wide variety of types of hearing staff, including lay citizens, law students, professional mediators, and lawyers. Clearly the use of trained members of the community as mediators is consistent and even requisite in a model of neighborhood justice which seeks to involve citizens in the remediation of community problems often inappropriately brought before the court. The use of lay citizens provides a project with a mediation staff who has a vested interest in the welfare of the community and the satisfactory reconciliation of disputing parties. Moreover, the opportunity to educate participating citizens regarding the functions and problems of the court may also serve an important function in altering community perceptions of official justice. The primary disadvantages of the use of lay citizens are the monetary costs and process time associated with the management of citizen mediators. The credibility of lay citizens may also be a factor to consider, particularly credibility with the project's major sources of referrals and its clients. Recent experience has shown that lay citizen mediator credibility is generally high.

The use of law students or other graduate students of any discipline offers a number of practical advantages, including a contained source of applicants, wage rates that need only be consistent with other part-time student employment opportunities, and the possibility of including some, if not all, initial and ongoing training activity in the graduate curriculum. A potential disadvantage of student mediators is the age of the group and their consequent lack of maturity. Law students have a further potential disadvantage in that their training emphasizes adversary skills which are inconsistent with the mediator's role. The Miami project employs professional mediators with backgrounds in such fields as law, psychology, social work, etc. The primary advantage of this practice is clearly the availability of a highly skilled mediation staff from whom the project can demand a level of professionalism and sensitivity not immediately available under a student or citizen model. Potential disadvantages include the costs of retaining professionals, the availability of a sufficient pool to cover project needs, given their competing professional demands, and the foregone opportunity to establish a strong sense of community justice. The Orlando, Florida project employs lawyers as mediators; the advantages are similar to those resulting from the use of professional mediators. The disadvantages are also similar, with the additional and very serious reservation regarding the inherent adversary, rather than mediational, orientation of law-trained persons. In summary, a number of factors bear on the issue of hearing staff qualifications, including the project's objectives, caseload, budget, and the availability of staff support services. While the lay citizen model is not without liabilities, it appears to be a particularly appropriate and timely model viewed in the context of the broad goal of citizen participation in the resolution of community disputes.

Hearing Staff Training

All of the projects reviewed offer training to their mediation staff. Boston and Rochester provide a full 40 hours of formal training for new mediation staff. New York exceeds this period at 50 hours, while Columbus offers 12 hours of initial training. In addition to theoretical and practical discussions of mediation and arbitration techniques, training typically includes sessions to orient participants to the criminal justice system, as well as project policies and procedures. Role playing and case studies are common methods advocated by projects, as is the opportunity to observe and co-mediate sessions with more experienced staff. Students and lay mediators can be expected to require the most extensive training and ongoing supervision.

Follow-up Techniques

The Boston, Columbus, and New York projects recontact disputants to determine whether the agreement has remained in force following the hearing. Boston recontacts the parties twice (two weeks and three months after the hearing), while other projects rely on a single contact 30 to 60 days after the hearing. Rochester has not been able to allocate the resources required for follow-up efforts; Miami plans to hire an intern who will initiate a follow-up procedure during the summer. Clearly, follow-up contact is an important function of a dispute processing project—both to monitor project achievements in terms of continuing client satisfaction and to identify needs for further mediation or social service assistance. Ideally, a project's role in enforcing non-binding agreements which may deteriorate following a hearing would be restricted to attempts to resolve the problem informally. Preparing charging documents or using information from mediation sessions to support official, criminal court action is inconsistent with the neutrality associated with the neighborhood justice concept and may raise due process concerns. Referrals to appropriate agencies, including small claims and criminal courts or social service agencies, are of course called for when project resources alone cannot resolve the problem.

Costs

The projects reviewed differ substantially in the volume and costs of referrals and hearings. Although the number of projects is clearly too small to draw any firm conclusions, it appears that high costs are associated with: private sponsorship; degree of advancement of the case in the criminal justice system at the time of referral; the use of arbitration; panels of mediators; and extensive follow-up processes. These findings are highly tentative and may be misleading in some cases. For example, the accounting procedures of public agencies may result in publicly sponsored projects not reflecting their full share of indirect costs, while an official location may have many material benefits, such as shared facilities, personnel, etc. It is difficult to relate the differences in costs among projects to project outcomes in order to derive measures of cost-effectiveness. Although rates of resolution breakdowns are available, these data are not uniform across sites, and differences presently observed can be partially attributed to variations in the definitions of outcomes and the type of follow-up effort. The development of uniform reporting categories and procedures would do much to provide projects with useful management information and would facilitate future comparative analyses.

Serious consideration should be given to the possibilities of future institutionalization in the city or county budgets when initial project budgets are planned. The only dispute processing project studied which has been fully institutionalized by its local government is the Columbus Night Prosecutor Program. As can be seen from Table 9.2, this project has the lowest overall budget and yet the highest caseload of all of the projects reviewed. Given the serious current problems with city and county government finances, every effort should be made to develop projects which are as inexpensive as possible. Possible mechanisms for cost savings include: the use of volunteers; efficient coordination with criminal justice screening staff in order to limit the need for project supported staff at referral sources; the use of graduate students on field placements to perform some office functions; the use of free public or private facilities for hearings, etc. Highly expensive projects are likely to face great difficulties in receiving continuation funding from local sources, and if such funding is available, it is likely to be a fraction of the project's original budget, necessitating the economical modifications suggested.

Evaluation and the Potential Contribution of Psychologists

It is clear that the newly forming Neighborhood Justice Centers raise provocative and fundamental issues regarding the relationships of individuals to one another and to their society. Research on these projects can provide insights regarding the most effective means of reducing interpersonal conflicts. In introducing the "Dispute Resolution Act" (S.957) on the floor of the Senate, Senator Kennedy noted, "If we are to insure that access to our legal system is available to all citizens on an equal basis, we must make it financially possible for States to act as laboratories in which to implement reforms where that system is found lacking. This amendment will do just that by providing the financial encouragement and initiative necessary for States to improve existing, or to create new, dispute resolution mechanisms."

Psychologists can and should play a major role in the effort to develop new mechanisms for reducing conflicts. First, the newly developing dispute resolution projects lend themselves to the research techniques of psychology. Psychologists have long had a preference for experimental methods, including random assignment of subjects to conditions and control of independent variables, as opposed to the preference in many other social sciences for observational, survey, and other research techniques. The likely availability of federal funds for project implementation and additional legislative plans to establish a research center for the study of dispute resolution processes may make possible the experimental assignment of disputants to both new projects and traditional processing mechanisms in many communities. The Vera Institute of Justice is already conducting a true random assignment experiment at a dispute settlement project in Brooklyn, New York. Disputants are asked whether they are willing to submit their disputes to mediation/arbitration and if so are randomly assigned to either traditional court processing or the new dispute center. Cases are being followed intensively to determine the effectiveness of the adjudicatory vs. mediation approaches and to estimate the costs of the two mechanisms. Psychologists have particular expertise in experimental methods, are well trained in the careful assessment of dependent variables, unobtrusive measurement, consideration of alternative explanations of results, etc. and should apply these tools to the investigation of the newly developing dispute processing mechanisms.

In addition to relevant research skills, psychologists have developed many theories which provide clues regarding how dispute projects might best be structured and which hypotheses might be most usefully explored. For example, attribution theory (Kelley, 1973; Jones and Davis, 1965) suggests that the degree of a disputant's attitudinal and behavioral change is likely to be inversely related to the degree of perceived external coercion in arriving at a dispute settlement. The relative effectiveness of techniques varying in levels of external coercion (conciliation, mediation, arbitration, adjudication) could be explored to determine if the laboratory predictions from research on intrinsic motivation (e.g. Deci, 1970) hold true in the real world settlement of disputes and may indicate which types of disputes are sensitive to this variable and which require the external imposition of coercion for successful settlement. Similarly, psychological research on bargaining and negotiation (e.g. Thibaut and Kelley, 1959; Deutsch and Krauss, 1961, etc.) provides many insights into how individuals attempt to resolve disputes. The new Neighborhood Justice Centers are likely to provide excellent laboratories for the study of many psychological processes. The combination of hypothesis testing research based upon psychological theories and straightforward project evaluative studies is likely to provide valuable information regarding ways to improve the American system of justice.

REFERENCES

Abel, R. Editorial Comment. *Law and Society Review* **11**:1 (1977).

American Bar Association. *Report of the Pound Conference Follow-up Task Force,* August 1976.

Burger, W. Agenda for 2000 AD—a need for systematic anticipation. *Federal Rules Decisions* **70**:83 (1976).

Danzig, R. Toward the creation of a complementary, decentralized system of criminal justice. *Stanford Law Review* **26**:1 (1973).

Danzig, R., and Lowy, M. Everyday disputes and mediation in the United States: a reply to Professor Felstiner. *Law and Society Review* **9**:675 (1975).

Deci, E. Effects of externally mediated rewards on intrinsic motivation. *Journal of Personality and Social Psychology* **18**:105 (1971).

Deutsch, M., and Krauss, R. Studies on interpersonal bargaining. *Journal of Conflict Resolution* **6**:52 (1962).

Felstiner, W. Influences of social organization on dispute processing. *Law and Society Review* **9**:63 (1974).

Fisher, E. Community courts: an alternative to conventional criminal adjudication. *American University Law Review* **24**:1253 (1975).

Fuller, L. Collective bargaining and the arbitrator. *Wisconsin Law Review* **23**:3 (1969).

Fuller, L. Mediation: its forms and functions. *Southern California Law Review* **44**:312 (1971).

Galanter, M. Why the "haves" come out ahead: speculations on the limits of legal change. *Law and Society Review* **9**:95 (1974).

Johnson, E., Kantor, V., and Schwartz, E. *Outside the Courts: A Survey of Diversion Alternatives in Civil Cases.* Denver: National Center for the State Courts, 1977.

Jones, E. E., and Davis, K. From Acts to Disposition. In L. Berkowitz (Ed). *Advance in Experimental Social Psychology* (vol. 2). New York: Academic Press, 1965.

Kelly, M. The process of causal attribution. *American Psychologist* **28**:107 (1973).

Kennedy, E. M. Floor Statement regarding S.957. *Congressional Record* 18904 (1977).

Koch, K., Sodergren, J., and Campbell, S. Political and psychological correlates of conflict management: a cross cultural study. *Law and Society Review* **10**:443 (1976).

Sarat, A., and Grossman, J. Courts and conflict resolution: problems in the mobilization of adjudication. *American Political Science Review* **69**:1200 (1975).

Sander, F. Varieties of dispute processing. *Federal Rules Decisions* **70**:111 (1976).

Shaver, K., Gilbert, M., and Williams, M. Social Psychology, Criminal Justice, and the Principle of Discretion: A Selective Review. *Personality and Social Psychology Bulletin* **1**:471 (1975).

Tapp, J. Psychology and the Law: An Overture. *Annual Review of Psychology* **27**:359 (1976).

Thibaut, J., and Kelly, M. *The Social Psychology of Groups*. New York: John Wiley & Sons, Inc., 1959.

Vera Institute of Justice. *Felony Arrests: Their Prosecution and Disposition in New York City's Courts*. New York: Vera Institute of Justice, 1977.

III

PSYCHOLEGAL ISSUES AFFECT-ING THE CARE AND TREATMENT OF PATIENTS

10

Confidentiality and Privileged Communication in Psychotherapy

Robert G. Meyer and Debora E. Willage

Much is assumed about what the consumer and the practitioner understand confidentiality and privileged communication to be, how important these are to the therapeutic process, and what effect a pledge of confidentiality has on the revelation of information. Such diverse groups as priests, journalists, psychotherapists, and attorneys have requested protection of confidentiality via privileged communication, apparently assuming that this is important to their effective functioning. Yet, all of these groups are similar in never having provided substantial, empirically established evidence that such an assumption is true.

We should note the difference between confidentiality and privileged communication or privilege: Confidentiality was not originally a legal concept, though it has increasingly attained that status; it primarily refers to codes of professional ethics designed to prevent unauthorized disclosures of information without the informed consent of the client. Privilege is a rule of law that permits a witness to the psychotherapy to refrain from providing any testimony that he or she might otherwise be compelled to give. The strength of most claims for privileged communication potentially derives from two factors, common or statutory law. Since there is very little support for the concept of a psychotherapist-patient privilege in common law, a claim for such a privilege must typically be established by statute.

The support for establishing any privilege by statute must come through fulfillment of certain legal criteria similar to those proposed by Wigmore

(1940). We refer to Wigmore since he is a highly respected authority on rules for evidence in the law. These rules are in essence a cost-benefit decision process, pitting the value gained from protecting the relationship versus the loss to society in not hearing all of the evidence that might act to protect its interests. There is certainly room for debate as to whether or not the psychotherapist-patient relationship privilege is upheld by the application of such cost-benefit rules. However, it does appear reasonable to say that logic, face validity, and the testimony of practitioners support the assertion that they are fulfilled, and thus the psychotherapist-patient privilege ought to be protected by privileged communication (Meyer and Smith, 1977; Cross, 1970). However, the lack of empirical evidence on this point, combined with a lack of clarity as to what people understand confidentiality and privilege to be, point to the following major issues which are accessible to empirical study:

1. Do potential clients or patients understand the relevant concepts of privilege and confidentiality?
2. Would accurate information in this regard affect potential clients in their decisions to enter into individual or group psychotherapy?
3. Would differing conditions of confidentiality and privileged communication affect the type of information disclosed?
4. Do providers of service understand the relevant concepts and laws?

In relation to the first point, there is already evidence that in related areas, people do not always understand what the relevant professionals assume they understand (Sales, Elwork, and Alfini, 1977). More specifically, Meyer and Smith (1977) in their study of group psychotherapy have collected data that bears on the issue of a potential client's understanding of the concepts of confidentiality and privileged communication.

A junior year, university-level class of 56 students was given a short questionnaire on which the initial question asked what the term "confidentiality" meant to the respondent. Responses were made anonymously and without coercion. Sixteen percent of those potential consumers stated that they understood this to mean only that a therapist would avoid discussion of relevant material in conversations and other communications and that he or she would not use these materials in professional communications or publications. What is most interesting is that the other 84% assumed that confidentiality included a refusal to testify about a case, even if validly ordered to do so by a court of law.

It is quite clear that there is very little accurate understanding of the issue in this subset of potential consumers. It has clearly been the position of the legal system, as well as of both the American Psychological Association and the American Psychiatric Association, that the pledge of confidentiality does not allow one to avoid a direct order by a valid court to provide relevant information. At a later point from the collection of this data, the same questionnaire was administered to a similar psychology class for the purposes of replication. In addition, it was administered to a group of lay people attending a workshop sponsored by the local mental health association, and the topic of confidentiality in psychotherapy was the issue under discussion. There were 50 persons in the psychology class and 26 in the mental health group who filled out the same questionnaire, and the results demonstrated a lack of understanding similar to that of the initial group.

Since at this juncture the data clearly suggests that potential consumers do not understand the implications of the term confidentiality, let us turn to the next question posed, i.e., whether accurate information in this regard would affect such potential clients in their decisions. Referring back to the group evaluated by Meyer and Smith (1977), these subjects were next provided a full description of the differences between the concepts of privileged communication and confidentiality and were then submitted to the following question, emphasizing a condition of no confidentiality in a potential group; it read as follows:

> Presume that you have now decided to seek entry into a therapy group, and the therapist tells you that information discussed in the group would not be considered confidential. Would you:
>
> a. Decide not to enter group therapy?
> b. Enter the group but with substantially less inclination to reveal relevant information in the group?
> c. Enter the group with approximately the same motivation and feelings you had before the therapist's statements?
> d. Enter the group with even greater motivation and willingness to reveal relevant information?

The very next question was exactly the same as this, except that respondents were told that "the therapist and the group members are pledged to confidentiality, and the therapist also states that, though very unlikely, if he were validly ordered by a court of law to reveal specific information, he would do so." Out of the 55 respondents, 45 (81.8 percent) answered a or b when the question emphasized the "no confidentiality" situation; when confidentiality had been emphasized as existent, only 26 of these 55 (47.2 percent) answered a or b. If one construes the answer order a to d to reflect a continuum from most problematic to most positive, a Wilcoxen test for two matched samples shows an F of .0000634 with a two-tailed test, significant well beyond the .001 level when the two questions are compared.

Those data clearly argue that perceptions and implications of confidentiality can affect the decisions as to the degree of involvement in group therapy; but information on point three is needed to supplement these prior data; i.e., would differing conditions of confidentiality affect the type of information disclosed. There has, in fact, been little data available to indicate that people actually do provide information differently depending upon under what conditions of confidentiality they perform.

Study 1—Method

The authors approached this problem by studying the amount and type of information a person would disclose under three confidentiality conditions: a pledge of complete confidentiality (C); no mention of confidentiality $(N\text{-}M)$; and clearly expressed non-confidentiality $(N\text{-}C)$. Data on 63 subjects were collected with subjects run in groups of approximately four people. Each group was randomly assigned to one of the three experimental conditions, for a total of 21 subjects per condition, and each group was read a set of instructions corresponding to the condition to which that group had been randomly assigned; i.e., Confidentiality (C), No Mention $(N\text{-}M)$, No Confidentiality $(N\text{-}C)$. After the instructions had been read, a questionnaire booklet was distributed, the first page of which was a personal information sheet.

Clients in therapy are identifiable even if they are assured of confidentiality, therefore, all subjects participating in the experiment were requested to put their names on the personal information sheet. This procedure also kept the effects of confidentiality from being confounded with the effects of anonymity.

The second section of the booklet contained the Marlowe-Crowne Social Desirability Scale $(M\text{-}C\ SD)$, a personality inventory that consists of 33 items that are either culturally acceptable but probably untrue statements or true but undesirable statements (Marlowe and Crowne, 1967). The $M\text{-}C\ SD$ scale was administered to determine if the extent of social desirability of the subjects' responses varied under the different conditions.

The third section consisted of the Hopkins Symptom Checklist $(HSCL)$, a self-report symptom inventory of 58 items. The checklist was initially designed to be used by psychiatric out-patients. Nevertheless, Derogatis, Lipman, Rickels, Uhlenhuth and Covi (1974) report that several studies have used the checklist successfully to detect differences in distress levels among nonpsychiatric (normal) medical patients. The *HSCL* allowed for a comparison between groups of the extent to which subjects report that are distressed by psychopathological symptoms.

The last section of the questionnaire contained the Rotter Locus of Control Scale (*RLC*), a 29-item, forced-choice test which is widely used to assess attitudes of how one perceives the cause for changes in one's world. People are scored as external or internal on the scale, depending on whether they view themselves as being able to control their world or under the control of external forces. It could be hypothesized that people who are 'external' or score high on the *RLC* would be more sensitive to the opinions of others, hence would respond differentially to the three conditions of confidentiality. However, the Rotter form does not tap such intrapersonal concepts so effectively as it might. Many of the items concern views of how political change occurs in society as opposed to more personal concerns; therefore, it was hypothesized here that it would be less sensitive to pressures of confidentiality than either the *HSCL* or the *M-C SD*.

The *M-C SD*, the *HSCL*, and *RLC* each permit the derivation of a single score. A high score value on the *M-C SD* suggests that subjects gave socially desirable responses; a high score on the *HSCL* indicates that subjects reported being bothered by a substantial number of physical and psychological symptoms. Finally, a high score on the *RLC* indicates that these subjects feel that events in the world and they themselves are controlled more by situational demands than by internal decisions.

Study 1—Results and Discussion

Review of the mean scores obtained on each questionnaire under the different levels of confidentiality (see Table 10.1) suggests that a definite pattern of responding occurred. The subjects in the No Confidentiality (*N-C*) condition provided the most socially desirable responses. They also reported being the least bothered by psychopathological symptoms and the most controlled by external reinforcers. Based on the results on the *M-C SD* and the *HSCL,* the subjects in the *N-C* condition are the least candid, while the subjects in the Confidentiality (*C*) condition are the most open about reporting distress. Subjects in the *C* condition reported being bothered more by symptoms on the *HSCL* than did the subjects in the other two groups. They also produced less socially desirable responses than did the subjects in the *N-C* condition on the *M-C SD*. Subjects in the *N-M* condition gave less socially desirable responses on the *M-C SD* than did the subjects in either of the other two groups, but their scores were only slightly less than that of the subjects in the *C* condition. On the

Table 10.1. Response scores under different levels of confidentiality mean scores and standard deviations: explicit instruction analysis.

Condition	N	Measure	M-C SD	HSCL	RLC
C	22	M	13.6	103.8	13.9
		SD	4.9	20.3	4.0
N-M	21	M	12.8	92.2	13.7
		SD	4.7	14.7	3.7
N-C	20	M	16.1	88.3	12.8
		SD	4.0	20.7	5.3

HSCL, subjects' scores in the *N-M* group indicated that they reported being bothered more by psychopathological symptoms than did the subjects in the *N-C* condition but less bothered than the subjects in the *C* condition. This suggests that the subjects in the *C* and *N-C* groups were affected by the manipulation of instructions and therefore responded in opposite directions from the subject who received no information about confidentiality.

In order to ascertain whether or not these differences were significant, the data from the questionnaires was analyzed by Multivariate Analysis of Variance (MANOVA) using Wilk's Lambda Criterion. Initial inferential analysis consisted of MANOVA being performed on the three levels of the independent variable (*C, N-M, N-C*) and on the three dependent variables (*M-C SD, HSCL, RLC*). The results ($F(6,116)=2.59$; $p<.022$) indicate that significant differences occurred in the types of responses subjects made under these particular conditions of confidentiality.

To determine to what extent each of the questionnaires contributed to the significance obtained with the MANOVA computations, Univariate Analysis of Variance (ANOVA) was performed on each of the dependent variables. The findings of this ANOVA suggest that the differences in the types of responses subjects made on the *HSCL* ($p<.024$) under the varying levels of confidentiality contributed most to the significance obtained with the MANOVA analysis. Thus, subjects were most influenced by confidentiality when they were required to report the more personal information. Even though the results of the ANOVA for the M-C SD were not significant ($p<.062$), the fact that the value approached significance would mean that the *M-C SD* could also have contributed to the significance of the results of the MANOVA and that the people respond differentially when reporting information that could influence others' opinions of them. The ANOVA analysis on the data from the *RLC* did not yield significant results, suggesting that the subjects did not vary their responses on this questionnaire as a function of the level of confidentiality.

As noted previously, it was hypothesized that the *RLC* would be less sensitive to the conditions of confidentiality than the *HSCL* or the *M-C SD*. Thus, a reanalysis by MANOVA was performed, using only the data from the *HSCL* and *M-C SD* which were the measures of interest. The result of the reanalysis (F(2,59=4.29; p<.018) was also significant, indicating that the types of responses subjects made on the *HSCL* and *M-C SD* questionnaires differed under the different conditions of confidentiality.

These findings indicate that degrees of confidentiality can act as an important variable in the types of responses people make, and the strength of the effect depends on the type of information requested. The more private the information asked and the greater the ability of the subjects to give socially acceptable answers, the stronger the effect of degree of confidentiality. Responses of the people who were told that the information they supplied might not be kept confidential were less candid on the *HSCL*, which requested the most personal information, than were those of the subjects who were informed that this information would be kept confidential. The differing effects of confidentiality were moderate in strength on the *M-C SD*, where the information requested was not so personal as that on the *HSCL* and were virtually nil on the *RLC*. Hence, the effects of the confidentiality variable were most marked when comparing people in confidential and non-confidential conditions.

Since it is difficult to obtain information about psychopathology without asking questions that are both quite personal and also can be answered in a socially acceptable direction, these two factors were not separated in the present study. Yet, we can say that there is solid initial data in response to point three; i.e., differing conditions of confidentiality do affect the type of information disclosed.

Study 2—Method

The fourth issue then asks whether or not the providers of therapeutic services themselves clearly understand the concepts of confidentiality and privileged communication. Data collected in a pilot study by the authors bear on this last point, at least in regard to the provision of information to group therapy clients and also to the degree of accuracy of beliefs that these therapists have about the issue.

Questionnaires were sent to 150 group psychotherapists, randomly selected from the register of the American Group Psychotherapy Association. Questions focused on their understanding of confidentiality and what types of information they gave either members or potential members of a therapy group. Information such as the therapist's professional identification, approach to therapy, and years of experience was also obtained. Forty-nine therapists returned adequately completed questionnaires for a response rate of 33 percent. The median number of years in independent practice was eight, with a range from one to 30 years, suggesting that they were experienced group therapists. A bare majority (52 percent) were primarily involved in private practice, and a high majority (90 percent) were primarily psychodynamic in orientation. Fifty-three percent of the group therapists indicated that they had participated in a court of law as an expert witness for either the plaintiff or the defense. Sixteen of the 49 therapists who responded also indicated that they were willing to have their group members fill out related questionnaires on these issues. A total of 196 questionnaires were sent out, and it was requested that they be filled out anonymously. Sixty-three client questionnaires were completed adequately and returned for a response rate of 32 percent. The mean number of months that they had been in group therapy was 12, with a range from one to 60 months.

Study 2—Results and Discussion

The most notable finding in the responses of the forty-nine therapists is that 65 percent of them assumed that confidentiality included a refusal to reveal information obtained in a group, even if validly ordered to do so by a court of law. It should be of some concern that only 35 percent of these individuals accurately reflect the law and position statements of the major professional organizations. This result is further reinforced by the probability that those individuals responding would be the most knowledgeable, since they were the ones from the overall group who were confident enough to allow themselves to be queried on the issue. As a side note, when respondents are categorized by profession, psychologists are even less accurate in their understanding of the issues than are the other professional categories, such as psychiatrists.

The respondents were also asked whether or not they made the issue of confidentiality an explicit part of the introduction to the group or discussed it in a group session, and 86 percent said that they did. As noted, a separate questionnaire was mailed out to a subsample of group therapy clients of these same therapists. It is interesting that out of those responding, only 38 percent reported that the issue of confidentiality was ever dealt with. One possible, though not necessarily probable, explanation for this inconsistency between therapist and client reporting is that, for the most part, those clients responding were inadvertently members of groups where the therapists said they did not deal with confidentiality. This could not be accurately assessed because of the anonymity used in the collection of data. More likely explanations are that either these individuals had forgotten that the therapist had dealt with the issue or they did not perceive the issue of confidentiality in the same way as the therapists did or possibly the therapist may have been inaccurate in reporting that they did discuss these issues.

Summary Discussion

The above two studies in conjunction with the data in Meyer and Smith (1977) provide information relevant to the four questions posed earlier concerning confidentiality and privileged communication in psychotherapy. Naturally, the above findings need to be replicated; this is particularly so for study two, since it was a pilot project. It would be important to vary the subsamples studied and, if possible, to study the effects of beliefs about confidentiality both on the actual decision to enter therapy and the consequent information disclosure subsequent to entry.

Replication of Study One should attempt to incorporate another target group, considering the reactions of those individuals who most directly reflect the reality of the ethical codes and laws regarding confidentiality and privileged communication. These would be individuals who have been told that all efforts would be taken to protect the disclosures made, but, in the rare event that such information were required by a court of law, it would be disclosed. It would also be interesting to see if these findings change, depending upon the theoretical orientation of the therapist, e.g., humanistic versus psychoanalytic versus behaviorist. In addition, while data from mock groups is an important entry point into this domain of information, it is ultimately crucial to obtain confirming data from actual groups in process. Gerbrasi, Zuckerman, and Reis (1977) point out the problems of generalizing from mock situations to the real world. Meyer and Smith (1977) detail the problems in the current laws relevant to group therapy in particular but also point to problems in individual therapy, as well. New legislation is needed to correct the significant and complex problems that have evolved in the area, but it is most important that an adequate information base be developed, so that these new ideas can be buttressed by more than tradition and testimony. The studies noted are a step in this direction, yet varying related and replication information is still needed on each of the four issues.

REFERENCES

Cross, W. Privileged communication between participants in group psychotherapy. *Law and Social Order* 191–211 (1970).

Derogatis, L. R.; Lipman, R. S.; Rickels, K.; Uhlenhuth, E. H.; and Covi, L. The Hopkins' Symptom Checklist (HSCL): A self-report symptom in inventory. *Behavioral Science* **19**:1–15 (1974).

Gerbrasi, K.; Zuckerman, M.; and Reis, H. Justice needs a new blindfold: A review of mock jury research. *Psychological Bulletin* **84**(2):323–345 (1977).

Marlowe, D., and Crowne, D. *The Approval Motive*. New York: John Wiley & Sons, Inc., 1964.

Meyer, R., and Smith, S. A crisis in group therapy. *American Psychologist* **32**:638–643 (1977).

Sales, B.; Elwork, A.; and Alfini, J. Improving comprehension for jury instructions. In B. Sales (Ed.) *The Criminal Justice System*, pp. 23–90. New York: Plenum Press, 1977.

Wigmore, J. *Evidence* (3rd Edition). Boston: Little, Brown, and Co., 1970.

11

Emergency Admission of Civil Involuntary Patients to Mental Hospitals Following Statutory Modification

Paul D. Lipsitt

A. BACKGROUND AND INTRODUCTION

In general medical practice, an emergency admission to a hospital occurs with the consent of the patient. If the patient is unconscious or otherwise in a physical or mental state which renders him incapable of providing consent, the inference is made that if the individual were competent to do so, he would wish to be treated.

In matters of mental illness, the notion of *parens patriae* has historically been the rationale in decisions for commitment. The logic is that since the person is mentally ill, he is not capable of making a reasonable decision for himself with regard to treatment, and therefore responsible others should make that decision. The psychiatrist or other mental health professional is initially designated to make this decision, with a court usually making the ultimate determination.

With the increasing attention to patients' rights, the current trend has

This research was supported by a grant from the Center for Studies in Crime and Delinquency, NIMH, Grant #MH25955-03.

I wish to acknowledge my appreciation to David Lelos, A. Louis McGarry, and John Monahan, for their critical comments of an earlier draft of this paper. Bruce Sales's evaluation of each draft has been invaluable.

been to narrow the population of those who may be committed. Traditionally, the criteria for involuntary commitment, which includes emergency admission, was that the person be mentally ill and in need of hospitalization. Under the more restricted, current rule, however, in addition to mental illness, an individual may not be involuntarily admitted to a mental hospital unless there is a likelihood of serious harm to himself or others or unless he is so gravely disabled that he is unable to care for himself and reasonable placement is not available in the community. This trend is consistent with the change in law in Massachusetts on this topic.[1] The new law, which emphasizes the presentation of evidence, obliges the Commissioner of the Department of Mental Health to articulate the definition of mental illness through administrative regulation and ultimately defines mental illness as "a substantial disorder of thought, mood, perception, orientation or memory which grossly impairs judgment, behavior, capacity to recognize reality or ability to meet the ordinary demands of life." Alcoholism is specifically excluded from the definition, defined in Massachusetts General Laws Chapter 123, Section 35, where independent procedures for hospitalization of alcoholics are provided. Harm to self or others is defined as:

1). a substantial risk of physical harm to the person himself, as manifested by evidence of threats of, or attempts at, suicide or serious bodily harm; 2). a substantial risk of physical harm to other persons, as manifested by evidence of homicidal or other violent behavior and serious physical harm to them; or 3). a very substantial risk of physical impairment or injury to the person himself, as manifested by evidence that such person's judgment is so affected that he is unable to protect himself in the community and that reasonable provision for his protection is not available in the community.

This study assesses the impact of the new law on the behavior of the decision-makers by analyzing the content of the documented decisions made by admitting physicians before and after the passage of the new law. It focuses on the parameters within which these decisions are made, based on the written reports of the psychiatrists certifying that the patient is in need of involuntary, emergency admission. The analysis was based on the new statutory and regulatory requirements for involuntary, emergency admissions and scored to reflect whether or not the admitting reports of the physician conformed to the various elements of the law.

This research is needed, since other studies of the civil commitment of the mentally ill have emphasized the decision making in court after there has been an emergency admission (Warren, 1977; Hiday, 1977) or have conducted a broad evaluation of the entire commitment process, such as the Enki report on the implementation of the Lanterman-Petris-Short

[1] Massachusetts General Laws, Chapter 123.

mental health law in California (Urmer, 1973), to the exclusion of how the law has affected the behavior of the expert witnesses—the mental health professionals.

The main hypothesis tested was that as a function of the change in the law and modification in the criteria for involuntary civil admission, there should be a reflected change in the content of the material certifying the need for involuntary emergency admission. In addition, the explicit reference to evidence under the new law should result in more detailed and explicit evidence of mental illness and the likelihood of serious harm after the change in the statute.

B. PROCEDURE FOR DATA COLLECTION AND EVALUATION

A random sample of 688 cases was obtained from the admissions reports from three state mental hospitals: Hospital 1 (234 cases) is a suburban hospital, serving several of the cities and towns within commuting distance of the major city, as well as more rural areas; Hospital 2 (233 cases) serves part of the major city but also includes an area of the suburbs that houses middle and upper middle class families; this hospital is also a major teaching and training facility for a medical school. Hospital 3 (231 cases) serves the inner major city area of predominantly lower class and racially mixed population; the majority of blacks in the city reside in this area.

From each of these hospitals samples were obtained for five selected fiscal years. The first year, chronologically, was 1965, which represented a period before the reorganization of the Department of Mental Health into regions and areas of the state under the Community Mental Health Center Act, Chapter 735 of the Acts of 1966, incorporated into Massachusetts General Laws as Chapter 19; the year 1968 represented a period under the old mental health code but after the reorganization of the Department of Mental Health; the third year examined was 1971, the last fiscal year under the old law. The revision of General Laws, Chapter 123 became effective on November 1, 1971. In order to allow a passage of time for the law to mature, the years 1974 and 1975 were selected, representing the third and fourth fiscal years after the modification of the mental health code.

In the analysis of the involuntary applications for admission, content reflecting each part of the mental illness definition and each aspect of likelihood of serious harm was coded, and senior staff were trained to a high level of reliability in scoring the content. Scoring was by the blind method, so that the scorers would not identify data according to year; reliability of over 80 percent was attained in scoring 13 cases by four raters (Table 11.1).

Table 11.1. Interrater reliability for the coding
of application for admission reports.

	Contingency Coefficients			
	1	2	3	4
R1 (.81)	—	.77	.81	.85
R2 (.81)	.77	—	.85	.82
R3 (.83)	.81	.85	—	.84
R4 (.84)	.85	.82	.84	—

The segments of mental illness consistent with the regulatory language
were identified for scoring purposes as follows:

Part I

Thought: Loose associations, tangential thoughts, "word salad"
             paranoid material, delusions

Mood: Depression, flatness of affect, manic, flight of ideas

Perception: Illusions, hallucinations

Orientation: Disoriented as to time, place or person, confused

Memory: Serious memory loss, including brain damage issues

Part II

Judgment: Talking about or making decisions that are clearly
             irrational

Behavior: Demonstrated acts must be described from ob-
             servations

Reality: An external phenomenon demonstrable beyond
             bare diagnosis

Demands of life: A life threatening circumstance, such as refusal or
             inability to eat, or in danger of freezing

Likelihood of serious harm was scored to conform to the statutory language:

To self: Demonstrated behavior of physically self-destruc-
             tive acts or serious threats to harm self.

To others: Clear evidence of life threatening behavior to others;
             very violent acts or placing others in reasonable fear
             of physical harm

Impairment of   Very substantial risk of physical harm to self due to
judgment   mental deterioration

C. PROTOTYPICAL CASES OF EMERGENCY ADMISSION

Examples of cases reporting the information upon which the involuntary emergency admission is made is presented to show in a more concrete manner how the two parts of the mental illness definition and likelihood of serious harm (LSH) were scored. These descriptive cases range from reports which provide no reference to the statutory and regulatory requirements, to others that partially comply, and to those that fully comply according to the scoring protocol.

An example of a report which contains no content in any of the categories of mental illness or LSH is the following:

Patient is unclean about herself and home, walks back and forth incessantly, annoys the neighbors, uncooperative during exam, smokes incessantly.

The next example includes Part I only:

Long history of depression, recent EST at hospital. Long history of barbiturate use. Private psychiatrist, Dr. J.

This case is an example of a report where the pathology is stated, but there is no sufficient evidence of functional disability (Part II) or individual risk; there is reference to medication, but no inference that this is inappropriate or that it creates a danger.

The following report describes Part II only, including deviant behavior but without a reference to pathology (Part I) or to the individual's likelihood of being a serious risk to himself or others:

Disturbed over school bussing. Shouts noisy screams, sings occasionally, recites poetry. Has been sleeping poorly the past five nights after she used up her medication.

Some cases reported clearly that the individual was a danger to himself or others but failed to indicate the relationship of that danger to mental illness; an example of such a case is one where an emergency admission was certified for a patient who was reported as violent towards others. The inference is drawn that he requires hospitalization. There is no reference to mental illness. This case is described as follows:

Patient attacked his mother, has threatened family members and on one occasion attacked his sister. He continues to be negative, overtly hostile, gets excited when thwarted, and threatens bodily harm to others. He is in need of further hospitalization.

This case would be scored for behavior in Part II as LSH to others.

Some reports rely on opinion only to meet the criteria for LSH to self. Since factual evidence of threats or attempts at physical harm to self are not present, statutory requirements are not met. For example, in the following case, there is insufficient descriptive and factual information to meet the criteria of Part I for mood and Part II for behavior:

> Twenty-nine year old white female, married, who has been chronically hospitalized with frequent overnight privileges. Symptoms include constant pacing, autism, speech only in symbolic gestures or words. Currently she is talkative, rather tearful and angry. Impulse control is now better than usual, although six weeks ago she ran from hospital. She is significantly depressed and a suicide risk.

An example of a case which meets Part I and Part II, as well as LSH by reason of severe impairment, is that of an 82-year-old man:

> Eighty-two year old man with chronic confusion, who fell down in his yard this afternoon and was confused and unable to talk. He soiled himself and suffers from senile dementia. He has chronic heart disease with angina pectoris.

D. DEMOGRAPHIC DATA

The sample consisted of 314 males (45.6 percent) and 374 (54.4 percent) females, of which 87 percent were white and 12 percent black. Forty-four percent were single, 28 percent were married, 18 percent divorced and 18 percent separated. Over half (52 percent) were Catholic, 27 percent were Protestant and 10 percent were Jewish. The mean age of the sample was 42 years, with a tendency toward a lower age, reflected in the median age of 38.6 years. The average level achieved in school was the 11th grade. Twenty-eight percent of the sample had had no prior admissions; 27 percent had been hospitalized once; 15 percent twice; 5 percent three times; and the remaining 21 percent four or more times. Ten persons had been hospitalized ten or more times.

The most common mode of referral to a mental health facility in this sample of emergency admissions was from a general hospital (36 percent). Police referral (21.4 percent) was the second most frequent method of hospitalization. Family and friends accounted for 18.5 percent of referrals.

The emergency admission patient is most likely to receive an entry in his record of schizophrenia as the diagnostic impression on admission, accounting for 37.4 percent of the sample; other affective disorders and organicity account for 27.3 percent and 16.9 percent respectively. On a scale of behavioral activity on admission, ranging from withdrawn to unmanageable, the written report indicated that about 40 percent were agitated but only 4 percent were unmanageable. The rest were almost equally divided among categories of withdrawn, passively conforming and actively cooperative.

Forty-one percent were discharged within two weeks; an additional 2–6 percent were discharged each week thereafter up to the tenth week. As the time extends to about two years, discharge frequencies were common in weekly increments of .1 percent to .7 percent. Ten patients had been hospitalized on their present admission for more than two years.

The comparative characteristics of the patients were analyzed for age, years of schooling, number of prior admissions, and length of the current admission. Since data on these variables were not consistently recorded, the number of cases is less than the total sample size. There is no significant difference in the years of schooling as a function of statute change. However, the age of those involuntarily admitted under the new statute was reduced by over three years from 43.6 to 40.3, which is significant with a probability of .026,* and the number of prior admissions increased from an average of 1.9 to 2.7, which is significant at the .001 level. Table 11.2 presents the number of prior admissions for each year examined.

Under the old law, the mean number of weeks of time hospitalized following the current admission was 21.4, in contrast to a mean of 11.3 weeks after the change in the law. This difference is significant at the .001 level, pooling the three old law years and the two new law years. Table 11.3 represents the differences for each of the five periods examined.

Table 11.2. Number of prior admissions for various yearly periods.

Year	Number of prior admissions
1965	1.6
1968	1.8
1971	2.4
1974	2.6
1975	2.9

Table 11.3. Current admission by weeks for each year.

Year	Mean
1965	17.9
1968	23.1
1971	23.9
1974	11.8
1975	10.5

*All statistical analyses in this study employ the chi square test for significance.

E. MENTAL ILLNESS REPORTING

For the purposes of this analysis, the basis for scoring the presence or absence of content reflecting mental illness followed the regulatory definition provided by the Department of Mental Health. As noted earlier, the scoring was in two major parts, identified as part I and part II: Part I reflected the psychopathology observed by the reporting physician, and part II refers to the deficits in function related to the pathology. For purposes of scoring the content, part I and part II were scored independently rather than scoring part II as a consequence of part I.

The five characteristics of part I are thought, mood, perception, orientation, and memory. In order to qualify for compliance with this part of the definition, at least one of these characteristics must be present. There were no significant differences in years in those reports with regard to meeting these requirements (old law—74.4 percent versus new law—72 percent). Thought and mood disorders were most frequently reported, accounting for about two-thirds of the cases, once again, without differences by year.

The functional aspects of the mental illness definition reflected in part II were scored on the four dimensions of judgment, behavior, capacity to recognize reality, and the ability to meet the ordinary demands of life. Behavior is by far the most common reference in this aspect of the psychiatrists' reports, being referred to in almost 70 percent of the cases; It was not distinguishable by year. An analysis of the compliance with part II reveals a significant difference by year ($P < .05$; 74.6 percent of the cases under the old law versus 81.2 percent under the new law) Table 11.4 presents the yearly percentages of those reporting each part of the commitment standard.

Table 11.4. Percentages of reporting of part I and part II by years.

Year	Part I	Part II
1965	71.1	74.8
1968	71.4	74.3
1971	80.2	74.0
1974	69.9	81.5
1975	74.3	79.4

F. LIKELIHOOD OF SERIOUS HARM REPORTING

Since the law clearly states that the physician must present evidence to make a finding that there is a likelihood of serious harm in one of the three categories, the cases were scored to reflect factual evidence versus opinion. If the report merely stated that the individual were suicidal, homicidal, or gravely impaired, without presenting demonstrable evidence of either a verbal or behavioral character, LSH was scored as "opinion only." A literal interpretation of the new law suggests that factual evidence must be stated to demonstrate the dangerous characteristic, such as threats or acts of attempted suicide, assault upon others, or life threatening circumstances, such as not eating, representing grave impairment. However, judges tended to give credence and some weight to opinion evidence when presented at commitment hearings.

There is an increase under the new law in the percentages of patients who meet the LSH criteria, both with and without opinion evidence, but the increase reached significance (P < .001) only when opinion evidence is included (Table 11.5).

Table 11.5. Percentages of cases meeting the LSH criteria under old and new law with factual and opinion evidence.

	N=406 Old Law	N=282 New Law
Factual Evidence Only	54.2	61.0
Factual and Opinion Evidence	62.8	78.4

For the purposes of conforming to the intent of the statute that there must be evidence of dangerousness, an analytic procedure was followed to tease this quality from the data. These data are followed to tease this quality from the data. These data are presented in independent categories by selecting first all cases that included "behavioral" material, regardless of other types of material and then selecting "verbal" material from the remaining cases and finally "opinion" material. Without overlapping cases, data total 100 percent with the inclusion of the "none" category. Giving validity to the rationale that "behavior" is of a higher order of dangerousness than "verbal," which in turn is higher than "opinion," all reports that contained "behavior" data, whether they contained any of the other categories, were parceled out first and so on down this hierarchical ladder. A residual category of "none" remained, containing no scoreable information on dangerousness whatsoever. Thus, these data can be considered as a scaling on a dimension of dangerousness. An examination of the LSH data reveals significant shifts under the new law in the categories of behavioral, verbal, opinion, and no LSH reference. Behavioral evidence increases, as does opinion evidence, but there is a slight decrease in verbal evidence, which represents only 8.7 percent of the data. In addition, there is a substantial decrease in the number of cases under the new law where no LSH reference is made (37.2 percent to 21.6 percent; Table 11.6). These differences are significant at the .0001 level.

Table 11.6. Percentages of behavioral verbal and opinion LSH material as a function of change in the law.

LSH	Old Law	New Law
Behavioral	44.8	53.2
Verbal	9.4	7.8
Opinion	8.6	17.4
None	37.2	21.6

An examination of the various categories of LSH by years reveals the increase in behavioral and opinion material after the change in the law (1974 and 1975). It is also apparent that fewer cases under the new law fail to include some evidence of LSH. However, it should be noted that there is a tendency, even under the old law, for references to LSH to increase. The "none" category decreases from 43.0 percent in 1965, to 35.7 percen in 1968, and to 32.8 percent in 1971 (Table 11.7).

Table 11.7. Percentages of reference to LSH by year for behavioral, verbal and opinion evidence.

LSH	1965	1968	1971	1974	1975
Behavioral	39.3	50.0	45.0	53.4	52.9
Verbal	10.4	5.0	13.0	7.5	8.1
Opinion	7.4	9.3	9.2	18.5	16.2
None	43.0	35.7	32.8	20.5	22.8

Of the 406 cases under the old law, 220 met the LSH criteria, while under the new law, 172 of the total 282 cases met the LSH criteria (Table 11.8). For the purposes of analyzing the relative distribution of the three categories of LSH before and after the change in the law, the percentages used were only for those that met the LSH criteria rather than the total sample. When more than one category of material was scored, dangerousness to others was the critical material for the first category, followed by dangerousness to self, and then severely impaired. The rationale for this option was based on levels of dangerousness as they appear on the hierarchical scale of decisions for involuntary admission. While this assumption may be challenged, a choice was necessary, since the naturalistic character of the research did not always allow for pure categories.

Table 11.8. Percentages of factual and opinion evidence for three categories of LSH as a function of change in the law.

	Factual Evidence Only			Factual and Opinion Evidence Only		
	Other	Self	Impaired	Other	Self	Impaired
Old Law	43.6	45.0	11.4	42.4	41.6	16.1
	(96)	(99)	(25)	(108)	(108)	(41)
New Law	54.1	28.5	17.4	48.4	29.4	22.2
	(93)	(49)	(30)	(107)	(65)	(49)

Analyzed in this way, these data reveal significant changes in the three categories after the change in the law. Examining for factual evidence only, there is comparatively more material in the admission reports dealing with LSH to others, increasing from 43.6 percent to 54.1 percent and less material alluding to LSH to self after the change in the law, decreasing from 45 percent to 28.5 percent. There is also a shift upwards for the LSH category of severe impairment. These shifts after the change in the law are significant at the .003 level. With the addition of opinion evidence to factual evidence, the number of cases meeting the criteria of LSH was increased to 255 under the old law and to 221 under the new law; the shift remains relatively stable and significant at the .02 level.

G. CONFORMING TO ADMISSION CRITERIA

In order to gain admission, the three factors for commitment must be met, as described in the introduction of this chapter: a pathology of mental illness, a functional component, and danger to self, others, or severe impairment. When we look for conformity to all factors, the data reveal that the strict criteria of LSH, factual evidence only, result in a total acceptable admission of 31.5 percent of the cases under the old law and 36.5 percent under the new law. While the difference is in the expected direction, it is not substantial enough to meet statistical significance beyond chance (P=.1995). When cases containing opinion content are included, the total increases to 37.9 percent under the old law and 47.2 percent under the new law which is significant at the .02 level.

Table 11.9 reflects the trend towards increased content for each of the five fiscal samples, combining part I and part II of the mental illness, with factual evidence only of LSH, and with expert opinion evidence added. Note, however, that there was a trend in increasing percentages of meeting the criteria, even prior to the change in the law, which dilutes the inference that the continuing change necessarily resulted from a change in the law.

Table 11.9. Percentages meeting admission for part I, part II and actual and opinion evidence of LSH.

Admission	1965	1968	1971	1974	1975
Factual Evidence Only (N=231)	25.2	34.3	35.1	37.0	36.0
Factual and Opinion Evidence (N=287)	28.6	41.4	43.5	47.3	47.1

H. SEX DIFFERENCES

Since dangerousness is frequently perceived differently according to whether or not the person is male or female, sex differences were also examined.

1. Mental Illness—Part I and Part II

In reporting females under the old law, part I was compiled within 79.8 percent of the cases, which is significantly different (.01 level) from the reporting of males, which occurred in only 68.4 percent of the cases. However, there were no significant differences under the new law (70.8 percent for females and 73.6 percent for males). There were also no differences in part II either before or after the law change.

2. Likelihood of Serious Harm

Under the old statute, there were no significant differences between males and females in the reporting of factual evidence of LSH (57.5 versus 51.2 percent); however, under the new law, these differences approached significant levels (67.8 versus 55.9 percent $p < .06$). The inclusion of opinion evidence increased the frequency of reporting under both the old and new law, but significant differences were still not reached (Table 11.10).

Table 11.10. Percentages of LSH with factual and opinion evidence as a function of sex.

	Male	Female
Old Law	67.4	58.7
New Law	83.5	74.5

3. Meeting Admission Criteria

The reporting of evidence of behavior that meets all the criteria for admission with factual evidence only of dangerousness tended to be higher for females prior to the change in the law (35.2 percent versus 27.5 percent), but these differences did not reach statistical significance. After the change in the law, there was a higher percentage of males who met the criteria for admission with factual evidence only (43.8 versus 31.1 percent) which is significant at the .04 level. With the inclusion of opinion evidence, the percentages increase for males and females before and after the change in the law but maintain comparable positions in relation to each other. Males and females who meet the total criteria for part I, part II, and LSH under the old law are 35.2 percent and 40.4 percent respectively. Under the new law, these percentages are 52.9 percent for males and 42.9 percent for females, reflecting the reversal observed when factual evidence only was scored. There are significant differences between males and females in the three categories of individuals meeting the commitment criteria, with or without opinion evidence. Males were more likely to be reported as dangerous to others, females more frequently were reported as dangerous to self and severely impaired (Tables 11.11 and 11.12). The differences in types of dangerousness in males and females are statistically significant (p < .0001).

I. COMPARISON OF HOSPITALS

The three state hospitals, while all under the administration of the Department of Mental Health, have varied characteristics as described in

Table 11.11. Percentages for three categories of LSH with factual evidence only as a function of sex.

	Others	Self	Impaired
Male	59.8	41.9	32.7
Female	40.2	58.1	67.3

Table 11.12. Percentages for three categories of LSH with factual and opinion evidence as a function of sex.

	Others	Self	Impaired
Male	60.5	41.5	32.7
Female	39.5	58.5	66.7

the beginning of this chapter. Each hospital was examined on the variables in the study for differences among them and for changes as a function of the law.

1. Mental Illness

Consistent with the findings for the whole sample, there were no significant changes in part I before and after the change in the law for any hospital. Each maintained about the same level of adherence to part I. It is notable, however, that there is considerable variation among the hospitals in the percentage of adherence to part I criteria under both the old and new law. Under the old law, Hospital 3 conformed to the definition of mental illness in part I, 13.6 percent more than Hospital 1, and, after the change in the law, the difference between the two hospitals was 19.6 percent (Table 11.13). These differences among hospitals are significant under both the old law ($P < .04$) and the new law ($P < .006$).

There were, however, changes under part II which occurred primarily in Hospital 1, where conformity to the criteria of the regulations increased from 71.9 percent to 88.4 percent in that hospital (significant at the .004 level; Table 11.14); increases in the other two hospitals were minimal. On part II, the differences among the three hospitals show no significant differences under either the old or new law, although the difference reaches the .06 level under the new law.

Table 11.13. Percentages under old and new law for each hospital on part I.

	Old	New
Hospital 1	67.6	60.0
Hospital 2	74.4	76.6
Hospital 3	81.2	79.6

Table 11.14. Percentages under old and new law for each hospital on part II.

	Old	New
Hospital 1	71.9	88.4
Hospital 2	79.1	79.8
Hospital 3	73.2	75.3

2. Likelihood of Serious Harm

Just as the data as a whole reflected no significant differences between the old and new law based on the evidence of factual material of LSH, so too, were there no differences for each hospital (Table 11.15). There were also no significant differences among the three hospitals in percentages of cases with factual evidence present either before or after the change in the law. However, as shown in Table 11.16, the inclusion of opinion evidence results in a significant increase in LSH content in Hospital 1 (P < .0008) and Hospital 2 (P < .02).

Table 11.15. Percentages under old and new law for each hospital for LSH factual evidence only.

	Old	New
Hospital 1	54.0	61.1
Hospital 2	58.9	66.0
Hospital 3	50.0	55.9

Table 11.16. Percentages under old and new law for each hospital for LSH factual and opinion evidence.

	Old	New
Hospital 1	61.9	83.2
Hospital 2	66.7	81.9
Hospital 3	60.1	69.9

3. Meeting Admissions Requirements

In order to meet the full admissions requirements, part I, part II, and at least one category of LSH must be satisfied. As noted earlier, the pooled data of the study sample revealed a significant level of difference with a change in the law when opinion evidence was added to factual evidence, but not significant when factual data stood alone.

These differences in smaller samples for each hospital did not reach statistical levels of significance when comparing data before and after the change in the law with or without opinion evidence (Tables 11.17 and 11.18). Hospital 3 reveals the largest increase in cases meeting all aspects of the admissions criteria after the change in the law but does not reach statistical levels of significance (P < .10, factual evidence only; P < .08, factual and opinion evidence). Hospital 2 more consistently met the requirements of the admissions criteria both before and after the change in the law.

Table 11.17. Percentages under old and new law for each hospital for full admissions requirements with factual evidence only.

	Old	New
Hospital 1	29.5	27.4
Hospital 2	34.9	40.4
Hospital 3	30.4	41.9

Table 11.18. Percentages under old and new law for each hospital for full admissions requirements with factual and opinion evidence.

	Old	New
Hospital 1	36.7	42.1
Hospital 2	40.3	50.0
Hospital 3	37.0	49.5

J. DISCUSSION

There are no significant differences in the frequency of appropriate admissions of involuntary patients to mental hospitals with the change in the law.

However, this conclusion does not obviate the necessity of examining the data in more detail for a content that has been modified during the ten-year period examined in the study. For example, part I of the criteria for commitment, the identification of pathology, is very similar under both the old and new laws, and, as would be expected, there has been no increase in the reporting of a person's pathology (part I) with the change in the law. Part II, however, is substantially different: The old statute simply referred to conduct "which clearly violates the established laws, ordinances, conventions or morals of the community;" the new regulatory language narrowed the criteria to "grossly impairs judgment, behavior, capacity to recognize reality, or ability to meet the ordinary demands of life." With this change, there has been an increase in the reporting of part II, the impairment of function. Thus, the significant difference in the reported material appears to reflect the awareness of this change.

The decrease in age of the sample appears to reflect the trend away from long term, involuntary admission of those who would earlier have been considered in need of treatment, particularly because of geriatric problems and other infirmities of age, both mental and physical. However, unless there is a very substantial risk that these infirmities place the individuals in physically threatening circumstances, involuntary admission is not statutorily acceptable. There has also been an increasing trend toward referring geriatric cases to nursing homes during the later period under the new law.

The trend for each of the sampled years also reflects the increase in the number of prior admissions, from 2.0 in 1965 to 3.6 in 1975, while the mean number of weeks of hospitalization was reduced by nearly half after the change in the law. Earlier hospital discharge is a factor which places some individuals in a greater risk of arrest, since anti-social behavior may lead to a return to the hospital, arrest, and both, in some cases; thus, the higher rate of recidivism. In addition, higher rates of arrest for both violent and non-violent offenses among mental patients have been found in recent research by Zitrin et al. (1976) and Sosowsky (1978). Furthermore, Sosowsky has found that since the narrowing of the criteria * in California for involuntary confinements, arrests for violent offenses involving

* Lanterman-Petris-Short Act of 1967, implemented July, 1969.

bodily harm have occurred three and one half times more frequently. His study examined a cohort of California patients hospitalized from June 1972 to December 1973, dates consistent with our study.

Earlier studies had found to the contrary, that mental patients were less violent or no more violent, than the general population (Pollock, 1938; Gulevich and Bourne, 1970). Our data suggests that there is an increased emphasis by mental health professionals and hospitals on issues of violence. Dangerousness has become the paramount concern in making a determination to hospitalize those in particular who are perceived as dangerous toward others.

The references to material reflecting a likelihood of serious harm were significantly increased under the new law when opinion data was pooled with factual evidence data; however, when factual evidence is presented alone, an increased frequency is found after the change in the law, which does not reach significance, though the trend is in the expected direction. These data suggest that since the change in the law, there has been a sensitization or awareness on the part of the admitting physician that material reflecting the risk of serious harm is important to justify an emergency admission. Yet, it appears that physicians often rely on opinions and not facts to support their belief in the need for hospitalization. Unless there is an adherence to factual evidence, the legislative intent to narrow the criteria for involuntary admission will be thwarted, and the intended protection of the subjects in emergency admission denied. Unfortunately, until case law interprets the statutory law, recognition of opinion evidence is likely to continue by some judges in Massachusetts.

Involuntary admissions based on danger to self significantly decreased after the passage of the new law. The increased emphasis on the protection of society as the primary reason for involuntary hospitalization appears to be reflected in these data. The increased civil libertarian stance on the right of the individual to be at liberty, unless the danger to self is clearly evident, may have resulted in a less frequent use of involuntary admissions in the harm to self category.*

In conclusion, the narrowing of the criteria for involuntary commitments has undoubtedly had a significant impact upon mental hospital census throughout the country. The increased emphasis upon community treatment programs has been another factor in reducing the hospitalized patient population in Massachusetts, as elsewhere. These changes in pol-

---

* All these data are presented in a relative sense, since the sum total of involuntary admissions on all grounds has been dramatically curtailed. In Massachusetts, total admissions to mental hospitals dropped from 14,803 in 1969 to 11,096 in 1975. During this period, voluntary admissions increased from 23% to 66.7%, and prolonged involuntary commitment (over ten days) has decreased from 8.1% to 1.3%.

icy have resulted in more freedom and less hospitalization for many individuals who would have been in locked wards in Massachusetts prior to the advent of the Community Mental Health Act. A proper order for involuntary hospitalization can be made only when dangerousness is documented. Yet, there are apparent trade-offs that must be carefully scrutinized. The deviant behavior reflected in part II of the mental illness definition and the LSH requirement bring criminal justice and mental health systems to the crossroads where joint decisions are essential and basic policies and values for both systems should be re-evaluated.

REFERENCES

Gulevich, G. D., and Bourne, P. G. Mental illness and violence. In D. Daniels; M. Gilula; and F. Ochberg (Eds.), *Violence and the Struggle for Existence,* pp. 309–326. Boston: Little Brown and Co., 1970.

Hiday, V. A. Reformed commitment procedures: An empirical study in the courtroom. *Law and Society Review* **11**:651–666 (1977).

Pollock, H. M. Is the paroled patient a menace to the community? *Psychiatric Quarterly* **12**:236–244 (1938).

Sosowsky, L. Crime and violence among mental patients reconsidered in view of the new legal relationship between the state and the mentally ill. *American Journal of Psychiatry* 1978. **135**:33–42 (1978).

Urmer, A. H. The burden of the mentally disordered on law enforcement. Enki Research Institute 1973.

Warren, C. A. B. Involuntary commitment for mental disorder: The application of California's Lanterman-Petris-Short Act. *Law and Society Review* **11**:629–649 (1977).

Zitrin, A.; Hardesty, A. S.; Burdock, E. L.; et al. Crime and violence among mental patients. *American Journal of Psychiatry* **133**:142–149 (1976).

12

Due Process of Law and the Attitudes of Professionals Toward Involuntary Civil Commitment

Lynn R. Kahle and Bruce Dennis Sales

INTRODUCTION

Involuntary civil commitment for mentally ill individuals has been sanctioned by society since the beginning of our nation (Brakel and Rock, 1971). This legal procedure is usually justified as being in the best interest of the mentally ill individual, since he or she will be subjected to treatment that could make him or her "more normal." A careful analysis of the treatment and care that institutionalized individuals have received once involuntarily committed and of the prognosis of cure as a result of this treatment has, however, led mental health lawyers and mental health professionals to raise the question of whether we are committing an individual in his or her best interests, or whether we are committing individuals in order to remove an eyesore from society's view. For example, in the now famous Supreme Court case of O'Connor v. Donaldson[1] the Court noted that, although Mr. Donaldson had been in a mental health institution for over 20 years, the only therapy that he had received was

The authors gratefully acknowledge the tireless efforts of Kathy Olson and Gene Schleppenbach in assisting with the collection of the data presented here. Earlier presentations of limited aspects of the research reported here may be found in Kahle and Sales (1978a,1978b) and in Kahle, Sales, and Nagel (1978).

"milieu therapy," which consisted of sitting in a room with other mentally ill people. The Court ruled that Mr. Donaldson must be set free.

In another landmark decision, a federal district court in Wisconsin was faced with a constitutional challenge to the very process whereby an individual is placed in an institution against his or her will (i.e., involuntary civil commitment).[2] After hearing all of the evidence, the court ruled that the Wisconsin statute was unconstitutional, because it did not afford the individual alleged to be mentally ill sufficient rights in order to contest the allegations during a fair and impartial hearing of the facts. The rationale behind the court's position was that involuntary civil commitment is a deprivation of liberty, similar to incarceration following a criminal offense. Because an individual loses his or her liberty and will be confined in a mental health institution, often for an unlimited length of time, it is mandatory that the individual receive a full and fair hearing. Since the Wisconsin case, a number of states have revised or are revising their commitment laws in order to insure that the commitment procedures provide adequate protection of the constitutional rights to a fair hearing and due process of law. Change has not come simply or easily: Some psychiatrists, and perhaps other mental health professionals as well, do not agree with the liberalization of the commitment laws (e.g., Treffert, 1975); for example, when a new bill[3] was introduced in the Nebraska Legislature, the psychiatric community represented through the Nebraska Medical Association attempted to introduce 27 different amendments, many of which would have decreased the due process rights of the subject of the commitment petition. These traditional attitudes may affect the implementation of revised statutes.

Conformity to the law has proven to be a problem in this area. In the much heralded case of Wyatt v. Stickney,[4] the federal district court in Alabama had to threaten the state with selling public property in order to force the institution to comply with previous orders to improve mental health services and care. A similar lack of conformity has occurred with lawyers: Wisconsin lawyers were found to be deficient in their representation of subjects of commitment petitions.[5] What makes that fact most disturbing is that Wisconsin was one of the leaders in changing its commitment statutes to provide for an effective hearing. When we combine the Wisconsin and Alabama cases, it is clear that there are examples of both lawyers and mental health professionals who are not fulfilling the statutory mandates.

An obvious problem arises: If the primary providers of the mental health services do not agree with the current trend in the law, will they then provide the kind of service that the law requires, and will they conform to the new patients' rights position? There are several questions that must be asked here: 1) What are the attitudes of lawyers and mental health professionals toward involuntary civil commitment? 2) Do mental health professionals differ from lawyers concerning their attitudes toward the purposes, functions, and best vehicle for commitment? 3) If attitudes diverge from the written law, will professionals then conform in their behavior to the law, or will they do everything possible to apply the law as they think it should be? and 4) Are the professional organization lobbies accurately representing their membership before legislative bodies on proposed changes in commitment laws?

The purpose of this study is to provide empirical evidence about the attitudes of psychiatrists, clinical psychologists, and mental health lawyers toward involuntary civil commitment procedures and the rights related to involuntary civil commitment, particularly due process safeguards. We chose these three professional groups because of their primary role during the commitment proceedings. Mental health professionals have been divided into psychiatrists and clinical psychologists, because the very different training that each group undergoes may lead to differences in attitudes towards commitment. It was initially expected that mental health lawyers as a group should be significantly more oriented toward protection of due process of law than mental health professionals because of their legal training. Furthermore, it was predicted that clinical psychologists should be more due process oriented than psychiatrists because of the greater emphasis in the training of clinical psychologists on data, empirical verification, and accountability. Even if no differences were found between the groups, this study should yield important information about the attitudes of these professionals toward the various aspects of the commitment process, which could substantially aid states in deciding upon what approach or approaches toward mental health law reform is viewed as appropriate by the primary professionals who interact with the mental health system. In instances where disagreements exist, we would hope that this research would provide a detailed agenda for discussions among the professionals, legislators, and others about the specific issues in involuntary civil commitment in need of change or support.

METHOD

Subjects for this study included 440 psychiatrists (general members, fellows, life members, life fellows, and distinguished fellows) randomly selected from the *Membership Directory of the American Psychiatric Association,* 440 clinical psychologists randomly selected from the *Biographical Directory of the American Psychological Association* (only members of the Division 12, the Division of Clinical Psychology), and all practicing attorneys who subscribed to the American Bar Association's *Mental Disability Law Reporter* (N = 64). Only people with addresses in the United States were selected.

It might be argued that our sample of lawyers is not representative of lawyers in general. In fact that may well be true: Lawyers who read the *Mental Disability Law Reporter* are probably actively involved in mental disability law and are responsible for much of the changing law; if this is true, then they are different from most lawyers, who may never handle a commitment case or do any work in this area. However, it is those lawyers who are active in mental disability law that we are interested in, since it is their opinions that are most knowledgeable and potentially most influential in shaping this area of law.

The general methodology for the survey followed approximately that outlined by Dillman, Christenson, Carpenter, and Brooks (1974). People on each list were mailed an introductory letter, the questionnaire, a reply envelope, and a reply post card. The reply post card allowed respondents to indicate that they had responded, while returning their questionnaires anonymously. Three days after the initial mailing, all people on the lists received a thank you/reminder post card. People who had not responded after approximately one month were sent a replacement questionnaire, and people who still had not responded after the second month received another replacement questionnaire by certified mail. Within each of the three professions, names were randomly assigned to receive their questionnaires with either a Psychology Department or a Law College return address.

The questionnaire consisted of 125 items which probed respondents' attitudes toward traditional, current, and potential future wordings (rules) in the law, as well as a variety of other general issues related to commitment. The nature of the items will become clear for the reader in the following section.

On most items respondents were asked to indicate their degree of agreement with a statement on a scale ranging from strongly *dis*agree (= 1) to strongly agree (= 7). We rather arbitrarily defined means in the lower third of the scale (1 to 3) as disagreement, means in the middle third of the scale (3 to 5) as undecided, and means in the upper third of the scale (5 to 7) as agreement. In a few instances we abandoned this system when the ranking of items offered more appropriate information for inference about opinions *within* groups.

For inferences about differences *between* the three groups, we used a one-way analysis of variance with alpha = .005; that is, we wanted to be at least 99.5% certain that observed differences between the groups were not due to random fluctuations in the data. Although some social scientists may object that this criterion is a bit conservative, we felt that it was appropriate for this research, because of the rather large sample sizes, the large number of tests performed, and because of the importance of our inferences. Throughout the remainder to this chapter, we shall present only the overall mean when the three groups do not differ, and three separate means when the three groups do differ at a statistically significant level, unless specifically noted otherwise.

RESULTS AND DISCUSSION

Response Rates

This three-mailing design yielded completed questionnaires from 67 percent of the subjects. Among psychiatrists there were 264 respondents (60 percent); among clinical psychologists there were 316 respondents (72 percent); and among mental health lawyers there were 50 respondents (78 percent). Non-respondents who indicated why they did not respond generally claimed, in order of frequency, that they were unfamiliar with the topic, retired, or found the length of the questionnaire too imposing. There was only one statistically significant difference due either to wave of response or to an interaction between wave and profession, which is less than one would expect by chance; therefore, this difference will be discounted.

Should Involuntary Commitment Be Abolished?

Although the three groups differed slightly on this question, they all rejected the statement, "Involuntary civil commitment should never be allowed" ($\overline{X}$ (psychiatrists) $- 1.54$; $\overline{X}$ (psychologists) $= 2.32$; $\overline{X}$ (lawyers) $= 2.20$). One might advocate abolishing involuntary civil commitment if one assumed that there is no such thing as mental illness (Szasz, 1961), that change (due to therapy) only occurs when the target person (patient) perceives that he or she has entered the situation voluntarily (Collins and Hoyt, 1971), or that mental illness problems are more expeditiously dealt with through legal channels other than involuntary civil commitment; however, respondents apparently rejected these positions.

Who Should Be Committed?

Table 12.1 shows that all three groups agreed with the current trend in the law toward requiring both dangerousness and mental illness for involuntary commitment. The respondents rejected the use of mental illness alone as a satisfactory standard for commitment. The reason for this current trend is that mental illness alone should not be used to justify a curtailment of liberty as great as involuntary civil commitment normally involves. Thus, courts and legislatures have generally added the criterion of dangerousness, which severely curtails the number of people subject to commitment, while at the same time ensuring it for those whom they believe are most in need of it.

Table 12.1. Items on which respondents agreed concerning who should be committed.

Means	Questions
	Involuntary civil commitment should be allowed if a person is:
6.35	dangerous to others and mentally ill.
5.89	dangerous to self and mentally ill.
3.08	mentally ill only.

What Is Mental Illness?

Some of the controversy over commitment laws in recent years has centered around definitions. Tables 12.2 and 12.3 present the respondents' views on how to define *mental illness*. Only psychosis was accepted by all three groups, although psychiatrists and lawyers were at least somewhat in favor of including organic mental illness. All three groups were slightly undecided about the sociopathic personality. The mental health professionals were additionally undecided about drug addiction, alcoholism, and custodial care cases.

These results imply that the respondents favored a restrictive definition of *mental illness* within the context of involuntary civil commitment law. None of the professions wanted to commit individuals with mild disturbances or who were simply difficult to manage. The indecision about the sociopathic personality may in part reflect the fact that it is not always possible to treat this malady with current methods. In addition, the indecisiveness of the mental health professionals on three of the four items in Table 12.3 may reflect the indecisiveness of recent legislative trends. Some states are adding drug addiction and alcoholism to their statutes, while others are deleting these conditions. The real issue may be one of administrative necessity in some states: If a state cannot commit a drug addict or an alcoholic to a mental health facility, there is often no other place to send these people; hence, the alternatives to commitment become either jail or ignoring the problems.

Table 12.2. Definitional components of *mental illness* on which respondents agreed.

Means	Questions
	When *mental illness* is used as a criterion for involuntary civil commitment, this phrase should include:
5.92	psychosis (severe inability to cope with reality).
2.51	neurosis (moderate inability to cope with reality).
3.03	sociopathic personality (inability to conform with prevailing social norms).
2.43	personality trait and pattern disorders (maladaptive character).
2.46	difficult for own family to manage, but not dangerous.
2.52	difficult for society to manage, but not dangerous.
1.90	neglects family obligations, but not dangerous.

Table 12.3. Definitional components of *mental illness* on which respondents disagreed.

Means			Questions
Psychiatrists	Psychologists	Lawyers	
			When *mental illness* is used as a criterion for involuntary civil commitment, this phrase should include:
3.89	3.24	2.92	drug addiction.
3.89	3.06	2.94	alcoholism.
5.23	4.38	5.02	organic mental illness.
3.61	3.11	2.91	in need of custodial care, but not in need of treatment.

What Is Dangerousness to Others?

In Tables 12.4 and 12.5 we find, once again, that respondents appeared to favor restricting whom society may commit involuntarily, this time with respect to defining *dangerous to others*. The only category which respondents wanted to include in this definition was physical harm. Respondents remained undecided about property damage, sexual imprudence, fear of harm, and psychological harm. The respondents favored the use of both past behavior evidence and predictions according to the last item in Table 12.4. In the case of past behavior, a comparison of items shows that all groups endorsed the use of both *recent* and *substantial*. In the case of predictions, all groups always preferred the use of "is *imminently* likely." In several cases the lawyers actually rejected a standard for defining *dangerous to others* for lack of the word *imminently*.

A bewildering result from Table 12.5 is that on the first item, respondents did not reject *dangerous to others* alone as a satisfactory criterion for involuntary civil commitment; in fact, clinical psychologists weakly

Table 12.4. Aspects of *dangerous to others* on which respondents agreed.

Means	Questions
	When *dangerous to others* is used as a criterion for involuntary civil commitment, one of the components of this phrase should be "a person who:
3.22	is imminently likely to make imprudent sexual decisions."
3.19	has recently made imprudent sexual decisions."
5.99	is imminently likely to harm another physically."
5.84	has recently harmed another physically and in a substantial manner."
5.24	has recently harmed another physically."
3.87	is imminently likely to damage another's property."
4.03	has recently done substantial damage to another's property."
3.66	has recently damaged another's property."
3.29	is imminently likely to harm another psychologically."
3.64	has recently harmed another psychologically and in a substantial manner."
3.26	has recently harmed another psychologically."
3.76	is imminently likely to place others in fear of harm."
4.04	has recently placed others in fear of substantial harm."
3.65	has recently placed others in fear of harm."
2.90	Each item beginning with "has" from above would be preferable if the word *recently* were omitted.
5.09	When *dangerous to others* is used as a criterion for involuntary civil commitment, this criterion should include both a recent occurrence *and* the likelihood of future occurrence.

Table 12.5. Aspects of *dangerous to others* on which respondents disagreed.

Means			Questions
Psychiatrists	Psychologists	Lawyers	
4.09	5.29	3.50	Involuntary civil commitment should be allowed if a person is dangerous to others. When *dangerous to others* is used as a criterion for involuntary civil commitment, one of the components of this phrase should be "a person who:
2.91	2.85	2.06	is likely to make imprudent sexual decisions."
5.33	5.10	4.24	is likely to harm another physically."
3.75	3.35	2.39	is likely to damage another's property."
3.11	3.01	2.27	is likely to harm another psychologically."
3.48	3.47	2.63	is likely to place others in fear of harm."

endorsed this criterion. If dangerousness without mental illness were a sufficient legal standard for involuntary commitment, commitment laws would have increased coercive power and could be used for preventive detention in this case; however, our current laws surely do not permit this type of preventive detention.[6] Furthermore, much of the research on the prediction of dangerousness shows that there is a strong tendency to overly predict. If this criterion were encompassed in the law, a number of individuals would probably be detained, due to predictions of dangerousness, who would not have done anything dangerous if they had been allowed to remain free (e.g., Monahan, 1975). We will further discuss problems concerning the prediction of dangerousness in the section on evidence.

What Is Dangerousness to Self?

Tables 12.6 and 12.7 show that respondents generally favored a restrictive definition of *dangerous to self*, too. On Table 12.6 items, all groups endorsed only the likelihood of suicide or serious physical harm as a sufficient definition of *dangerous to self*, although the groups were undecided about whether an inability to provide for one's own basic needs should fall within commitment laws. In addition, although each of these criteria is based upon an assessment of *likelihood*, which necessitates a prediction, the last item in Table 12.6 shows that respondents favored the use of both past behavioral evidence and the use of prediction in the determination of dangerousness to self. This combination should decrease the number of committable people and increase the accuracy of judgments about dangerousness to self. This result also clarifies much of the ambiguity of the middle three items in Table 12.7: Although the clinical psychologists were undecided about the use of past behavioral evidence alone, they clearly supported its use in conjunction with predictions. The last item in Table 12.7 shows that psychologists and lawyers favored only *recent* behavioral evidence, although psychiatrists also approached this view.

To summarize the results thus far, it appears that the most acceptable criterion for involuntary civil commitment, according to the respondents, would read as follows:

A person may be involuntarily committed if he or she is psychotic *and* if he or she *both (a)* is imminently likely to and (*b*) has recently:

1. attempt(ed) suicide or
2. cause(d) serious physical harm to self or
3. harm(ed) another physically in a substantial manner.

Such a definition limits considerably who may be committed when compared with many current laws, but it is consistent with the present trend in new commitment laws. Although some people hold a stereotype that mental health professionals want wide discretionary powers in determining who should be committed, the respondents disprove this belief.

Table 12.6. Definitional components of *dangerous to self* on which respondents agreed.

Means	Questions
	When *dangerous to self* is used as a criterion for involuntary civil commitment, one of the components of this phrase should be "a person who:
5.80	is likely to commit suicide."
4.33	is unable to provide for own basic needs."
2.75	is likely to make imprudent economic decisions."
5.61	is likely to cause serious, physical harm to self."
5.18	When *dangerous to self* is used as a criterion for involuntary civil commitment, this criterion should include both a recent occurrence *and* the likelihood of future occurrence.

Table 12.7. Aspects of *dangerous to self* on which respondents disagreed.

Means			Questions
Psychiatrists	Psychologists	Lawyers	
4.76	4.63	3.04	Involuntary civil commitment should be allowed if a person is dangerous to self.
			When *dangerous to self* is used as a criterion for involuntary civil commitment, one of the components of this phrase should be "a person who:
5.42	4.61	5.10	has recently attempted to commit suicide."
3.27	2.39	1.80	has recently made imprudent economic decisions."
5.45	4.85	5.02	has recently caused serious, physical harm to self."
3.05	2.73	1.86	The above three items would be preferable if the word *recently* were omitted.

When Should Commitment Hearings Be Held?

One possible response to this question would be, "Never"; our respondents did not give this response, however. All groups agreed that "Commitment hearings should be mandatory" ($\overline{X}$ (psychiatrists) = 5.20; $\overline{X}$ (psychologists) = 6.08; $\overline{X}$ (lawyers) = 6.36). In addition, respondents' views about the timing of the hearings, presented in Table 12.8, conform to the general legal trends of recent years. The right to a hearing within a reasonable period of time is critical for insuring that other due process protections are afforded to the subject of a commitment petition. Thus, this section also supports the emerging picture that all of our respondents are concerned with providing legal protections for the subjects of petitions.

Table 12.8. When decisions about commitment should be made.

Means	Questions
6.56 days	If a preliminary hearing is required to evaluate the evidence prior to a final hearing, how long after the individual was taken into custody should the hearing be held? Please give, *in days,* the longest wait which should be allowed.
15.25 days	How long after the individual was taken into custody should the final hearing be held? Please give the longest wait which should be allowed, again *in days.*
3.20 months	How frequently should status and treatment reviews be held after an individual has been involuntarily committed? Please give the longest duration between reviews which should be allowed, *in months.*

Who Should Make the Decision to Commit?

The groups showed very little agreement concerning whom society should entrust with the power to commit, at least with respect to the options with which we provided respondents in Table 12.9. The psychiatrists do not rate any potential decider above five; from their rank orderings, we might conclude that psychiatrists would like to make the decision themselves, but the lawyers rejected this option, and the psychologists were undecided. Lawyers endorsed judges, but the mental health professionals were undecided about this possibility. Interestingly, none of the groups were sold on having juries make commitment decisions.

The compromise solution favored by the psychologists—a board of people—was at least not rejected by the psychiatrists and the mental health lawyers. If a board decides whether a particular person should be committed, all respondents agreed that a psychiatrist and a judge should be on the board. Lawyers and psychologists supported the inclusion of a clinical psychologist, and the indecision about whether lawyers should be included was at least in the direction of having lawyers on this board.

One criticism that may be made against such a board is that it would not provide due process protections during a hearing so adequately as a court of law would. Although this is possible, it need not be the case: The legislature could authorize the board to provide full due process rights during the hearing and require that there be an automatic right of appeal to the district court *de novo.* This combination should give subjects of a commitment petition the same rights which they would receive in a court of law, except that there could be the added benefit of having the case heard before individuals knowledgeable about mental illness.[7] In addition, recent research in social psychology leads one to expect that decisions made by a board would more closely approximate societal values than would individual decisions (see Pruitt, 1971).

Table 12.9. Items concerning who should make the decision to commit.

Means			Questions
Psychiatrists	**Psychologists**	**Lawyers**	
			The decision to commit a person involuntarily should be made by:
4.77	4.20	5.81	a judge.
2.85	3.37	3.78	a jury.
3.83	4.15	4.94	a jury, if the person in question, or his legal counsel, requests a jury.
4.88	4.11	2.88	a psychiatrist
3.48	2.58	2.24	a physician.
3.16	4.16	2.63	a clinical psychologist.
4.03	5.60	3.33	a board of people.
4.64	5.20	4.29	person or people *un*associated with the institution to which the person in question will be sent.
			If the decision to commit a person is made by a board of people, this board should necessarily include:
6.41	5.92	5.60	a psychiatrist.
4.57	3.63	4.28	a physician.
4.49	6.03	5.23	a clinical psychologist.
4.86	4.05	4.53	one of the above three.
4.81	4.93	5.00	a lawyer.*
5.48	5.34	5.33	a judge.*

* On this item the means for the three groups do not differ significantly.

The psychologists were sensitive to the potential conflict of interests which might arise if the decision to commit someone were to be made by someone from the same institution to which the person in question would be sent if committed. Especially in some rural areas where hospitals may be underpopulated, the economic advantage of additional patients may taint the appearance of objectivity, if the decision to commit were made by someone who stands to gain from it. An additional reason to avoid this conflict of interests is that the therapist-patient relationship should start more cordially after commitment if the therapist has not been an adversary of the patient at a recent hearing.

Where Should Commitment Hearings Be Held?

In Table 12.10 lawyers rejected the hospital as a satisfactory alternative, but, in all other cases, the groups were undecided. The mental health professions ranked informal settings highest; the lawyers ranked court rooms highest. Flexibility in hearing locales may be essential. Ideally, hearings should not be held in a hospital, because the hospital environment may lead to an unconscious presumption of mental illness on the

Table 12.10. Means concerning where the commitment hearing should be held.

Means			Questions
Psychiatrists	Psychologists	Lawyers	
			Commitment hearings should be:
4.73	4.66	3.84	in an informal setting.
3.19	3.37	4.92	in a court room.
4.63	3.26	2.76	in a hospital.
3.88	3.87	3.78	in any place that provides a formal setting.

part of the person(s) deciding whether to commit an individual; nevertheless, in some cases, holding a hearing in a hospital may be essential, given an acute disability of a particular person facing commitment.

We might speculate that lawyers associate due process protection with the court room, viewing the setting as one important contributor to the frame of mind of the person(s) making the decision to commit. The assumption about the importance of stimulus control in this setting is particularly intriguing and should be further explored. Lawyers, however, may simply be more at ease in the court room, and mental health professionals may prefer informal settings, because of the emphasis on flexibility and informality in their training. Whatever the reason, further research needs to be done on what environment will promote the fairest hearing for both the individual's and society's interests.

What Evidentiary Rules Should Be Used in Commitment Hearings?

For the first three items in Table 12.11, we borrowed Stone's (1975) percentage definitions of the most common evidentiary standards used in the law. Although these percentages are nowhere sanctioned by the law, they do illustrate the rank order of these standards. We thought that they would be helpful to mental health professionals who may be less familiar with evidentiary standards than lawyers.

All the groups endorsed "on a clear and convincing proof," although the clinical psychologists ranked "beyond a reasonable doubt" even higher. Both of these criteria are currently being used,[8] although the trend is more toward using the former criterion. For example, involuntary commitment for mental illness and dangerousness is a civil (not criminal) action; thus, only a civil standard of proof would normally be required (preponderance of the evidence; on a clear and convincing proof).[9] Unless a legislature would set the standard at "beyond a reasonable doubt," it is doubtful that a court would impose this higher burden. However, since a person's liberty is at stake, the preponderance standard may be unacceptable even if mandated by the legislature.

Table 12.11. Means concerning commitment hearing evidentiary criteria.

Means			Questions
Psychiatrists	Psychologists	Lawyers	
			The decision in an involuntary civil commitment hearing should be based:
4.74	3.66	3.02	on a preponderance of evidence (at least 51% certainty).
5.10	5.08	5.06	on a clear and convincing proof (approximately 75% or more certainty).*
4.04	5.44	4.12	beyond a reasonable doubt (approximately 90% or more certainty).
2.57	3.78	3.80	on criminal law rules of evidence (more stringent than civil law rules of evidence).
4.28	4.10	4.35	on civil law rules of evidence.*
3.71	4.93	4.00	on separate rules of evidence which closely approximate criminal law rules of evidence but which do not employ the label "criminal."

* On this item the means for the groups do not differ significantly.

As noted earlier, all three groups favored the use of predictions of dangerousness as a prerequisite criterion for involuntary civil commitment. Table 12.12 shows the respondents' estimates of the predictive accuracy of current methods of assessing dangerousness. It is surprising that the lawyers, who typically have no training in data analysis, did not differ from the mental health professionals in their impressions of the predictive accuracy of dangerousness assessments. All three groups tended to overestimate the utility of dangerousness predictions when compared with most estimates presented in the research literature (e.g., Monahan, 1975; Morris, 1974); however, the respondents' estimates nevertheless illustrate an evidentiary paradox when compared with the standards of evidence which respondents supported in Table 12.11. On the one hand, it is necessary to establish, with at least 75 percent certainty, that a person is dangerous; but, on the other hand, we are not able to predict dangerousness with even 50 percent accuracy. Thus, we can never establish that a person is dangerous with sufficient certainty to comply with the evidentiary standards. Since any argument based on probabilities can never be better than its weakest component, any conclusion based on dangerousness and all other information necessary for commitment would still not comply with the percentage of certainty which the respondents wanted the evidence to meet. This paradox will undoubtedly be the focus of considerable controversy concerning involuntary civil commitment in the near future.

Another area of considerable controversy over evidence, at least

Table 12.12. Estimates of the predictive accuracy of dangerousness judgments.

Means			Questions
Psychiatrists	Psychologists	Lawyers	
			Please estimate the percentage of accurate predictions which are made with current methods of predicting dangerousness:
49.13%	46.64%	46.03%	to self.
39.57%	45.56%	42.00%	to others.

Note: The above means are not significantly different statistically.

among the three groups we surveyed, has to do with the evidentiary stature of the clinical psychologist's testimony. Table 12.13 displays the means which suggest that clinical psychologists would like to have a larger role when testifying than they are accorded in some jurisdictions. Except for the interpretation of biochemical or clearly medical information, clinical psychologists wanted equal evidentiary stature with psychiatrists; the psychiatrists and lawyers were undecided about granting this equality. For psychiatrists, this rating may reflect their traditional concern over protecting their guild interests. For lawyers, however, a plausible reason is not self-evident: It may be that lawyers assume psychiatrists are more qualified than psychologists, since law schools predominantly label their mental health law course, "Law and Psychiatry." The real issue is, however, whether either group is qualified by its training and experience to provide expert testimony. Some authors have forcefully argued that neither clinical psychologists nor psychiatrists should have prominent evidentiary stature (Ennis and Litwack, 1974; Morse, 1978). Since psychological and psychiatric tests and methods often have suspect reliability and validity, there appears to be no simple solution to this professional controversy.

Table 12.13. Means concerning the evidentiary status of psychologists' testimony.

Means			Questions
Psychiatrists	Psychologists	Lawyers	
			The clinical psychologist's testimony should have equal weight with the psychiatrist's testimony in a commitment hearing:
2.50	5.52	3.47	always.
3.30	1.41	2.04	never.
4.90	2.05	3.91	only in matters of interpreting psychometric data.
4.28	5.89	4.74	except in matters of interpreting biochemical or clearly medical information.

What Rights Should Be Accorded with Respect to Commitment?

Tables 12.14 and 12.15 display data on the respondents' views about rights during and after involuntary civil commitment proceedings. These rights are at the center of the discussion about whether there should be more attention to due process of law in civil commitment. One view of commitment maintains that ensuring the protection of rights could be detrimental to the recovery and treatment of a mentally ill person because of intense emotion which can be associated with legal hearings. Another view of commitment holds that in matters of deprivation of liberty, it is essential to protect the alleged mentally ill person from the possibility of arbitrary, capricious, or malevolent decisions and that thus careful attention should be paid to rights and the due process of law. Most often, the respondents apparently favored the second alternative, although there was some indecision, especially among the psychiatrists.

One important right for an individual facing commitment is that of legal counsel; this right is necessary, because the individual is almost certain to have little legal knowledge about commitment proceedings. If the individual wishes to contest a commitment, legal counsel will be indispensable in the preparation and presentation of a defense. Yet Stone (1975) reports that while 42 jurisdictions provide for a right to legal counsel in commitment proceedings, only 24 provide for the appointment of counsel when the individual facing commitment is indigent; thus, poverty creates unequal justice. It is laudatory that all three groups of respondents

Table 12.14. Rights on which respondents agreed.

Means	Questions
	During the process of involuntary civil commitment proceedings, the person in question should have the right to:
6.49	legal counsel.
6.47	legal counsel, even if indigent.
6.36	adequate written notice of all hearings relevant to the case.
6.07	have an independent examination, even if indigent.
6.01	have own witnesses.
5.88	have adverse witnesses cross examined.
	An individual who has been involuntarily civilly committed should have the right to:
6.55	treatment.
6.16	keep and wear own clothing.
5.58	communicate without censorship by telephone in privacy.
5.74	communicate without censorship by sealed envelope through the public mails.
6.30	keep a small amount of funds for personal expenses.
6.40	have access to a patient grievance procedure.
5.40	independent review of case at any time upon request.

Table 12.15. Rights on which respondents disagreed.

Means			Questions
Psychiatrists	Psychologists	Lawyers	
			During the process of involuntary civil commitment, the person in question should have the right to:
6.08	6.38	6.76	adequate written notice of reasons for invoking commitment proceedings.
5.83	6.39	6.54	adequate written notice of the way the hearing will be conducted and the rules governing it.
5.87	6.30	6.66	adequate written notice sufficiently early to prepare a defense.
4.88	5.69	6.40	be informed of his or her diagnosis.
4.87	5.62	6.70	have access to prior mental records if the person's history is to be brought up in the hearing.
4.34	5.61	6.34	have access to prior mental records.
			An individual who has been involuntarily civilly committed should have the right to:
4.10	5.33	5.14	refuse treatment.
4.92	5.71	6.00	challenge the treatment plan.
3.35	4.76	5.08	have access to all records regarding his or her case.
4.24	5.23	5.36	have access to all records regarding his or her case, unless harmful.
4.98	4.95	5.30	have a date specified upon commitment of when the commitment will cease.
3.30	3.11	2.16	Involuntary commitments should be for an indefinite length of time to prevent patients who are not fully well from being discharged.
			When the right to refuse treatment is in the law, this right should apply *unless:*
6.20	5.49	5.68	a short term imposition of drugs is necessary because there exists an imminent danger of serious harm to self or others.
4.89	3.98	3.38	treatment will lead to a more prompt cure.
4.79	3.80	3.30	treatment will lead to an earlier release.
3.67	2.91	2.42	Individuals who enter a mental hospital on a voluntary basis should *not* be permitted to leave the hospital at their own discretion if it is not advisable from a medical standpoint.

strongly support the right to legal counsel for all people facing commitment.

Legal counsel may not, however, be very helpful in preparing a defense if adequate written notice about the time, place, issues, and procedures for the hearing are not supplied. Furthermore, adequate written notice may be useless if it does not arrive sufficiently early to prepare a defense. Although the three professions differed statistically in their level of support for three of the four questionnaire items which inquired about adequate written notice, in all cases each group was well within the range of agreement for granting these rights.

Once an individual facing commitment has written notice and counsel, the next task is to gather and present information concerning his or her case. Respondents favored a right to independent examination, even if a person were indigent. They also supported the rights to have witnesses and to cross examine adverse witnesses. On other rights related to the gathering of information, however, only the psychologists and lawyers assented. The psychiatrists were undecided about whether the alleged mentally ill person should know his or her diagnosis and should have access to prior mental records. The lack of this information would greatly hinder the preparation of a convincing defense, since the two sides in the dispute would have unequal information.

All three groups agreed that a number of rights should also be afforded to an individual who has been involuntarily committed. This consistent concern for rights by all three groups shown in the bottom half of Table 12.14 is interesting, because it conflicts with the stereotype of mental health professionals as individuals unconcerned with patient rights. All three groups supported the right to treatment, which will be discussed in more detail below. All three groups favored the rights to communicate by telephone and by mail, to keep and wear one's own clothing, and to keep a small amount of funds for personal expenses. Especially important for protecting the other rights of patients are the rights to a patient grievance procedure and to independent review at any time upon request. Again, all three groups were willing to grant these rights.

Only psychologists and lawyers were willing to establish rights to challenge the treatment plan and to have access to all records regarding one's case, unless harmful; the psychiatrists remained undecided. Psychiatrists were even undecided about whether voluntary patients should be allowed to leave a hospital at their own discretion. Yet, at least with regard to the right to challenge the treatment plan, psychiatrists may not be opposed to challenge, since, as noted above, they supported the right to independent review at any time upon request; they simply appear to favor challenge by another professional.

Switching to the right to refuse treatment, psychologists and lawyers favored such a right, but the psychiatrists were undecided. All three groups favored an exception to the right to refuse treatment, if it is in the law, which would allow for a short term imposition of drugs when there exists an imminent danger of serious harm to self or others. In some cases, such an exception to the right to refuse treatment may be necessary to maintain order in a mental health institution. This exemption could be abused, however, if one acknowledges that all patients who are committed under statutes in which dangerousness is a criterion for commitment are by definition dangerous.

Respondents were undecided about two other potential qualifications in the right to refuse treatment. Perhaps respondents realized that the right to refuse treatment involves a number of very complex issues when applied to mental health: To what extent should a therapist respect the religious convictions of a patient? To what extent may the nature of a patient's mental illness influence his or her ability to decide (e.g., in cases of paranoid or masochistic patients) to refuse treatment? Should the right to refuse treatment apply only to some types of controversial treatment (e.g., psychosurgery or electroconvulsive shock therapy)? Particularly complex issues arise in connection with the right to refuse treatment when one considers that many mental health professionals are also research scientists. The ethical questions associated with research on human subjects are myriad. The researcher has obligations both to protect his or her research subjects and to help future generations of patients.

The opposite of the right to refuse treatment, the right to treatment, appears to be one of the most controversial topics in the literature on involuntary civil commitment (e.g., Golann and Fremouw, 1976). It was the least controversial right among these respondents (see Table 12.14). Nevertheless, the data in Table 12.16 raise some questions about the nature of the conviction in the right to treatment among the respondents. Although respondents supported a right to treatment, the mental health professionals were undecided about whether to allow commitment if no treatment were available, and all three professions were undecided about whether involuntary civil commitment should be allowed only if treatment is likely to be effective. To take either equivocal position is problematic. If patients have the right to treatment, but are involuntarily committed when no treatment is available, commitments would undoubtedly be overturned on appeal.[10] Furthermore, this logic may partially imply a reluctance to make mental health professionals accountable for their treatment. But commitment without effective treatment is tantamount to no treatment at all. In either case commitment becomes a form of preventive detention—something which is unpermissible under current law when done to individuals who are dangerous only. Since persons labeled mentally ill and dangerous hve been shown to constitute no greater danger to society than persons from the rest of the population (Stone, 1975), there is no justification for allowing preventive detention solely because the dangerous individual is also mentally ill.

Table 12.16. Means of treatment availability prerequisites for commitment.

Means			Questions
Psychiatrists	Psychologists	Lawyers	
			Involuntary civil commitment should be allowed *only* if:
4.34	4.25	5.10	treatment is available.
3.46	3.83	4.29	treatment is likely to be effective.
4.73	4.79	5.88	a less restrictive alternative for treatment with about equal likelihood of effectiveness is *not* available.

The indecision of mental health professionals with respect to the use of less restrictive alternative therapies also is disturbing. It again raises the question of whether *treatment* is sometimes a euphemism for *preventive detention*.

Are There Other Issues in Commitment?

Of course. A few of these issues are raised in Table 12.17. The first three items deal with a few professional issues in commitment. Surprisingly, the mental health professionals and the lawyers do not differ in their view of civil commitment as a legal versus a medical problem. The mental health professionals do differ in the importance which they attach to medical versus psychological aspects of mental illness, as one might expect, given their different training experiences. The third item was initially included in the questionnaire for coding purposes,[11] but the results from it are nevertheless interesting. All three groups wanted a more important role in the development of civil commitment laws. The mental health lawyers expressed the strongest interest in increased power, although the psychiatrists, who currently appear to have the most power, did not differ from the mental health lawyers too much. These results imply that all three groups will have a great deal of interest in both testifying before and aiding legislatures in shaping new laws in this area.

The fourth item in Table 12.17 refers to a recent case in California[12] where a court ruled what the question states. All three groups were undecided about this issue, perhaps because it involves both questions about responsibility to potential victims and about the confidentiality of the therapist-client relationship.[13] Given that mental health professionals often overly predict dangerousness and that public prophecies often have a way of becoming self-fulfilling, it is not clear whether mental health professionals should have a legal obligation to warn every potential victim of a patient's threats.

Table 12.17. Several other issues.

Means			Questions
Psychiatrists	Psychologists	Lawyers	
4.27	4.45	4.45	Civil commitment is more a legal than a medical problem.*
4.45	2.18	3.34	Mental illness is more a medical than a psychological problem.
5.85	5.50	5.96	Civil commitment laws would be more effective if (your profession) had a more important role in their development.**
4.11	4.74	4.06	If a person is judged dangerous to others and not institutionalized, that person's therapist should have a legal obligation to warn potential victims of the danger.
5.23	5.83	5.60	Involuntary civil commitment could conceivably be used as a tool for political suppression.

* This difference is not statistically significant.
** In place of "(your profession)," the name of the profession of the respondent was inserted (i.e., psychiatrists, clinical psychologists, or mental health lawyers).

The last item in Table 12.17 shows that all groups were concerned about the potential for political abuse in involuntary civil commitment. This potential was recently underscored when the World Psychiatric Association censured Soviet psychiatry for allowing political dissidents to be classified as mentally ill. The concern for political abuse may account for the general tendency of all our respondents to want due process protections provided to subjects of commitment petitions.

DIFFERENCES RELATED TO RETURN ADDRESS, EMPLOYER, AND THEORETICAL ORIENTATION

In addition to profession, we were able to separate our respondents along several other dimensions. As mentioned in the Method section, some respondents thought that they were responding to a survey sponsored by a law college, while other respondents thought that they were responding to a survey sponsored by a psychology department (actually both of these assumptions were true because the second author has a joint appointment to both a law college and a psychology department). We were also able to divide respondents according to whether their major source of employment was government, private practice, or academic, based on replies to a question near the end of the schedule. Finally, we examined whether major, theoretical differences in psychiatry/psychology influenced how respondents completed their questionnaires. The categories which we offered respondents for theoretical classification were behavioristic, humanistic, psychoanalytic, and other; we added one additional category, humanistic-psychoanalytic, because a number of respondents selected both of these classifications. For all of the analyses reported in this seciton (which are all statistically significant), we used the same alpha level as above (.005) to determine statistical significance, but we were unable to include mental health lawyers in these analyses because of insufficient sample size. As above, the statistic we used was analysis of variance. The below interactions do not represent all interactions which were statistically significant, only those interactions which were of particular interest to us; nevertheless, overall, we found far fewer interactions than we had initially anticipated.

Dividing the respondents according to return address revealed some troubling findings: On certain questions, respondents appeared to change their views based upon whether their responses were to be sent to a law college or a psychology department; for example, when estimating the accuracy of predictions of dangerousness to others in Table 12.18 (previously discussed with respect to Table 12.12), both psychiatrists and psychologists were less confident in predictions when responding to a psychology department than when responding to a law college. Perhaps this difference is due to the greater likelihood of a psychologist to be involved in data analysis, compared to a lawyer. Hence, respondents were more cautious when they expected that their responses would be compared with previous research by someone well equipped to interpret that research.

Table 12.18. Interaction between profession and return address in estimates of percentage of accurate predictions of dangerousness to others with current methods.

| | | Return Address | |
		Law Coll.	Psych. Dept.
Profession	Psychiatrists	40.63%	38.26%
	Psychologists	46.78%	44.17%

In response to the statement, "Involuntary civil commitment should be allowed if a person is dangerous to others" (alone), which we first discussed in connection with Table 12.5, we found an additional main effect; responses to a law college were more likely to be undecided ($\overline{X} = 4.47$) than were responses to a psychology department ($\overline{X} = 5.06$). There are at least two possible interpretations which could be given to this finding: On the one hand, respondents may have been under the stimulus control of the return address; thus, when responding to a law college, respondents may in general have been more conscious of the law and consequently less certain of using preventive detention for dangerousness. On the other hand, respondents may have tried to project an image which they thought would be more acceptable to the interviewers. Only further research can isolate which of these interpretations, or others, is appropriate.

Finally, Tables 12.19 and 12.20 (previously discussed in Tables 12.15 and 12.17, respectively) display more means which show differences in how mental health professionals respond to different audiences. Psychiatrists were less in favor of indeterminant commitments when responding to a law college than when responding to a psychology department, whereas psychologists opposed indeterminant commitments only when replying to a psychology department. Psychiatrists were slightly more likely to agree that civil commitment is more a legal than a medical problem when responding to a law college than a psychology department, whereas psychologists took the opposite tactic. In general, psychologists gave more polar responses when responding to a psychology department, whereas psychiatrists gave more polar responses when responding to a law college. Psychologists may have been more at ease and therefore more forthright when responding to fellow psychologists, whereas psychiatrists may have been more emphatic when they expected to accomplish more in terms of legal reform. Moreover, it appears that caution must be exercised in accepting the views of any advocate of a particular

Table 12.19. Interaction between profession and return address in response to the statement: "Involuntary commitments should be for an indefinite length of time to prevent patients who are not fully well from being discharged."

		Return Address	
		Law Coll.	Psych. Dept.
Profession	Psychiatrists	3.03	3.65
	Psychologists	3.32	2.85

Table 12.20. Interaction between profession and return address in response to the statement: "Civil commitment is more a legal than a medical problem."

		Return Address	
		Law Coll.	Psych. Dept.
Profession	Psychiatrists	4.45	4.04
	Psychologists	4.11	4.82

position without first recognizing that for whatever reason, the respondent may alter conclusions to different audiences. Often people attempt to manage impressions when presenting their attitudes (Kahle, 1978), and it is important to recognize that this process can occur in situations such as this one. People who conduct surveys on the attitudes of a particular target group toward some area of the law have to be sensitive to the possibility that respondents, answering the same questions, may express different opinions to different people.

When dividing the respondents according to their source of employment, we likewise discovered several differences which suggest that careful attention must be given to the employment of the professional in understanding his or her attitudes toward this area of the law. For example, private practice psychiatrists were more likely to be undecided about rights to communicate without censorship (originally discussed with respect to Table 12.14) than were the remaining psychiatrists and all psychologists. For communication by telephone, the private practice psychiatrists ($\overline{X} = 4.88$) were the only group with a mean below 5.40; for communication without censorship by mail, private practice psychiatrists ($\overline{X} = 5.09$) were the only group with a mean below 5.50. One possible explanation for this finding may be that private practitioners are more worried that clients' communications can hurt their image or reputation, which directly affects their chance of obtaining new patients and therefore their income level. Academicians and government employees would not share similar concerns, because the former are less dependent upon clients for income, and the latter are less dependent upon reputation for attracting clients. But why did psychologists in private practice not react the same way? The reason may lie in the fact that psychologists are overall more due process oriented, and this orientation may overcome any effects of private practice concerns. In addition, many psychologists in private practice work for psychiatrists and are thus not truly independent; hence, they would not have to worry about client behavior in the same way psychiatrists would. These reasons are speculative, but the important point is that employment does affect attitudes in this area.

An additional interaction effect related to source of employment showed that respondents who worked for the government were more likely to be undecided about the potential for political suppression as a result of involuntary civil commitment when responding to a law college than when responding to a psychology department, but academicians were more emphatic about this potential problem when replying to a law college than to a psychology department, according to the data in Table 12.21 (previously in Table 12.17). Once again we can speculate on the reason: Responses to a law college are more likely to have an impact on

Table 12.21. Interaction between major source of employment and return address on the question about whether involuntary commitment could be used for political suppression.

Source of Employment	Return Address	
	Law Coll.	Psych. Dept.
Government	4.93	5.97
Private Practice	5.70	5.53
Academic	5.94	5.38

the law than responses to a psychology department. The government employees may have wished to appear concerned about political abuses to fellow mental health professionals but feared further legislation on this topic which would restrict them. Academicians, on the other hand, would be less likely to experience the direct effects of such new laws and hence may be more concerned about obtaining laws which would protect their profession's image. Moreover, one may expect that the divergent interests, responsibilities, and pressures on mental health professionals in different employment categories will influence their views on other issues as well. When examining the response of a particular mental health professional, it is not sufficient to assume that one person represents his or her entire profession, since even within a profession there may be considerable variability, depending upon the major types of professional activities in which the person engages. It is important to take a careful look at the person's source of employment.

Finally, we observed several differences among mental health professionals attributable to the theoretical orientation of the respondents, and these differences are ones which may easily escape people outside of the mental health professions. Although we did not find as many differences due to theoretical orientation as we had initially expected, it is inevitable that in some areas of law, the differences in goals and philosophies about human nature will lead to different legal prescriptions; for example, the means in Table 12.22 show the considerable variability associated with theoretical orientation. Beyond the tendency of psychiatrists to rate this item lower, which we have already discussed with respect to Table 12.15, several other factors appear to be operating here: This significant interaction appears in part to be due to the low ratings given by the humanistic-psychoanalytic and "other" psychiatrists when responding to a psychology department. Another significant interaction, this time on the right to keep and wear own clothing after commitment (originally from Table

Table 12.22. Interaction between profession, theoretical orientation, and return address on the right to adequate written notice sufficiently early to prepare a defense.

Profession: Return Address: *Orientation*	Psychiatrists		Psychologists	
	Law Coll.	Psych. Dept.	Law Coll.	Psych. Dept.
Behavioristic	6.15	6.33	6.36	6.38
Humanistic	5.35	5.94	6.32	6.41
Psychoanalytic	5.98	6.12	6.49	6.45
Humanistic-Psychoanalytic	6.09	5.31	5.40	6.44
Other	5.79	5.16	5.92	6.57

12.14), existed between theoretical orientation and profession; it was apparently due to the lower rating by the psychoanalytic psychiatrists ($\overline{X}$ = 5.76). We might venture an explanation for this finding by assuming that psychoanalytic psychiatrists would place more emphasis than other groups on having the authority to control the patient's identity by such means as control over attire, since identity is a more important construct in psychoanalytic theory (e.g., Erikson, 1963) than in other theories and since psychiatrists are more likely to endorse traditional psychoanalysis than are psychologists. The above two differences underscore the importance of theoretical orientations for mental health professionals; therefore, it is important for lawyers and legislators, who rely on mental health professionals for expert advice, to be aware of the fact that mental health professionals do not all approach the world in the same manner.

CONCLUSIONS

The above data should be particularly useful: 1) to legislators contemplating revisions in their state's commitment statutes who want to balance the interests of the professions involved with the mental health system; and 2) to other people who wish to understand and discuss areas of controversy and agreement with respect to commitment law. Attitudinal paradoxes exist with respect to such topics as dangerousness, the right to treatment, and the right to refuse treatment, but the general trend of thought on commitment laws is toward increased concern for the rights of individuals facing commitment rather than toward increased protection of the power of mental health professionals. As we predicted, the lawyers were more emphatic in their support of the due process of law approach to commitment than the psychologists, who in turn were more concerned with due process of law than were the psychiatrists. Even the psychiatrists, however, would be better characterized as supporting the increased concern over rights than opposing it. Where psychiatrists did not endorse a particular right, they were usually undecided rather than in opposition to that right.

In general the results of this survey are encouraging both for people who advocate commitment statutes which emphasize rights more strongly and for people who wonder whether such laws would be followed even if enacted. Of course, attitudes are often, but not always, predictors of behavior (Kelman, 1974). Sometimes situational constraints will lead to deviations from the ideals which people express in a survey; for example, if a legislature enacts a law which guarantees all of the due process rights we have discussed, but fails to appropriate sufficient funds for the mental health system to ensure that the rights can be protected, all of the positive attitudes toward due process of law in the world may not help individuals facing commitment to receive a fair and impartial hearing.

REFERENCES

Brakel, S. J., and Rock, R. S. (Eds.) *The Mentally Disabled and the Law*. Chicago: Ill.: University of Chicago Press, 1971.

Collins, B. E., and Hoyt, M. F. Personal responsibility-for-consequences: An integration and extension of the "forced compliance" literature. *Journal of Experimental Social Psychology* 8: 558–593 (1972).

Dillman, D. A., Christenson, J. A., Carpenter, E. H., and Brooks, R. M. Increasing mail questionnaire response: A four state comparison. *American Sociological Review* 39: 744–756 (1974).

Ennis, B. J., and Litwack, T. R. Psychiatry and the presumption of expertise: Flipping coins in the courtroom. *California Law Review* 62: 693–752 (1974).

Erikson, E. H. *Childhood and Society* (2nd ed.). New York: W. W. Norton, 1963.

Golann, S., and Fremouw, W. T. (Eds.) *The Right to Treatment for Mental Patients*. New York. Irvington, 1976.

Kahle, L. R. Dissonance and impression management as theories of attitude change. *Journal of Social Psychology* 105: 53–64 (1978).

Kahle, L. R., and Sales, B. D. The attitudes of clinical psychologists toward involuntary civil commitment. *Professional Psychology* 9: 428–439. (a) (1978).

Kahle, L. R., and Sales, B. D. Provocative novelty revisited. *Mental Disability Law Reporter* 3: 677–678. (b) (1978).

Kahle, L. R., Sales, B. D., and Nagel, S. On unicorns blocking commitment law reform. *Journal of Psychiatry and Law* 6: 89–105 (1978).

Kelman, H. C. Attitudes are alive and well and gainfully employed in the sphere of action. *American Psychologist* 29: 310–324 (1974).

Monahan, J. The prediction of violence. In Chappell, D., and Monahan, J. (Eds.) *Violence and criminal justice*. Lexington, Mass.: D.C. Heath (Lexington Books), 1975.

Morris, N. *The Future of Imprisonment*. Chicago: University of Chicago Press, 1974.

Morse, S. Crazy behavior, morals, and science: An analysis of the mental health legal system. *Southern California Law Review* **51,** in press.

Pruitt, D. C. Choice shifts in group discussion: An introductory review. *Journal of Personality and Social Psychology* **20:** 339–360 (1971).

Stone, A. A. *Mental Health Law: A System in Transition.* Rockville, Md.: National Institute of Mental Health, 1975.

Szasz, T. S. *The Myth of Mental Illness: Foundations of a Theory of Personal Conduct.* New York: Harper, 1961

Treffet, D. A. The practical limits of patients' rights. *Psychiatric Annals* **5:** 91–96 (1975).

FOOTNOTES TO CHAPTER 12

[1] O'Connor v. Donaldson, 422 U.S. 563 (1975). Since the purpose of this article is not to review current developments in commitment law, only illustrative case and statutory examples will be cited. The reader interested in keeping abreast of legal changes in this and related areas should consult the *Mental Disability Law Reporter.*

[2] Lessard v. Schmidt, 349 F. Supp. 1078 (E.D. Wes. 1972), *vacated and remanded on procedural grounds,* 414 U.S. 473 (1974), *on remand,* 379 F. Supp. 1379 (E.D. Wis. 1974), *vacated and remanded on other grounds,* 412 U.S. 957 (1975), *on remand,* 413 F. Supp. 1318 (E.D. Wis. 1976).

[3] NEB. REV. STAT. §83–1001 *et seq.* (1976).

[4] Wyatt v. Stickney, 325 F. Supp. 781 (M.D. Ala. 1971); 334 F. Supp. 1341 (M.D. Ala. 1971); *enforced by* 344 F. Supp. 373, 344 F. Supp. 387, *appeal docketed sub nom.* Wyatt v. Aderholt, No. 72–2634, 5th Cir., filed Aug. 1, 1973. Wyatt v. Stickney, 344 F. Supp. 373, 376, 379–385 (M.D. Ala. 1972).

[5] State of Wisconsin ex rel. David Memmel and Judith Pagels v. Edwin A. Mundy, No. 441–417 (Milwaukee County Circuit Court, Wisc., August 18, 1976).

[6] There is also an irony in the fact that the addition of mental illness as a criterion makes this type of deprivation acceptable, "especially since the evidence suggests that . . . mental illness is an especially poor indicator of future criminal conduct" (Stone, 1975; p. 49).

[7] E.g., NEB. REV. STAT. *supra,* note 3.

[8] E.g., ARIZ. REV. STAT., §36–540 (1974), uses "clear and convincing proof." Examples of "beyond a reasonable doubt" include: In re Ballay, 482 F.2d 648 (D.C. Cir. 1973); Lessard v. Schmidt, *supra,* note 2.

[9] Doremus v. Farrell, 407 F. Supp. 509 (D. Neb. 1975).

[10] O'Connor v. Donaldson, *supra,* note 1.

[11] This item enabled us to identify the profession of the respondent in cases where a respondent did not sign his or her questionnaire.

[12] Tarasoff v. Regents of University of California, 529 P.2d 342, 118 Cal. Rptr. 129 (1974), *vacated,* 17 Cal. 3d 425, 551 P.2d 334, 131 Cal. Rptr. 14 (1976).

[13] See, e.g., Comment, The therapist's duty to potential victims: A non-threatening view of Tarasoff. *Law and Human Behavior* **1:**309–318 (1978).

13

Factors Affecting the Patients' Rights Ideology of Mental Hospital Personnel

Paul P. Freddolino

INTRODUCTION

In recent years, concern for patients' rights issues in mental health has become increasingly dramatic. Court challenges and new mental health legislation, based on civil liberties and constitutional rights, have led to new patterns of treatment and care, institutional due process, and even discharge of previously institutionalized patients. This has led to backlashes from mental health professionals ostensibly concerned with patient care issues, from employees of state institutions fearing loss of jobs, and from community residents terrified by the presence of mental patients in their neighborhood.

Responses of personnel in the mental health field to extending patients' rights have been varied. For some, the main issue has been maintaining high treatment standards for all patients; for another group, it has been the

Some of the material contained in this study appeared in my doctoral dissertation (Freddolino, 1977). The research on which it is based was supported by a grant from the Foundation for Mental Health Research, Inc. Additional financial assistance was provided by the Rackham School of Graduate Studies at The University of Michigan, and support for all computer work came from the Department of Sociology at The University of Michigan. Preparation of this study was also supported by a NIMH Postdoctoral Fellowship (USPHS 1T32–MH 14583). I want to express my special thanks to Professor Oscar Grusky for his extensive comments on an earlier draft of this manuscript.

maintenance of civil liberties and due process in dealings with patients; for still others, it has been safeguarding the prerogative of mental health professionals to make final decisions about treatment. There is also a basic difference in values concerning the role of large state hospitals. Some people see large mental hospitals as a functional and necessary part of treating mental health problems. Others seem unalterably opposed to large mental health institutions as dehumanizing and useless (Goffman, 1961; Vail, 1966; Ennis, 1972).

In addition to treatment and civil libertarian concerns, there is a theme of self-interest related to job security evident in responses to patients' rights issues. For example, the American Federation of State, County, and Municipal Employees has published a short monograph (Santiestevan, 1975) criticizing the pattern of releasing patients from state hospitals. Throughout the discussion, the threat of job loss to staff who provide direct care and who are members or potential members of the organization is implicit. Attitudes of staff members toward patients and mental illness constitute an important component of the ambiance of any mental hospital. Although a number of researchers have attempted to assess the attitudes of both the general public and mental health workers (Rabkin, 1975), few have examined staff attitudes toward specific patients' "rights" as defined by legal statutes. One exception is the national study of psychiatrists, psychologists, and mental health lawyers by Kahle and Sales, appearing in this collection, which examines attitudes toward involuntary civil commitment.

Much of the work that has been done concerning patients' rights has focused on a single issue, such as the right to treatment (Pfohl, 1975; National Association of Attorneys General, 1976) or the overuse of medications (Chandler and Sallychild, 1977). A large number of studies have dealt with the impact of legislative and judicial action on the mental health system (Stone, 1975). Frequently, these studies have examined the variance between legislated intent and actual implementation of changes in mental health codes (Warren, 1977; Lipsitt, 1980); unfortunately, little attention has been paid to the role of administrative and staff perspectives as causative elements determining the final outcomes of legislated change.

The central problem in this study is to account for the differing responses toward patients' rights issues made by and acted upon by planners, administrators, practitioners, and advocates in the field of mental health. This chapter will discuss the effect of four factors on state hospital personnel's view of patients' rights issues: demographic characteristics, position in the hospital, profession, and extent of direct patient care responsibilities.[1] The description of various ideological responses to patients' rights issues and the analyses of causative factors presented below are designed to extend our knowledge of the organizational and interpersonal context in which legislative and judicial mandates are implemented.

It is hoped that this analysis of patient's rights ideology (PRI) will provide information of use to planners and administrators in their attempts to implement legislative and judicial mandates. Although we cannot assume a one-to-one relationship between attitudes and actual behavior, studies of the attitudes of influential people in a system do provide us with a way of understanding how they view important parts of their work (Schuman and Johnson, 1976).

STATEMENT OF THE PROBLEM

State hospitals, as people-processing institutions, share a number of characteristics that affect the behaviors of the people within them, both staff and patients; the most salient characteristics of these institutions are summarized below: [2]

1. As in other types of medical facilities and other total institutions, daily life in state hospitals tends to be dictated by factors other than strictly medical considerations; specifically, these factors are *patient management* (control) and *staff convenience* (Goffman, 1961:346–347; Freidson, 1970:312).

2. State hospitals are characterized by a confusion of functions or goals. In addition to the medical function of treatment, which justifies the hospital's existence, two other functions can be identified, both of which may conflict with the treatment function. The custodial function (Parsons, 1957:110) reflects pressures to protect society from "the danger and nuisance of certain kinds of misconduct" (Goffman, 1961:352); that this function exists is in part demonstrated by the fact that the rules by which individual patients enter hospitals are usually controlled by other societal institutions (e.g., state legislatures) that are in turn directly responsive to community sentiment. The second alternate function of state hospitals is the *waiting room function,* by which hospitals must retain patients only because there is no room in other, more appropriate facilities. Thus, many people who may not have "medical" problems requiring "treatment" are held because hospitals have been assigned these functions: For example, a 1970 study by the National Institute of Mental Health showed that 56 percent of the patients at a mental hospital in Washington, D.C. needed "outplacement" in a less restrictive setting, but, due to an absence of such facilities, these patients were kept in the hospital. [3]

3. The conflict among functions is exacerbated by the involuntary character of many admissions to state hospitals. Even when patients

admit themselves, the action is frequently taken under threat of court action by family members or community agencies (Stone, 1975:43). Staff in state hospitals thus confronts large numbers of patients who are angry and hostile, because they are being held against their will.

4. Unlike other loci of expert treatment, state hospitals cannot be seen as benign agents that have no negative effects upon those entering them (Goffman, 1961:356; Scheff, 1966:114). Two major negative effects can be cited. First, commitment to state hospitals carries a stigma that remains with the individual even after discharge (Goffman, 1961:355); Perrucci (1974:22–27) notes that this stigma is often attached to the staff as well. Second, patients often become so accustomed to the institutional routine and so afraid of the justifiably great risks of leaving (including the need of confronting the community's reaction to them as "former mental patients") that they do not want to leave the institutions (Goffman, 1961:356).

These characteristics and their inherent conflicts define the arena in which patients' rights ideology will be examined. It is an arena marked by constant conflict between humane standards—reflecting the view of patients as people—and institutional efficiency—reflecting the need to maintain order and control. As Goffman (1961:111) has expressed it, "the social reality in a total institution is precarious. I think we should not be surprised by these weaknesses . . . but rather wonder that more flaws do not appear."

These characteristics and conflicts lead to two predictions concerning the relationship between control and patients' rights ideology at the level of respondent characteristics: First, those who possess more interpersonal "power" in terms of their positions in the hospital organization, the relative prestige of their professions, or other social and economic characteristics, are more likely to be "pro-patient" in their responses to patients' rights issues; the elements of this statement must be examined separately.

Position

More powerful positions in the hierarchy of the state hospital bring increased contact with agencies and institutions outside the hospital, including such groups as the Department of Mental Hygiene, other state and local agencies, and professional mental health groups; thus, people in these positions have a reference group composed largely of high level professionals outside the hospital. Similarly, if the hospital and its policies come under attack, such as when a patient advocate sues for release of a patient, higher level administrators must interact with the judicial system and defend the policies of the institution.

The individuals who occupy more powerful positions in the organization might therefore be expected to have a perspective that is more cosmopolitan and, consequently, more liberal in nature (Rogers and Shoemaker, 1971). This prediction is consistent with results of research in other institutional arenas. For example, Stouffer, et al. (1949) found that officers tend to be more liberal than enlisted men on a number of issues; other studies have shown that principals tend to be more liberal than teachers (Carlson, 1965). Lieberman (1956) has shown that a change in role causes changes in attitudes, rather than the reverse. Thus, individuals higher in the power hierarchy of hospitals should be more inclined to support patient rights. As used in the analyses below, the variable POWER is meant to categorize the actual position of individual respondents within the organization. It expresses the difference between, for example, an LPN and a nurse administrator, or between a Psychologist I (a beginning position) and a social worker in the position of treatment team leader. The measure ranges from therapy aide assistants to hospital directors.

When considering an individual's position in the system, it is also necessary to consider the individual's adherence to the "medical model" of mental illness. This model holds that mental illness has its source in the individual, not in the environment; that its treatment should be pursued through such mechanisms as psychotherapy, not manipulation of the environment; that power in mental hospitals should be in the hands of mental health professionals; and that state mental hospitals can be beneficial (Bardach, 1972:65). Since granting more rights to patients is inconsistent with many aspects of the medical model, respondents who show higher levels of agreement with the tenets of this model could be expected to have lower scores on PRI; it should be noted, however, that a perfect, negative relationship between scores on these two measures is not expected because they reflect different ideological clusters. The "medical model" reflects a much broader set of issues than PRI, and some differences in the relationships between other factors and these two ideological scales should result. The basic theoretical perspective of this study leads to a prediction that respondents who occupy more powerful positions will have higher PRI scores. However, at the same time, because these respondents have reached positions of power within the system, they will probably show more commitment to the medical model that legitimates that system.

Ten items developed by Bardach (1972) to measure respondents' attitudes toward a number of issues of "ideological cleavage" in mental health are used to measure the extent of agreement with tenets of the "medical model." Scores on these items are then summed to provide a single variable (TRAD), with higher scores indicating more support for the traditional medical model.

Profession

Certain professional groups, such as psychiatrists and psychologists, possess more power and prestige in state mental hospitals (Freidson, 1970:52–54), and they are less likely to feel directly threatened by granting more rights to patients. At the same time, these professional groups should also show high levels of commitment to the traditional "medical model" view of mental health. In the data described below, the variable PROF is coded to reflect the relative power and prestige positions of the professions in state mental hospitals (Freidson, 1970:52–54). It ranges from therapy aides to psychiatrists, with a total of six categories.

Socioeconomic Variables

Sex, race, and education are generally viewed as factors influencing individuals' social class position and thus their power (Lenski, 1966; Bendix and Lipset, 1966). It follows from the perspective noted above that these factors will also influence attitudes toward patients' rights, over and above their effects on professional and organizational achievement. Specifically, whites, males, and respondents with higher educational levels will probably show more support for the extension of patients' rights, since they will generally rank higher on a scale of power.

The socioeconomic variables utilized in the analyses are:

Sex (SEX). This is a simple, dichotomous variable.

Race (RACE). This is also a dichotomous variable, coded for whites and nonwhites; it should be noted that Blacks constitute about 80 percent of the nonwhite group in the total sample.

Education (EDUC). This variable is coded incrementally from low to high levels of education, ranging from no schooling to doctoral degrees.

The second general prediction relates to the nature of all mental hospitals. As a result of working in a "total institution" (Goffman, 1961), individuals who have day-to-day responsibility for maintaining the control function of the institutions—namely, those whose primary tasks involve direct patient care—will be less likely to be "pro-patient" in their responses to patients' rights issues. The patient care responsibility variable

(PTCARE) divides respondents into two groups, according to whether or not direct patient care was a major responsibility of their positions.

The staff with patient care responsibilities must maintain the discipline required for efficient operation of hospitals, and they must deal with the angry reactions of patients who have been involuntarily committed; thus, they would experience most directly the impact of giving patients more rights. Following this logic, it is expected that they would have scores lower in support of patients' rights, because they directly face the task of effectively implementing the hospital's control over patients on a daily basis. In addition, because the pressures that result from patient care responsibility heighten the need for legitimation of their activities, these staff could be expected to support strongly the medical model of mental illness.

This analysis led to the formulation of the perspective that has guided the research: *An individual's response to the complex set of issues regarding patients' rights in state mental hospitals is directly related to the amount of power or control which (s)he possesses relative to patients and to other respondents.*

To summarize, this perspective leads to four predictions regarding power, control, and support for patients' rights:

Hypothesis 1: Individuals who occupy positions of greater power in the mental hospital will be more inclined to support patients' rights.
Hypothesis 2: Those respondents whose socioeconomic status reflects greater power in the society will be more inclined to support patients' rights.
Hypothesis 3: Respondents in professions with higher prestige in the mental hospital will be more inclined to support patients' rights.
Hypothesis 4: Those respondents who are directly involved in patient care will show less support for patients' rights.

An additional hypothesis deals with the relationship between position in the organization and extent of support for the traditional medical model:

Hypothesis 5: Respondents who occupy positions of greater power in the hospital will be stronger in their support for the medical model of mental illness.

METHODS

An extensive data set concerning patients' rights ideologies of staff and administrators was gathered during 1975 at six state hospitals in New York. The status of patients' rights had undergone some important changes in the State as a result of a recodified Mental Hygiene Law which took effect in January, 1973, thus making it an ideal setting for a study of attitudes toward patients' rights and the implications for change mandated by legislation.

In-depth interviews were conducted with 96 administrators and staff, covering respondents' perspectives on patients' rights; these interviews were complemented by extensive background material on the respondents. The administrators included the Hospital Directors, Clinical Deputy Directors, and Directors of Nursing, while staff included a wide range of respondents from chiefs of service through therapy aides (or attendants), from a variety of professional backgrounds: psychiatry, psychology, social work, nursing, etc. The interviews were also supplemented by 459 self-administered questionnaires completed by staff members at the same six hospitals. Tables 13.1 and 13.2 below describe the sample in more detail. The response rate for the self-administered forms was 60.5 percent; only one person chose not to be interviewed. The self-administered forms were pre-coded, making data preparation easier; this was also true for those interview items identical to questions in the self-administered forms.

Open-ended questions used in the interviews necessitated the development of a coding system drawn from the responses. For each question, all 96 responses were read and grouped into a number of categories which were then defined. These were combined into a coding system for the entire interview, which was used to code responses a second time. The coding system and interviews were then turned over to other judges, who coded them again. Any discrepancies in coding were then discussed until mutual agreement was reached on each response. When grouped into the categories used in the analysis presented below, the inter-coder reliability

Table 13.1. Position of inter-view respondents.

POSITION	N
Directors *	7
Clinical Deputy Directors	6
Directors of Nursing	5
Unit Chiefs	7
Team Leaders	6
Psychiatrists	6
Psychologists	8
Social Workers	6
Activity Specialists	5
Nurses	22
Psychiatric Aides	18
	96

* and Acting Directors

Table 13.2. Profession of respondents in interview and questionnaire samples.

	Interview		Questionnaires	
	N	%	N	%
Psychiatry	22	22.9	10	2.3
Psychology	9	9.4	14	3.2
Social Work	11	11.5	23	5.3
Nursing	29	30.2	78	18.1
Activities	7	7.3	15	3.5
Therapy Aides	18	18.8	292	67.6
TOTAL	96	100.1 *	432	100.0
Unknown	—		27	

* rounding error

rate was 0.84. The major focus of the analyses presented below is on the interview data. Corresponding analyses from the questionnaire data are occasionally presented to verify relationships uncovered through specific analyses of the interview data, to the extent such results are available.[4]

Although a large number of the specific patients' rights issues noted above were included in the research reported here, primary analysis focused on a subset of nine key issues, each measured separately; the nine issues included the effects of emphasizing due process, the right to refuse treatment, patients' role in decision-making, and shifting resources to aftercare, community treatment, among others (see Table 13.3). These nine items showed the greatest amount of variance among the respondents, and they were also the nine most highly clustered items in the cluster analyses of all interview items.[5]

Each item was measured on a scale from one to five, with higher scores indicating responses more favorable to patients' rights. The "pro-patients' rights," or civil-libertarian pole, of each scale was decided upon by referring to the major themes and positions defined and advocated by Ennis (1972), Ennis and Siegel (1973), Szasz (1961 and 1970), and Vail (1966); the "anti-patients' rights" pole on each item was defined by the responses which came closest to the antithesis of the "pro" pole. A summary measure, called IDEOLOGY, was also utilized. It was computed as the unweighted sum of responses to the nine issues. The potential range of this latter measure is from nine to 45; the actual range among interview respondents was from ten to 41.

The use of cluster analysis and constrained factor analysis (Jöreskog, Gruvaeus, and van Thillo, 1970) made it possible to determine the five items (marked with asterisks in Table 13.3) which are the strongest indicators of the overall concept of patients' rights ideology. The computer

Table 13.3. Operational measures of patients' rights ideology (PRI).

Label	Measures		
IDEOLOGY	Responses to the following 9 interview questions are summed for each respondent.		
STEPS	I13	Should any steps be taken to make them (patients) more aware of their rights? Why or why not? What steps?	
REFUSE	*I14	Do you believe that patients should always have the right to refuse specific treatment modalities? Does it make a difference if a patient is voluntary, involuntary, or criminal order?	
VOICE	*I15	How much say should patients have in making decisions concerning themselves and their treatment?	
HAMPER	I17a	Some people have argued that the emphasis on due process has hampered the attempts to treat patients. Do you agree or disagree? Why?	
CMH	*I21	Assuming that state funding for mental health has an upper limit, should a larger percentage of resources be geared toward "aftercare," community facilities and staff, even at the expense of psychiatric center budgets?	
DECIDE	I23a	Who should ultimately decide whether or not a person is "ready" to be released?	
CRITERIA	I23b	On what criteria?	
DELTA	*I27	Should changes in the way patients are handled in the New York Psychiatric Centers be initiated from within the Department of Mental Hygiene or by groups and individuals outside the Department?	
TREAT	*I2	How would you define a patient's "right to treatment?"	

* Indicates items which most strongly influence the measure of patients' rights ideology.

program used for the constrained factor analysis provides values for the coefficients (or loadings) of each of these five items, together with the corresponding error term for each item.[6] These values can thus be fixed at the levels indicated in the confirmatory factor analysis and utilized in this form in additional analyses. The measure combining these five items with the loadings described here is called ISSUES; it should be noted that the issue with the greatest impact on the overall concept of patients' rights ideology, defined by these variables, is the right to refuse treatment (REFUSE).

Before presenting the data, two additional variables must be mentioned:

Experience in Mental Health (EXPER)

This variable, which is measured in terms of the number of years of experience in the mental health field, is utilized in part as a surrogate for the age of the respondent. No *direct* relationship between this variable and PRI is hypothesized, because the increases in "power" that may come with age would be offset by a stronger tendency toward "conservatism."

General Political Orientation (RADICAL)

This variable reflects respondents' self-evaluation of their views on public policy, and it ranges from very conservative to very liberal and radical. No direct relationship with PRI is hypothesized, because of the individualistic nature of the issues involved; in other words, these issues dealt with rights of individual mental patients and may thus have been perceived as liberal, "civil-libertarian" issues. If, however, the focus had been placed on the role of state mental hospitals as an extension of government used to control people, a greater similarity in ideologies could be expected between very conservative and very liberal respondents, although perhaps derived from basically incompatible political perspectives.[7] Although no direct relationship to PRI is hypothesized for these two variables, they are included in the causal models because they are expected to affect other independent variables, such as power in the organization and traditionalism.

RESULTS

Intercorrelations among these independent variables and the dependent measure IDEOLOGY are presented in Table 13.4, where the matrix entries are the standard Pearson product-moment correlation coefficients; they are based on the 81 interview respondents for whom there were no missing data on any of the variables included. A quick glance at the matrix indicates that POWER, TRAD, and PTCARE show the highest intercorrelations with IDEOLOGY, the interview measure of PRI. These three correlations were in the direction anticipated by the above discussion. High scores on IDEOLOGY correlated with high POWER scores ($r = .425$), low TRAD scores ($r = -.390$), and holding positions which do not involve patient care ($r = .419$). Correlations of the other variables with IDEOLOGY are all in the direction predicted in the hypotheses, but their magnitude is not as great as these three. The correlation matrix, however, provides only an estimate of the extent of covariation between each pair of variables in the matrix. Neither causal relationships nor multivariate interpretations can be addressed. In order to pursue such analyses, it is necessary to utilize additional analytic techniques; two such approaches were utilized: path analysis and linear structural equation systems.

Path analysis, as an approach to examining causal relationships, was

Table 13.4. Correlation coefficients.

	SEX	RACE	EDUC.	PROF.	EXPER.	RADICAL	POWER	TRAD.	IDEOLOGY	PTCARE
SEX	1.000									
RACE	-.059	1.000								
EDUC.	-.323 **	-.021	1.000							
PROF.	-.374 **	-.133	.854 **	1.000						
EXPER.	-.113	-.037	.158	.249 *	1.000					
RADICAL	-.180	.018	.212	.161	-.059	1.000				
POWER	-.224 *	-.115	.771 **	.754 **	.474 **	.188	1.000			
TRAD.	-.101	.001	-.059	.018	.195	-.310 **	.066	1.000		
IDEOLOGY	-.103	-.178	.298 **	.152	.059	.219 *	.425 **	-.390 **	1.000	
PTCARE	-.123	-.067	.363 **	.315 **	.420 **	.091	.639 **	.048	.419 **	1.000

R @ .05 = .218
R @ .01 = .285
N = 81

* significant at .05 level
** significant at .01 level

introduced by Wright (1960), made popular by Duncan (1966), and more recently described in detail by Land (1968) and Heise (1968, 1975); it is basically a method for examining causal relationships by decomposing and interpreting linear relationships among a set of variables based on two assumptions:

1. that there is a weak causal order among variables, which is either empirically known and/or theoretically justified; and

2. that the relationships among these variables are causally closed—that is, that their covariation is not due to their partial or total dependence on a common outside cause.[8]

Given these assumptions and the causal ordering implied by the theoretical perspective outlined above, a model was developed that utilized the variables as illustrated in Figure 13.1. The initial formulation of the model specified that the causal system was recursive; in other words, each variable was seen as being caused by a linear combination of some or all of the variables that preceded it in the causal chain, plus an error term. The only exception to this was the relationship between RACE and SEX. Here the assumption was made that their covariation was noncausal. All of the independent variables noted above were included in the model except the patient care responsibility variable, since the inclusion of this important dimension, solely by means of a dichotomous variable in equations that already specified numerous terms, could have obscured important information.

The structural equations that express the relationships among these variables (in standardized form) implied by this initial model are as follows:

$$X_3 = \beta_{31}X_1 + \beta_{32}X_2 + U_3$$
$$X_4 = \beta_{41}X_1 + \beta_{42}X_2 + \beta_{43}X_3 + U_4$$
$$X_5 = \beta_{51}X_1 + \beta_{54}X_4 + U_5$$
$$X_6 = \beta_{61}X_1 + \beta_{62}X_2 + \beta_{63}X_3 + \beta_{65}X_5 + U_6$$
$$X_7 = \beta_{71}X_1 + \beta_{72}X_2 + \beta_{73}X_3 + \beta_{74}X_4 + \beta_{75}X_5 + U_7$$
$$X_8 = \beta_{81}X_1 + \beta_{82}X_2 + \beta_{83}X_3 + \beta_{84}X_4 + \beta_{85}X_5 + \beta_{86}X_6 + \beta_{87}X_7 + U_8$$
$$X_9 = \beta_{91}X_1 + \beta_{92}X_2 + \beta_{93}X_3 + \beta_{94}X_4 + \beta_{95}X_5 + \beta_{96}X_6 + \beta_{97}X_7 + \beta_{98}X_8 + U_9$$

Each equation relates a set of the independent variables to one dependent variable. For example, in this initial model, respondents' position in the hospital (X_7 = POWER) is defined as the sum of their sex (X_1), race (X_2), education (X_3), professional field (X_4), and amount of experience in mental health (X_5), plus an error term (U_7).

Using the technique of least squares multiple regression, these equa-

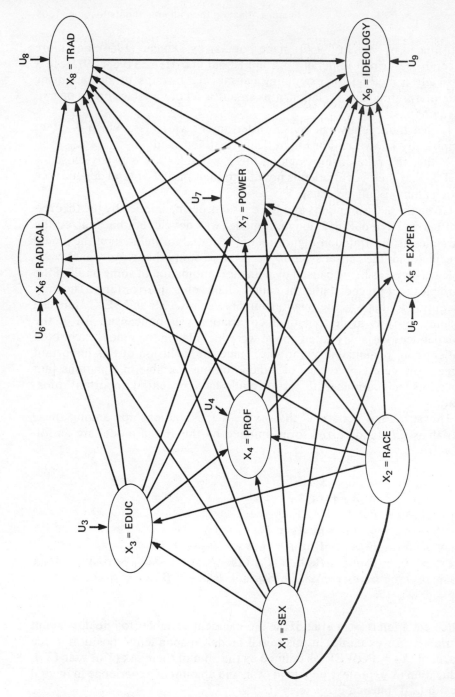

Figure 13.1. Initial path model.

tions were estimated in turn. For each equation, the initial estimates of the coefficients for the various component elements were examined to determine whether or not they were significantly different from zero. Although the computer program utilized for the analysis provided a statistical test of the significance of each coefficient, this was not applied in the absolute manner in making decisions concerning the retention of a particular path. Heise (1975:194–195) notes that statistical tests with small samples may be too insensitive and lead to rejection of causal effects that actually exist; thus, two different criteria were utilized in making the decision to retain a particular relationship in the model and to consider it in the analysis. A relationship was retained if:

1. the magnitude of the coefficient was at least twice the size of its standard error, and the standard error itself did not exceed 0.15; or

2. its coefficient was comparable to the other effects being considered in the model (Heise, 1975:195) on the basis of the first criterion. By taking this conservative position in eliminating paths, I hoped to retain theoretically interesting paths in the model. (When paths of particular theoretical interest were nevertheless eliminated from the model, they will be noted and discussed in the course of this presentation.)

Following these procedures did lead to the elimination of some paths. The results of the process are presented in Figure 13.2, which is the final estimated model relating the variables in the system. All coefficients are in standardized form. Given the theoretical perspective described above, three of the equations comprising this model deserve particular attention, and each estimated equation will be examined in turn.[9]

$$(\text{Eq. 1}) \quad \text{POWER} = (.577)\text{EDUC} + (.204)\text{PROF} +$$
$$(.312)\text{EXPER} + .495 \qquad (R^2 = .755)$$

The coefficients for RACE and SEX were both too small to be retained in the equation, indicating that respondents' power positions in the organization were caused by a combination of their education, length of experience in mental health, and professional ranking. This equation explains the highest percentage of variance in the dependent variable of any equation in the model.

$$(\text{Eq. 2}) \quad \text{TRAD} = (-.182)\text{SEX} + (-.284)\text{EDUC} + (-.337)\text{RADICAL} +$$
$$(.301)\text{POWER} + .918 \qquad (R^2 = .158)$$

Recalling that traditionalism is a measure of the respondents' agreement with the tenets of the medical model, this equation indicates that

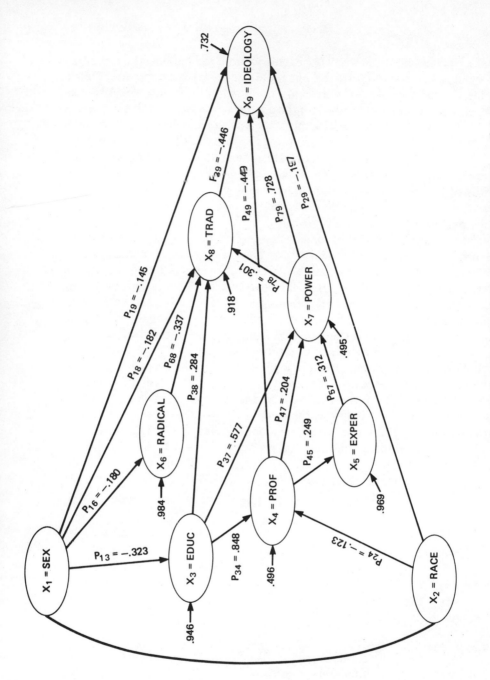

Figure 13.2. Final path model with estimated standardized coefficients.

there is no causal relationship between RACE or PROF and traditionalism, when we control for the other variables in the equation. Furthermore, when we partial out the effects of respondents' power positions and the self-evaluation of their political perspectives, there does not seem to be any difference among the professions in their support of the medical model.

Perhaps the most interesting coefficient is that relating POWER to TRAD. This positive coefficient indicates that holding a more powerful position leads to a more traditional medical model view of mental health. This finding is consistent with the perspective outlined above, and it suggests that the people who "make it" in terms of success within the mental hospital's organizational hierarchy are led to higher levels of agreement with the ideology that legitimates that system.

$$\text{(Eq. 3)} \quad \text{IDEOLOGY} = (-.145)\text{SEX} + (-.197)\text{RACE} + (-.449)\text{PROF} + (.728)\text{POWER} + (-.446)\text{TRAD} + .732$$
$$(R^2 = .464)$$

As predicted by the theoretical perspective, this equation indicates that men and whites have higher PRI scores and that occupying a position of power in the hospital leads to higher PRI scores. The equation also indicates that higher scores on traditionalism lead to lower approval of the extension of patients' rights, when we partial out the effects of the other variables.

The negative coefficient obtained for professional prestige was not expected, since it was assumed that greater professional power and prestige would lead to higher levels of support for patients' rights. When Equation 3 is re-estimated using the square of PROF, a larger proportion of variance is explained, suggesting that the relationship is curvilinear.[10] This indicates that the relationship between respondents' profession and their PRI scores is affected by more than the prestige of the profession itself, and it suggests a closer examination is needed of the roles and responsibilities of the various professional groups in the state hospitals.[11]

The path analysis model estimated for the interview data used IDEOLOGY as the measure of respondents' PRI scores. This variable is a summary measure of nine interview items, with each item equally weighted; however, a more efficient measure of PRI is available. It is based on the component items shown empirically to be the most strongly related to the underlying dimension of patients' rights. This measure, as noted above, is derived from the confirmatory factor analysis of the interview items. The most direct way to make use of this measure of PRI is to utilize ISSUES as a true dependent variable defined by the five most salient items. This requires a technique that allows for multiple indicators of unmeasured variables.

The means of accomplishing this goal is provided by using LISREL, "a general computer program for estimating a linear structural equation system involving multiple indicators of unmeasured variables" developed by Jöreskog and van Thillo (1972). This program enables the user to estimate the unknown coefficients in the set of linear structural equations, including the coefficients of the indicators of unmeasured hypothetical constructs (such as PRI) and the appropriate error and residual terms. The procedure produces maximum likelihood estimates of the coefficients, which can then be scaled so that each has a variance of 1.0. Once the maximum likelihood estimates of the parameters have been calculated, it is possible to test the goodness of fit of the original model using a likelihood ratio technique with an approximate chi-square distribution (Jöreskog and van Thillo, 1972:8).

In the model prepared for the LISREL program, the relationships among the predictor variables and between the predictors and the measure of PRI are essentially the same as in the initial path model before estimation (Figure 13.1 above). The important difference lies in the measurement of the dependent variable. In the LISREL model, PRI is taken as a latent unmeasured construct, and the five interview items with the highest loadings are shown as measures of this hypothetical construct.[12] The results of the LISREL approach were similar to those generated by the path analysis described above. Although the magnitudes of some of the coefficients are different, all of the paths in the LISREL model that appear in the path analysis model have the same signs, and all of the LISREL paths that were dropped from the path model are small in absolute value. The similarity between the two sets of results gives added credence to the validity of the theoretical model utilized in the analysis. The most salient result of this comparison is that the linear structural equation system, which makes maximum use of the information available concerning the components of PRI, indicates the same complex relationship among respondents' profession, power position, and PRI scores. It also confirms that a higher position of power leads to higher scores on both traditionalism and patients' rights ideology.

DISCUSSION

The discussion of state hospitals as people-processing institutions presented earlier pointed to a number of dimensions expected to influence respondents' orientations toward patients' rights. In conceptualizing the influence of interpersonal power on respondents' reactions to the rights of mental patients, three related elements are included: the level of respondents' positions within the hospital organization (measured by POWER), the relative prestige of their professions (measured by PROF), and certain socioeconomic characteristics which reflect relative power in the society at large (measured by SEX, RACE, and EDUC). The use of the multivariate procedures described above enabled examination of the net effects of each of these variables, while controlling for the effects of the other variables included in the models. [13]

First let us examine the socioeconomic and hospital-position dimensions, then we will consider the effects of professional field. Finally, we will review the results dealing with the structural characteristic of patient care responsibility, the fourth major factor seen as related to support for patients' rights. The results of the two causal modeling approaches support the idea that respondents' racial and sexual backgrounds affect their support for patient's rights, while their level of education has no independent effect outside of the influence through their profession or organizational position. Although the coefficients for RACE and SEX are small, they are statistically significant, and they suggest support for the idea that whites and males will be more likely to support patients' rights because their own socioeconomic positions give them more power in the society, and hence they are less likely to feel threatened by any extension of patients' rights. [14] The analyses presented above also clearly demonstrated that higher levels of support for patients' rights are related to high positions in the organizational structure of the hospital (controlling for the effect of profession). At the same time, respondents in higher positions also show more support for the dominant, mental health ideology (as measured by TRAD). [15] Both results are congruent with theoretical expectations.

Several interpretations of these results must be considered. It has been noted already that as one ascends the power hierarchy in a state hospital, positions increasingly involve contact with agencies and institutions outside the hospital. This, in turn, leads to the development of a more "cosmopolitan" perspective than might be expected for lower-level staff. At the same time, stronger agreement with the tenets of the medical model of mental illness is developed, and this includes support for the idea that mental illness requires *treatment* and that state hospitals can be effective agents of that treatment. In the presence of internal conflict concerning the functions of treatment, custodial care and residual care (for those awaiting alternate placement), in the absence of clear indications that the treatment function is being executed, and in the face of conflicting community demands that hospitals be humane and yet effective by not releasing the "wrong people," individuals in positions of power are expected to be enlightened, humanitarian administrators. Although some parts of the community may want an efficient dictator, this will not be openly acknowledged. Thus, the role of individuals in more powerful positions may indeed require a more liberal ideology in order to deal with certain groups. Another aspect of this interpretation can be seen in the relationships with the Department of Mental Hygiene and the State Legislature, both of which constitute part of the responsibility attached to more powerful positions. To the extent that meeting the demands of patients' rights advocates will cost more money (e.g., for more staff), supporting patients' rights may be an effective strategy for obtaining larger budget allocations.

A complementary interpretation derives from the internal responsibilities of higher level staff. Within each hospital, the conflict of functions between treatment and control confronts lower-level staff most directly. The lower-level staff, who have to deal directly with the patients, must personally present institutional demands to those patients and then must deal with their hostility and aggression.[16] For lower-level staff, the issue of control takes on an immediate and threatening reality, especially given their task of disciplining involuntary patients. Thus lower-level staff see the extension of patients' rights as making their jobs more difficult and dangerous. Higher-level staff can "afford" to be more sympathetic to the extension of patients' rights, because they will not have to confront the disruptions in discipline that might result (Goffman, 1961:113-114). As long as the control function remains critical—that is, as long as large numbers of involuntarily committed patients are institutionalized with small numbers of staff—there is little likelihood that lower-level staff will respond very favorably to patients' rights issues.[17]

This analysis demonstrates that power, deriving from respondents' positions in society and in the organizational hierarchy of the mental hospital, is an important factor in determining orientations toward patients' rights, as well as commitment to the traditional medical model of mental illness. These results appear when respondents' profession is controlled for.

Turning now to the effects of professional prestige, the results of the multivariate procedures described above indicate that the relationship between PROF and IDEOLOGY is curvilinear, suggesting that professional prestige is not directly related to support for patients' rights; rather, a more complex relationship exists between respondents' professions and their PRI scores. A direct examination of scores on IDEOLOGY by profession (Table 13.5)[18] enabled a fuller exploration of the nature of this relationship. From the table, it is clear that social workers have the highest mean score and therapy aides the lowest, while psychiatrists, psychologists, and nurses were grouped together near the center.[19] The standard deviations of the scores indicate a wide variation in response to

Table 13.5. PRI scores by profession.[18]

Profession	N	Average PRI Score on Ideology	Standard Deviation
Therapy Aides	18	19.588	6.0834
Nurses	29	24.448	6.5552
Social Workers	11	31.545	4.2980
Psychologists	9	24.778	4.9441
Psychiatrists	22	25.364	7.6192

these issues, possibly due to differences in responsibilities within professional groups. This makes it imperative to discuss some characteristics of professional training and roles in interpreting these differences.

Therapy Aides

The general role of therapy aides or attendants has been treated at length in the literature (see, for example, Simpson, 1961, and Strauss, et al, 1964:93–140). They are responsible for basic housekeeping functions, personal hygiene of patients, preparation of daily notes and records, and various other routine tasks; primarily, however, they are charged with the responsibility of maintaining order in the wards and with spending a great deal of time with patients. In many wards visited during the research, especially on the evening and night shifts, the therapy aides were the only staff on duty. Thus, in terms of actual patient care and patient contact, therapy aides have by far the most contact with patients. In some wards, a number of therapy aides have been trained to dispense medications, so that there is no routine need for nurses to be present.

Given the combination of low status (bottom rung on the ladder) and high levels of patient care responsibility, it was not surprising that therapy aides had the lowest PRI scores. Their role epitomizes the conflicts inherent in the mental hospital: they are the staff who must maintain order in the wards, even though they are greatly outnumbered by their patients; thus, the custodial function of the hospital is most clearly visible in their role. The vulnerability of their position is reflected in their low PRI scores. In addition, therapy aides are quite strong in their support for the medical model of mental illness, having traditionalism scores almost as high as those of psychiatrists and nurses, as noted in Table 13.6.[20] This result is also not surprising since it is the medical model, and perhaps nothing else, which can and does provide the legitimation for the custodial tasks that they must perform and for the strict disciplinary role that they must maintain with patients. For therapy aides more than any other staff group, the conflict between closeness and distance in dealing with patients is critical. To maintain order they must not identify with, nor be identified with, the patients (Goffman, 1961:122).

Table 13.6. Traditionalism scores by professional group.[21]

Profession	N	Traditionalism Score	Standard Deviation
Therapy Aides	16	29.25	2.79
Nurses	27	30.07	3.40
Social Workers	10	27.00	3.02
Psychologists	8	27.88	3.64
Psychiatrists	21	30.95	4.60

Nurses

Although nurses are almost as strong as psychiatrists in their support of the medical model of mental illness (and thus show some similarity to therapy aides), their average PRI scores are considerably higher than those of the therapy aides (Table 13.5). Part of this difference most likely results from their position in the hospital. As the direct supervisor of the therapy aides, nurses are one step removed from the immediate control function which the aides must execute. Furthermore, many nurses have responsibilities in more than one ward, which again dissipates some of the impact of the control issue. Nurses often serve as intermediaries between professional staff and the aides (Strauss, et al., 1964:146–153).

Within nursing ranks, there is a dichotomy between those with direct patient care responsibilities in the ward and those who hold more supervisory positions and have little direct contact with patients. As seen in Table 13.7, those nurses with primarily administrative and supervisory responsibilities have significantly higher PRI scores than the ward nurses. Thus, their higher position and lack of direct care responsibilities provide them with a buffer that makes the extension of patients' rights less threatening to them.

Table 13.7. Mean PRI scores for patient care and non-
patient care groups by profession.

Profession	Patient Care			Non-Patient Care		
	N	Mean	Standard Deviation	N	Mean	Standard Deviation
Aides *	16	19.8	6.2	1	16.0	—
Nurses **	17	22.1	5.4	12	27.8	6.8
Social Workers	4	32.5	5.0	7	31.0	4.2
Psychologists **	7	22.7	3.0	2	32.0	2.8
Psychiatrists **	7	23.4	9.6	15	26.3	6.7
Other **	4	21.3	3.3	3	31.3	3.2

* too few cases in non-patient care group
** differences in means statistically significant using t-test

Psychologists

The small number of psychologists included in the sample makes it difficult to draw conclusions about them, but some tentative remarks may be made. In most state hospitals, psychologists function under the supervision of the ward psychiatrist, and their duties usually include psychological testing and research, in addition to some therapeutic functions. Although they are supervised by psychiatrists, many psychologists in institutional settings become advocates for milieu therapy (Schwartz, 1957) and as such come into conflict with psychiatrists. In many respects, their position is similar to that of the social workers, and both groups tend to show less support for the medical model of mental illness (Table 13.6).

On the subject of support for PRI, however, psychologists appear to be closer to psychiatrists than social workers. This may be due to their attempts to be accepted in a number of arenas as possessing skills equivalent to the psychiatrists, so as to enable them to function without direct supervision. This is an issue of interprofessional conflict that will probably not be resolved for some time. In the interim, it is conceivable that the more psychologists attempt to be dealt with as equivalent to psychiatrists, the more they will perceive issues in a similar manner (Zander, et al, 1957).

Social Workers

Social workers share with psychologists the commitment to milieu therapy and a lower level of support for the medical model. However, they are much more positive in their support of extending patients' rights than all the other professional groups. Two factors may contribute to this finding:

First, as a major function of their position in the hospital, social workers are heavily involved in making arrangements for the discharge of patients. In this role, they are acutely aware of the problems of transferring patients out of the hospital, even when they believe that the patients are ready. They are also forced to deal with the bureaucratic processes which impinge upon the rights of patients as human beings. Finally, in dealing with getting patients out of the hospital, social workers can become acutely aware of the negative effects of institutionalization and stigma on these patients. Second, in the interprofessional arena, social workers have been attempting to attain a status equivalent to that of psychiatrists and psychologists, while at the same time maintaining a perspective different from these groups. Their support for the patient and patients' rights may be part of this process. In any case, social workers in the organization do not have to deal with direct control of patient activity in the manner that aides and nurses must. At the same time, they do not have to bear the legal (or even intraorganizational) responsibility of the psychiatrist. They are the only professionals that show no difference in support of patients' rights between those with and without direct patient care responsibilities.

Psychiatrists

The response of psychiatrists to the extension of patients' rights presents an opportunity to study the vagaries of power and authority. As might be suspected, psychiatrists are the strongest group in support of the medical model view of mental illness which is, after all, the source of their professional, therapeutic legitimation. However, despite their position of relative power in the organization, psychiatrists have PRI scores significantly below those of social workers and only slightly above those of nurses and psychologists (Table 13.5). Even when only those psychiatrists not involved in patient care (that is, the administrators) were considered, they scored below those of other non-patient care professionals (Table 13.7).

The power of psychiatrists in the organizational structure of mental hospitals is quite real. While other staff members may be called upon to give their opinions on a variety of issues and to share their knowledge of patient behavior, in the final analysis usually only the psychiatrists have the right to compose an overall assessment of the patient and make the critical decisions concerning disposition (Goffman, 1961:357–358). They alone can sign orders for medication and treatment, and they alone have the official authority to release a patient.

This official power of psychiatrists carries with it a tremendous burden. Although they have the authority to make these critical decisions, they also carry sole legal responsibility for the effects of their decisions (Perrucci, 1974:159–160). If the treatment they prescribe proves to be harmful, or if a patient they release injures another person, they may be liable. These official responsibilities make them potentially vulnerable, and this makes them less inclined to be supportive of an extension of patients' rights. As the official representatives of the medical model, psychiatrists are faced with the responsibility of ensuring that patients remain obedient and controlled, by coercion if necessary (Freidson, 1970:316). This often entails allowing lower-level staff a fair amount of liberty in executing this mandate. At the same time, psychiatrists are expected to maintain treatment standards and demonstrate that the treatment goals of the institution are in fact being realized (Parsons, 1957:109–112).

The training of psychiatrists has a significant impact on the manner in which they execute their responsibilities (Buchner, 1965; Becker and Carper, 1956). We have already seen the strong negative correlation between support for patients' rights and support for the medical model (Figure 13.2 and Table 13.4). Thus psychiatrists, who have the highest level of support for the traditional medical model (Table 13.6) and who have had extensive training in it, are not likely to be highly supportive of patients' rights, although some specific rights will be supported and others will not be opposed. This lack of support becomes inevitable in the face of the conflict among the functions of state hospitals.

To a certain extent, regardless of their power in the organization and/or removal from the direct contact with patients that characterizes the role of aides, psychiatrists are still left in the position of defending as "therapeutic" an institution that enforces some clearly anti-therapeutic processes (Goffman, 1961:356; Scheff, 1966:114). In the face of this contradiction and the expected resistance of involuntarily committed people, psychiatrists show levels of support slightly below the neutral range, indicating neither great support nor great resistance. When we examine only scores for psychiatrists without patient care responsibilities, they show more support, but the scores still remain below the mean; thus, contrary to my initial hypothesis, the higher prestige of psychiatrists does not lead in general to higher levels of support for patients' rights. Those psychiatrists in administrative and supervisory positions show significantly higher levels of support than their colleagues with direct patient care responsibilities, but even they fall below support levels shown by social workers.

The psychiatrists' role thus brings full circle the discussion of power and control issues in the state hospital. In the role of therapy aides, tension created by direct contact with involuntarily committed patients appeared. The aides, with little organizational power, nevertheless have day-to-day responsibility for maintaining order in the wards. The extension of patients' rights would mean a direct and immediate threat to their position relative to those whom they control. The psychiatrists, with tremendous organizational power and with little immediate contact with the subjects of organizational control, must maintain the legitimacy of the entire enterprise in the face of many nontherapeutic activities. They must continually defend the notion that state hospitals are indeed therapeutic organizations, in spite of the authoritarian regimen required to maintain order; for psychiatrists, then, the extension of patients' rights could mean an attack on the very foundation of their profession.

Perrucci (1974:33) describes the instability of the psychiatrists' role in relation to lower-level staff. His analysis is equally penetrating as an explanation for the psychiatrists' position on patients' rights:

The combination of marginality and stigma makes the physician especially vulnerable to challenges to his authority. He faces the classic dilemma inherent in bureaucratic authority in which the holder of a position of authority does not or cannot validate positional authority with demonstrated expertise. Authority based upon position alone is unstable and will be eroded eventually in relations with subordinates.

Thus, therapy aides, with the day-to-day burdens of enforcing the control functions of the hospitals demonstrate the lowest levels of support for patients' rights, while social workers, who are often the most involved in assisting patients to return to the community, show the highest levels of support. Although psychiatrists possess the most power and prestige, the responsibilities of the profession mute the effect of these characteristics, and thus psychiatrists show levels of support about equal to those of nurses and psychologists. The finding of similar scores for psychiatrists and psychologists is consistent with results reported in the study by Kahle and Sales appearing in this collection. This suggests a three-tiered relationship between profession and support for patients' rights—a result statistically confirmed by the one-way analysis of variance results presented in Table 13.8. These results confirm that support for patients' rights shows no statistically significant differences among nurses, psychologists, and psychiatrists. Therapy aides are different from all of the other groups at the lower end of the scale, and social workers are different from all other groups but at the higher end of the scale; Figure 13.3 displays these results visually.

The fourth major factor examined in this chapter—the extent of respondents' direct patient care responsibilities—has been shown to be an important element affecting support of patients' rights (see Table 13.7). The data indicate that among nurses, psychologists, and psychiatrists, there are significantly higher levels of support for patients' rights from respondents in administrative or supervisory positions, compared to re-

Table 13.8. Comparison of mean scores on ideology by profession from Anova.[a]

	F-Statistics				
	Aides	Nurses	Social Workers	Psychologists	Psychiatrists
Aides					
Nurses	6.19 *				
Social Workers	23.35 *	9.82 *			
Psychologists	3.88 *	0.02	5.54 *		
Psychiatrists	7.82 *	0.26	6.85 *	0.05	

* P < .05
a) ETA = .4716
   ETA − SQUARE = .2224
   Equality of Variances established (F = 1.1965, df = 4,6711.9, p = .31)

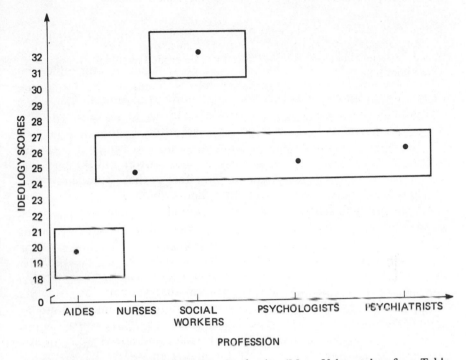

Figure 13.3. Mean Ideology Scores by Profession (Mean Values taken from Table 13.5).

spondents with primarily direct patient care positions. Social workers are more supportive of patients' rights, regardless of the extent of patient care responsibilities. No comparison is possible for therapy aides, since only one was in a primarily supervisory position. The significant differences in resistance to patients' rights between staff with and without patient care responsibilities can be attributed to differences in both the structurally given demands of the positions they occupy, and staff conceptions of how those demands must be met (Levinson, 1959).

Staff without patient care responsibilities generally occupy positions that demand interaction with two principal groups: other staff and people outside the hospitals. In such positions, staff are likely to have less direct contact with patients and, thus, less of a feeling for problems of relating to patients for a full, eight-hour shift. Their sense of "doing a good job" is not tied directly to interactions with patients; furthermore, since their "significant others" include individuals and groups which may be patients' rights advocates, they must be concerned about the visibility of their role performance to these outsiders. In other words, for staff without patient care responsibilities, a sense of accomplishment and fulfillment does not require close working relationships with patients; it *does* require some measure of compromise on patients' rights issues with others who are or have to be concerned with these issues—advocates or administrators, respectively. For staff with patient care responsibilities, however, patients form an important part in their role definition. Spending time with patients is demanded by the very nature of their positions in the organization, and how they deal with patients is an important component of their own role definition.

Finally, let us consider one last issue. In the introduction to this chapter, it was noted that responses of mental health personnel to extending patients' rights were in part affected by the theme of self-interest concerning job security. Although the theoretical analysis has focused on the roles of power and professional responsibilities, the economic, self-interest perspective should also be considered.[22]

According to this perspective, an individual's response to this complex set of issues is directly related to perceptions of the impact of extending patients' rights on his/her job security. These perceptions are not constant across all respondents but vary according to such contextual factors as the availability of alternative jobs in the same geographical location. In discussing this perspective the following premise must be noted: extension of patients' rights implies a direct threat to the present system of involuntary, inpatient hospitalization and thus to the jobs of some personnel. Let us compare the interpretation of significant differences between personnel with and without direct patient care responsibilities. According to the structural power perspective discussed above, staff with direct patient care responsibilities have the immediate task of controlling largely involuntary patient groups which greatly outnumber staff. Thus any extension of patients' rights would be resisted, because it threatens to give patients more power and thereby to make the job of direct patient care staff even more difficult.

The interpretation of these findings from the economic, self-interest perspective is more straightforward. Staff with direct patient care responsibilities are more resistant to extending patients' rights because of a strong fear that such changes will eventually lead to the closing of many inpatient units, thus costing them their jobs. In general, hypotheses derived from an economic self-interest model are fairly consistent with the statistical analyses presented above. There are no serious contradictions between the two interpretations, and indeed there appears to be some complementariness.

CONCLUSIONS

This chapter has demonstrated that support for patients' rights is affected by respondents' power positions in the organization, by their socioeconomic status in society, and by the nature of the roles and responsibilities of their professional groups in state hospitals. However, this analysis is not meant to imply that these patterns are static; for example, there may well be fluctuations in the amount of personal involvement in the lives of different patients, sometimes leading to more closeness, then followed by a distancing phenomenon in the face of the inherent conflicts involved (Goffman, 1961:82). However, the basic patterns remain the same. As implied in the discussion above, this is due to the organizational structure of state mental hospitals, and the conflicting functions which they must execute. These functions all involve "patient care" in one form or another. In discussing the roles and responsibilities of the various professions, the study has touched on some of the intragroup differences between those whose responsibilities emphasize direct patient care and those whose positions are primarily administrative and/or supervisory. The results suggest that this is the most significant difference among respondents.[23]

Those without direct patient care responsibilities in general do not face the task of direct control over involuntarily confined patients. At the same time, there may be less fear that changes in the mental health system brought about by extending patients' rights will cost them their jobs. Supervisory and administrative tasks will remain, whether the predominant structure is inpatient or outpatient.

The complementarity between these two perspectives stems from the relationship between ends and means. The structural power perspective strongly suggests that until our present system of involuntary inpatient units is changed, staff with direct patient care responsibilities will strongly resist extending patients' rights.[24] They experience more directly the problems of executing the control function of the institution and thus have more to lose.

The economic self-interest perspective suggests a mechanism for dealing with this resistance if the response to direct patient care staff can indeed be attributed to fear of job loss. Such resistance may be diminished by providing training opportunities—with no loss of pay or seniority—to prepare inpatient staff for new positions in community-oriented facilities; to be effective, however, such a program must practically guarantee that no jobs will be lost and that few people will have to be relocated.[25]

The relationships between, and implications of, these two perspectives must continue to be examined; however, it is clear from the above analyses that power in the organization, profession, socioeconomic status, and extent of direct patient care responsibility are the critical variables affecting the patients' rights ideology of mental health personnel in state hospitals.

The present study suggests that in the absence of extensive structural change, resistance to, or lack of support for, extending patients' rights in state hospitals can be expected to continue. Constant monitoring by groups with real power and adequate resources will be needed to ensure compliance. Although less resistance will be found among non-patient care staff and top level administrators, direct patient care staff will feel threatened by a loss of power and an increase in perceived threat.

This study was not designed, nor intended, to demonstrate that ensuring patients' rights means better treatment. That complex issue is a question deserving investigation. Similarly, the present research does not include measurement of actual behavior in the hospitals, and it may be that patients' rights are in fact being honored. However, the resistance of some of those who have direct care responsibilities, and the lack of support of patient rights amongst many other staff make it difficult to believe that such is the case at the present time. On the contrary, until such positive actions have been documented, there should be continued scrutiny of events in the daily life of state hospitals; furthermore, these results should alert administrators, legislators, and judges to the need for providing enforcement mechanisms as an integral part of any change imposed on state hospitals from outside the organization.

REFERENCES

Bardach, Eugene. *The Skill Factor in Politics: Repealing the Mental Commitment Laws in California.* Berkeley: University of California Press, 1972.

Becker, Howard S. and James Carper. "The development of identification with an occupation." *American Journal of Sociology* **61**:289–298 (1956).

Belknap, Ivan. *Human Problems of a State Mental Hospital.* New York: McGraw-Hill, 1956.

Bendix, Richard and Seymour Martin Lipset (Eds.). *Class, Status, and Power.* Second edition. New York: Free Press, 1966.

Bucher, Rue. "The psychiatric residency and professional socialization." *Journal of Health and Human Behavior* **12**:119–130 (1964).

Carlson, R. O. *Change Processes in the Public Schools* Eugene, Oregon: Center for the Advanced Study of Education Administration, 1965.

Chandler, Daniel and Andrea Sallychild. *The Use and Misuse of Psychiatric Drugs in California's Mental Health Programs.* Sacramento: Assembly Office of Research, 1977.

Duncan, O. D. "Path analysis: sociological examples." *American Journal of Sociology* **72**:1–16 (1966).

Ennis, Bruce J. *Prisoners of Psychiatry: Mental Patients, Psychiatrists, and the Law*. New York: Harcourt, Brace, Jovanovich, Inc., 1972.

Ennis, Bruce J. and Loren Siegel. *The Rights of Mental Patients: The Basic ACLU Guide to a Mental Patient's Rights*. New York: Avon Books, 1973.

Fox, Daniel J. and Kenneth E. Guire. *Documentation for MIDAS, Michigan Interactive Data Analysis System*. Ann Arbor, MI: The Statistical Research Laboratory, University of Michigan, 1974.

Freddolino, Paul P. *Patients' Rights Ideology and the Structure of Mental Hospitals*. Doctoral dissertation. The University of Michigan, Ann Arbor, MI, 1977.

Freidson, Eliot. *Profession of Medicine: A Study of the Sociology of Applied Knowledge*. New York: Harper & Row, 1970.

Goffman, Erving. *Asylums*. Garden City, N.Y.: Doubleday Anchor, 1961.

Heise, David R. "Problems in path analysis and causal inference." In E. F. Borgatta (Ed.), *Sociological Methodology 1969*, pp. 38–73. San Francisco: Jossey-Bass, 1968.

Hobbs, D. "Mental health's third revolution." In A. Bindman and A. Spiegel (Eds.), *Perspectives in Mental Health*, pp. 32–49. New York: Behavioral Science Press, 1969.

Jöreskog, Karl G., and van Thillo, Marielle. *LISREL: A General Computer Program for Estimating a Linear Structural Equation System Involving Multiple Indicators of Unmeasured Variables*. Princeton: Educational Testing Service, 1972.

Jöreskog, Karl G.; Gruvaeus, T. Gunnar and van Thillo, Marielle. *ACOVS, A General Computer Program for Analysis of Covariance Structures*. Princeton: Educational Testing Service, 1970.

Kahle, Lynn, and Sales, Bruce D. "Due process of law and the attitudes of professionals towards involuntary civil commitment." In P. D. Lipsitt and B. D. Sales (Eds.), *New Directions in Psycholegal Research*. New York: Van Nostrand Reinhold Co., 1980.

Kim, Jea-Om and Frank J. Kohout. "Special topics in general linear models." In N. H. Nie, et al. (Eds.), *Statistical Package for the Social Sciences* (Second Edition). New York: McGraw-Hill, 1975.

Kolb, Lawrence C. *The 1977 New York State Five-Year Plan for the Development and Provision of Comprehensive Mental Health Services*. Albany: New York State Department of Mental Hygiene, 1977.

Land, Kenneth C. "Principles of path analysis." In E. F. Borgatta (Ed.), *Sociological Methodology 1969*, pp. 3–37. San Francisco: Jossey-Bass, 1968.

Lenski, Gerhard. *Power and Privilege*. New York: McGraw-Hill, 1966.

Levinson, Daniel J. "Role, personality, and social structure in the organizational setting." *Journal of Abnormal and Social Psychology* **58**:170–180 (1959).

Lieberzan, S. "The effects of changes in roles on the attitudes of role occupants." *Human Relations* **9**:385–402 (1956).

Lipsitt, Paul D. "Emergency admission of civil involuntary patients to mental hospitals following statutory modification." In P. D. Lipsitt and B. D. Sales (Eds.), *New Directions in Psycholegal Research*, New York: Van Nostrand Reinhold Co., 1980.

National Association of Attorneys General. *The Right to Treatment in Mental Health Law*. Raleigh, N.C.: Committee on the Office of Attorney General, 1976.

Parsons, Talcott. "The mental hospital as a type of organization." In Milton Greenblatt, et al (Eds.), *The Patient and the Mental Hospital*, pp. 108–129. Glencoe, Ill.: The Free Press, 1957.

Perrucci, Robert *Circle of Madness: On Being Insane and Institutionalized in America*. Englewood Cliffs, N.J.: Prentice-Hall, Inc., 1974.

Pfohl, Stephen J. *Right to Treatment Litigation: A Consideration of Judicial Intervention into Mental Health Policy*. Columbus, Ohio: Ohio Department of Mental Health and Mental Retardation, 1975.

Rabkin, Judith G. "The role of attitudes toward mental illness in evaluation of mental health programs." In Elmer Struening and Marcia Guttentag (Eds.), *Handbook of Evaluation Research*, pp. 431–482. Beverly Hills, CA: Sage, 1975.

Revelle, William. *Cluster Analysis and Scale Construction*. Ann Arbor, MI: Center for Research on Learning and Teaching, 1971.

Rogers, Everett M. and F. Floyd Shoemaker. *Communication of Innovations: A Cross-Cultural Approach*. New York: The Free Press, 1971.

Scheff, Thomas. *Being Mentally Ill*. Chicago: Aldine, 1966.

Schuman, Howard, and Johnson, Michael P. "Attitudes and behavior." In Alex Inkeles, et al, *Annual Review of Sociology*, pp. 161–207, Volume 2. Palo Alto, CA: Annual Reviews, Inc. 1976.

Schwartz, Morris S. "What is a therepeutic milieu?" In M. Greenblatt, et al (Eds.), *The Patient and the Mental Hospital*, pp. 130–144. Glencoe, Ill.: The Free Press. 1957.

Simpson, Richard L. *Attendants in American Mental Hospitals*. Chapel Hill: Institute for Research in Social Science, University of North Carolina, 1961.

Stanton, A. H. and M. S. Schwartz. *The Mental Hospital*. New York: Basic Books, 1954.

Stone, Alan A. *Mental Health and Law: A System in Transition*. Rockville, Md.: National Institute of Mental Health, 1975.

Stouffer, A. S., et al. *The American Soldier*. Princeton, N.J.: Princeton University Press, 1949.

Strauss, Anselm L., et al. *Psychiatric Ideologies and Institutions*. New York: The Free Press, 1964.

Szasz, Thomas. *The Myth of Mental Illness*. New York: Hoeber-Harper, 1961.

Szasz, Thomas. *The Manufacture of Madness*. New York: Harper and Row, 1970.

Vail, David J. *Dehumanization and the Institutional Career*. Springfield, Ill.: Charles C. Thomas, 1966.

Warren, Carol A. B. "Involuntary commitment for mental disorder: the application of California's Lanterman-Petris-Short Act." *Law and Society Review* 11:629–649 (1977).

Wheeler, Stanton, "The structure of formally organized socialization settings." In O. G. Brim, Jr. and S. Wheeler, *Socialization After Childhood*, pp. 51–116. New York: John Wiley, 1966.

Wright, S. "Path coefficients and path regressions: alternative or complementary concepts?" *Biometrics* 16:189–202 (1960).

Zander, Alvin, et al. *Role Relations in the Mental Health Professions*. Ann Arbor, MI: The University of Michigan Press, 1957.

FOOTNOTES TO CHAPTER 13

[1]A much more extensive analysis can be found in my doctoral dissertation (Freddolino, 1977).

[2]This analysis of hospital organization draws heavily on the work of Stanton and Schwartz (1954), Belknap (1956), Parsons (1957), Goffman (1961), Scheff (1966), Wheeler (1966), Freidson (1970), and Perrucci (1974).

[3]This situation later became the basis for a landmark patients' rights case, *Dixon v. Weinberger*, 405 F. Supp. 974 (D.D.C. 1975).

[4]Additional analyses using the questionnaire data are currently in progress.

[5]Cluster analyses utilized two computer programs with somewhat different algorithms: the CLUSTER program in MIDAS (Fox and Guire, 1974:36–39), and the ICLUST program developed at The University of Michigan's Center for Research on Learning and Teaching (Revelle, 1971). Results from the two analyses were very similar.

[6]The coefficients and error terms for the five items are as follows:

Item	Coefficient	Error Term
REFUSE	.626	.780
VOICE	.477	.879
CMH	.520	.854
DELTA	.368	.930
TREAT	.530	.848

[7]This interpretation was reinforced by a conversation with Thomas Szasz which took place during the data collection stage of the study.

[8]This is equivalent to saying that their disturbance variances are uncorrelated.

[9]The remaining equations in the model are:

$$EDUC = (-.323) \, SEX + .946 \qquad (R^2 = .105$$
$$PROF = (.848) \, EDUC + (-.123) \, RACE + .496 \qquad (R^2 = .754)$$
$$EXPER = (.249) \, PROF + .969 \qquad (R^2 = .062)$$
$$RADICAL = (-.180) \, SEX + .984 \qquad (R^2 = .032)$$

[10]This approach was suggested by Joseph C. Fisher. The resulting equation is:

$$IDEOLOGY = (-.181) \, SEX + (.186) \, RACE + (-.503) \, PROF^2 + (.746) \, POWER + (-.434) \, TRAD + .715 \, (R^2 = .489).$$

See also Kim and Kohout (1975:371–372). Both terms cannot be included simultaneously because of their high intercorrelation ($r = .9850$).

[11]See the DISCUSSION section below.

[12]A much more detailed presentation of my use of LISREL with this model can be found in Freddolino (1977:134–138).

[13]This statistical control is critical to the analysis of *net* effects. For example, in examining the coefficients for RACE, one can see the effects of respondents' racial background on IDEOLOGY *over and above* the impact through the influence of respondents' profession and power position.

[14]From the results of Equation 2, it appears that men are also more likely to support the tenets of the traditional medical model for mental illness, while there is no difference in support for the model between whites and nonwhites.

[15]This finding supports the idea that patients' rights ideology is different from broader ideologies in the mental health field. The coefficient for RADICAL in Equations 3 and 4 were statistically insignificant and were dropped from the equations, indicating no difference in PRI scores between those who identified themselves as conservative and those identified as liberal or radical, suggesting that PRI is not easily amenable to a simple liberal-conservative dichotomy. Equation 2, however, shows that TRAD is influenced by RADICAL, with self-

identified conservatives more likely to show high scores on traditionalism. Finally, it should be noted that the large, negative coefficient for TRAD in Equation 3 (which indicates that when POWER and PROF are controlled for, respondents who are high in traditionalism will be low in their scores on patients' rights ideology) suggests that the two ideologies may be somewhat antithetical.

[16]Among the respondents, the correlation between power position in the organization and patient care responsibilities is equal to .639, indicating that lower-level staff are more likely to have direct patient care responsibilities.

[17]A much more thorough examination of patient care responsibilities in this context is presented in Freddolino (1977:160–177).

[18]The mean score for the miscellaneous, professional category (which includes activity specialists, vocational rehabilitation specialists, etc.) is not included. The mean score for this group is 25.571±4.6341.

[19]Scores on the questionnaire equivalent follow the same basic pattern, although therapy aide scores are not as divergent from nurses' scores.

[20]Traditionalism scores for the questionnaire respondents follow basically the same pattern.

[21]The mean TRAD score for the miscellaneous, professional group in the interview sample is 30.00±3.96.

[22]My current research attempts to develop this perspective more fully.

[23]Additional analyses to support this conclusion can be found in Freddolino (1977:160–177).

[24]It should be noted that very few respondents are fully *supportive* of extending patients' rights. For the most part, they vary on the extent of their resistance.

[25]It is of interest to note that the first steps in developing such a plan have appeared in a recent New York mental health five-year plan (Kolb, 1977:99–102).

Index

Index